Tools for Thinking
and Problem Solving

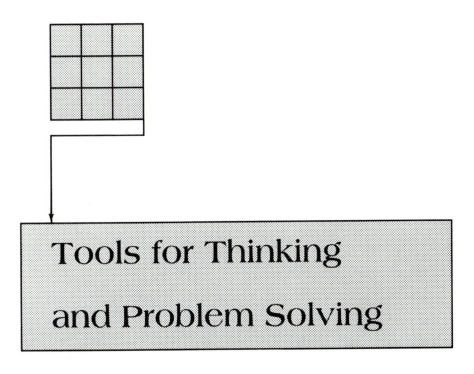

Tools for Thinking and Problem Solving

Moshe F. Rubinstein

University of California, Los Angeles

PRENTICE-HALL, INC., Englewood Cliffs, New Jersey 07632

Library of Congress Cataloging in Publication Data

Rubinstein, Moshe F.
  Tools for thinking and problem solving.

  Bibliography: p.
  Includes index.
  1. Problem solving. 2. Mathematical models.
I. Title.
QA63.R84 1986   153.4'3   85–6428
ISBN 0-13-925140-5

Editorial/production supervision
  and interior design: *Joan L. Stone*
Cover design: *Debra Watson*
Manufacturing buyer: *Rhett Conklin*

Moshe F. Rubinstein, *Patterns of Problem Solving,* © 1975, pp. 74, 78, 165, 167, 188, 247, 251, 253, 256, 257, 261, 287, 290, 291, 324, 328, 330, 357, 387, 388, 389, 412, 429, reprinted by permission of Prentice-Hall, Inc., Englewood Cliffs, N.J.

Printed in the United States of America

10 9 8 7 6 5 4 3 2 1

ISBN 0-13-925140-5 01

PRENTICE-HALL INTERNATIONAL (UK) LIMITED, *London*
PRENTICE-HALL OF AUSTRALIA PTY. LIMITED, *Sydney*
PRENTICE-HALL CANADA INC., *Toronto*
PRENTICE-HALL HISPANOAMERICANA, S.A., *Mexico*
PRENTICE-HALL OF INDIA PRIVATE LIMITED, *New Delhi*
PRENTICE-HALL OF JAPAN, INC., *Tokyo*
PRENTICE-HALL OF SOUTHEAST ASIA PTE. LTD., *Singapore*
EDITORA PRENTICE-HALL DO BRASIL, LTDA., *Rio de Janeiro*
WHITEHALL BOOKS LIMITED, *Wellington, New Zealand*

To my family—
a lively arena to practice problem solving

Contents

CHAPTER 3

Tools for Representation, 78

Contents

CHAPTER 7

Tools and Concepts for Decision Making, 227

CHAPTER 8

Structuring Decision Situations, 271

Preface

This book is based on notes developed in teaching courses and seminars on problem solving at universities and in industry during the past ten years. The participants in these courses and seminars represented diverse backgrounds, interests, and levels of experience. They included executives, managers, professional staff in many fields from industry and government, and students, faculty, and administrative staff from universities.

The purpose of the book is to develop tools for imaginative and rational thinking most suitable for the era of computers, and to prepare the reader to become more creative and productive in professional work and in dealing with personal everyday life situations. To form an effective human-computer symbiosis, we humans must focus on nonprogrammable activities that include rich and imaginative perceptions of context, wisdom to ask appropriate questions, identifying reasonable goals in the context of human values, and representing problems from complementary as well as conflicting points of view. To enhance the potential for imaginative thinking, we must learn to devote more time to problem representation before plunging into a problem solving mode. We must develop attitudes and tools that enable us to take risks, tolerate errors, and function effectively in the presence of ambiguity.

The age of computers requires that we cultivate the unique human capacity to observe, recognize, discover, and spark ideas in the form of untested hypotheses. Motivation is enhanced when we pursue our own ideas, and productivity is promoted by our strong desire to test their validity. We can use the computer to apply tools for testing our ideas and to perform analysis, extrapolation, prediction, and verification. These scientific tools of rational thinking complement our capacity for the imaginative humanistic powers to observe, recognize, discover, and generate ideas.

Combining imaginative and rational thinking, we can develop the capacity to recognize higher orders in the form of new patterns and new common principles that unify diverse phenomena and make complex situations more simple. This is the essence of creative and productive thinking and problem solving. Much of human endeavor is a quest for simplification.

To maintain viability in the face of continuous change in the world around us, we must be receptive to new information, store it, process it, and continue to monitor for change. If we accept only information that fits our models and reject that which does not fit, all learning stops. Learning takes place when we are receptive to information that does not fit and creates conflict with our models, as well as that which fits and is in harmony with our models. Complacency thrives on harmony. Learning takes place when the stress of conflict from information that does not fit leads us to change our models. Imaginative thinking and the courage to make errors can replace complacency with vigilance so we can act in advance in anticipation of change rather than react to it unprepared.

The first chapter sets the stage for the entire book by introducing problem situations in medicine, law, farming, and business, and identifying common features of context, representations, uncertainty, information, culture, and frames of reference. Chapter 2 introduces attitudes and heuristic guides to acquisition of knowledge, problem representation, and search for solutions. We identify a global holistic phase that can tolerate fuzziness and ambiguity and a sequential step-by-step phase in which each aspect is studied in depth. Chapters 3 and 4 introduce tools for representation and discuss their powers and limitations in applications. Chapters 5 and 6 develop tools for dealing with uncertainty and ambiguity. Chapters 7 and 8 provide a foundation for sound judgment in decision making by developing attitudes, tools, and concepts important to professional practice and to personal vitality and viability.

The subject matter treated in the book is presented with a balance between qualitative guides and quantitative tools and examples are used to demonstrate a wide range of applicability to all fields.

The book can be used as a textbook for a course in problem solving or for self study. Exercises in the body of the text and at the end of each chapter are designed to stimulate thinking and guide the reader to explore ideas for new applications of the tools and concepts discussed in the text. Topics are presented in a hierarchical structure of headings and subheadings. Summaries at the end of each chapter review the material.

Many people have contributed to my learning during the time in which the material for this book was developed. The members of the teaching staff in the UCLA program "Patterns of Problem Solving" have been an ever present source of ideas and stimulation. Their excitement in teaching and learning problem solving provided thousands of young people with the kernel of a true education.

My colleagues, Professors Robert S. Elliott, Gary Hart, Paul Johnson, Walter J. Karplus, Peter Likins, and Bill VanVorst, taught the course as an extra load in their teaching assignment.

Over the years the teaching staff kept changing as instructors who were graduate students in various fields completed their studies. I wish to thank the dedicated efforts of Dr. Alex Ratnofsky, Ben Rodilitz, Edward Kazmarek, Michael Brooks, Dan Levy, Dr. Iris Firstenberg, Dorit Mileikowsky, Andrew Mishkin, Kristy Mutschler, Dr. Yannis Phillis, Filipe Diez-Canedo, Dr. Esfandiar Lohrasbpour, Richard Rose, Dr. Soroosh Sorooshian, Dr. Tom Sabol, and Sergio Alvarado.

Professor Robin Keller, Dr. Kenneth Pfeiffer, Professor Ileana Costea, and Professor David Kay helped me shape the form and content of the course and contributed much to my learning.

Captain David Ramm, Captain Robert Dees, and Major Buckner Creel shared with us their experience in teaching "Patterns of Problem Solving" at the West Point Military Academy. Their active participation in the UCLA summer training programs for instructors and peer teachers made a profound impact on all of us who were in attendance.

Gary and Jean Gasca were part of the course from its inception. Their loyalty and devotion were exceptional and beyond the call of duty. No words can do justice to the warmth and delight I feel when I think of the many years of my association with them as their professor, mentor, and colleague.

Special thanks go to Gary Pastre and Ez Nahouraii who were first to recognize the potential of teaching problem solving to managers and professional staff at IBM and who invited me to try my ideas in many seminars that they had organized.

Dr. Victor Tabbush, Associate Dean and director of executive education in the Graduate School of Management at UCLA, gave me the opportunity to lecture on problem solving in the School's Executive Program. This provided an arena to test my ideas with audiences of a broad range of interests from industry and government. The National Science Foundation Chautauqua short course program sponsored by the American Association for the Advancement of Science provided me with a similar arena in academia.

Joan Stone was an outstanding production editor. Fumi Kawamoto displayed exceptional dedication and loyalty and typed several versions of the material without losing interest in the project.

My daughters, Dr. Iris Firstenberg and Dorit Mileikowsky, and my wife, Zaffa, helped with researching some of the topics in the book, assisted with proofreading, and provided constant encouragement with their insights and constructive evaluations.

Moshe F. Rubinstein

Imagination is more important than knowledge,
for knowledge is limited
whereas imagination embraces the entire world,
stimulating progress giving birth to evolution.

Albert Einstein

Tools for Thinking
and Problem Solving

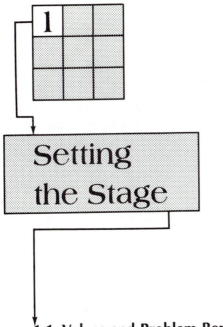

Setting the Stage

1.1 Values and Problem Representation

THE DOCTORS

In the spring of 1967 a 5-year-old boy was admitted to a hospital in Palo Alto, California, complaining of back pain. Preliminary x-rays revealed that two vertebrae had collapsed. Tests to establish possible causes of this phenomenon were all negative. Subsequent x-rays indicated that a third vertebra had collapsed and a fourth one was beginning to deteriorate. There were serious chances for damage to the spinal cord that could result in paralysis or even death.

Let us put ourselves in the position of the two doctors who were assigned to the case and construct a representation of the situation.* First we wish to distinguish between *what we can do* and *what may happen*. At this stage let us suppose that we can choose to *wait* for further observations or we can choose to *treat*. Let us suppose also that what may happen to the boy is one of three states: *cure, paralysis,* or *death*.

Figure 1.1 is a model in which we separated the words describing *what we can do* from those describing *what may happen*. The model consists of a matrix with two rows and three columns. The row labels *Wait* and *Treat* are the *actions* that *we can control* directly. The column labels *Cure, Paralysis,* and *Death* are the *states* that *we cannot control* directly. Each of the six boxes in the matrix is an *outcome* representing an intersection of an action and a state such as Wait–Cure, Wait–Death, Treat–Death, and so forth.

*This particular case was studied in detail by Ginsberg and Offensend in 1968 [1].

1

Figure 1.1   The doctors: representation of what we can do and what may happen.

The model of Figure 1.1 is highly abstract; that is, it is void of detail, as it should be in the early stages of a representation. The words *Wait* and *Treat* are aggregations of various waiting periods and various treatments, respectively. Similarly, the words *Cure, Paralysis,* and *Death* can each be expanded by adding more detailed information, such as how soon they will occur, the level of cure, and the degree of paralysis. For our discussion here let us assume that by *Cure* we mean complete cure, that *Paralysis* is from the neck down, and that these two states as well as *Death* may occur within six months. The actions *Wait* and *Treat* are mutually exclusive; that is, we can choose only one of the two. If we wish we may expand the model of Figure 1.1 and add a row that is a combination of waiting for observation and treating alternately, and label this row *Combined Wait–Treat.*

When I tell the story of Figure 1.1, people agree that the *goal state* is *Cure.* But which of the remaining two states, *Paralysis* and *Death,* is most undesirable: paralysis from the neck down for a 5-year-old child, or death before the age of 6? I have never received complete agreement on this question regardless of how small a group is responding to it. Is this a *relevant* question? Let us explore this. In the present situation we must choose between *Wait* or *Treat.* The question is *relevant* if the answer can make a difference in our choice of an action, or can change the level of confidence that we have in a choice. Otherwise, it is *irrelevant.*

Suppose that in the past a decision to wait resulted in paralysis from the neck down, and a decision to treat resulted in cure in only one in a thousand cases and in death in all other cases. If you consider *Paralysis* the most undesirable state, you may proceed with the treatment at the risk of death. If you consider *Death* the most undesirable state, you may decide to forgo the treatment. You can now see that how we rank the states *Paralysis* and *Death* may influence the choice of an action, and that the *choice of an action can be governed as much by what we may wish to avoid as by what we wish to achieve,* namely, Cure.

The ranking of the states in Figure 1.1 depends on our values. The values may be those we hold as individuals, as well as group values of society to which we may or may not subscribe. Let me illustrate this point by a story related to me by a brain surgeon. The surgeon was in his office one day when he was called to the street to help with an injury in a traffic accident. A quick look told him that the injury was most likely a brain hemorrhage and that the pressure on the brain caused by the outflow of blood must be relieved immediately. The injured person was rushed to the office, where the surgeon prepared for an emergency operation. When the surgeon stood over the injured person with a scalpel in

2

hand, he suddenly froze. This was the time when malpractice suits were becoming a major issue. He remembered how hard he worked to support himself during his years as a student. He was now in his mid-forties, a prominent member of the community with a successful practice and a nice family. Was he risking all this by operating on this stranger?

In effect, thoughts about a malpractice law suit interfered with the surgeon's action. The introduction of new group values to which he personally did not subscribe influenced his problem-solving ability, although only for a moment. He confided in me that in cases where there was no emergency his actions were often governed by concerns over potential malpractice law suits.

Before malpractice became a major issue I asked doctors which of the outcomes in the last column of Figure 1.1 they considered worse: *Wait–Death*, or *Treat–Death*. The common response was that *Wait–Death* was worse because there was always the nagging thought that at least you could have done something about the problem. With the advent of malpractice law suits the response to the same question became more elaborate and less committed to a position. The response might begin with, "It all depends. . . ."

Now let us return to our story of Figure 1.1. The two doctors assigned to the case did not agree in their rankings of the states. One considered *Death* to be worse and the other, *Paralysis*. Which of the two doctors should handle the case? Recall that the choice of action may be governed as much by what a doctor wishes to avoid as by what he wishes to achieve. The doctors disagreed because their *attitudes* toward death and paralysis were different; their *values* were different. They may still agree on the diagnosis and may be equally competent as physicians, but since their values differ they may choose different courses of action.

The *form* of representation employed in Figure 1.1 can be used in other situations in which the content is entirely different from the one we used to this point. This will be shown in the next two examples.

THE JURY

My wife served on a jury once and I watched her agonizing for weeks over a decision on her vote. Finally, the hour of decision arrived and she had to cast her vote of Guilty (G) or Innocent (I). These were the two actions that she could control. There were two corresponding true states that she could not control: *Innocent* or *Guilty*. The four entries in the matrix of Figure 1.2 designate the four

		True State (what we cannot control)	
		Innocent, I	Guilty, G
Verdict (what we can control)	Innocent, I	II Free the innocent	IG Free the guilty
	Guilty, G	GI Punish the innocent	GG Punish the guilty

Figure 1.2 The jury: representation of jury verdicts and true states.

possible outcomes, or intersections of verdicts and true states. The first letter indicates the verdict, and the second the true state. Thus *IG* is the outcome with a verdict innocent when the true state is guilty and results in freeing a guilty person. Outcome *II* corresponds to setting free an innocent person, and outcome *GG* corresponds to punishment of a guilty person. Although the jury has control over the choice of a *verdict*, it has no control over the *true states*. One of these states, whichever is true, happened already.

Two errors may be committed: punishing an innocent person, outcome *GI*, or freeing a guilty person, outcome *IG*. Which of these errors should we consider worse? Most people consider punishing an innocent person worse and wish to make this error as seldom as possible. However, once all relevant information in a trial has been introduced and deliberated, an attitude that favors reducing the number of errors *GI* can be achieved only at the cost of increasing the number of errors *IG*. This is a version of the uncertainty principle* which suggests that there is a trade-off between the two errors. Your choice of which is the most undesirable error is value laden, and your vote on a jury will be influenced by it. The values that guide the choice of which type error to make smaller, punishing an innocent person (error of commission) or freeing a guilty person (error of omission), may change for the person and for the group of which he is a part. In the Western world a person is innocent until proven guilty. Therefore, punishing the innocent is considered the worst outcome. But during World War II, after Pearl Harbor, when the American people felt a threat to the fabric of their society, innocent Japanese-Americans were put in special internment camps for the duration of the war. During that period in our history punishing the innocent was not considered as undesirable as freeing the guilty, and we acted accordingly. The pendulum can swing one way or the other in terms of which error is considered worse.

While the judge rules on *relevance* of the evidence presented in court, the jury decides on its *credibility* in reaching a verdict beyond reasonable doubt. What constitutes "reasonable" depends on individual values. Often the decision of what constitutes reasonable doubt in the mind of a member of a jury is established more by moral law than legal law, that is, more by human values than by reasoning on the basis of evidence. However, both values and reasoning are present in the final analysis of human reasonable behavior.

THE FARMER'S DAUGHTER

Mr. Johnson must decide what to do next year on his farm. It has been a tradition with farmer Johnson to employ tools for thinking to represent a situation before making a decision. After considering many alternative courses of action, he derived the model of Figure 1.3 with three courses of action and three states of nature representing weather conditions. The model is abstract in a number of ways. The number of alternative actions is smaller than the number available in general. This could be due to constraints, such as availability of crops, financial resources, or other factors. The alternatives could be expanded

Patterns of Problem Solving [2, p. 219].

		Perfect	Fair	Bad
	Plant crop *A*	$100,000	$10,000	−$20,000
Action	Plant crop *B*	$80,000	$40,000	$0
	Lease the land	$30,000	$30,000	$30,000

Figure 1.3 The farmer: representation of what the farmer can do and what may happen.

to include various combinations of crop *A* and crop *B*. The states of nature such as rainfall, levels of temperature, winds, and so on, which are relevant to the success of the crops, could be described to various degrees of detail. The simplification to the three states of *Perfect, Fair,* and *Bad* constitutes a high level of abstraction that includes many variable conditions within some bounds. For example, the state *Perfect* may imply that yearly rainfall is between certain bounds, and that the number of days of above 100°F temperature does not exceed a certain number, and so on.

The array of numbers in Figure 1.3 is called a *payoff matrix* and represents the outcomes in the form of profits or losses farmer Johnson believes will result. For example, when he plants crop *B* the profits will be $80,000, $40,000, or $0, depending on whether the state of nature is respectively Perfect, Fair, or Bad.

Normally, we would consider profit in dollars as the measure of success in the enterprise described by Figure 1.3. But people are concerned with other factors even in what appear to be matters of money. Farmer Johnson has an 18-year-old daughter who has been begging him for a chance to go to college. He has given her a number of reasons why she cannot go. He is supporting a son in college, his parents are old and need his help, and his financial resources are not sufficient. The daughter could help on the farm if she were to stay at home rather than go to college and become an additional financial burden. Besides, Mr. Johnson does not believe it is important for a woman to have a college education. This is part of his value system.

In the past 10 years farmer Johnson has been planting crop *A*, always hoping for the big profit from this crop under *Perfect* weather. In the first two years he was lucky, but five of the 10 years the weather was *Bad*, and in three years it was *Fair*. This put him in a poor financial state. If he plants crop *A* and the weather is not *Perfect*, he cannot send his daughter to college. If he plants crop *B* and the weather is *Bad*, he cannot send his daughter to college. However, if he leases the land, he can send his daughter to college regardless of what the state of the weather might be. But then he will have to forgo the dream of buying the adjoining farmland and the new farm equipment for the expanded farm. This dream could be realized if he plants crop *A* under *Perfect* weather conditions two more times in the next two years. The farmer is beginning a new set of 10 years in farming; maybe he will be as lucky these first two years as he was in the first two of the preceding 10. But what if the weather is only *Fair,* or worse yet, *Bad?*

After thinking more about the expenses of the next two years, farmer Johnson decided that if he could attain a profit of at least $140,000 in the next two years combined, he could realize his dream and still send his daughter to college. This could be achieved with the following outcomes. (For simplicity we consider that the model of Figure 1.3 will apply for the next two years.)

First year and second year: Plant *A*–perfect weather

or

First year and second year: Plant *B*–perfect weather

or

First year: Plant *A*–perfect weather
Second year: Plant *B*–perfect or fair weather

or

First year: Plant *B*–perfect or fair weather
Second year: Plant *A*–perfect weather

The model of Figure 1.3 can help *structure* the elements of the problem, facilitate *communication*, gain *understanding*, and enhance the ability to *predict* consequences of actions. But the structure itself is no substitute for thinking. It is an aid to thinking. Reasonable thinking includes values and related qualitative features that cannot always be translated to quantitative equivalents.

Farmer Johnson used the model of Figure 1.3 as an aid to thinking. He decided to lease the land. His daughter went to college.

IMPORTANCE OF PROBLEM REPRESENTATION

The preceding three examples of problem situations for the doctors, the jury, and the farmer had a common structure, a similar form of representation. We *did not* show how to solve the problems but rather how to represent their relevant elements in a form that can serve as a tool for thinking. The representation is a framework for thought and it may provide new insight that did not exist before; it may suggest new alternatives, new connections, or cues to information known but not retrieved before; or it may help us identify the need for unknown information. It may even lead to the conclusion that there is no problem, or that a problem exists but should be ignored.

The key point is that often we move too quickly into a problem-solving mode when we should spend more time on problem representation. Think of the word representation as if it were written in the form re-presentation. A problem well understood and well stated is often half solved. Understanding and clarity in statement can be aided by presenting a problem from one point of view and then re-presenting it from another. This enhances the potential for alternative ways of perceiving a situation and thinking about it. Our creativity is often sparked not only by what we do but by how we think about something and how we perceive it. You see more of an object when you look at it from a number of positions. What may have been hidden from one vantage point is revealed from another. A new representation (a re-presentation) may be likened to changing your position as you move around an object. A representation is a frame of reference. The picture changes as you change the frame of reference.

1.2 Anatomy of a Problem

What is a problem? Let us develop the following broad definition as a frame of reference. A problem exists when the following elements are present in the mind of a human problem solver:

A perceived present or initial state
A perceived desired goal or end state
Perceived obstacles that prevent bridging the gap between the present and goal state

The level of difficulty of a problem is determined by the perception of how insurmountable the obstacles are. An obstacle may be the inability to identify a process that might bridge the gap between an initial and goal state. For example, in Figure 1.1 we may be unaware of any treatment that can bring the sick boy closer to the desired state of *Cure*. When a process is known, we may consider the level of uncertainty in the consequences of applying it as an obstacle to overcome. The obstacle may even be our inability to define properly the initial state, in which case our present state is "a poorly defined initial state" and the goal state is "a well-defined initial state." Similarly, the obstacle may be a poorly defined goal state. Both the initial and goal states may be poorly defined.

Many erroneous problems are a result of errors in the assessment of an initial state, an ill-defined or incompletely articulated goal state, or both. Using the most powerful techniques and ideas to solve the wrong problem will not only do no good but may sometimes do harm by destroying what we already have.

Even when you consider the present state to be no different from the goal state, and you wish to preserve the status quo, you may still have a problem because there may be obstacles in the form of disruptive forces that can change the status quo.

The elements of a problem in general that we have identified here are broad enough to encompass any kind of problem we wish to deal with, from the problems described in the models of Figures 1.1, 1.2, and 1.3, to puzzles, playing chess, personal problems, professional problems, social problems, political problems and so on.

The anatomy of a problem focuses on three main elements, *initial state, goal state,* and *processes,* as shown in Figure 1.4. A process may consist of

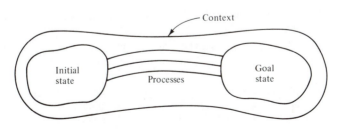

Figure 1.4   Anatomy of a problem

actions that can bridge the gap between the initial and goal states. The goal state must include what we wish to achieve as well as what we wish to avoid.

The greatest efforts in education are devoted to the process, that is, to teaching what to do under given conditions and how to do it. Many problems in mathematics begin with the word "given" and conclude with "find. . . ." Namely, the initial state and goal state are specified, and the student is instructed to identify and apply a process to bridge the gap between the given and desired states.

Most problems encountered in life normally require great effort to achieve well-thought-out descriptions of what we have and what we desire. Often, we do not devote sufficient time to generate well-defined initial and goal states, and we rush to generate and apply a process that does more harm by disturbing what we wish to preserve than it does good by achieving new goals. An additional feature that should be included is the *context* of the problem, the frame of reference that the problem solver considers. The situation of farmer Johnson as represented by Figure 1.3 changed drastically when it was considered in a context that included his daughter's desire to go to college. Problems are not solved in a vacuum; the context must be considered in the representation as shown schematically in Figure 1.4. Often, as the context changes the nature of the problem changes. In general, the values of a problem solver constitute a very important context and frame of reference for problem representation and solution. The model of Figure 1.4, despite its high level of abstraction, can serve as a useful and practical structure to remind us of the need to consider all three elements in the anatomy of a problem as an integrated whole embedded in a context. The context and each of the elements must be examined carefully. The solution to a problem can take on various forms. It may consist of going around an obstacle without ever removing it, or it may even use an obstacle to an advantage. The solution may have the form of a new perception that there is no problem, as a result of a reassessment of the present and goal states.

In the following we present four examples of problem situations focusing on key points from the discussion above.

Example 1: Is There a Problem?

A friend of mine, who was the president of a large company engaged in research and development, related to me the following story. A division of the company was awarded a contract by a local government agency to solve a problem relating to the English reading abilities of children in the third grade of a public school in a Mexican-American community. The initial and goal states in the anatomy of the problem were as follows:

> *Initial state:*   The children in the third grade of the school cannot read English at their grade level.
>
> *Goal state:*   The children should be able to read English at their grade level within six months.

The initial and goal states were identified in more detail in terms of the specific vocabulary; the requirements for reading, writing, and spelling; and general comprehension. But in essence the given and desired states were stipulated just as they are stipulated in drill-type problems in a mathematics textbook. It was implied that the problem existed because obstacles were present such as the language spoken at home, the limited help children could receive at home, economic issues that deprived the children of a good education, and other obstacles. These obstacles created the gap between the given and desired states. The solution was perceived as a process that could bridge the gap that existed between the actual and desired states. The president described to me such a process that included, among other features, a computer-aided instruction component. The solution process was impressive. But was there a problem? As it turned out, the reading ability of the students was determined from a test. Each page of the test had a picture and five words. The instructions on top of each page read as follows: "Underline the word that corresponds to the picture below." The children could read the five words, but most of them had never encountered the words *underline* and *correspond* before. Therefore, the test results were more a measure of the students' abilities to read and comprehend the test instructions than their ability to read English at their grade level. When a new examination was administered without the written instructions, and instead the teachers explained to the students by example what they were expected to do, there was no evidence that the students could not read at their grade level. The perceived initial state was in error, leading to an erroneous problem.

Example 2: Context? What Is the Context?

The "Brazilian killer bees problem" started in Brazil when the government sponsored an effort to introduce a new breed of bees to the country. Brazil's predominantly Italian bees were becoming lazy and unproductive and it was thought that by breeding them with a species of an industrious African honeybee the production of honey would be increased. The difficulty was the evil temper of the African bees. Therefore, 70 queens each with 100 workers were collected in Africa and taken to Brazil for study at a research center. The queens had their wings clipped so they could not escape and the hives were protected by wire screens to prevent the escape of new queens born in captivity. Only the much smaller worker bees could squeeze through the screens to collect nectar for the production of honey. One day a technician removed the screens from the hives at the research center where the African bees were studied. More than two dozen new queens, each with its swarm of workers, escaped the beehives into the wilds of Brazil. About seven years after this accident, stories began to float around about swarms of wild bees stinging animals and people to death. Thus had started the story of the Brazilian killer bees. By 1974 when the last death was reported, 16 people and many animals had died from bee stings.*

How do we deal with such a problem? What should be the goal state? What is the proper context? The initial state description in terms of the killings as the only context can lead to an emotional reaction and the selection of a process to get rid of the bees. But this would eliminate the honey these bees could produce. In the context of the need for honey the thinking may focus on alternative processes for making the bees more docile without affecting the production of honey to a large extent.

Example 3: The Role of Values

In 1958 the people in the San Francisco Bay area brought to a halt the construction of the Embarcadero Freeway, which was partially built. The construction of the freeway was perceived as a process to bridge a gap between an existing and a goal state inasmuch as transportation and mobility in the Bay area were concerned. But the solution process

*The killer bee story appeared in the *Wall Street Journal,* January 15, 1980.

put in jeopardy an aesthetic value when the elevated portions of the new freeway structure obstructed the beautiful view of the bay. The people in the area were not willing to pay the price of aesthetics for the gain in mobility. The context of the problem was not fully explored at the stage of problem representation.

Example 4: Benefits of a Model

A mathematics instructor used the model of Figure 1.4 in teaching a remedial arithmetic class. When the students were given mathematics word problems, she asked them to present the problem by considering four elements:

WHAT IS GIVEN?   WHAT DO YOU WANT?

PROCESS NEEDED   ESTIMATE

She introduced the idea of asking for an *estimate* of the answer in the form of a flexible preliminary assessment of the "ballpark" for an answer. Repeated use of the model by the students yielded the following results as reported by the teacher:

There was a change in focus from the solution process to the sorting of information.

There was a marked improvement in problem-solving ability.

The model helped the students to organize their work.

The model helped the students to discover the processes needed. Instead of wild guesses, they tried to identify a *process* that could connect *what was given* with *what was desired*.

A side benefit of the model was an improvement in reading comprehension. It helped students pick out the important sentences in mathematics word problems and it apparently helped them do the same for their general reading—as reported by their English teachers.

1.3 Elements of Problem Structure

Figure 1.5 is another way of looking at important elements of problem structure in general. First we identify a *need* to bridge a gap between an initial

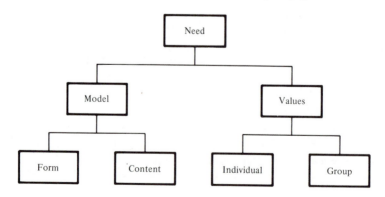

Figure 1.5 Elements of problem structure.

and a goal state. A model is constructed to help us communicate the elements of the problem to others or to clarify them to ourselves. This may improve our understanding of the relationships between the elements and thus enhance our ability to predict consequences of actions that we can take. A model has both a *form* and a *content*. In Figures 1.1 to 1.3 the form was a matrix with the rows identifying the actions we can control directly and the columns identifying states over which we have no control. The form was identical for the three problems, as shown in Figure 1.6. The content, however, was different.

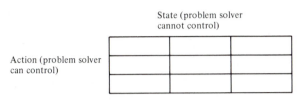

Figure 1.6 General form of model for Figures 1.1, 1.2, and 1.3.

At the same level as the *model* in Figure 1.5 we have the *values* of the problem solver and values of others that the problem solver considers important. These values influence the construction of the model. Actions may be included or excluded based on your values and the values of others important to you, depending on your motivation to comply with what you believe is expected of you. *Values* make references to what matters to us, and to our predispositions in the form of general *attitudes* to people, objects, and experiences. Our attitudes span the spectrum from unfavorable to neutral to favorable. For example, our attitude to a problem we face may be viewed as a source of frustration—an unfavorable attitude, or as a challenge—a favorable attitude. The attitudes we hold are a function of our past experiences and the beliefs or opinions we hold. There are a number of attitudes that appear to be productive in human problem solving. These will be discussed later.

1.4 Models, Uncertainty, and Values

In our discussion in the preceding pages we used the words *model, uncertainty*, and *values*. These words represent concepts that are central to thinking and problem solving, and therefore we explore them here in more detail.

MODELS

A model is a simpler representation of a real-world problem. The models of Figures 1.1 to 1.3 are such simpler representations. A *model* is created to help us *communicate*, gain *understanding*, and enhance our ability to *predict* consequences of actions that we can take. *A model should aid the thinking process. A model is a tool for thinking*. To serve this general purpose it must be simple enough, in particular in the early stages of thinking about a problem, so that we can comprehend it. Therefore, only the most important elements are included in the model. We suppress detail but try not to oversimplify the representation to the point where the model is no longer useful. Models can be expanded to include more detail and they become more complete as we gain understanding from working with simpler models first.

UNCERTAINTY AND INFORMATION

Uncertainty is present in most situations that we face. It is part of the human condition. We must learn to accept this fact and deal with uncertainty in two fundamental ways: *develop tools to reduce it when we can,* and *learn to tolerate it when we cannot reduce it anymore.* The fact remains that in most real-life problems we cannot eliminate uncertainty altogether unless we create unrealistic models of the world. The predisposition to tolerating uncertainty is a crucial attitude for creative human thinking and problem solving.

Uncertainty can be reduced by the acquisition of *information.* But before information is acquired it must be studied for *relevance, credibility,* and *worth,* in that order. Information is *relevant* when it matters whether we have it or not. Information can be *relevant* in one context and irrelevant in another. For example, if farmer Johnson in Figure 1.3 can obtain $100,000 instead of $30,000 from leasing the land, information regarding the weather is irrelevant to his decision. However, such information is relevant in the problem as given in Figure 1.3.

Information is *credible* when it is accurate, and we can trust its source. The degree of accuracy can vary, but it is important not to ignore accuracy. This is not to suggest that inaccurate information cannot be used. To the contrary, sometimes a perfectly inaccurate source tells a great deal. For example, if only two mutually exclusive events A or B can occur in a model, the prediction of A by a perfectly inaccurate source is as good as the prediction of B by a perfectly accurate source, as long as we know that the inaccurate source is always wrong in its predictions.

If we are satisfied with the relevance and credibility of the information, we must next establish its *worth.* Namely, we must calculate the additional benefit gained from the availability of the information and compare this gain with the cost (in the form of time, money, etc.) of the information. The preceding evaluation of information in three steps in terms of relevance, credibility, and worth is summarized in the tree of Figure 1.7.

VALUES

Each of our three stories involving doctors, a jury, and farmer Johnson was value laden. Values affect the choice of a solution to a problem, they affect the choice of the problem to be solved, and they affect the choice of representation. Whenever a human problem solver applies a general precept of problem solving such as constructing a model, identifying alternative courses of action, or reacting to uncertainty, all these activities are performed by a person rooted in a

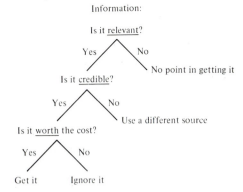

Information:

Is it relevant?

Yes / No

No point in getting it

Is it credible?

Yes / No

Use a different source

Is it worth the cost?

Yes / No

Get it   Ignore it

Figure 1.7 Evaluating information in three steps.

culture and a community with distinct attitudes and associated values. This perspective influences the choice of problems, the solution to problems, and the way problems are perceived. Values are a fundamental frame of reference for thinking and problem solving.

1.5 The Role of Culture in Thinking and Problem Solving

The ways we perceive reality, the ways we think, and the ways we solve problems are all embedded in a context. The context is structured in levels. At the highest level is the context of the culture of which we are a part. At lower levels we have the context of individual values and values of the community and family. The context of culture may determine whether individual or community values are at a higher level. For example, in the culture of the Far East, community values take precedence over individual values. In the Western world, values of the individual may prevail. Culture constitutes a frame of reference that can explain as well as predict the behavior of its members. A culture normally preserves those features of perception, and of representation in language and in art, that served the cause of its survival in the environment where the culture had developed.

These preserved features of perception and representation have served as guides to behavior for the members of a culture, to enhance the probability of survival. For example, the Eskimos created many words to distinguish different kinds of snow. The Bassa language spoken in Liberia created only two words for the entire spectrum of color, one word for purple, blue, and green, and another word for yellow, orange, and red. In the Wintu language spoken by the Wintu Indians of California, representation of spatial situations is governed by the topology of form. For instance, when a Wintu Indian sees what we describe in English as "There is a book on the table" he says in Wintu "The table bumps." Namely, the surface, or terrain, is not flat. This shows that the Wintu-speaking Indians have a strong orientation to perceiving and thinking in terms of the topology of form and this overshadows the feature of relationship between the position of the book with respect to the table, or the presence of the two objects in the first place. The feature of relationships between objects reflects the context of Western culture.

CULTURE AND ART

The influence of culture finds expression in art. The value and importance of the individual compared to the entire community, the significance attached to life here and now compared to eternity, and the difference between what we see and what we believe is really out there are manifested in the different ways that art developed in the East and West. Japanese artists did not paint shadows, because to them a shadow was only a temporary short-lived change in appearance, not an important permanent aspect of reality shared by all observers. When the Dutch treatises on perspective were introduced in Japan at the end of the eighteenth century, the Japanese artists adopted it in a form that was compatible with the context of their culture. European painters considered that reality, as it appeared to an individual observer, was an important feature. Therefore, their paintings had a central perspective in which lines that were actually parallel were shown progressively converging, appearing closer together, at larger distances from the observer. In Japanese paintings, parallel lines in reality remained parallel in the painting. In the Eastern culture it was more important to capture on canvas the way things were rather than the way they appeared to an observer.

CLASSIFICATION OF CULTURES

Cultures can be described and classified in many ways. What we wish to do here is isolate dominant features that can be used as high-level values that guide, to some extent, thinking and problem-solving behavior. These high-level values can be viewed as a context and frame of reference to explain and predict behavior. The context of culture is a major element in constructing models for human thinking and problem solving. The following key features characterize the cultures of the Middle East, East, and West.

In most *Middle East cultures*, prestige, dignity, and being in control, whether real or perceived, are dominant.

In *Eastern culture* the preservation of human harmony and group membership are dominant.

In *Western culture* getting the job done and achieving tangible results are dominant.

In the following two sections we focus attention on aspects of the cultures prevalent in the Middle East and in Japan, as compared to Western culture, using stories to illustrate how the context of a culture serves as a frame of reference to guide thinking and problem-solving behavior.

1.6 The Importance of Control and Prestige

THE ELEVATOR STORY: WHO IS IN CONTROL HERE?

Story has it that when elevators were introduced in some of the large cities in the Middle East it was not uncommon to witness the following episode. An office worker is standing at the ninth floor of a multistory building and wishes to go down to the first floor. He notices from the numbers on the lighted panel above the elevator door that the elevator is on the second floor. He therefore pushes the "up" button to summon the elevator to the ninth floor. Once inside the elevator he pushes the button for the first floor only to discover that the elevator ignores his command and keeps going up to pick up and deliver other passengers. The worker gets very upset. There is something wrong with the technology of the twentieth century, he claims. Things do not work right. What is going on?

When you explain to the office worker that by pressing the "up" or "down" buttons you do not instruct the elevator what to do, but rather "tell" it where you wish to go, he may look at you as if you were a lunatic. He will tell you that it is none of the elevator's business to know where he wants to go. In the culture of the Middle East it makes no sense to tell a machine where you want to go. This compromises dignity. It is much more sensible to tell the machine what it ought to do and expect it to respond—so that you remain in control.

In the Western world we do not question who is in control; we indeed tell the elevator where we wish to go and let it take over and decide when and where to stop. We accept the fact that by pressing the "up" and "down" buttons we tell the elevator where we want to go, not command it to go up or down.

We could, of course, design elevators to follow our instructions directly but then they would not operate efficiently to reconcile the conflicting desire of many users waiting for an elevator at the same time. However, is efficiency so important that we are willing to compromise our "dignity" and tell a "dumb" machine what we want to do? In Western culture it is efficiency that serves the cause of achievements which is important. In other cultures this may not be the case.

THE TWO SONS: ACHIEVEMENT VERSUS RESPECT

A missionary who was a student of cultures once wanted to test the behavior of an Arab audience in the Middle East. He presented the audience with the following story of the two sons in the parable of the New Testament (Matt. 21:38):

"A certain man had two sons; and he came to the first and said, 'Son, go to work today in my vineyard.'

He answered and said, 'I will not!' but afterwards he repented and went.

And he came to the second, and said likewise. And he answered and said, 'I go sir!' and went not."

The Arabs in the audience had a strong preference for the second son because he showed respect by his answer. The achievement of the task was secondary in importance compared to the control perceived through apparent obedience and respect. To disobey the father is to challenge his control, his dominance. The only way the father assures himself of his control is by exercising it and seeing to it that it is not challenged; achievement is not of equal importance.

1.7 The Quest for Harmony

HARMONY AND PRODUCTIVITY

A great deal has been written in recent years on the productivity of Japanese industry [3]. To emulate the Japanese style may be very difficult because their productivity must be viewed in the context of their culture. It is a culture in which group affiliation is of prime importance, where the desires and expectations of the team guide individual behavior, where doing what is expected of you by the group takes precedence over individual desires. The quest for human harmony constitutes an overriding frame of reference—a contextual guide to explain and predict behavior.

CONTROL MECHANISMS IN ORGANIZATION

In a paper on organizational dynamics, Ouchi and Price [4] suggest that organized efforts can be managed or controlled through one of three basic social mechanisms: *markets, bureaucratic hierarchies,* and *clans*. Each mechanism can provide motivation to pursue acceptable goals and provide the information required for productive efforts to achieve them.

A *market* has a control mechanism in the form of a *price*. When a price is properly set it motivates people to act in a way that satisfies both individuals and the organization.

A *bureaucratic hierarchy* has control that depends on *employees who agree to be monitored* by their superiors and told what to do. This normally leads to high job specializations. In a bureaucratic hierarchy, employees have less freedom than in a market pricing mechanism.

A *clan* has a mechanism of control that derives from a *shared set of values* by its members. The clan is a social unit, in which the goals of the individual merge with those of the organization. This provides the motivation to pursue the common goals with information flowing freely to ensure high productivity in individual efforts.

For successful control in organized efforts, the market mechanism requires accurate price mechanisms to assess values of contributions. The bureaucratic hierarchy requires rules for control. The clan requires harmony and stability.

There is no pure single control mechanism in an organization. The label of each mechanism of control, such as *market, bureaucratic hierarchy,* or *clan,* merely indicates which is the dominant one in an organization.

Japan provides the most striking examples of industrial clans, where average absentee rates in industry are below 2 percent and productivity in the last three decades has increased two to three times over that in the United States.

Japanese society is hierarchical in nature, but it does not depend on bureaucratic hierarchy of organization as a mechanism of control as do organizations in the Western world. Decision making does not follow a rigid "top-down" sequence in which orders flow from the top down. In the business world, for example, planning is a slow process, with information flowing from the bottom of the hierarchy up and back, until each member in the group understands what is expected of him or her. Only after consensus has been reached does the implementation phase begin, and it normally proceeds quite smoothly and rapidly. Thus the Japanese approach to business decision making is to take more time for planning so that less time is required for implementation.

THE ROLE OF LANGUAGE

In 1965, I was invited by one of the largest construction companies in Japan to give a series of lectures to their engineering and management staff. Hiroshi Nei, an engineer with the company and a former student of mine in the United States, was assigned to act as my official host. The evening before my lectures were to begin I presented Hiroshi with two plans, plan *A* and plan *B*, that I was considering for the lectures and I asked: "Hiroshi, should I use plan *A* or plan *B?*" Hiroshi responded very politely with: "Yes." Thinking for a moment that perhaps I did not make myself clear, I repeated the question and received the same response. It became clear that this was the answer, "yes," I should use plan *A* or plan *B*.

The Japanese language has its grammar and syntactical rules, but these play a less important part in communication than the issues of courtesy and the preservation of human harmony. When teachers and parents ask children to speak correctly, the reference is most likely to aspects of courtesy involved in speaking Japanese, not to the grammar.

For example, there are a number of ways of saying "you," one when addressing a brother, one for a friend, one for an uncle, a boss, a subordinate, and so on. To speak properly means choosing the proper words for the occasion. By employing the appropriate "you," the speaker indicates that he knows the relative position or relationship between himself and the listener, and this leads to a corresponding level of courtesy that preserves the harmony in the encounter.

When a Japanese is not sure what is expected of him, communication will deliberately include a built-in ambiguity and vagueness to leave room for discussion, consideration, and further assessment. This was the reason for Hiroshi's answer. In his mind what was most important were the issues of harmony and courtesy, not a focus on his opinion on the matter, although I asked for it. A vague ambiguous response leaves room for more discussion and is less likely to lead to conflict and to a disruption of harmony. What if Hiroshi had said immediately that plan *A* was better and I reacted by saying that I thought plan *B* was better? Hiroshi thought that under the circumstances, courtesy called for letting me decide alone. I was his former professor and he was my host in his home country. Hiroshi was withholding judgment for the cause of courtesy and harmony.

LAW, LAWYERS, AND DOING BUSINESS

The preservation of human harmony is manifested in other aspects of Japanese life. In the United States there are approximately 600,000 lawyers; California alone has about 80,000 lawyers. Japan, with a population that is about one half the population of the United States has approximately 12,000 lawyers. The culture in Japan is founded on human harmony. Lawyers are therefore required only in extreme cases when conflict and resulting disharmony occur. A lawyer in Japan is used as an agent for *corrective measures* to remedy conflict and disharmony, not as an agent to provide *preventive measures* via contractual agreements between parties as is the custom in the United States. These different attitudes toward lawyers are best illustrated in the conduct of business in the United States and Japan. In the United States it is considered prudent to employ the services of a lawyer in business contracts of all sorts. We use lawyers in advance to avoid possible disputes in the future. The basic premise is to hope for the best but be ready for the worst. The attitude of readiness for the worst is tantamount to viewing the parties to an agreement as adversaries and writing the terms of the agreement accordingly.

When Japanese negotiate a contract they do not think that they are negotiating with adversaries. There is a higher context of preserving harmony. Bringing in lawyers would be considered offensive—a signal of distrust, and thus disruptive to harmony.

I am reminded of a book that I read about the Japanese culture [5]. The author describes how salesmen would go about selling cash registers in Japan and in the United States. The salesmen in the two countries, representing different cultures, would use entirely different approaches to persuade a potential customer to make a purchase. In the United States the basic premise would be that human beings are weak and can be tempted to become dishonest in dealing with cash. Thus to keep clerks in a business honest, a cash register may be a good safeguard. In Japan you would not sell a single cash register using such an approach. The Japanese strive to preserve harmony in human relations. In this context a salesman would argue that human beings are prone to making unintentional mistakes. Thus a clerk working long hours is prone to errors in calculations. When errors are discovered at the end of a day because sales records do not agree with the amount of cash, they lead to unpleasant feelings which are disruptive to the harmony in the organization. The introduction of a cash register is then featured as a good way to reduce errors of this kind, and thus contribute to the preservation of harmony among the people in a business.

MASLOW'S HIERARCHY OF HUMAN VALUES

Maslow's hierarchy of human needs [6] has also been used to explain the Japanese propensity for productivity and achievement by suggesting that achievement is a human need that follows the need for membership in a group. The five basic human needs according to Maslow are, in order from lowest to highest:

Home
Unthreatened (safety)
Membership
Achievement
Novelty (self-actualization)

I chose the words describing Maslow's hierarchy of human needs so that the first letters of the five words spell HUMAN. *Home* stands for shelter and basic physiological needs. *Unthreatened* represents the need for safety. *Membership* is the need to belong. *Achievement* is manifested by the need for esteem and respect from peers and colleagues. Beyond achievement, *Novelty* represents actions taken for self-fulfillment. According to Maslow, the needs surface in hierarchical order. When the physiological needs are not satisfied, the higher-level needs hold little meaning for the individual. When physiological needs are satisfied, safety becomes important, then belonging, then esteem, and finally comes self-actualization after all the preceding four needs have been satisfied. I recall a situation during a war when my safety was threatened very seriously. I made a vow not to ask for esteem, or novelty, in fact for anything, if I only survived. I survived, and then the other needs surfaced despite my vow.

In many Japanese businesses the practice is to give people job security so that the need to be unthreatened is satisfied. The strong commitment to harmony and group affiliation leads to the satisfaction of the need to belong, or membership. Thus the way is open for the need to achieve to surface.

GROUP AFFILIATION

Although it is difficult and time consuming to change behavior, it is still worthwhile to learn from the Japanese culture a number of lessons in the conduct of human affairs. In listening to others speak, we ought to focus on what they say and delay judgment. In working with groups, the initial efforts should be devoted to sorting out facts, not to expressing opinions. As members of a group we should attempt to seek a balance between our individual needs and the need for harmony in the group. In making decisions, as individuals or in a group, we ought to take sufficient time to plan so that less difficulty is likely to be encountered in the implementation of decisions.

1.8 Frames of Reference and How They Change

Thomas Kuhn discusses frames of reference in science in his book *The Structure of Scientific Revolution* [7]. The frames of reference are the established patterns of thinking and problem solving, namely the established context that guides work on new hypotheses, models, theories, experimentation, and interpretation of observations. Kuhn uses the word "paradigm" to describe the scientific frames of reference. These include the paradigms of Copernican astronomy, Newtonian mechanics, the theory of relativity, and so on. Kuhn maintains that most scientific work is performed in the context of an existing paradigm. Emphasis is placed on facts in observed phenomena that are important to the paradigm, and attempts are made to explain observation by using the models of the paradigm. The basic aim is to continue the search for understanding by standing on the shoulders of the existing paradigm. A change in paradigm comes about as a result of a scientific breakthrough that shakes the foundation of the existing paradigm and replaces it with a new one. The new paradigm creates a new context, a new frame of reference. Sometimes the new frame of reference becomes a higher-level context that includes the old frame as a subset. Sometimes the two frames of reference exist side by side, permitting alternative ways, or complementary ways, of viewing aspects of reality.

A rigid commitment to a paradigm may lead you to reject an observed fact when it does not fit a paradigm, or to accept as fact what has not been observed when the paradigm model predicts its existence. This is illustrated by the stories on the observation of the planet Uranus and the prediction of the existence of Vulcanus, a planet that has never been observed, as we relate in the following.

THE PLANETS

Kepler knew of six planets revolving around the sun. In 1781, about 150 years after Kepler's death, the astronomer Herschel observed a seventh planet,* Uranus, revolving beyond Saturn. The following six planets (written in order of their distance from the sun), Mercury, Venus, Earth, Mars, Jupiter, and Saturn, were known from the early days in the history of civilization. The model included only these planets and no more. Kuhn relates that when the object in the position of Uranus was observed on several occasions before Herschel observed it, it was not identified as a planet because it did not fit the accepted frame of reference of only six planets with no planets beyond Saturn. Even Herschel first interpreted his finding as a comet and not a planet because it had a visible disk. It was many months later, after continued observations and study, that the scientific community concluded that it must be a planet and thus changed the paradigm by permitting additional planets in the solar system.

The observed orbit of Uranus did not agree with the predictions of Newton's model.† Using the new paradigm, astronomers hypothesized that the deviations of Uranus from the orbit predicted by the model must be attributed to attraction from a planet beyond Uranus. Leverrier, a French astronomer, investigated this hypothesis and predicted the existence of an ultra-Uranian planet. He mapped the orbit of this planet on the basis of the orbit of Uranus,

---

*Hundreds of minor planets have been observed since then to revolve between the orbits of the major planets.

†Newton's model is referred to here as a more general model which contains Kepler's model for the solar system.

using Newton's model, and assigned its position in the skies. He wrote about his findings to a colleague at a well-equipped observatory and asked that the planet be observed on the night of September 23, 1846. The letter arrived on that day, and the same evening the new planet was found within 1 degree of the location predicted by Leverrier. The mass and orbit were later also determined to agree with Leverrier's prediction.

The ultra-Uranian planet predicted by Leverrier is the planet Neptune. It is interesting to note that after the discovery of Neptune, irregularities were observed in its orbit. These were also explained by Newton's model and were attributed to the existence of a small planet beyond Neptune. This small planet is Pluto, which was discovered in 1930.

Astronomers were overwhelmed by the mounting evidence that was continually enhancing the credibility of Newton's model. The model explained the irregularities in the orbit of Uranus by predicting the existence of Neptune. Then it explained the irregularities in the orbit of Neptune by predicting the existence of Pluto. It is not surprising, therefore, to learn that astronomers predicted the existence of another planet in the vicinity of Mercury to explain the irregularities observed by Leverrier in its orbit. So strong was their conviction that they even named this planet Vulcanus. To the present day no trace of Vulcanus has ever been found.

Vulcanus was one of a number of failures that started casting some doubt on the domain of validity of Newton's model. It took the general theory of relativity to explain the irregularities in the orbit of Mercury, which is the nearest planet to the sun (see Table 1.1). These irregularities were attributed to the curvature of space-time in the neighborhood of a large mass, such as the mass of the sun. The paradigm of general relativity took over at the point where Newton's paradigm reached the limit in its ability to explain and predict natural phenomena. Newton's model became, then, a subset of the more general and more powerful paradigm of relativity.

In a similar vein, when biologists and geologists suggested, on the basis of studies in their fields with associated paradigms, that geological times must go back millions of years, the famous British physicist and mathematician Kelvin (1824–1907) dismissed this idea because it did not fit his paradigm.

Table 1.1 Distances of the planets from the sun

Planet	Distance from the Sun (millions of kilometers)
Mercury	58
Venus	108
Earth	150
Mars	228
Jupiter	778
Saturn	1400
Uranus	2900
Neptune	4500
Pluto	5900

Kelvin allegedly said: "That's absurd; why don't you people be scientific? We can prove that the sun cannot have lasted that long" [8]. Indeed, it could not, on the basis of his model for solar energy generation. The commitment to the model caused Kelvin to reject the new evidence that was consistent with models in other fields, but not his field.

LEARNING AND FRAMES OF REFERENCE

In general, the conceptual constructs, or images that we create as frames of reference, are rich and complex. Boulding discusses these images in a masterpiece of philosophical presentation entitled *The Image* [9]. We all have a number of basic concepts that enable us to form constructs that constitute frames of reference for judgments and action in the world we live in. A simplified and reduced list of these concepts includes the following:

A concept of space

A concept of time

A concept of cause–effect relationships

A concept of uncertainty

A concept of value

A concept of abstraction or level of remoteness of our images from the "reality" they symbolize or represent

A concept of levels of subscription by others to our constructs or images

Using these concepts we form representations and models as our frames of reference. When our frames of reference are fixed and rigid, they become a substitute for thinking. Learning takes place when we have the flexibility to change our frames of reference. The most creative efforts of human beings involve departing from existing frames of reference and constructing new ones.

In the following we discuss the contributions of Einstein and Picasso to the changes in frame of reference that occurred in science and art in the twentieth century.

EINSTEIN, PICASSO, AND THEIR FRAMES OF REFERENCE

Newton viewed the world through a fixed spatial frame of reference with its origin fixed in the center of gravity of the universe. Einstein revolutionized science by introducing a moving spatial frame of reference in which the observations became relative and dependent on the observer and his frame of reference.

Picasso revolutionized the approach to art in a similar way. A painting usually captured a scene from a single spatial frame of reference. Picasso introduced multiple spatial frames of reference in the same painting. In his painting *Woman of Arles* the woman's head is seen in full face and double profile as if it is in motion and the observer is taking a walk around the woman.

It is remarkable that Einstein and Picasso arrived at parallel creative developments by departing from a fixed spatial frame of reference. However, science and art are not so far apart, not quite the two separate worlds as some "frames of reference" suggest. A scientific diagram or equation reduces detail to a minimum, not unlike an abstract painting. An electron, a scientific construct, is not more "real" than Picasso's *Woman of Arles*.

The concept of time has also undergone change, and again both Einstein and Picasso contributed to the new image. Picasso departed from painting a scene as if capturing a fixed moment in time. The multiple spatial frames of reference represent different points in time as the observer is moving around the object, or if we wish to view it another way, the woman in the *Woman of Arles* is turning her head and this departs from the fixed time frame of reference.

When Einstein introduced his celebrated twin paradox, many people found it difficult to accept, because they could not depart from relating the concept of age to their fixed concept of time. In this paradox one of a pair of twin brothers goes on a space trip in which time "slows down." When he returns to earth, he is still a young man, whereas his brother has died of old age many, many years before his return, say 200 earth years earlier. How is this possible? Some may be inclined to say that they will believe this when they see it, or experience it. But how could they? Often we "see it when we believe it." That is, when we have a frame of reference that is flexible and can change, we can appreciate and comprehend or "see" new constructs or images. Let us return to Einstein's twins. We normally measure time by counting cyclic events. From sunrise to sunset is a day. The number of cyclic revolutions of the hands on a clock measures hours, minutes, and seconds. Atomic clocks of high precision count the number of particles that are emitted, and so on. The age of a human being is counted by years, which are again cyclic events, the rotations of the earth around the sun.

Suppose that we devise a new way for establishing age as follows. We will count the number of heartbeats in a lifetime. On that basis we can establish that the average age of a human being is some number x of heartbeats. If we assume that each of our twins has the same number of average heartbeats x for his lifetime, the following can happen. Imagine that for some reason the motion of the twin who is in outer space causes his heart to complete one heartbeat while the heart of the twin on earth completes 100 beats. If all biological processes "slow down" at the same rate of one cycle for the twin in space for every 100 for the twin on earth, then when the twin on earth has used up all x heartbeats, the twin in space has used up only 1% of his heartbeats. Thus he stays younger!

HOW WE SEE THINGS

A preacher once wanted to demonstrate to an audience the harmful effects of alcohol. He placed one worm in a glass of water and another in a glass of pure alcohol. The worm in the glass of water made its way to the edge of the glass and crawled out; the other worm disintegrated in the alcohol. The preacher was pleased with the demonstration, and thinking he had shown the harmful effects of alcohol, asked rhetorically: "Do you see the message of this experiment?"

Someone in the audience who was known to be a heavy drinker responded: "I see the message. If you drink alcohol you will be free of worms in your stomach" [10].

The preacher saw the events from his frame of reference, the heavy drinker from his.

THE IMPORTANCE OF FLEXIBILITY

Flexibility in employing frames of reference is crucial if we wish to enrich the ways we perceive, represent situations, use models, think, and solve problems. The psychologist Abraham Maslow said the following when he discussed the influence of rigid strict behavior in psychology: "If the only tool you have is a hammer, you tend to treat everything as if it were a nail" [11]. Maslow is warning us that the person who has only one tool in the form of a method or an instrument that he or she applies rigidly will become tool oriented and not problem-solving oriented. Thus it appears desirable to have alternative frames of reference and a number of tools for thinking and problem solving and to employ flexibility in their use.

1.9 Summary

Human values are an integral part of problem representation. They are reflected in our perception of what we can and cannot control.

The actions we choose in problem situations can be governed as much by what we wish to avoid as by what we wish to achieve.

Models can facilitate communication, contribute to understanding, and enhance our ability to predict consequences of actions. Models are aids to thinking. Human thinking and problem solving may include qualitative features that are not represented in a quantitative model. Models helps structure our thinking, but they do not tell us what to do. We decide what to do.

Models can help organize our thinking for processing information in creative ways. A model has both form and content. A model is a tool for thinking.

In most cases we do not spend sufficient time on problem representation. Problems should be presented and re-presented to change the frame of reference and enrich how and what we perceive.

A problem consists of a present state, a goal state, and obstacles that interfere with efforts to bridge the gap between the two states. Every problem is embedded in a context. The problem may change when the context changes. A different context may require a new approach and a different solution path to a problem.

Uncertainty and human values should be reflected in our models whenever possible. Uncertainty can be reduced by the acquisition of information. Before we acquire information we should consider its relevance, credibility, and worth. It is important for us to tolerate a measure of uncertainty since it is part of the human experience.

Culture influences how we perceive and describe reality. Cultures can be classified on the basis of which of the following is a dominant feature of the culture: control, harmony, or achievement.

Examples are given of how the importance of control in the Middle East influences behavior, and how the quest for harmony in Japanese culture explains the propensity to group achievements in that culture.

Maslow's hierarchy of human values includes basic physiological needs, security, group membership, achievement, and self-actualization.

Examples are given of how new frames of reference and theories come into being as a result of a revolution or shakedown of existing paradigms.

The frames of reference introduced by Picasso and Einstein are discussed. These frames of reference caused a revolution in the arts and sciences.

PROBLEMS

1.1. Describe the initial state and goal state for the problem in Figure 1.1. Discuss the role of values in this problem. How can values influence the choice of a course of action?

1.2. Describe the initial and goal states for a jury, for a person on trial, for the prosecution, for the defense, and for the judge. Discuss the role of values in judicial problems.

1.3. How could you explain the action of farmer Johnson of Figure 1.3 when he decided to lease the land so that his daughter could go to college?

1.4. Formulate a personal problem in terms of initial and goal states. Describe the context of the problem. How would the problem change as a result of change in context?

1.5. Discuss the relationship between individual and group values in Problems 1.1 and 1.2.

1.6. Describe how people deal with uncertainty. Is uncertainty always an undesirable element in a problem situation? Discuss.

1.7. Give examples of information that may be relevant in one context and irrelevant in another.

1.8. Give examples of situations in which relevant and credible information that is available but will require time for its acquisition is not worth waiting for.

1.9. Discuss the idea that uncertainty is part of the human experience and therefore we must learn to live with it.

1.10. How does culture influence thinking and problem solving?

1.11. If you were assigned to deal with "up the down elevator" story of Section 1.6, how would you state the problem in the light of the given information of perceived difficulties by the users? How would you solve the problem?

1.12. How would a father in Western culture react to the two sons in the story of Section 1.6?

1.13. Discuss how natural language and culture are interrelated.

1.14. Discuss how Maslow's hierarchy of human values could be used to predict human behavior.

1.15. How do new theories arise in physical science and in human affairs?

1.16. How do models influence learning and thinking?

1.17. How would you measure the thickness of page 180 of this book? What assumptions would you make and what frame of reference would you use?

1.18. Suppose that you are a member of the Western culture, and you negotiate a business deal with a company in the Middle East. What guidelines would you use?

1.19. What guidelines would you use if you had to negotiate with a Japanese company?

1.20. Give two examples from your own personal experience in which you moved too fast into a problem-solving phase and did not spend sufficient time in the problem representation stage.

1.21. If we cannot control states of nature, why should we be concerned with them?

1.22. Why should a model be highly abstract in the early stages?

1.23. Discuss how you believe learning takes place in your experience.

1.24. Give examples of rigid and flexible frames of reference and how they influence thinking and learning.

1.25. What is the lesson we learn from the discoveries of Neptune and Pluto and the failure to confirm the existence of Vulcanus?

1.26. Give three examples of how two people can see different things in identical messages.

1.27. Give an example of how language can reflect attributes of a culture.

1.28. What must be done to ensure the credibility of information in a large computer data base?

1.29. Show how the elements of problem structure of Figure 1.5 fit a problem of your choice.

1.30. Use circles, lines, or any other figures in combination with key words to summarize the content of the chapter on a single page. Be imaginative.

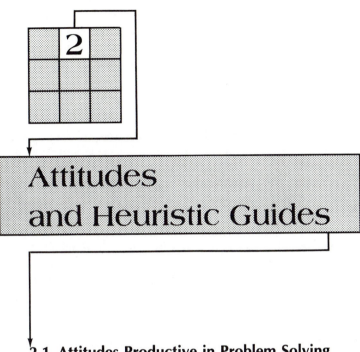

2.1 Attitudes Productive in Problem Solving

It has been said that education provides a repertoire of solutions to life's problems. In fact often our solutions apply to problems that do not arise, and we are confronted with new problems for which we have no solutions. To deal with such new problems we need to resort to a mode of behavior that is based on attitudes that are appropriate for unfamiliar situations. These attitudes should include tolerance for uncertainty and ambiguity; willingness to deal with complexity, confusion, and conflict without breaking down; accepting dissonant information; courage to take reasonable risks; and a fundamental desire to enhance our capacity for thinking and problem solving. It is easier to state the attitudes than to develop them. Nevertheless, as a first step we must become aware of their existence, and then through repeated practice and experience, we stand a good chance of developing and integrating these productive attitudes.

HOW ATTITUDES DEVELOP

Attitudes are inclinations, predispositions that guide our behavior. Attitudes develop and change with time and experience. When your general attitude to problem solving is negative, you are inclined to avoid problems. This may be the result of experiences that caused the negative aspects of problem-solving situations to outweigh the positive. You may have, for example, a negative attitude to any activity that has to do with numbers, from balancing the checkbook to doing any sort of arithmetic, let alone more advanced mathematics. This attitude may stem from a variety of experiences that were associated with unpleasant feelings when numbers were involved. I recall a story about a successful psychologist who had such a negative attitude to numbers, because of the following traumatic experience. One day when she was in the first grade the teacher had written on the blackboard the following numbers:

$$1 \; 9 \; 2 \; 3 \; 6 \; 8 \; 5$$

The teacher then asked the 6-year-old heroine of our story to walk up to the blackboard and show the class which of the numbers was the largest. With great confidence she pointed to the 2. The teacher corrected her and pointed out that 9 was the largest number. The class started laughing. The child blushed with deep embarrassment. She thought the question had to do with the size of the symbols on the board, not their numerical values. The damage was done.

In the old Jewish tradition, children were taught the alphabet with letters covered with honey. A child would point to a letter, repeat its sound after the teacher, then touch it with the forefinger and lick the honey. Here is one way to instill a positive attitude to an activity by associating it with an experience that is viewed positively. No wonder the Jewish people became known as the people of the book.

POSITIVE ATTITUDE TO THINKING AND PROBLEM SOLVING

A positive attitude to problem solving is associated with a view that considers a problem as a challenge, an enrichment of the repertoire of tools for thinking, a learning experience. With a positive attitude a frustrated effort to identify a solution process is compensated for by the elation of finding a solution or by the lessons learned from no success. Creative people have such a positive attitude to problem solving. They view an obstacle in a problem situation as an intellectual and emotional adventure. Creative people can tolerate complexity, uncertainty, conflict, and dissonance. They enjoy new experiences. They are more active than passive and have a capacity for producing results. They are doers. They seem to be in control. They radiate self-confidence. All these attributes are consistent with the positive attitude that creative people, in every field, have to problems and problem solving.

ENHANCING POSITIVE ATTITUDE TO PROBLEM SOLVING

A positive attitude to thinking and problem solving cannot be separated from the feelings generated from these activities. The more positive and enjoyable the feelings associated with an activity, the more positive the attitude to the activities. It is a delightful experience to watch the face of a child who has just solved a problem by himself, with no help, and is eager to tackle another problem. This holds true for adults as well as children.

To increase the potential for a positive attitude to thinking and problem solving, we should develop guides and tools of thinking and problem solving that are consistent with human nature and human information-processing capabilities—tools that we enjoy using; guides and tools that will enhance the likelihood of success in our efforts. Such general guides and tools will help us discover and invent new ways of thinking, different ways of perceiving reality, and new patterns of problem representation and problem solving. These enriching experiences will continue to develop our thinking and problem-solving capabilities as a lifelong learning activity. In the following sections we introduce general guides and tools that serve the cause of discovery and creative invention. These guides are called heuristics. Heuristic guides are plausible, provisional, reasonable, but not complete or certain to lead to success all the time. Heuristic guides and heuristic reasoning can enhance thinking and problem-solving efforts most of the time, but not always. Heuristics can help us in the acquisition of knowledge, in problem representation, and in a search for solutions. Heuristics may apply to thinking and problem solving in general, or they may be domain specific, as will be shown in the following sections.

2.2 Heuristic Guides [12]

ALGORITHMS AND HEURISTICS

The store of information and knowledge we possess by virtue of our past experiences includes *factual information* such as the multiplication table for digits 1 to 9, *algorithms* for generating information such as the steps required to obtain the result of $(397.5 \times 149)/20.1$, and *rules of thumb,* or general plans to guide our actions in problem solving. Such rules of thumb are known as *heuristics.* For example, in trying to obtain an answer to $(397.5 \times 149)/20.1$, we may employ a heuristic of rounding off the numbers to $(400 \times 150)/20$ so that the calculations can be performed in our head as

$$\frac{400}{20} \times 150$$

yielding $20 \times 150 = 3000$. This general plan of "estimating" or "approximating" does not guarantee the correct solution but provides a reasonable ballpark value and can serve as a check to the calculations conducted by the algorithms for multiplication and division. In fact, since in the rounding off in the example above we increased the numerator and decreased the denominator, the estimate of 3000 for the answer is an upper bound to the correct answer. Under some conditions we may use heuristics to establish upper and lower bounds for a solution. This is helpful, in particular when the search for the correct or best solution may require excessive effort.

Heuristics may also be viewed as guided procedures that increase the probability of finding solutions with less time and effort than that required by a random search or an exhaustive search by an algorithm. Heuristics place limitations or constraints on random or exhaustive search by identifying domains for the search with increased probability of leading to the answer. For example, suppose that you are asked to rearrange the letters EHT to form an English word. There are six ways of arranging the letters. Because there are three ways to choose the first letter for a position in a word, each of these three choices is followed with a choice of any of two of the remaining letters, and finally the last letter is placed in position. The tree structure of Figure 2.1 shows the six arrangements starting with the letter in the first position in the formed word, followed by the letters in second and third positions. The procedure for generating the tree can be considered an algorithm that can guide an exhaustive search for the right word at the bottom of the tree.

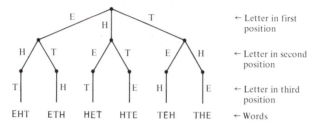

Figure 2.1 Tree structure using an algorithm.

Suppose that the letters are selected in such a way that the solution is limited to a single word; then the probability of obtaining a solution by a random search in our case of three letters is one out of six possible letter sequences, namely, 1/6. However, if we use the heuristic guide that T and H occur frequently in the combination TH and use TH as one entity and E as the other, we limit the search to two possibilities, as shown in the tree of Figure 2.2. Thus we increase the probability of finding a solution by trial and error from one out of six (1/6) possibilities to one out of two (1/2) possibilities. However, if we change letter E to O in Figure 2.2 and apply this heuristic guide, we obtain OTH or THO, neither of which is a solution. Since heuristics may sometimes fail, they must be used with caution.

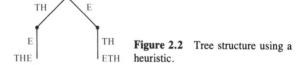

Figure 2.2 Tree structure using a heuristic.

2.3 Heuristic Guides to the Acquisition of Knowledge

A great deal has been written about learning, memory, the representation of knowledge, and the transfer of knowledge. There are some general guides that can help us organize knowledge in a way that will increase the probability of its retrieval when we need it and which will make it more likely that we transfer knowledge acquired in the past to new situations where it may be relevant and useful. These guides are based on active rather than passive involvement on our part, and on use of our imagination.

Teaching is an active rather than a passive mode of learning. Instead of studying material passively, a better technique is to teach the material to someone else. The presence of a goal to teach others requires thinking in terms of different frames of reference, such as learners with different backgrounds. This creates opportunities to perceive the subject from different points of view and it provides a number of indices for storing the material for future reference. The questions that students raise provide further insight and understanding. The act of teaching itself is a form of retrieval of the knowledge, and each retrieval constitutes an *active effort* that enhances the potential for future retrievals.

Active involvement works effectively in storing information even in the absence of an opportunity to teach. For example, when you study a subject from a book, close the book periodically and become an active learner. Write a brief summary of what you studied using your own words. This is better than the passive approach of rereading the material, highlighting it in various colors of ink, or copying it from the book using the author's words and sentences. If you cannot recall an item immediately, let it be a challenge and keep trying. If you fail to recall it, look it up but pause to devise an active scheme for storing it. Invent indices for storage that can later help you with retrieval. When you wish to memorize something, an active search for interesting acronyms is a productive process. Even when you fail to find a suitable acronym, the act of trying will contribute to a more successful future retrieval.

ACRONYMS

Acronyms can be viewed as indices for storage and retrieval. When I pointed this out in a lecture once, I used the example of the acronym HOMES for the names of the Great Lakes (Huron, Ontario, Michigan, Erie, Superior). Someone in the audience suggested that I must be aware of a more powerful acronym than HOMES. When I asked what it was, he responded, "your name." For a brief moment I was puzzled; what has "Rubinstein" got to do with the Great Lakes? When someone near me whispered my first name, I recognized the connection between MOSHE and the lakes. I walked over to the person who made the connection, thanked him, and assured him that because of his creative discovery I shall never forget my name, nor will he and the rest of the audience. As for the lakes, it provided me with an additional index for retrieving their names.

Many years ago I tried to invent an acronym for the names of the planets in the order of their distance from the sun. After many attempts I wrote down the sequence of initial letters from each name.

MVEMJSUNP

I noticed that by adding an "i" in two places I could sound the sequence as two words:

MiVEM   JiSUNP

I retrieved these two words so many times since I first created them that by now they are part of my vocabulary. Thus I have an index for retrieving the names of the planets in the order of their distances from the sun (see Table 1.1).

MODEL OF MEMORY

Human memory has more the nature of a warehouse with a very large supply of building materials and working tools than the nature of a storehouse with a fixed number of filing cabinets for storing information. The building materials model permits us to use scaffolding to build structures to various levels with intricate multiple connections between them. Adding the acronym MOSHE to HOMES can be viewed as building more paths or bridges for retrieving the information they lead to. The idea of a dynamic and evolving structure for storing information suggests that more structure will improve successful recognition and recall. The fixed warehouse model would suggest that the more cabinets we fill up, the less room is left for new information.

PRODUCTION RULES AND STORIES

In addressing the issue of human ability to transfer knowledge from one area to another, Simon [13] points out that empirical evidence for the ability of human problem solvers to transfer knowledge and skills to new task situations is mixed at best. Simon suggests that people should become aware of how guides to problem solving are organized in memory. The organization is in the form of sets of production rules in which a repertoire of learned problem-solving actions is associated with conditions, to form condition–action pairs. Once recognized in a situation, the conditions constitute cues or indices for corresponding actions.

Stories or concrete examples can serve the same indexing function for the transfer of knowledge to new situations. Stories are compact storage capsules that have the added feature of facilitating easier retrieval of the messages stored in them. One story may contain a number of concepts, and you may retrieve these concepts by recalling the story. A story may store information in the form of condition–action pairs, to use Simon's terminology. We have all experienced how much easier it is to recall the lyrics of a song when we begin by humming the tunes of the melody. A story is the melody of ideas and concepts. What good is stored knowledge and wisdom if you cannot retrieve it?

The Talmud, the Jewish writings dealing with morals, ethics, laws, human attitudes, and exercises in logic, has two main elements: *Halacha,* which is the formal or legal part, and *Agada,* the legend or story part. Messages of productive attitudes for behavior and techniques for logical thinking are embedded both in the well-structured precepts and in the stories. The Talmud has been a powerful source for sharpening formal logical thinking and for enhancing human problem-solving abilities for many generations. We should revive the art of storytelling to enhance learning for problem solving.

2.4 Heuristics for Problem Representation

A common error in approaching problems is to move too quickly into a problem-solving mode. There are, of course, situations where quick action is required, but in most cases more time can be devoted to structuring the problem, presenting it, and re-presenting it, each time discovering new elements from a different perspective. Allowing sufficient time for representation is conceptually similar to taking a walk around an object and inspecting it. What is seen and what is hidden change with the position of the observer. A number of guides can help you take such a walk around the problem and devote more time to representation. This will make it more likely that you will not embark on a problem-solving mode too soon.

GET THE FACTS

Imagine that while driving a truck on a freeway you approach an overpass. A sign informs you: "CLEARANCE 12 FEET." A sign posted in the truck cabin tells you that the top of the truck is 12 feet and 2 inches high. There is no way to turn back, and there are no side roads. What are you going to do? Most people suggest deflating the tires to lower the truck and clear the overpass. Anyone who would proceed to do so would be moving too soon into a problem-solving mode. The first step is to represent the problem. Identify the initial state, the goal state, and the obstacles. But do so by getting the facts. Get out of the truck and inspect the clearance with your eyes. If necessary, try to measure the height of the overpass as well as the height of the truck. There may be no problem at all.

Get the facts and pay attention to the distinction between facts, opinions, and judgments whenever possible. It is true that to decide what is fact requires judgment. But at least when statements can be verified by inspecting the facts, do so. We often accept information as if it were factual when it is an expression of opinion or belief. Sometimes we make an observation, modify it by judgment, and then treat our judgment or belief as fact.

When you ask for information be sure that you are given facts, not opinions. Statements such as "I think our sales are ahead of last year" or "I believe we tested the equipment before shipment to the customer" suggest that perhaps more judgment and opinion are present than fact. When you do not have the key to a closed door that you wish to open, do not conclude that it is locked and start searching for the key. The prevailing opinion that a locked door can be opened by the appropriate key is one representation that may apply to the situation. Get the facts; try the handle; the door may be closed but not locked. If this does not work, take a walk conceptually around the obstacle, the locked door in this case. Imagine that you are inside the room. I once suggested this to a friend as we were standing in front of a locked door with no keys, and he responded by saying "Moshe, if we were inside we would have no problem, but the fact is that we are outside." This was indeed a fact, but there were other facts we had not explored. I knocked on the door. It was opened immediately; there was someone inside the room who could open the door. The cartoon of Figure 2.3 illustrates how common it is to use judgment and opinion when it is so easy to establish the facts and the consequences of not getting the facts.

Figure 2.3 Consequences of not getting the facts.

I once drove with a friend into the subterranean parking garage of an office building when we discovered that the horizontal arm guarding the entrance could not be raised. It was seven o'clock in the evening and there was no parking attendant at that hour. Conclusion: We could not get in. This conclusion holds true most of the time. But then I remembered the overpass story. I got out of the car and inspected the situation to get the facts. I stood by the car, then next to the guarding arm at the entrance, and measured them against my body. I noticed that immediately past the guarding arm the driveway had a steep slope leading down to the garage. This gave me an idea. Perhaps if I moved the front wheels forward while the nose of the car cleared the arm, the car would be lowered enough under the arm to clear it all the way. I started moving the car while my friend took hold of the end of the arm and lifted it as much as he could without breaking it. We cleared the arm by about an inch.

After we parked the car my friend changed expression as he exclaimed: "My God, how do we get out?" For a moment I was petrified. Then we both burst into laughter when he said that we could back out the way we came in. Of course going out was no problem. The exit was open. But in retrospect we moved too soon into a problem-solving mode. We should have continued our efforts in representation so that we might have raised the question of getting out before we moved in.

It has been said that a smart person manages to escape from unpleasant situations that a wise person would avoid in the first place. The wise person devotes more time to structuring problems by considering potential consequences before acting. This leads to better judgments, better foresight, and to behavior that increases the probability of desired outcomes, or decreases the probability of undesired outcomes.

2.5 Changing Representation

Change in representation is often a creative heuristic problem-solving tool. For example, when an obstacle appears to be insurmountable and has negative features, try to change the representation by focusing on what could be its possible positive features. Initially, it may be very difficult to think of anything positive, primarily because your state of mind has been tuned to the negative. But by going over the facts and suppressing judgments and opinion you may come up with new ideas.

Consider, for example, the story about an apple grower who was about to pick a crop of apples from the trees when a hailstorm hit the area [14]. The hail left marks on the skin of the apples that turned into brown spots. These marks constituted a serious obstacle in trying to market the crop successfully. It appeared that the obstacle had only negative features. Changing the representation to focus on the possible positive aspects led to the following line of reasoning. Why did the apples get the brown marks? Because it had hailed. Why then grow apples where it may hail before the crop is harvested? Because apples grow best in mountain areas where chills from storms give the apples a chance to develop the sugars for outstanding taste. In such areas you may have a hailstorm before the fruit is picked from the trees.

The positive feature that was identified from these facts is that the brown marks on the skin of the apples constitute evidence that the apples are grown in an area most suitable for enhancing their sweetness. Therefore, when the grower shipped the apples to his customers, each box contained a card with the following information:

Apples grow best in mountain areas where chills from storms toughen the skin and delay the ripening to permit the sugar to develop and yield the most delicious apples. The apples in this box contain evidence that we grow our apples in such an area. The small brown marks on the skin of some of the apples are a result of a hailstorm just before we picked them from the trees. When you taste these apples you will know how important these chills are in developing sweetness and flavor.

In some situations a solution to a problem can be viewed as a change in the representation of the problem [2, 15]. The solutions of many problems in algebra, and mathematics in general, consist of transformations of the given information so as to make the solution, which is obscure, become transparent in a new form of representation. Most mathematical derivations follow this route.

Changes in representation by a transformation may form an auxiliary step that simplifies the solution process. The use of logarithms reduces multiplication and division to the simpler operations of addition and subtraction, respectively.

Consider the game "number scrabble" in which two players draw from nine cards numbered 1 to 9. The cards are placed in a row, face up. The players draw alternately one at a time, selecting any card remaining in the row. The goal is to be first to select three cards with a total value of exactly 15. If all nine cards are drawn with neither player securing 15 in a set of three cards, it is a draw. How can this game be represented to help the player form a strategy? Try it.

Does the array of Figure 2.4 help you construct a strategy? This array is also called a magic square in which the numbers in each row, column, and main diagonal add up to 15. Will the transformation to a game of tic-tac-toe be helpful?

4	9	2
3	5	7
8	1	6

Figure 2.4 Magic square representation for the game number scrabble.

Another problem that can be solved by an appropriate change in representation comes from chess. Two black and two white knights are positioned as shown in Figure 2.5. Only the nine squares shown can be used in moving the knights.

Devise a plan to move the knights one at a time until the black and white knights trade positions. A knight can move three squares in the sequence (1, 2) or (2, 1), in which the first number indicates the number of squares in one direction, and the second is the number of squares in a perpendicular direction. A square can be occupied by one knight only. Knights can skip over each other in making the moves. For example, the knight in the upper left corner can move (2, 1) and land in the square in row two, column three, or in row three, column two. The same results can be obtained by the move (1, 2). The objective is to achieve a trade in positions of the knights, using the minimum number of moves.

The change in representation from Figure 2.5 to the form shown in Figure

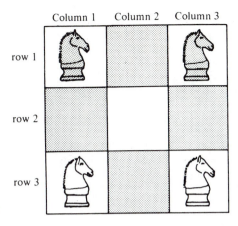

Figure 2.5

2.6b, in which the idea of the circular mobility of the knights is brought into focus, makes manipulation of content, movement of knights, so much easier that the solution becomes almost transparent. Figure 2.6a repeats Figure 2.5 with the squares numbered. Figure 2.6b shows the initial state in terms of the position of each knight and those squares in the array into which each can move from the initial state. To change positions, each knight must move four steps in either a clockwise or a counterclockwise direction.

Language in all its forms is a most powerful tool for problem representation. Asking the right question, uttering the correct word, or hearing it, may direct your processing to the appropriate region in your long-term storage to retrieve information that will guide you to a successful change in representation.

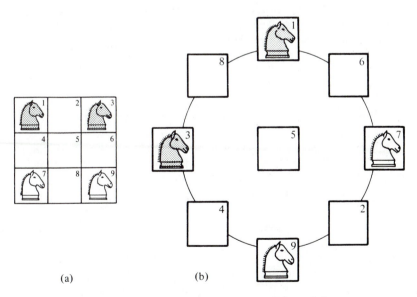

(a)   (b)

Figure 2.6   Change of representation of Figure 2.5.

A particular word or an idea may cause you to restructure old knowledge and produce new representations and creative solutions to problems.

Hammurabi in Babylon changed the course of history by changing the representation when dealing with the problem of an inadequate water supply. Instead of asking how to get the people to the water, he asked how to get the water to the people. This led to the invention of canals. A similar situation arose during World War II in Europe when it was necessary to design hangars so that airplanes could be removed quickly in an emergency. Initially, it was difficult to achieve a successful solution with conventional hangar designs. An outstanding creative solution was finally obtained by changing the representation and asking how the hangars could be rapidly removed from the airplanes so that they could take off. A folding-type mobile configuration for the hangars offered the design solution.

A change in representation may transform a negative to a positive response, as was the case with a clergyman who was a heavy smoker. When he asked his superior whether he could smoke while praying, the response was a strong no. A wise friend suggested that next time he ask whether he could pray while smoking.

In Figure 1.5 we noted that two fundamental features characterize models in general: a *form* and a *content*. It is possible to describe different contents by the same form of a model, and one content can be fitted into different model forms. The choice of form, which signifies here a form of representing the content, establishes the ease of manipulating the content and detecting errors of omission and commission. The choice of form therefore establishes the facility to refine and improve the model to better serve its purpose. For example, the Hebrews and Greeks used letters to represent numbers. This mode of representation was not productive or useful for manipulation of the content that these forms represented. The same was true for Roman numerals. The invention of the positional number system provided a new form with much greater power of manipulation.

2.6 Changing Verbal to Graphic Representation

A problem may be presented in a verbal form that makes it difficult for us to see the relationships that prevail among elements. In such situations a change to a graphic representation may enhance the ability to see. For example, suppose that five towns A, B, C, D, and E are directly connected by links of equal length of travel time as follows. You can go from town A to town B, from A to D, from B to C, from B to E, from C to D, from C to E, from D to A, from D to E, and from E to D.

If you must find the path of shortest time from town A to town E going through towns B and C, it can be assessed from the representation given above using the English language. However, a change in representation from English to a *digraph* ("digraph" is a contraction of the words "directed graph," namely, a graph with its arcs having arrows showing direction) with nodes representing towns, and edges (or arcs) with arrows showing direction of direct connection between towns, gives a much better way to "see" the given information and a way to respond more easily to questions regarding routes. Figure 2.7 shows such a representation.

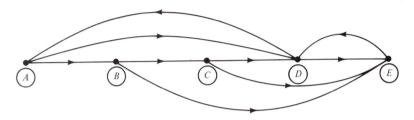

Figure 2.7 Direct ties between five towns.

A change in representation may create a form that is more compatible with our human information-processing capabilities. For example, a diagram or a graph may be more suitable than a verbal or a mathematical description. The new representation can make it easier for us to identify features that were not apparent before the change, or were not easily seen in earlier presentations. These added features may serve as cues to alternative solutions, or suggest changes in the goal state by identifying surrogate or proxy goals when we see no way to achieve the desired goal directly.

THE SEVEN FARMS: AN EXAMPLE IN CHANGING REPRESENTATION

In 1907 there lived seven families on large farms in Australia. The farms were separated by distances ranging from 5 to 7 miles. When the families learned that a telephone company was willing to provide them with a telephone communication system, they accepted the offer. The telephone company was inexperienced and the communication system that was installed left a lot to be desired. The family on farm 1 could call directly only the families on farms 2 and 4; farm 2 could call only farms 3 and 5; farm 3 could call only farm 1; farm 4 could call only farms 5 and 7; farm 5 could call only farms 4 and 7; farm 6 could call only farms 2, 3 and 5; farm 7 could not initiate any calls, but could receive calls from farms 4 and 5.

The following two columns show *from* where *to* where calls can be made directly.

From	To
1	2, 4
2	3, 5
3	1
4	5, 7
5	4, 7
6	2, 3, 5
7	None

This condensed representation leaves out redundant words such as "could call" that appear in the verbal representation, and makes it easier to see the connections between farms. We can change this condensed representation further to the form of the digraph in Figure 2.8. Now the direct communication ties between the seven farms are seen at a glance. The digraph provides an efficient visual representation compatible with human information-processing capabilities.

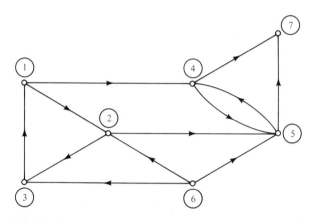

Figure 2.8 Digraph of direct communication ties between seven farms.

Now if farm 3 must establish contact with 6, the digraph represents possible solutions far better than does the verbal description. From the digraph we see that there is no way 3 could call 6. In fact, no one can call 6. 6 does not receive any calls, only initiates them. But 3 could call 1. How will this help? He could tell 3 (if 3 is not talking to 2 or 4) to call 2 and tell him that should he, 2, happen to hear from 6 to have him call 3 immediately. 3 could also ask 2 to call 5 and convey the same message. But let us wait. While 3 is calling 1, 6 might be trying to call 3 for some reason. So 3 should be very brief in his conversation with 1. Also, if 2 is talking to 5, 6 cannot talk to either of them. Therefore, it is better for 4 instead of 2 to convey the message to 5. This could be done by 1 calling 4 and asking him to call 5, requesting him not to use his phone, and in case he hears from 6 to have him call 3.

Suppose 2 is a gossip. Then 3 should remember this and ask 1 to tell 2 not to call him (3) to find out what's up, because the lines to 2 and 3 must be kept open.

What are other alternatives? Let us look at the situation from another perspective and change the representation by identifying a surrogate goal. 6 could initiate a call to establish contact with 3 if he had a reason to do so. 3 could create such a reason or incentive for 6 to call him. As soon as this surrogate goal is identified, you begin to explore new directions. You may suggest that 3 set his barn on fire. This may catch 6's attention and he may get on the phone. But 3 should not set his barn on fire before he warned 2 through 1 of his plan, or else 2 will be the first to call, blocking a potential call from 6.

In summary, a good representation is one that aids thinking and problem solving.

2.7 Changing Representation by Adding, Removing, and Rearranging

A few years ago, when my daughter Iris was in a junior-year-abroad program, there was a long period when we did not receive a letter from her, although we wrote weekly. We were worried, but there was no way for us to get in contact with her by phone. So we changed the representation of the problem by introducing a surrogate goal: to create an incentive for her to call us. I wrote her a short letter and added a postscript that read: "Just in case you ran out of money, I am enclosing a $500 check with this letter." I dispatched the letter and four days later we received a telephone call from her. I had mailed the letter without the money.

Heuristics for change in representation include the addition of elements, removal of elements, rearranging or combining of elements, and combinations of these activities. A change in representation may involve moving from verbal to visual representation or to mathematical representation or the reverse. We may change an abstract to a concrete representation or the other way around. We may focus on a small part of a problem in detail by ignoring the rest, or view the entire problem with respect to a global feature by filtering out or ignoring any other features that may be present.

THE MONK PROBLEM

The following problem was posed by Carl Duncker. A monk starts walking up a mountain at six o'clock in the morning one day and reaches a temple on the summit at six in the evening. The following day he rises early and starts on his way down from the summit at six o'clock in the morning and reaches the bottom at four o'clock in the afternoon. He follows the same narrow path on both days. Is there a spot on the path that the monk passed or occupied on both days (going up and going down) at precisely the same time? Think about it. Try a change in representation.

THE HAT RACK PROBLEM: REARRANGING ELEMENTS

The following problem is known as Maier's Hat Rack Problem [16]. Imagine that you are in a room that is 20 feet wide and 40 feet long with a ceiling that is 8 feet high. On the floor you have two boards of lumber with dimensions of 2 inches × 1 inch × 60 inches and 2 inches × 1 inch × 43 inches, respectively, and a clamp wide enough to hold the two boards together. Your task is to use the lumber and the clamp to build a hat rack in the middle of the room approximately 10 feet away from any wall. The hat rack must be stable enough so that a jacket could also hang from it. Try it before you read on.

To study this problem you may use a concrete representation by finding two pieces of lumber and a clamp. You may use two smaller pieces of lumber and a suitable clamp to create a scaled down hat rack under a table. Or you may use past experience and knowledge to create visual representations of similar situations.

Trying various representations may lead you to rearrange your past knowledge and recognize that a ceiling can support a column when it is wedged between a floor and a ceiling. You may be reminded of a lamp that is supported by a post made up of two tubes, one sliding inside the other with a spring connection. The spring is compressed when the post is forced between the floor and ceiling.

Rearranging elements may help us not only reproduce or retrieve knowledge we have, it may lead us to produce or create new knowledge by restructuring old knowledge. In the present example, old knowledge in the form "columns support ceilings" can produce new knowledge in the form "ceilings support columns."

REPRESENTATIONS OF THE MOUNTAIN CLIMBING PROBLEM: ADDING ELEMENTS

Now let us return to the monk. Try combining the two parts of Figure 2.9. Imagine two monks, one going up the mountain in Figure 2.9a and one coming down in Figure 2.9b. Now superimpose parts (a) and (b). Think of two buses beginning at two different ends of the same street and moving in opposite directions. This is a visual representation that can help make transparent a solution to the problem that was obscured by the verbal representation we gave.

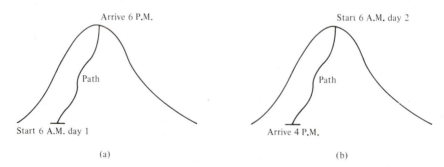

Figure 2.9 Concrete pictorial representation of mountain-climbing problem: (a) going up; (b) going down.

Figure 2.10 gives an abstract representation in the form of two curves showing position on the path versus time of day for both days on the same set of reference coordinates. We discover that the curves must intersect at a point representing a specific spot on the path at a particular time of day.

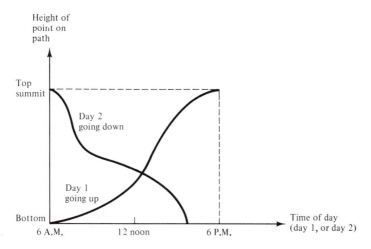

Figure 2.10 Abstract pictorial representation of mountain-climbing problem.

CLEARING THE OVERPASS

Remember the overpass story of Section 2.4? Try to use change in representation to deal with the following situation. Consider yourself driving the same truck but this time you are transporting a giraffe to the zoo. The giraffe is standing on the top of the truck with its neck oriented forward in the direction of travel. While the top of the truck can clear the overpass by about 4 inches, the head of the giraffe is about a foot higher than the clear passage height. There are no side roads and no way to turn back. What are you to do?

2.8 Removing Elements by Focusing and Filtering

In his book *Godel, Escher, Bach,* [17] Hofstadter describes two related ways to remove information from a representation which he calls "focusing" and "filtering." *Focusing* entails description of a part in detail to the exclusion of all else. *Filtering* involves a feature to describe the whole by excluding, or filtering, all other features. For example, we can study and describe a part of a painting in detail and say that it is a head of a man in the upper right corner of the painting. Or we can study and try to describe the entire painting after we take a picture of it using a series of filters to remove all colors except for red. The only feature left is red, and what will appear to us is a red house. The examples Hofstadter gives are in terms of pattern recognition problems from the book *Pattern Recognition* by the Soviet scientist Bongard [18]. The book contains a collection of 100 problems of the kind shown in Figures 2.11 and 2.12. The objective is to identify a feature that will help classify any one of the 12 squares as a member of one of two groups. The two groups consist of the six squares on the left and the six

Figure 2.11 Adapted from Bongard problem 55. (Ref. 18.)

squares on the right of the vertical line separating the two groups. This task of classification was intended for human beings or computers as pattern recognizers, with the computers using an artificial intelligence program for the recognition task. Hofstadter points out that in Figure 2.11, recognition comes from focusing on the little circle and its relationship to the indentation, to the exclu-

Figure 2.12 Adapted from Bongard problem 22. (Ref. 18.)

sion of all else in each box. If you stand inside the indentation facing the figure, the circle is on your left for the six figures on the left of the vertical line, and on your right for the figures on the right. In Figure 2.12 we filter out all features except size. On the left each box has the same size figures; on the right each box has mixed sizes.

Try to identify features for the boxes in Figures 2.13, 2.14, and 2.15. Be

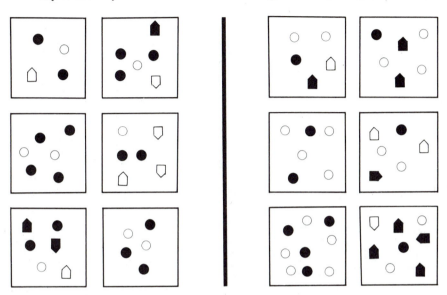

Figure 2.13 Adapted from Bongard problem 28. (Ref. 18.)

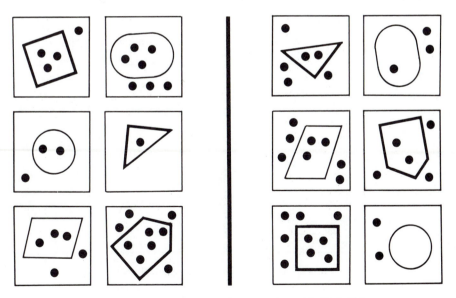

Figure 2.14 Adapted from Bongard problem 29. (Ref. 18.)

Figure 2.15 Adapted from Bongard problem 30. (Ref. 18.)

flexible by moving back and forth between focusing and filtering, naming shapes, counting objects, or counting all dark objects but ignoring their shape (shape filtered out).

Now try Figure 2.16. Some people will say that the figures on the left are

Figure 2.16 Adapted from Bongard problem 4. (Ref. 18.)

geometrical or regular figures. It turns out that they label as geometrical or regular those figures for which they have common names. The figures on the left have common names such as circle, square, triangle, ellipse, and pentagon, whereas we have no comparable common names for the figures on the right. People with knowledge of the concept of convexity say that the figures on the left are convex and on the right nonconvex. A figure is convex if you can select any two points inside the figure and connect them with a straight line and no part of the line will be outside the figure. The figures on the left in Figure 2.16 are convex and on the right, nonconvex. For each figure on the right we can find two points inside the figure such that when we connect them by a straight line, part of the line will be outside the figure.

One day I presented Figure 2.16 and asked people to identify a distinguishing feature to classify the two groups. One person suggested that the figures in the six boxes on the right represent cookies that can be broken into two parts in an easier manner than the cookies on the left. Here is a new concrete contextual representation that uses imagination.

Try to identify features for Figures 2.17 to 2.21. You will have little difficulty seeing the "raisins" in the cookies of one figure and noting what happens to them when you break the cookies into two parts.

Figure 2.17 Adapted from Bongard problem 5. (Ref. 18.)

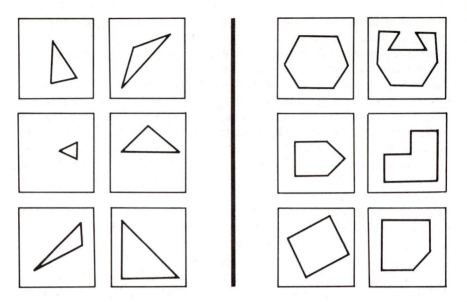

Figure 2.18 Adapted from Bongard problem 6. (Ref. 18.)

Figure 2.19 Adapted from Bongard problem 19. (Ref. 18.)

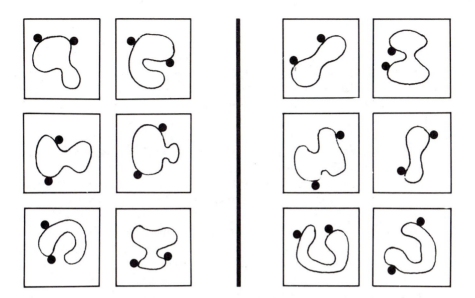

Figure 2.20 Adapted from Bongard problem 20. (Ref. 18.)

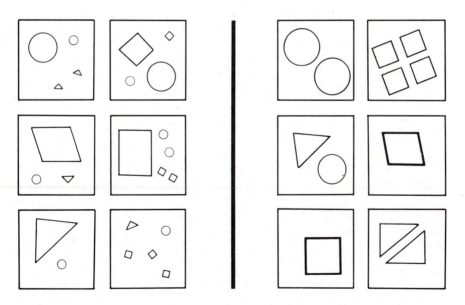

Figure 2.21 Adapted from Bongard problem 21. (Ref. 18.)

2.9 Testing Hypotheses

Look at Figure 2.13. A quick scan may give you an idea about a feature for classification. Suppose that you inspected two or three boxes and had the idea that counting the dark and open "houses" and circles will provide a feature. You come up with an idea that there are more dark figures than open ones on the left and the reverse on the right. Your idea is an untested hypothesis. You test it by going through all the boxes and counting the dark and open circles and "houses."

The hypothesis is rejected. Let us focus on the circles and filter out the "houses." Counting the circles for one or two boxes on each side we may come up with the hypothesis that each box on the right has more open than dark circles and the left boxes have more dark than open circles. Now we test the hypothesis. It works.

The procedure we outlined here is the heart of the scientific method. Using some limited observation we come up with an idea for generalization. We treat the idea at this stage as an untested hypothesis. Next we test the hypothesis by acquiring more information and making a decision whether to accept the hypothesis, reject it, or continue testing. Even ideas that do not work out have value. They may constitute platforms for better ideas.

2.10 Heuristic Guides to Problem Solving

Heuristics can be classified in a number of ways. Our classification into those that apply to acquisition of knowledge, representation, and solution is one such classification. Use the heuristics wherever and whenever they work for you. Be flexible, and take the time to structure a problem situation before you move into a solution phase. It may prove helpful to consider the following heuristics to guide problem structuring and problem solving.

PERMIT SUFFICIENT TIME FOR GENERATING ALTERNATIVE SOLUTIONS

Do not begin evaluation and selection of solutions too soon. A common unproductive tendency in problem solving is to evaluate and choose among a small number of alternatives before sufficient time has been devoted to generating additional alternatives. Once an alternative is chosen, you may develop resistance to considering additional alternatives and prejudge negatively new alternatives.

CONCENTRATE ON WHAT YOU CAN DO

Focus attention on surmountable obstacles that block the way to a solution. Before attempting a solution to a problem, make sure that the obstacles have been identified. There may be obstacles that can be overcome and others that cannot. In such situations try to focus on those that you can overcome, provided that success in overcoming these obstacles will lead to the goal.

CONSIDER IMPLEMENTATION

Focus on both quality and acceptability for success in implementing a solution to a problem. The search for a solution to a problem normally receives much more attention than the implementation stage. This may lead to failure to solve the problem. In particular, when implementation requires the cooperation of other people, it is very important to devote attention to both the quality of a solution and to the acceptance by the agents of implementation. The leaders of the Sony Company in Japan would not have made their success story a reality if they had not done just that. They considered tape recorders to be excellent tools for teaching and learning. But to market the product successfully they started by teaching the public about the power of the tape recorder and thus created the market for the product.

MAINTAIN GROUP HARMONY

When a group is involved in problem solving, pay attention to everyone's feelings. Try to maintain harmony. Sometimes when a group member takes a strong position too early in a problem-solving situation, his ego may get in the way of reason. Subsequent efforts to preserve the integrity of the ego may lead to distorted thinking and rejecting even common sense. Reason, not pride, should govern intelligence in problem solving. Watch out for distorted thinking in efforts to preserve the integrity of a bruised ego.

BE A GOOD LISTENER

When you interact with the group, be a good listener. Try not to formulate your response while you are listening to others talking. Do not judge the ideas of others when they are first stated by saying "you are wrong," "I disagree with you," "this is nonsense," and other such gems. These may promote ill feelings and become obstacles to solving problems. Listen as if you will be required to take an examination on what the other person is saying. This shows respect, making the speaker feel important. It generates goodwill. If you do not agree with the position taken by a colleague and you have a different position, state your position. It will be evident to you and your colleague that the two positions are different if both of you are good listeners.

FOCUS ON WHAT YOU CAN CONTROL

Identify actions that you can control in a problem situation, and exercise control whenever it can help you achieve your goals. Studies have indicated that not only actual control, but even the perception of control that may be illusionary, enhances human problem-solving performance. Giving up control, or perceiving no control when there is control, erodes the ability to perform well and achieve goals. When you perceive no choice, you act as if you have no alternatives, and the perception becomes a self-fulfilling prophecy. On the other hand, when you stop to ask who is in control, you will be surprised how often you will discover more control than you ever thought you had. ,

2.11 The Importance of Control in Problem Solving

Examination papers normally consist of a number of questions, some short, some long. Although the questions may be numbered, you need not begin by attempting to answer the questions in the order given. The instructor selects the order for the questions, but you need not accept this order to control the sequence of answers. You can control this sequence. You can select any order you please. What will be the best for you?

From experience you know that to begin with questions that you can answer gives you confidence, lifts your spirits, and enhances your performance. On the other hand, when you begin with a question that appears beyond your knowledge, you worry, your confidence begins to erode, your spirit breaks, and your performance suffers. Therefore, attempt to use a sequence of answering questions to achieve what is best for you. Do not give up your control.

Start by scanning the entire examination paper using the following filtering process. Identify questions that appear easy for you to answer. Ignore questions that appear too wordy and complex or time consuming to read through in a first scan. Commit yourself to return to these questions after you try the problems you believe you can handle.

This brief holistic scan is a good investment of your time; it establishes the sequence of answers that will boost your morale. Next, start a sequential focus of attention by answering the easiest questions first and work your way progressively to more difficult ones. In some cases you will discover that time is up before you get to the most difficult question.

Students who start with the difficult questions, because they believe they can answer the easy ones later, often find themselves still stuck with these questions when the time is up. It is said that a wise person sometimes succeeds by beginning at the end, while the fool ends in the beginning.

CONTROL AND CHOICE

A doctor related to me that she spends hours to supply detailed information about patients. In one case in which she treated a patient for a minor ailment, a letter arrived from a lawyer's office requesting that she supply the answers to 45 questions on an interrogatory form enclosed with the letter. The questions were very specific with regard to date of treatment, nature of treatment, charge for treatment, and so on. The doctor told me that it took a nurse two hours to retrieve the patient's records, identify the specific information requested, and type it on the forms. I asked the doctor why she did all that. She responded with a surprised look saying that she had to do so because there was a legal matter involved and she had no choice. But she did have a choice. She could have selected the form for supplying the factual information. To use the form that was designed by the outside source amounts to letting that source dictate and thus control the form in which the information is to be supplied, and probably, to the convenience of that source. The doctor could have made copies of the records and mailed them to the lawyer with a note stating that all the facts were included. By avoiding the transfer of the information to the lawyer's forms she could have saved time and eliminated the possibility of human errors that sometimes result in such efforts.

Each year I receive many requests for recommendations on former students. Sometimes a number of forms are sent for the same person, each requesting information in a different format. I could spend days trying to respond to these requests for information. Instead, I have my own form in which I give the important details about the student on the basis of my experience, stating all pertinent factual information and the basis for my evaluations. The letter is attached to the form on which I write: "Information supplied in attached letter." It is even possible that my form gets more attention than the standard forms of the source requesting the information.

2.12 Removing Relations and Decomposing Complexity: A Heuristic for Simplification

The complexity of a problem can often be traced to the number of relationships between the elements. If we can remove relationships that are of minor importance, we may reduce a complex problem to a number of independent simpler problems. For example, if you consider 28 elements relevant to the design of a teakettle, such as weight, color, size, or cost, we may have to list 2^{28} subsets as design groupings of the elements. This is because each of the 28 elements may be included or excluded in a subset. The creative effort of human problem solvers is to reduce considerably the size of such a list, which, incidentally, contains more elements than the entire English language. In principle, we attempt to simplify the real-world problem through modeling, by aggregating elements that are strongly connected through structure and function, or both, and selecting the chunks so the connection between them in terms of structure and function is weaker than that within the chunks. This is shown schematically in Figure 2.22. The process permits tearing or decomposing a complex problem into smaller parts. The weakly linked parts are studied separately and then the complete solution is synthesized from the constituent parts. Complexity is a function of the number of links between elements, not the number of elements.

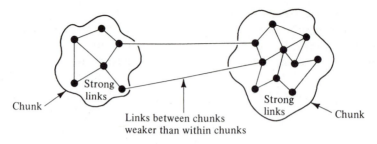

Figure 2.22

Therefore, to reduce complexity, we aggregate elements with many links into chunks that are then viewed as single elements, but in the chunking process we are also guided by the criteria of minimizing the number and strength of links between the chunks selected so that each chunk can be treated separately.

NEWTON'S MODEL AND THE HEURISTIC FOR SIMPLIFICATION

Newton's inverse-square model of gravitation was an ingenious application of the heuristic of simplification through the removal of elements and relationships. Newton considered only the force of attraction between two masses M_1 and M_2, and disregarded the presence and influence of other masses. Thus he simplified the model by removing all elements and relationships except for two masses and their interaction. This led to the conclusion that the force of attraction, F, between masses M_1 and M_2 increases in direct proportion to their product, and decreases in proportion to the square of the distance, r, that separates them. The equation that expresses these relationships has the form

$$F = c \, \frac{M_1 M_2}{r^2}$$

The symbol c in the equation is a constant representing the magnitude of force F for $M_1 = M_2 = 1$ and $r = 1$. c has a magnitude equal to that of the force of attraction between two unit masses 1 unit of distance apart.

2.13 The Mixed-Scanning Heuristic [19]

THE BRAIN

Studies of the brain have revealed that the cerebral cortex is divided into two hemispheres. The left hemisphere is connected to the right side of the body and predominantly controls analytical, logical, and sequential thinking as manifested in mathematical skills and language. The right hemisphere is connected to the left side of the body and predominantly controls the orientation in space, the identification and recognition of patterns, faces, and sites, and in general the more artistic and less analytical functions. Whereas the left hemisphere is primarily *sequential* in its operations, the right hemisphere is primarily *holistic*.

The two hemispheres are connected by a bundle of fibers known as the "corpus callosum," and each hemisphere can thus transfer information from one side of the brain to the other. Damage to either hemisphere or to the connection between hemispheres can lead to serious impairment in the ability to perform normal human functions. For example, damage to the left hemisphere can limit or severely impair the language ability; damage to the right hemisphere can limit spatial awareness and the ability to recognize people and sites. Severing the connection between the two hemispheres produces the following phenomenon. A person with such a split brain holding a familiar object in the right hand will be able to name it although it is out of sight. However, if the object is in the left hand and out of sight, he will not be able to describe it because the left hand is connected to the right side of the brain, which has little capacity for language. Since there is no connection between the two hemispheres and the left hand is connected to the right hemisphere, the left hemisphere where the "language machine" primarily resides is simply unaware of what is in the left hand [20].

People may have a more dominant left or right hemisphere. The dominance of each side of the brain manifests itself in creative endeavors of different kinds. Thus an artist normally has a more dominant right side with strong holistic, intuitive, and spatial orientation and with an ability to assimilate many inputs simultaneously. The organization of the information processed is somewhat loose and diffused with no strong sequential attachment, but there is a rather general and sometimes fuzzy relationship between the elements processed. This is consistent with right-hemisphere dominance.

On the other hand, a scientist normally has a more dominant left side, with a sequential, rational, and logical orientation. Information is processed in serial fashion, step by step, with limited tolerance for fuzzy and holistic assimilation of inputs.

CREATIVE PEOPLE

Some of the most creative human problem solvers have an unusual capacity to integrate the two modes of conscious functions of the two hemispheres, and move back and forth between the holistic and sequential, between intuition and logic, between the fuzzy large field of a problem domain and a clear specific small segment of the field. Such people can be outstanding artists and scientists because they combine the strong attributes of both. Thus Leonardo da Vinci (1452–1519) had strong creative capabilities in art and science and Einstein (1879–1955) was a great scientist and an accomplished violinist.

Although we cannot emulate an Einstein or a da Vinci, use of both modes of consciousness can lead to greater creativity and enhance problem-solving ability in general. First we must develop an awareness of our problem-solving styles, whether predominantly intuitive-holistic or logical-sequential, and our ability to tolerate fuzziness, vagueness, and uncertainty. Such awareness will help us exercise better control when a need arises to shift from one mode of problem solving to another, that is, from holistic to discrete, step-by-step detail, and vice versa. The key is a need for a flexible, open-ended approach, a mixed scanning of the field of the problem domain, oscillating between a tacit, holistic, diffused stage on the one hand and an explicit, analytical, focused stage on the other.

THE MIXED-SCANNING STRATEGY

Etzioni [21] proposes a mixed-scanning strategy as an active approach to societal decision making similar to the strategy employed by a master chess player. The master chess player does well when he combines two modes of behavior alternately, going from a vague but encompassing scan of the field to a detailed study of a subset of moves and then to further detailed examination of a single sequence of steps, finally leading to a move. This process is repeated each time the player responds to a move by the opponent. Etzioni discusses in a similar vein the scanning of the field by infantrymen in hostile territory and the scanning of the sky by weather satellites. The vigilant mixed scanning by the infantrymen calls for a rough overall scan of the entire field of visible territory for signs of danger, such as movements, shadows, and unusual objects. Following this low-precision, all-encompassing scan, a smaller portion of the field, in the vicinity of the infantrymen, is examined more closely for possible smaller movements. Then the holistic scan is repeated, followed by close scrutiny of the immediate area. In a weather satellite two cameras perform the functions of a broad holistic scan and specific bit-by-bit sequential examination of a small portion of the sky. One camera takes broad-angle pictures covering large portions of the sky in low precision, while a second camera takes high-precision, high-resolution pictures of small portions of the sky identified by the first camera as candidates for closer examination on the basis of preestablished criteria. The investment of time and energy in each mode of scanning depends on the situation, but in general it is important not to persist too long in either mode. Persisting too long in a broad encompassing scan may lead to the onset of boredom and carelessness with a loss of vigilance to look out for areas worthy of detailed examination. On the other hand, persisting too long in examining a detail may blur the overall objective.

2.14 Application of Mixed Scanning

Let us consider examples in which a mixed-scanning strategy can prove useful. An architect designing a house begins with a holistic image of the spatial layout consistent with some idea of the ballpark figure for budget, the client's needs, and the general site of the house. This stage is followed by more detailed examination of floor plans, location of doors, closets, and so on. The study of detail may require adjustments in the holistic picture of the previous stage, and then a detailed examination of new features. The actual construction of the house requires detailed working plans for a step-by-step implementation of the design. In contrast, the renderings of the house in the early stages of the design are artistic images of a holistic nature, void of detail. The renderings show relationships between the house and its surroundings, the front view, side view, and views in perspective, with the prime focus on the aesthetic values, namely the right-hemisphere domain. The detailed plans for implementation are more sequential and logical, oriented to step-by-step operations—the domain of the left hemisphere.

In many ways the writing of a book involves a mixed-scanning strategy. In my writing I begin with a vague idea of a complete subject, followed by an outline of chapters. Next I normally identify one chapter, not necessarily the first, that appears the most fundamental, and start writing. The stage of detailed work of choosing words, creating sentences, and paragraphs may take a few days. Then comes a scan of the outline which undergoes some revisions, and a second chapter is selected for detailed step-by-step effort, and so on. As the work continues, chapters written in the early stages may be rewritten. In one case a colleague of mine and I rewrote one chapter four times before the book was published. We used a mixed-scanning strategy, being firm about our prime goal to write a book that would have strong potential for survival. Therefore, the topics were selected carefully so that their relevance would not be eroded with the passage of time. Because of this strategy the book has survived for 18 years, was translated into foreign languages, and continues to be used, although it is a book in a field of engineering that has undergone constant change in the past two decades.

2.15 Problem Solving Using Mixed Scanning

We now apply the mixed-scanning strategy to two example problems as an illustration of how our thinking moves back and forth between holistic general ideas and the sequential detailed testing of ideas.

Example 1: Deciphering a Cryptogram

Consider the following cryptogram in which each letter represents another letter in the English alphabet:

MZQPQ LPQ AZQ XUCMX CT FQXAQPFQLP?

Using a mixed-scanning strategy to decipher the cryptogram, we first scan it holistically in an encompassing sweep as if trying to put music to the sentence. We note the punctuation and classify the cryptogram as a question. We also note the high frequency of Q. Now comes the more specific bit-by-bit detailed stage. What is unique about a question? It begins with such words as *How, Where, Which, Who.* Which letter has the highest frequency in English? The letter e. The combination of the answers to these two questions suggests the word "Where" at the beginning. An attempt to read the question starting with "Where" will quickly suggest holistically, and with support from some of the detail already uncovered in identifying Q as e and P as r, that the question begins with "Where are the . . . " The next word is likely to be a plural noun ending with S. Thus X stands for S.

Continuing with the next word, CT will suggest "of," "or," "on," "in." We leave the solution as an exercise for the reader.

Example 2: Going to Planet X

A rocketship must go from the earth to planet X. It is a 5-day trip, but the rocketship holds only enough fuel for a 3-day trip. Fuel stations A, B, C, are on the route to planet X and are, respectively, 1, 2, and 3 days' flight from the earth. The rocketship can store fuel at these stations. Find the minimum number of days required for the rocketship to reach planet X.

Let us begin by considering overall features. The trip requires 5 days of fuel and the rocket can hold fuel for only 3 days. Therefore, fuel for 2 days must be stored in intermediate fuel stations. Without working any detail, we show in Figure 2.23 six options for storing fuel for 2 days. In options a, b, and c, the needed fuel for 2 days is stored in stations A, B, and C respectively. In the remaining options d, e, and f, two fuel stations are selected in each case with 1 day of fuel in each. Continuing with general considerations, it is also apparent that once the trip is made there is no way to get back because the rocketship cannot arrive at planet X with more than 1 day of fuel. But this is not a concern in the problem if the flight is unmanned or other larger rockets will arrive in the future. In the present problem the rocket must arrive in a minimum number of days, so it should arrive with no fuel to spare.

The objective of a minimum number of days for the flight suggests that we spend the least amount of time on the subgoal of implementing a fuel storage plan. Holistically, we feel that the closer the stored fuel is to the earth, the less time will be required to get it to the storage locations. On this basis option a appears best, followed by option d.

Now let us examine in detail option a. The fuel for 2 days is stored in fuel station A. But from A there is a 4-day trip to planet X with no fuel stored in any intermediate station between A and X. Since the rocketship can only hold fuel for 3 days, option a will not work. If we examine option d, which is the next best option in terms of proximity of the stored fuel to the earth, we find that it will work.

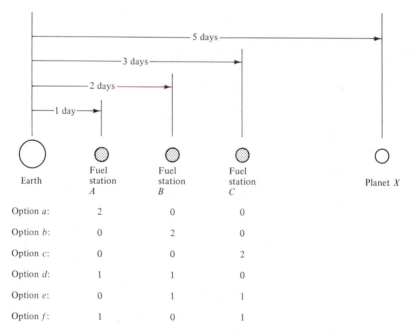

Figure 2.23 Rocketship problems with fuel storage options.

Now we must deal with the subgoal of implementing option *d* for fuel storage. This requires a detailed examination that will reveal an interesting result. While option *a* cannot serve as the final storage plan before the rocketship leaves the earth for planet *X*, it will turn out to be an intermediate step required to implement option *d* because to deposit fuel for 1 day on station *B* will require a minimum of 2 days' fuel at station *A*. Thus options rejected at one stage of problem solving may become feasible options at another stage. Commitment to accepted or rejected options should be done cautiously to maintain flexibility in the problem-solving process.

2.16 Learning Strategies and Mixed Scanning

Pask and Scott in their study of learning strategies classify learners as Holists or Serialists [22, 23]. The Holist tends to learn better through an encompassing general view of the field of study before pursuing detail. At times the Holist images the entire field of knowledge with a tendency for over-generalization. The Serialist tends to learn better from step-by-step procedures similar to an algorithm for a computer program. The Serialist may at times get lost in detail and become unable to see the forest for the trees. When a Serialist learner is asked to "teach back" what he has learned, he will tend to preserve the precise sequence in which detailed information was acquired. The Holist's teach-back may include some major rearrangements of the order in which details were learned casting them in new structures, but preserving the coherence of the body of knowledge assimilated. Pask and Scott have conducted studies demonstrating that the Holist learns best when the subject matter is presented in a holistic encompassing manner with details embedded in the total presentation. The Serialist learns best when the subject matter is presented sequentially, in a step-by-step orderly fashion. A mismatch between learner classification and teaching style or material presentation leads to inferior learning performance.

These studies suggest dominance of one style or the other in some people, but for each person there must exist some optimal mix of the two modes of behavior in a particular problem situation. It is important to learn to use both styles in a mixed-scanning approach, which will enhance our capabilities as learners and problem solvers.

2.17 Human–Computer Symbiosis

In the past three decades we have seen an unprecedented progress in the area of computers. In the early stages of computer technology the emphasis was on hardware—the physical makeup of the computer. Next came the surge in software studies—programming languages for effective computer use by human beings. Although developments in both hardware and software are continuing, emphasis is now shifting to the user. We are increasingly becoming direct users of computers. As writing was once the magic tool of priests and is now shared almost universally by all, so is computer programming ceasing to be the exclusive knowledge of computer programmers.

The computer provides a revolutionary aid to problem solving and decision making. As the computer is taking over more and more programmable functions, more of human thinking and problem solving is shifting to nonprogrammable activities. These activities include finding appropriate problems, identifying goals in the context of human values, representing problems and constructing models from complementary points of view or frames of reference, and identifying reasonable goals and answers that will do when the "best" answer cannot be obtained in reasonable time with reasonable effort, or cannot be recognized when attained. These nonprogrammable activities require the attitudes and general problem solving techniques discussed in this book.

The activities of problem solving begin with the highly nonprogrammable tasks and progress toward the programmable. But even after results are obtained by extensive calculations using computers there is still the need for an interpretation of the results, and this again is often a nonprogrammable human activity. A productive symbiosis of human beings and computers will assign the nonprogrammable tasks to human beings and the programmable to computers. The nonprogrammable include the holistic, global activities involving heuristics, values, attitudes, emotions, and humor, while the programmable include sequential step-by-step detailed algorithms. The programmable and nonprogrammable interact just as the two hemispheres of the brain exchange information through the corpus callosum. This division of functions and their interaction is shown schematically in Figure 2.24. The width of each triangle in the figure represents the relative amount of effort devoted to the activities. At the beginning, the top of the figure, effort is virtually all nonprogrammable. At the end, the bottom of the figure, effort is all programmable. In the middle, when we have a reasonable initial grasp of the problem, there is the largest amount of mixed scanning. At this stage we move back and forth, testing our ideas in a form of mental or computer simulation algorithm and using the results to infer global conclusions or new ideas for changes in the model that we are constructing.

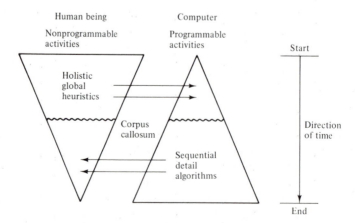

Figure 2.24 Human–computer symbiosis.

2.18 Connections: From the Spinning Wheel to the Printing Press

The following account, which takes us from the spinning wheel to the printing press, should serve to stimulate our thinking about possible *connections* between diverse experiences and observations. When we are preoccupied with predictions for what the future holds in a particular field, it helps to go back to lessons of history and probe the genesis of past developments. This is in the nature of a mixed-scanning approach with a holistic view of many fields and developments, and detailed probing of one field or one development. It can help us identify connections between fields and developments that on first sight appear vastly unrelated. The connections may provide the spark for new ideas.

PRODUCTION OF BOOKS

When parchment was used to produce books, between 200 and 300 sheep or calves were required to generate the parchment for a single Bible [24]. The preparation of a scroll of the Bible was expensive, with the cost of material considerably higher than the cost of labor for the work of the scribe who recorded the text of the Bible on the parchment. There was therefore no incentive for replacing scribes and their rather slow pace of work with more efficient means of writing. However, developments in completely different fields brought about a drastic change in the materials used for book production, shifting the production of books from a material-intensive activity to one that was labor intensive, namely to one in which the wages of the scribe became the major cost.

PRODUCTION OF THREAD

Before the spinning wheel made its appearance, thread was produced by a spindle. A spindle is a wooden rod, tapered at each end, that was used by the spinner to twist the fiber drawn from a mass of wool or flax into thread. The thread was wound on the spindle as it was spun. The production of thread was such a slow process that one weaver using a loom to produce cloth could use the thread produced by many spinners. The bottleneck in the production of cloth was the slow and costly process of producing the thread. This changed dramatically with the advent of the spinning wheel.

THE SPINNING WHEEL

The spinning wheel was invented in China and it appeared for the first time in a Chinese painting in the middle of the eleventh century [24]. It was not until the thirteenth century that this invention reached Europe. The influence of the spinning wheel on the production of yarn was monumental. A single instrument could produce in one day what many spinners took several days to produce. The result was a considerable reduction in the cost of labor for the production of plain cloth. This lowered the prices of cloth and increased its use. Linen was particularly reduced in price and its use increased because it was normally plain, with no patterns, and very seldom dyed. By the fourteenth century the use of linen for underwear, shirts, sheets, and towels increased to the point that a new by-product became more available: cloth rags.

PAPER USED FOR BOOKS

With increasing use of cloth, cloth rags proved to be a suitable material for making paper. As the price of cloth continued to decline, the availability and use of paper rose. By the end of the thirteenth century the cost of paper was down to one-sixth of the cost of parchment. Paper began to be used more and more in the production of books, although the Bible and other special works in deluxe editions continued to be produced on parchment. For ordinary book production the cost of material became relatively small compared to the wages of the scribe. This provided the incentive for developing less costly means of writing, thus giving birth to the printing press.

THE PRINTING PRESS

The printing press had its origin in the wooden wine press that had been in use for many years before Gutenberg came out with the new invention in the 1450s. The printing press brought about a revolutionary increase in the rate at which written material could be produced. The Gutenberg printing press could produce 30 printed pages per hour, an astonishing speed of production compared to the pace of a scribe at work [25].

The technology of book production changed very little in the following 360 years. But in the nineteenth century two developments further improved the printing process: the steam engine and the production of paper from boiled wood chips.

In 1813, Friedrich Koenig, a Saxon printer, saw the connection between the labor required in operating the printing press and the steam engine. He invented a metal rotary press and ran it with steam one year later in 1814. The new invention increased the production rate from 30 to 300 pages per hour, an order-of-magnitude increase in efficiency. Within a year enough improvements were introduced to increase the rate of production to 550 pages an hour.

As steam power was supplanting human labor in production, the 1840s saw the introduction of boiled wood chips as a replacement for rags of cloth as the basic material for paper. This reduced the cost of materials for books further, thus increasing the incentive for greater efficiency in the printing process. By 1850, as experience with steam engines and the metal rotary printing press increased, the rate of production reached 10,000 pages per hour.

THE GROWTH OF PUBLISHED WORK

An interesting parallel development to the production of printed materials is the growth in the number of scientific journals published. In 1750 there were only 10 scientific journals in the world. From 1750 the number of journals increased by a factor of 10 every 50 years, leading to the following proliferation [25]:

Year	Number of Scientific Journals
1750	10
1800	100
1850	1,000
1900	10,000
1950	100,000

This represents a doubling time of 15 years.

BE VIGILANT

The brief historical trace of factors that led to the development of the printing press suggests that although one could see how the introduction of the spinning wheel to thirteenth-century Europe could have an impact on production of textiles, to see in advance the impact of the spinning wheel on book production would have required clairvoyance. But a flexible attitude, coupled with a vigilant mixed-scanning approach to problem solving and a readiness to follow developments in different fields, may sometime come close to achieving clairvoyance. When this happens we will remember how the spinning wheel helped give birth to the printing press.

2.19 Exercises in Applications of Heuristics

Exercise 1

In his book *Problem Solving and Creativity in Individuals and Groups* [16], Maier discusses the following elements in a repertoire of behavior which he identifies as productive problem-solving attitudes:

Focusing on the present and future rather than the past
Solving a particular rather than a general problem
Locating one's position in relation to obstacles and goals
Distinguishing among goals, obstacles, and solutions
Attending to interpersonal conflict
Promoting variety
Avoiding commitment

Discuss these seven problem-solving attitudes as they may apply to problem solving by an individual and a group, and give examples in each case. Examples based on your experience are desirable. When such examples are not available, invent some.

Exercise 2

Select an introductory textbook in a subject that is not in your field. Suppose that you are asked to study the textbook for a course. Describe the role of each of the following three strategies for mastering the textbook:

1. Purely holistic
2. Purely sequential
3. Mixed-scanning strategy

Describe the advantages and disadvantages of each strategy.

Identify three situations under which a different strategy will be most appropriate for each condition.

Exercise 3

In *Problem Solving and Education—Issues in Teaching and Research,* Cyert [26] summarizes the following heuristics from *Patterns of Problem Solving* by Moshe F. Rubinstein. Study these 10 heuristics, then classify them in two or more categories and write what they mean to you using your own words. Give one example for each, either based on an experience you had or use imagination to invent a suitable story. The heuristics are numbered for ease of reference, not necessarily in order of importance or use.

1. *Total picture.* Before you attempt a solution to a problem, avoid getting lost in detail. Go over the elements of the problem rapidly several times until a pattern or a total picture emerges. Try to get the picture of the forest before you get lost in the trees.

2. *Withhold your judgment.* Do not commit yourself too early to a course of action. You may find it hard to break away from the path but may find it to be the wrong one. Search for a number of paths simultaneously and use signs of progress to guide you to the path that appears most plausible.

3. *Models.* Verbalize; use language to simplify the statement of the problem; write it down. Use mathematical or graphical pictorial models. Use abstract models such as symbols and equations, or use concrete models in the form of objects. A model is a simpler representation of the real-world problem; it is supposed to help you.

4. *Change in representation.* Problem solving can also be viewed as a change in representation. The solutions of many problems in algebra and mathematics in general consist of transformations of the given information so as to make the solution, which is obscure, become transparent in a new form of representation. Most mathematical derivations follow this route.

5. *Asking the right questions.* Language in all its forms is a most powerful tool in problem solving. Asking the right question, uttering the correct word, or hearing it, may direct your processing unit to the appropriate region in your long-term storage to retrieve complete blocks of information that will guide you to a successful solution.

6. *Will to doubt.* Have a will to doubt. Accept premises as tentative to varying degrees, but be flexible and ready to question their credibility, and, if necessary, pry yourself loose of fixed convictions and reject them. Rejection may take the form of innovation, because to innovate is, psychologically, at least, to overcome or discard the old if not always to reject it outright.

7. *Working backward.* Do not always start at the beginning and follow systematically step by step to the end goal. The solution path is as important as the answer and, in problems where the goal is specified, the path is the solution. It may be easier to start with the goal and work backward to the beginning.

8. *Stable substructures.* In complex problems it helps to proceed in a way that permits you to return to your partial solution after interruptions. Stable substructures that do not collapse or disappear when you do not tend to them will serve this purpose.

9. *Analogies and metaphors.* Use an analogy whenever you can think of one. An analogy provides a model which serves as a guide to identify the elements of a problem as parts of a more complete structure. An analogy also helps to recognize phases as elements of a complete process.

10. *Talk.* When you are stuck after an intensive effort to solve a problem, it is wise to take a break and do something else. It is also helpful to talk about your problem at various stages in your search for a solution. Talking to someone may help you pry loose of the constraints we mentioned, because your colleague may have a different world view and may direct you to new avenues of search when he utters a word or asks a question.

2.20 Problems to Stimulate Thinking

STORY TIME

After working with a friend on a crossword puzzle from the *New York Times,* my daughter Dorit told me with great excitement how her friend figured out a verbal description for the expression

$$\frac{0}{BA + MS}$$

that fit into the puzzle. I suggested jokingly that perhaps it stands for "There is nothing above being alone with (+) myself." But then Dorit told me that the description had to fit into a row of 19 boxes in the puzzle.

I worked on this problem for two months. The expression

$$\frac{0}{BA + MS}$$

would pop into my head at the most unusual times. I would dream about it and wake up thinking about it. Dorit began to regret having mentioned the problem, thinking perhaps that my failure to get the answer was not helping my ego. It was obvious she wanted to help me, but I assured her that I was having fun. Indeed I was. While on a 10-day lecture tour, the hours on the airplane felt like minutes. Not a dull moment, I had the puzzle to work on.

My efforts had a certain fixation to them. I kept treating BA and MS as two university degrees. At one point my daughter suggested that I might be too rigid in my approach, namely that "above" was not the only possibility. That immediately suggested "below," but I begged Dorit to let me do it alone. I had a new stream of ideas but could not fit my creations into 19 letters.

At the end of May, Dorit and a guest joined my wife and me for dinner at the UCLA faculty center. It had been a very warm day. The conversation turned to the heat and temperature when Dorit and her guest excused themselves to go to the restroom. I suddenly experienced a flash of thought, grabbed a pen, and started writing on a card that was on the table. I exploded with excitement; I had it! But now I had to share my finding with Dorit. So without thinking I got up and ran after her. I came to a screeching halt in front of the door that read WOMEN. I paused for a second and then knocked on the door. A woman came out. You should have seen the look on her face when I explained: "You wouldn't believe my story if I told you, but could you please give this card to my daughter Dorit, who is inside there?" The excitement on my face must have moved the woman to heed my request. Seconds later came the scream from inside: "Daddy, you got it!"

The talk about the heat brought to my mind the word "degree" in a different context, and thus after more than two months, in a flash, I tried "Two degrees below zero" and I knew I had the answer. But I gained much more than an answer. I gained insight into some aspects of my own problem-solving style and became aware of features I believe I can better control now. But above all, I had fun, and I added a story to my problem-solving repertoire.

I have often thought that we should plan programs for mental fitness in much the same way that we plan for physical fitness. Continued efforts with mental exercises lead to new ways of thinking and may improve our performance as problem solvers.

One difficulty with puzzles and problems posed to us by our friends is that often they give us the answers before we have had a chance to try working them ourselves. It is very frustrating to be given an answer when you want the opportunity to find it yourself. When this happens you feel robbed of the joy and excitement that comes with the cry: "I have got it!" So the next time you present puzzles to your friends, do not give hints, offer no help, leave them alone. Give them a chance to come to you with the cry: "I have got it!"

I often let students ponder a question for days and even weeks. The glow on their faces when they come to share the triumph of success evokes my greatest satisfaction as a teacher.

Now that I have robbed you of the joy of working out Dorit's puzzle, I will compensate for it with the following puzzles and games. I hope that the hours of effort you may devote by persevering with patience and continued vigilance, looking for clues from unusual sources, will stimulate your thinking and motivate you to consider attitudes and heuristic guides discussed in the book.

PROBLEMS, PUZZLES, AND GAMES

Problem 1

Three blindfolded people, Abe, Beth, and Chuck, each take one hat from a barrel containing three black and two white hats. Abe and Beth remove their blindfolds and can each see the hats on the heads of the other two, but not the hat on their own head. Abe says: "I cannot tell what color my hat is." Upon hearing this, Beth says: "I cannot tell the color of my hat either." Hearing these two statements, Chuck, who is still blindfolded, says: "I know what color my hat is." How did he know, and what was the color of his hat?

Problem 2

Joe rows his boat upstream in a river at a constant velocity by exerting a constant effort on the oars as he pushes them against the water. Just as Joe passes under a bridge that spans the width of the river, his hat falls in the water. Joe only becomes aware of the missing hat 10 minutes later. He immediately turns the boat around (assume that this action is so quick that it takes no time) and starts rowing the boat downstream, exerting the same effort on the oars as he did going upstream. Joe catches up with his hat 1 mile downstream from the bridge. How fast does the river flow?

Problem 3

Two ferryboats start at 8:00 A.M. from opposite sides of a river. They each maintain constant velocity, but one is faster than the other. They pass each other at a point that is 2100 feet from the shore that the slower boat left. Each boat continues to the opposite side and after a 15-minute stop starts on its way back. On the way back the boats pass each other at a point that is a distance of 1300 feet from the shore that the slower boat is leaving now on its return trip. How wide is the river? Try to solve the problem by using one linear equation in one unknown.

Problem 4

There are 100,000 blue marbles in a blue barrel and 100,000 red marbles in a red barrel. A blindfolded person transfers 100 marbles from the blue to the red barrel, mixes the marbles in the red barrel, and transfers 100 marbles from it back to the blue barrel. This is repeated again with 100 marbles taken from the blue to the red barrel and then 100 randomly chosen marbles are taken back from the red to the blue barrel. After this blue-to-red, red-to-blue transfer of 100 marbles is repeated three times, which of the following statements is true?

1. There are more blue marbles in the red barrel than red marbles in the blue barrel.
2. There are more red marbles in the blue barrel than blue marbles in the red barrel.

Problem 5

The following conversation takes place between two friends A and B, who have not seen each other for a long time but have kept up their mental exercises:

    A: I have three sons.
    B: How old are they?
    A: The product of their ages is 36.
    B: That is not enough to answer my question. Can you give me another clue?
    A: Yes, their ages are integer numbers whose sum is the same as the number on the store across the street.
    B: Give me a few minutes to work it with pencil and paper.
    B: (a few minutes later) I have almost got the answer but I need another clue.
    A: O.K. The oldest one has red hair.
    B: I have got it.

What are the ages of the three sons?

Problem 6

The 9 foot × 12 foot carpet shown in Figure P2.6 with a 1 foot × 8 foot hole must be restored to a square 10 foot × 10 foot carpet by introducing only two cuts (along a line of any shape) between the inner boundary (around the hole) and the outer boundary, and sewing the parts together. How should the carpet be cut?

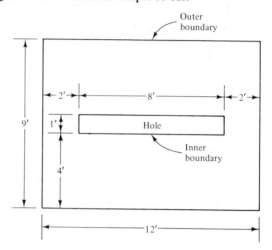

Figure P2.6

Problem 7

The game of the star shown in Figure P2.7 can be played with pennies. The objective is to cover as many of the circles as possible with pennies, subject to the following rules. The game begins with all circles empty and to cover a circle you start at any empty circle, skip one circle and continuing along a straight line from where you started, cover the next circle. For example, you can start at 1 when 1 is empty and cover 7 or 9, start at 10 when 10 is empty and cover 4 or 2, start at 3 when 3 is empty and cover 6 or 9, and so on. You may skip over a covered circle, but you can only start at an unoccupied circle.

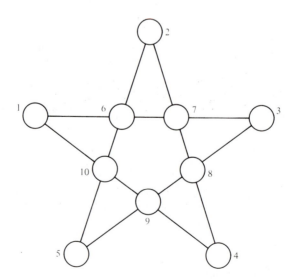

Figure P2.7

What is the largest number of circles that can be covered?

Devise a systematic way for covering the maximum number of circles.

Problem 8

The triangle game shown in Figure P2.8 is played as follows. First cover the 14 circles numbered 2 to 15 with pennies. The objective of the game is to remove as many pennies as possible. A penny is removed when you skip over it with another penny adjacent to it by moving the penny along a straight line to an unoccupied circle. For example, at the beginning of the game we can only move with the penny at 4 or 6. 4 can skip over 2, removing it, and land in 1. Or 6 can skip over 3, removing it, and land in 1. Suppose that we start by removing the penny at 2 with 4 landing in 1. Now with circles 2 and 4 unoccupied, 11 can skip over 7 into 4, or 13 can skip over 8 into 4, or 6 can skip over 5 into 4, or 9 can skip over 5 into 2.

What is the maximum number of pennies that can be removed?

Devise a plan for removing the maximum number of pennies.

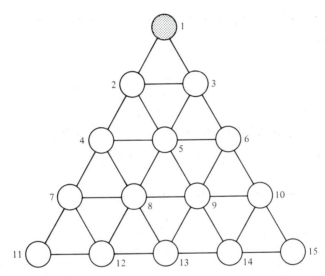

Figure P2.8

Problem 9

Alice, Bob, Chuck, David, and Elsa live in five different houses that are numbered 101, 102, 103, 104, and 105, along a street that runs from south to north, with 105 being farthest north.

Alice does not live in 105.

Bob does not live in 101.

Chuck does not live in either 101 or 105.

David lives in a house farther north than Bob.

Elsa does not live in a house adjacent to Chuck.

Chuck does not live in a house adjacent to Bob.

Identify the occupants of the five houses.

Problem 10

A dispatcher can run twice as fast on the turf as she can on the sand. The strips of sand and turf are 2 kilometers (km) and 3 km wide, respectively, as shown in Figure P2.10. B is 5 km north and 7 km east of A. What is the quickest route that she can take from A to B?

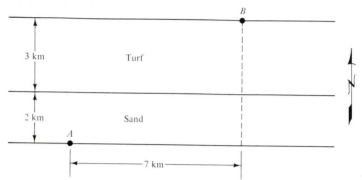

Figure P2.10

Problem 11

You are playing three games against two opponents. You win the contest if you win two consecutive games in the sequence of three. You must alternate playing against the opponents, playing them one at a time. One opponent, S, is a stronger player than you are, and the other, W, is weaker. You have a probability of 1/3 of winning against the strong player, and 2/3 of winning against the weak player. You can choose the first opponent. If you choose S for the first game, you will then play W and finally S again. If you choose W first, you play them in the sequence W, S, W.

What would you do, and why?

Problem 12

One hundred identical sacks with 1000 gold coins in each are delivered to a bank. There is reliable information that one sack contains counterfeit coins. The bank has a large scale that can weigh up to 100,000 coins at one time. It is known that a good coin weighs 10 grams and a counterfeit coin weighs 11 grams. The counterfeit coins cannot be distinguished from the good coins other than by the fact that they are heavier. What is the smallest number of weighings required to identify the sack of counterfeit coins?

Problem 13

Of 12 coins, 11 are identical and one is only different in weight. Using a balance, how can you identify the odd coin and tell whether it is heavier or lighter than the other coins with no more than three weighings?

Problem 14

A train from town α to town β makes one 30-minute stop at a station on the way. If you start from α on foot when the train leaves α, you will be 4 miles from α when the train reaches the station, and you will reach the station just when the train leaves it. If you go on walking with no stop you will be 1 km from town β when the train arrives there. However, if you board the train when you get to the station, you get to town β 15 minutes later than if you ride the train from town α to the station and immediately continue on foot from the station to town β. What is the distance between towns α and β?

Problem 15

Jane and Jim working together can sort a crate of apples in 10 minutes. Jim and Joyce can do it in 15 minutes, and Jane and Joyce can do it in 20 minutes. How long does it take each of the three to sort seven crates of apples alone?

Problem 16

Three men A, B, and C participated in a *truel* in accordance with the following rules. Each man was given a pistol and two bullets and positioned himself at the vertex of an equilateral triangle, 30 meters from the other two men. A was to fire one bullet first, next B, next C. They were to repeat this sequence until all bullets were fired or one man survived. The probabilities of each man hitting a target 30 meters away were 2/3 for A, 3/4 for B, and 1 for C. This explains the reason for the sequence of firing.
What should A do with his first bullet?

Problem 17

A thin line of gold coating on the surface of a cylinder must connect points A and B. The cylinder is 16 centimeters (cm) long and has a circumference of 24 cm (a radius of $12/\pi$ cm) as shown in Figure P2.17. What is the minimum length of gold coating required? How would you trace it on the face of the cylinder?

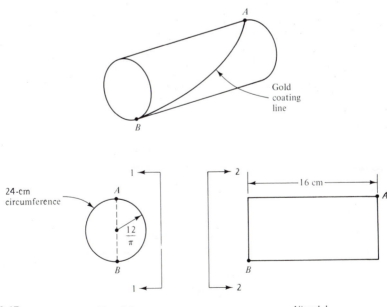

Figure P2.17   View 2-2   View 1-1

Problem 18

Using 12 toothpicks you can form three square boxes as shown in Figure P2.18. Use the same 12 toothpicks to construct a figure with a closed continuous boundary in the plane of the paper so that its area is equal to the three square boxes in Figure P2.18 and no more than two toothpicks meet at the boundary of the figure. In our figure four toothpicks meet at two points.

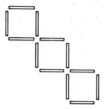

Figure P2.18

Problem 19

Try the following cryptarithmetic problem in which each letter stands for a different digit.

$$D O N A L D$$
$$+ G E R A L D$$
$$R O B E R T$$

$D = 5$. What digits are represented by the other letters?

Problem 20

What does each letter represent in this cryptarithmetic problem?

$$S E N D$$
$$+ M O R E$$
$$M O N E Y$$

Problem 21

Rearrange the following letters so that they spell a single English word.

$$T E R A L B A Y$$

Problem 22

Try the following cryptograms. Each cryptogram is a sentence in which each letter represents a different letter in the alphabet. The code is different for each sentence.

AZCOC'P FG UJNFJMJCU ODE MGO GFC AG PHJX GF D AOJTYE PJUCQDHY. PG-QDATZ EGBO PACX.

CIFLMPK FSH QPMGK ML MIJDKCQKQ FSHD NCJK ECGHK.

XPZMLPKKL BQBKTZQV: SQCMW-XPRTSQL DRYYQT, BJFMQ VWTRF,
DRXGCPQJY FJSXJGQV.

Problem 23

Using a balance scale, show that only four weights are required to weigh objects of weights from 1 to 40 pounds (all weights are given in integers).

Problem 24

Two teams are digging a tunnel from vertical shafts at two ends as shown in Figure P2.24. How can each team establish the direction of digging so that the teams will not deviate from a straight line connecting the two ends of the tunnel?

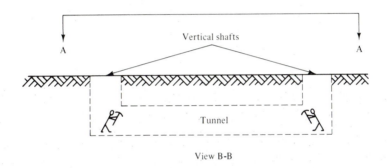

View B-B

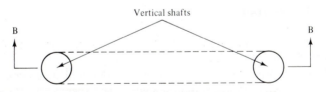

Figure P2.24   Top view A-A

Problem 25

Take three objects of equal heights, such as three cups, and three knives of equal length. Position each of the three cups at the vertex of an equilateral triangle at a clear distance *d* from the other two cups that is slightly larger than the length of a knife. Now using the three knives, place a glass of water in the middle of the triangle with its bottom at the level of the tops of the three cups as shown in Figure P2.25.

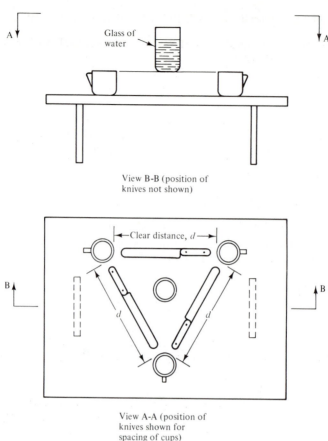

View B-B (position of
knives not shown)

View A-A (position of
knives shown for
spacing of cups)

Figure P2.25

2.21 Summary

A positive attitude to problem solving considers a problem as challenge, an opportunity to enrich thinking and learning.

Heuristics are general guides or rules of thumb that can help us in acquisition of knowledge, problem representation, and search for solutions. Heuristics may apply to thinking and problem solving in general, or they may be domain specific.

Active rather than passive learning and storing of information enhances the potential for retrieving information when it is needed. For example, inventing your own acronyms to store information is much more effective than using acronyms invented by others.

Heuristic guides to problem representation include sorting out facts from judgments and opinions; looking for positive as well as negative features in obstacles; trying more than a single representation; changing representation by

Attitudes and Heuristic Guides   Chap. 2

adding, removing, and rearranging elements in a structured situation; and focusing on details and filtering out features.

Testing hypotheses is the heart of the scientific method.

Heuristic guides to problem solving include devoting sufficient time to identify and generate alternative solutions; concentrating on surmountable obstacles; considering implementation in the planning stage; maintaining harmony in a group of problem solvers; taking time to be good and active listeners; and focusing on actions that we can control.

The perceived and actual control in problem situations can contribute greatly to achieving desired goals.

Heuristics can be used to reduce complexity by decomposing large problems to smaller subsets.

The structure of the human brain permits us to deal with both holistic and sequential operations. We can tolerate general fuzzy information in holistic fashion, and we can process specific clear information in logical, sequential, step-by-step fashion. The ability to move back and forth between the holistic and sequential modes of thinking is the basis of a mixed-scanning heuristic that can be used very effectively in learning and problem solving.

A productive symbiosis of human beings and computers will delegate the nonprogrammable activities requiring heuristic thinking to the human beings and the programmable activities that can be reduced to algorithms to the computer.

The impact of the spinning wheel on the printing press suggests that connections between diverse experiences and observations can spark novel ideas.

The chapter concludes with exercises in applications of heuristics, and problems to stimulate thinking.

PROBLEMS

2.1. Describe your own attitudes to problem solving.

2.2. What do you consider to be productive attitudes in problem solving?

2.3. What is the difference between heuristics and algorithms?

2.4. How can you be active rather than passive in learning?

2.5. Describe your strategy to play the game of Figure 2.4.

2.6. How would Figure 2.10 change if the monk started on his way down at 11:00 A.M. and reached the bottom at 7:00 P.M.?

2.7. Identify a feature to distinguish between the two groups of six boxed drawings in each of Figures 2.13 to 2.17.

2.8. In what way does the activity in Problem 2.7 compare with testing hypotheses?

2.9. Discuss the importance of control in problem solving.

2.10. Give two examples, other than those given in the book, where you could use the mixed-scanning heuristic.

2.11. Why is it important not to evaluate alternative solutions before you devote sufficient time to generating alternatives?

2.12. How could mixed scanning be used in a video game when you are in a spaceship and other ships are closing in from all directions?

2.13. Give your own three examples of change in representation.

2.14. List five attitudes that may hinder problem solving.

2.15. Discuss the roles of imagination and logic in human problem solving.

2.16. List attributes shared by creative people you have known.

2.17. Discuss how we can develop a productive attitude to problem solving in general.

2.18. Using your own words, describe what is meant by the word "heuristic." Give an example.

2.19. Suppose you had a calculator that gives answers with no decimal point. What could be the contribution of such a calculator to learning and generating heuristics for calculations?

2.20. Discuss the importance of stories in learning.

2.21. Give examples where you may use one or more of the following: opinions, judgments, facts.

2.22. What is the advantage of having graphical representations?

2.23. Let us suppose that the family of farm 3 in Figure 2.8 has a sick child who was treated by the doctor who lives in farm 6. The doctor had prescribed two red pills when the child goes into convulsion and two blue pills 2 hours after the convulsions stop. The child goes into convulsion. The mother rushes to the medicine cabinet and freezes when she is not certain which color pills to give first. The doctor has warned her not to switch the order of the given pills. She cannot find the note with the instructions. There is no information on the bottles. What is she to do? She knows the doctor is in his farm 6 because it is 8:00 A.M. Monday and he does not leave for town before 9:00 A.M. His buggy can be seen outside the farmhouse.

2.24. Give examples of situations where focusing and filtering can help you think more clearly.

2.25. Describe how we can go about becoming good listeners.

2.26. Give examples of situations in your own experience when you gave up control when there was no justification to give it up.

2.27. Describe a situation that you would label as complex and suggest ways to make it simple.

2.28. Is the solution to the problem of Figure 2.23 unique? Explain your answer.

2.29. Describe activities that human beings do well but cannot be performed by computers at the present state of our knowledge.

2.30. To what extent do you think a physician could be assisted by a computer? Describe specific areas.

2.31. How would you develop procedures for a balanced use of the right and left hemispheres of the brain?

2.32. Discuss how you envision a human–computer symbiosis by the year 2000.

2.33. How can education promote and enhance the transfer of knowledge across boundaries between various disciplines?

2.34. Discuss how changing the frame of reference can help solve Problem 2 of Section 2.20.

2.35. Create a simple concrete model to simulate the barrels and marbles of Problem 4, Section 2.20. Go through the actual operations of three round trips as described in the problem. How will the results of the simulation (after you did it) help deal with the problem? Will the answer be changed if we did not mix the marbles in each barrel after each move and did not select 100 marbles randomly in each move?

2.36. What are the difficulties people encounter with Problem 5, Section 2.20? What can we learn from this problem? What becomes evident when you put yourself in the position of the friend who is trying to figure out the ages?

2.37. Use the mixed-scanning heuristic to find the worked-out solution to Problem 13 of Section 2.20.

2.38. Does Problem 18 of Section 2.20 have a unique solution? Discuss.

2.39. Discuss why some ideas may be viewed as untested hypotheses.

2.40. Why should idea generation be separated from idea evaluation if we wish to enhance the potential for generating novel and creative ideas?

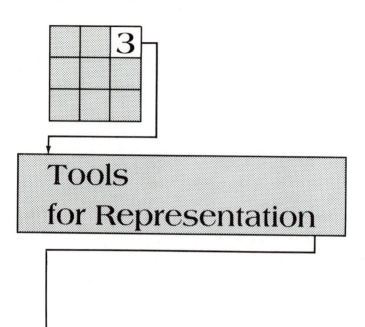

Tools for Representation

A main theme of this book is the need for human reasonable thinking; the kind of thinking that is flexible and can adapt appropriate tools and attitudes to a situation. Thinking that requires a rich repertoire of tools and attitudes as well as an appreciation of their potential use and limitations. This chapter begins with a discussion of such tools for representation as applied to one of the most fundamental human activities, that of classification. We show how these tools can be applied and how they can be used to develop important concepts. Subsequently we use these tools to discuss information and uncertainty and to prepare us to deal with decision situations in a structured manner.

3.1 Matrices or Tables

Suppose that we wish to classify people in terms of two attributes, "American" and having "British ancestors." Let A stand for American, meaning a U.S. citizen, and let B stand for having British ancestors. $\bar{A}$ and $\bar{B}$ will stand for "not American" and "not having British ancestors," respectively. We can have four different classes of people with respect to the presence or absence of the two attributes A and B. These are AB, $A\bar{B}$, $\bar{A}B$, and $\bar{A}\bar{B}$. The four classes can be shown by a matrix or table of two rows and two columns as shown in Figure 3.1. The two rows of the matrix are labeled A and $\bar{A}$, and the two columns B and $\bar{B}$. Each box in the matrix is identified by the row and column labels to which it belongs. Suppose that we have 1000 people with 800 classified as A and 700 classified as B. This means that 200 are $\bar{A}$ and 300 are $\bar{B}$. These four numbers

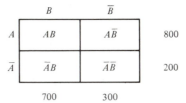

Figure 3.1 Matrix or table for classification.

	B	$\bar{B}$	
A	AB	$A\bar{B}$	800
$\bar{A}$	$\bar{A}B$	$\bar{A}\bar{B}$	200
	700	300	

give us the sums of the entries in the two rows and two columns in Figure 3.1. But we do not have the distribution of numbers to the four classes AB, $A\bar{B}$, $\bar{A}B$, and $\bar{A}\bar{B}$ in the four boxes of the matrix.

   Suppose that we wish to know the number of people with attributes A and $\bar{B}$, namely the number of people in class $A\bar{B}$. How can we use the representation of Figure 3.1 for this purpose? Our initial reaction may be that we do not know the answer. But let us be reasonable. To say that we do not know the answer may suggest that the answer could be any number. This, of course, is not true because we have some information. Let us reason together. Since we have 1000 people, certainly the answer cannot be larger than that. But we can do better than that. $A\bar{B}$ is at the intersection of row A and column $\bar{B}$. The largest value $A\bar{B}$ can assume on the basis of the sum for row A is 800, but then this will violate the sum of 300 for column $\bar{B}$. Therefore, 300 is the upper bound for $A\bar{B}$, in which case $\bar{A}\bar{B}$ must have a value of zero. The other values will be as follows.

	B	$\bar{B}$	
A	500	Start with 300	800
$\bar{A}$	200	0	200
	700	300	

   Now that we have established an upper bound on the value of $A\bar{B}$, we can establish a lower bound. The absolute lowest value would be zero. But is this consistent with the information we have? Let us try it by inserting a zero in the box for $A\bar{B}$ and fill in the values for the other boxes to satisfy the row and column sums given to us as shown.

	B	$\bar{B}$	
A	800	0	800
$\bar{A}$		300	300
	800	300	

   To satisfy the sums of 800 and 300, respectively, for row A and column $\bar{B}$ in which $A\bar{B}$ is nested requires 800 in box AB and 300 in box $\bar{A}\bar{B}$. This makes the sums for row $\bar{A}$ and column B too high by 100 each. Therefore, $A\bar{B}$ must be at least 100, as shown next. This requires that $\bar{A}B$ be assigned the value of zero.

	B	$\bar{B}$	
A	700	Start with 100	800
$\bar{A}$	0	200	200
	700	300	

The value of $A\bar{B}$ is therefore a number between 100 and 300. This is an accurate answer, although it is not as precise as 259 if this were the actual answer. It is certainly an improvement over no answer at all.

A TOOL FOR THINKING

Consider the matrix of Figure 3.1 as a tool for representation to aid our thinking in the context of the following situation. A man has just learned that he may be afflicted with a rare disease. He is considering an operation. The information available about this operation is as follows. 1000 people are known to have had this rare disease, 200 survived, designated by S, and 360 underwent an operation, designated by P. How can the man find the number of people who did not undergo the operation and did not survive, $\bar{P}\bar{S}$? It would be difficult to attempt an answer by merely looking at the three numbers 1000, 200, and 360 without resorting to a tool such as that of Figure 3.1. Let us try to answer the question beginning with the representation of Figure 3.2.

	Survived, S	Not survived, $\bar{S}$	
Operated, P	PS	$P\bar{S}$	360
Not operated, $\bar{P}$	$\bar{P}S$	$\bar{P}\bar{S}$	640
	200	800	**Figure 3.2**

The largest value that $\bar{P}\bar{S}$ can assume can be no larger than the smallest sum for the row and column in which $\bar{P}\bar{S}$ is nested, namely, 640 in our case. If we choose the value of 640 for $\bar{P}\bar{S}$, the other entries in the matrix will be as follows:

	S	$\bar{S}$	
P	200	160	360
$\bar{P}$	0	640	640
	200	800	

The smallest value that $\bar{P}\bar{S}$ can assume occurs when the values for $\bar{P}S$ and $P\bar{S}$ in the row and column of $\bar{P}\bar{S}$ are as large as possible, and this will happen when PS is as small as possible or zero. With zero for PS, $\bar{P}\bar{S}$ becomes 440 as shown next.

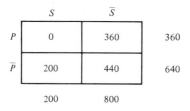

	S	$\bar{S}$	
P	0	360	360
$\bar{P}$	200	440	640
	200	800	

Hence $\bar{P}\bar{S}$ has a value between 440 and 640.

Find the bounds on the number of people who underwent the operation and did not survive. The answer is between 160 and 360.

3.2 Venn Diagram

The classification of people in accordance with the two attributes A (American) and B (British ancestors) can be represented by a *Venn diagram* as shown in Figure 3.3. The region marked A is equivalent to row A of the matrix in Figure 3.1 and the area outside A is equivalent to row $\bar{A}$ in the matrix. The region B is equivalent to column B of the matrix representation, and the area outside B is equivalent to column $\bar{B}$. The four regions AB, $A\bar{B}$, $\bar{A}B$, and $\bar{A}\bar{B}$ are marked in Figure 3.3. If we wish we can adjust the area of each region to represent the number of items with the particular attributes. For example, if we have 1000 people of which 800 have attribute A, 600 attribute B, 550 are AB, and 150 are $\bar{A}\bar{B}$, the relative areas representing these numbers will be as shown in Figure 3.3 in which each $1/1000$ of the total area of the rectangle represents one person.

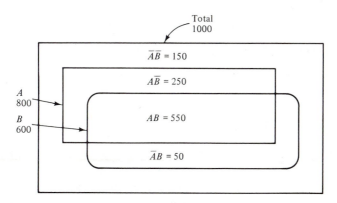

Figure 3.3 Venn diagram for classification.

3.3 Tree Diagram

The tree of Figure 3.4 shows another representation for classification in terms of presence or absence of two attributes A and B. We can start the tree with either A or B and proceed with the remaining attribute below the first one. In

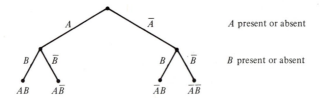

| | A present or absent |
| | B present or absent |

Figure 3.4 Tree for classification.

Figure 3.4 we first separate the A's from the $\bar{A}$'s; then each of these subsets is separated in terms of B and $\bar{B}$ to yield the four classifications at the bottom of the tree. For 1000 people with 800 of type A, 600 type B, 550 type AB, and 150 type $\bar{A}\bar{B}$ the tree would appear as follows:

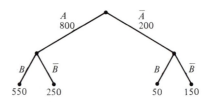

3.4 Equation

The following equation will also yield the four labels for classifying subsets in terms of two attributes A and B.

$$(A + \bar{A})(B + \bar{B}) = AB + A\bar{B} + \bar{A}B + \bar{A}\bar{B}$$

The multiplication is regarded as an *AND* operation and the addition (+) represents an *OR* operation.

3.5 Karnaugh Map

The Venn diagram of Figure 3.3, also known as a Euler diagram, need not have regions described by any particular geometric form. For example, we can use rectangles, circles, triangles, or any arbitrary shape, as shown in Figure 3.5 for two attributes A and B. An alternative form of a diagram for classification

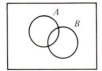 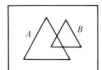 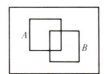 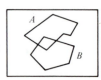

Figure 3.5 Venn diagrams for two attributes.

Tools for Representation   Chap. 3

that employs rectangles that extend to the boundaries of the entire figure is known as a Karnaugh map. Figure 3.6 shows a Karnaugh map for two attributes A and B. The regions A and B occupy the areas marked by lines inclined to the right and to the left, respectively. The four classifications AB, $A\overline{B}$, $\overline{A}B$, and $\overline{A}\overline{B}$ are shown in the figure.

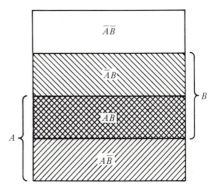

Figure 3.6 Karnaugh map for two attributes A and B.

3.6 Summary of Representations for Two Attributes

Figure 3.7 (see page 84) shows the five representations for classifying objects according to the presence or absence of two attributes A and B.

3.7 Representations for Three Attributes

Suppose that we have three attributes A, B, and C and wish to classify objects on the basis of presence or absence of each of these attributes. We will have eight distinct classifications. Figure 3.8 (see page 85) shows these eight classifications from ABC to $\overline{A}\overline{B}\overline{C}$ using five different representations. Figure 3.8a extends the matrix in Figure 3.7a to a cube partitioned into eight boxes. The four front boxes are identical to those of Figure 3.7a with the addition of attribute C. The four boxes in the back have $\overline{C}$. For the Venn diagram we added a region C in addition to A and B of Figure 3.7b. The tree diagram of Figure 3.8c extends the tree in Figure 3.7c with the addition of branches C and $\overline{C}$ at the bottom of the tree. For the equation we added the factor $(C + \overline{C})$. In the Karnaugh map, the region C is identified by the rectangle marked with vertical lines.

3.8 Representations for Four Attributes

Figure 3.9 (see page 86) is an extension of the representations in Figure 3.8 to four attributes. Figure 3.9a has two rooms marked D and $\overline{D}$, respectively. Each of these rooms has the cubes as well as labels of Figure 3.8a with the

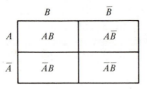

(a) Matrix or table

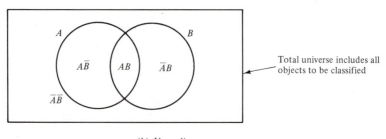

(b) Venn diagram

Total universe includes all objects to be classified

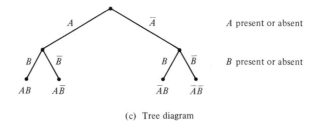

A present or absent

B present or absent

(c) Tree diagram

$$(A + \bar{A})(B + \bar{B}) = AB + A\bar{B} + \bar{A}B + \bar{A}\bar{B}$$

(d) Equation

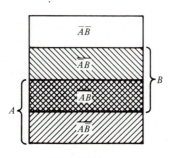

(e) Karnaugh map

Figure 3.7 Representations for classifying in terms of two attributes.

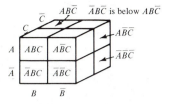

(a) Matrix expanded to cube

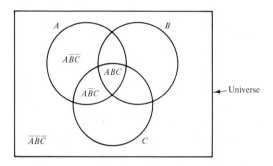

(b) Venn diagram

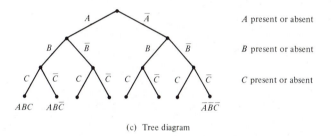

(c) Tree diagram

$(A + \overline{A})(B + \overline{B})(C + \overline{C}) = ABC + AB\overline{C} + \cdots + \overline{A}\overline{B}\overline{C}$

(d) Equation

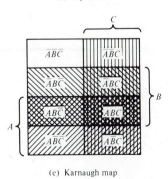

(e) Karnaugh map

Figure 3.8 Representations for classifying three attributes.

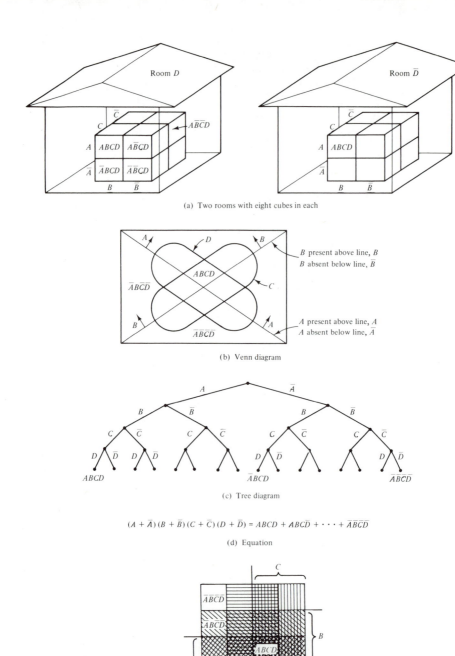

(a) Two rooms with eight cubes in each

(b) Venn diagram

(c) Tree diagram

$$(A + \bar{A})(B + \bar{B})(C + \bar{C})(D + \bar{D}) = ABCD + ABC\bar{D} + \cdots + \bar{A}\bar{B}\bar{C}\bar{D}$$

(d) Equation

(e) Karnaugh map

Figure 3.9 Representations for classifying four attributes.

symbol D added to each label in room D, and $\overline{D}$ added to each label in room $\overline{D}$. The Venn diagram of Figure 3.9b has a region A above the diagonal line from the upper left to the lower right corner. $\overline{A}$ is below this line. Regions B and $\overline{B}$ are separated by the other diagonal line from the upper right to the lower left corner. Regions C and D are shown by the elliptical shapes. For the tree diagram we added branches D and $\overline{D}$. The equation is expanded by factor $(D + \overline{D})$. In the Karnaugh map we added region D marked by horizontal lines. Regions C and D in this diagram divide the total area into vertical rectangles in a way that corresponds to the way regions A and B divide it into horizontal rectangles.

3.9 Which Representation to Use?

If we were to proceed with a classification for five or more attributes, it would become apparent that representation in the form of expansion of matrices into cubes, cubes placed in rooms, and then two rooms in each of two buildings and next two buildings in each of two cities becomes awkward. The same can be said about Venn diagrams and Karnaugh maps. Equations and tree diagrams present no difficulty. For trees we add branches at the end of the tree as we add an attribute, and for the equation we add a factor in parentheses. For example, classification in terms of the presence or absence of n attributes A_i ($i = 1$, $2, \ldots, n$) would require a tree with n levels with a total of $2 \times 2 \times \cdots \times 2 = 2^n$ end branches. The equation would have the form

$$(A_1 + \overline{A}_1)(A_2 + \overline{A}_2) \cdots (A_n + \overline{A}_n)$$

or in shorter notation,

$$\prod_{i=1}^{n} (A_i + \overline{A}_i)$$

in which $\prod_{i=1}^{n}$ designates multiplication of the factors in parentheses for values of i from 1 to n. The equation is a compact form of representation, but it is not useful as a working tool that we can use in a way similar to the use of the matrix representation of Figure 3.1.

The tree diagram is most useful for any number of attributes. However, we shall demonstrate that the Venn diagram is useful as a tool for thinking to explain some important concepts, and matrices may be useful in other situations, as will be shown by the discussions that follow.

3.10 Attributes with More Than Two Levels

Suppose that we wish to classify a set of objects in terms of two attributes: color and shape. The colors consist of blue $\equiv C_1$, red $\equiv C_2$, and white $\equiv C_3$. The shapes are circle $\equiv S_1$, square $\equiv S_2$, triangle $\equiv S_3$, and rectangle $\equiv S_4$. Each object can have only one color and one shape, that is, the colors $C_i (i = 1$,

2, 3) are mutually exclusive, and the shapes are mutually exclusive. We can represent the 12 ($3 \times 4 = 12$) classifications in the following matrix:

	S_1	S_2	S_3	S_4
C_1	C_1S_1	C_1S_2		
C_2				
C_3				C_3S_4

or by an equation

$$(C_1 + C_2 + C_3)(S_1 + S_2 + S_3 + S_4) = C_1S_1 + C_1S_2 + \cdots + C_3S_4$$

or in a tree:

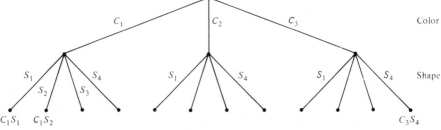

Of course, we could reverse the positions of S and C in the representations above and obtain

	C_1	C_2	C_3
S_1	S_1C_1		
S_2	S_2C_1		
S_3			
S_4			S_4C_3

$$(S_1 + S_2 + S_3 + S_4)(C_1 + C_2 + C_3) = S_1C_1 + S_1C_2 + \cdots + S_4C_3$$

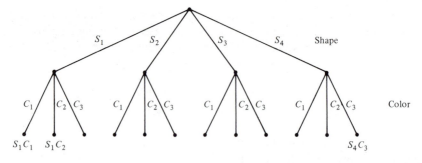

A Venn diagram or a Karnaugh map would appear similar to the matrix representation and would offer no advantage.

3.11 Application of Tree Diagrams: Scan the Field before Acting

We shall now show how a tree representation for classification can be employed as a tool for scanning a field of possibilities before embarking on a course of action, thus enhancing the potential for rational and imaginative thinking.

THE NEWSPAPER BOY

Jerry was 11 years old when he was selling newspaper subscriptions in the neighborhood with an unusual record of success. Each week he sold considerably more subscriptions than any other boy who worked for the same newspaper distribution agency.

The key to his success was a careful classification of the people in the neighborhood as shown in the tree of Figure 3.10. First, he divided all people into two sets: those who have a subscription, S, and those who do not have one, $\bar{S}$. The group S was not of interest because there were no potential buyers in this group. Group $\bar{S}$ was divided further into those who read newspapers, R, and those who do not, $\bar{R}$. The subgroup with classification $\bar{S}\bar{R}$ on the rightmost

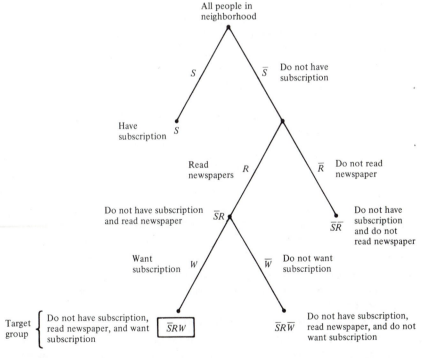

Figure 3.10 Classification of people in a neighborhood to study potential for newspaper subscriptions.

branch of the tree did not seem to include potential buyers. This left him with subgroup $\bar{S}R$ that included two parts: $\bar{S}RW$, namely those who do not have a subscription, read newspapers, and may want a subscription; or those who have no subscription, read newspapers, and may not want a subscription. Jerry decided to find a way of identifying members of the subgroup of newspaper readers without a subscription, classification $\bar{S}R$, so he could ask them whether they wanted one.

One Sunday morning Jerry went with his parents to a restaurant in the neighborhood. He noticed people stopping to buy newspapers at the newspaper stands in front of the restaurant. Chance events favor the prepared mind, as by serendipity he discovered a connection between the people stopping at the newspaper stands and the class of people with the label $\bar{S}R$, those who have no subscription and read newspapers.

On the following weekends, Jerry positioned himself next to the newspaper stands in various locations in the neighborhood, and in a period of a few weeks he sold more subscriptions than some other boys sold in a year. While other boys went indiscriminantly from house to house unsure of the classification of the occupants, Jerry focused on a subgroup with the highest potential of becoming new subscribers, and in so doing he achieved the highest return per hour of effort. Jerry scanned the field before he acted and it paid off.

ELECTION CAMPAIGN

Frank, a former student, was involved in a campaign to elect a Democratic candidate to the U.S. Congress and wanted to develop a strategy to achieve victory. The candidate lost the race to the Republican candidate in the last election by a small margin and preparations were in progress for a new campaign. Frank asked me how the tools of problem solving might help in the campaign to increase the prospects of a victory for his favorite candidate. I stressed the need for careful classification of the relevant constituency before resources of time, money, and energy were allocated. To drive home the point, I told him the story about Jerry and the newspaper subscriptions.

Frank reviewed the records of the last elections. There were four offices on the ballots, with Republican and Democratic candidates competing for each. One of the offices was a seat in Congress. On the basis of this information he classified all voters in one of 16 categories as shown in Figure 3.11. A voter could choose one of 16 sequences in the voting process. On the extreme left branch of the tree a person voted for the Democratic candidate in each case. On the right-hand side, the vote also went with the party line, but this time Republican. Between these extremes there were people who split their vote between Democrats and Republicans.

The conclusion he reached was that people who vote the party line are not likely to change their minds, but people who split their votes, in particular 2, 2, may be paying attention to who the candidates really are, and might be convinced to vote for what they perceive as the better candidate regardless of political affiliation.

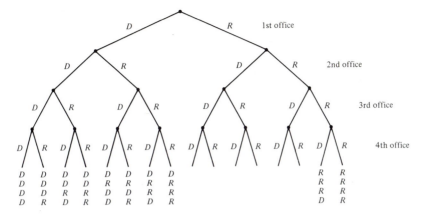

Figure 3.11 Classification of voters for four candidates.

The question was how to identify this class of voters. Questions lead to a search for answers, and when you know what you are looking for there is a good chance that you will recognize it when you see it. Frank studied the returns of the last election and noted that some precincts had given a majority to all four Democrats, others to the four Republicans, and others split their vote. There were 500 precincts in the congressional district. Precincts could be classified the same way as individual voters in Figure 3.11. So while the classification of each individual was not possible, aggregates or groups could be classified by precincts. Being a mathematician, Frank proceeded to establish upper and lower bounds on the number of people who must have split their votes in each precinct. From this, he identified 60 of the 500 precincts as having a high potential of responding favorably to a strong campaign. The 60 precincts were clustered in 13 geographic regions and a vigorous campaign was launched in them.

You must have guessed the results. Frank's candidate won the elections and has been serving as a successful and respected congressman. Would I tell the story otherwise?

MANAGEMENT STYLES

In a study of mismanagement styles Adizes [27] classifies managers in terms of presence or absence of each of the following roles: administrator, *A*; producer, *P*; integrator, *I*; entrepreneur, *E*. *A* is a bureaucrat who goes by the book; *P* is bent on producing results; *I* focuses on achieving consensus; *E* engages in the role of entrepreneur and innovator. Figure 3.12 shows the 16 possible classifications in terms of presence and absence (shown by an overbar) of these roles.

At the extreme left and right of the tree we have, respectively, the "textbook manager" *APIE* with all roles present, and the "dead wood" manager, with no role of *APIE* present. Some classifications are more common in managers in terms of compatible roles such as *AP̄IĒ* and *ĀPIĒ*; others are very

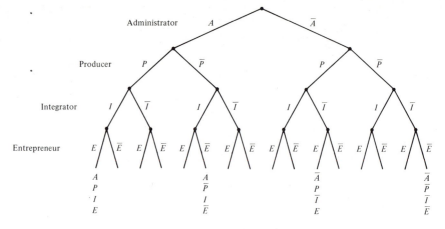

Figure 3.12 Classification of management styles.

uncommon because of incompatible roles such as $AP\overline{IE}$ and $\overline{AP}IE$, or the ideal supermanager $APIE$.

Adizes uses these classifications for diagnosis of an organization to detect presence or absence of the various managerial roles and to recommend actions compatible with the needs of the organization. The thesis advanced by Adizes is that a healthy organization requires a balance of these four attributes and a management team should be selected accordingly.

KNOWLEDGE AND MOTIVATION

Workers in industry and students in schools can be classified in many ways. One classification that can be useful to a manager or a teacher considers knowledge, K, and motivation, M, as shown in Figure 3.13 (see also reference 28).

The approach a manager or teacher should take in managing or teaching depends on the classification. People in classification KM are those who know

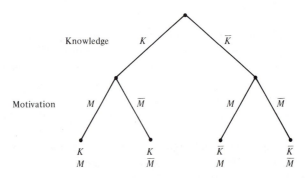

Figure 3.13 Classification of workers or students in terms of knowledge and motivation.

what to do and are motivated to do it. The best strategy to employ with these people is to stay out of their way, leave them alone. The class $K\overline{M}$ needs to be motivated, the class $\overline{K}M$ needs to be shown or taught what to do and how to do the task, and the class $\overline{K}\overline{M}$ represents a serious challenge. A different strategy is required for each class. A choice of proper strategy is predicated on, and must be preceded by, a proper classification, scanning the field and identifying the presence and absence of relevant features.

3.12 Applications of Venn Diagrams

For many years I have been using a Venn diagram whenever a situation arises that requires a distinction between a condition that is *necessary* and a condition that is *sufficient*. For example, Figure 3.14 shows the relationship between the city of Los Angeles and the state of California. The city is completely nested inside the state. Therefore, the following statements are true:

1. If I am in Los Angeles, then *I am* in California.
2. If I am outside California, then *I am* outside Los Angeles.
3. If I am outside Los Angeles, then *I may be* in California.
4. If I am in California, then *I may be* in Los Angeles.

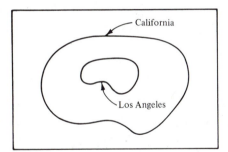

Figure 3.14 Relationship between Los Angeles and California. Being in Los Angeles implies being in California.

DEMONSTRATIVE REASONING

Statements 1 and 2 have conclusions that are definitive: No one will argue that if Figure 3.14 is true, namely Los Angeles is in California, and if I am in Los Angeles, then *I am* in California. Similarly, if I am outside California, *I am* outside Los Angeles. This form of reasoning that leads to definitive conclusions is called *demonstrative reasoning*.

PLAUSIBLE REASONING

Statements 3 and 4 suggest conclusions that are reasonable, plausible, but not definitive. When I am in California, the conclusion that there is a chance that I am in Los Angeles is plausible, and the chance would become greater if the area of Los Angeles were to become larger and almost approach the size of

California but still preserve the relationship of Figure 3.14, namely that the city remain wholly inside the state. Similarly, when I am outside Los Angeles, the conclusion that there is a chance that I am in California is reasonable, plausible, but not definitive. The chance would become greater as the area of California outside Los Angeles increases relative to the area of the rectangle outside California. The rectangle could represent the United States, the "universe," or boundaries of the problem at hand that contains California.

The reasoning of statements 3 and 4 is called *plausible reasoning*. The conclusions in plausible reasoning indicate direction in the following sense: If I am outside California, the statement "I am in Los Angeles" is false. However, if I am in California, the statement "I am in Los Angeles" is moving in the direction of possibly being true.

NECESSARY CONDITION

To be in Los Angeles it is *necessary* to be in California, *but it is not sufficient*.

SUFFICIENT CONDITIONS

To be in California it is *sufficient* to be in Los Angeles, *but it is not necessary*.

GENERALIZATION

Consider the two regions P and Q of Figure 3.15, with P completely inside Q. We designate such a relationship by an arrow going from P to Q as follows:

$$P \rightarrow Q$$

This notation is equivalent to the statement P *implies* Q, or *when P is true, then Q is true* or *P is a subset of Q*. In the regions P and Q of Figure 3.15, $P \rightarrow Q$ means that whenever we are inside P we are inside Q, and therefore,

P is *sufficient* for Q *but not necessary*

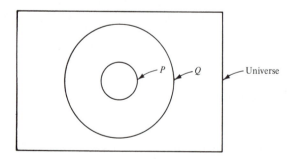

Figure 3.15 $P \rightarrow Q$, P implies Q.

Tools for Representation   Chap. 3

and

> Q is *necessary* for P *but not sufficient*

When P and Q are identical in size and completely overlap we write $P \leftrightarrow Q$ and we have

> Q is *necessary and sufficient* for P

and

> P is *necessary and sufficient* for Q

The imply statement $P \rightarrow Q$ is very useful in testing the validity of arguments, as demonstrated by the following discussion, which expands the exposure to this concept as introduced here.

3.13 Testing the Validity of Arguments: The Imply Statement

Suppose that we believe the premises; would we accept the conclusions?

Joe claims that if he takes a shower, he sings at the top of his voice. In fact, he says that whenever he takes a shower he sings. We could accept this as a cause–effect relationship by claiming that the water of the shower stimulates Joe to sing. But Joe also claims that if the phone rings, he is in the shower. Now, it is difficult to see any cause–effect relationship between the ringing of the phone and the taking of a shower.

Philosophers have tried for many years to establish a connection between causality and implications represented by sentences of the type: *If p is true, then q is true*. Causality may be involved in an implication. However, for our purposes we shall define an implication, in the form of an if–then statement, as merely the simultaneous occurrence of two events or the simultaneous truth of two classifications.

To be more explicit, let us return to Joe. Joe will state

> If I shower, then I sing

Suppose that we designate by $\sim$ the negation of a statement. Then if

> r denotes "I shower,"
> $\sim r$ denotes "I do not shower."

And if

n denotes   "I sing,"

$\sim n$ denotes   "I do not sing."

Joe's statement can now be written in the compact form:

If r, then n.

Namely, if r is true, then n is true. But this makes three situations possible:

1. $r \wedge n$ ($\wedge$ denotes "and")
2. $\sim r \wedge n$
3. $\sim r \wedge \sim n$

Using a Venn diagram, the three possibilities are identified in Figure 3.16. The imply statement *If r, then n* does not permit $r \wedge \sim n$ to be true, namely, shower and not sing.

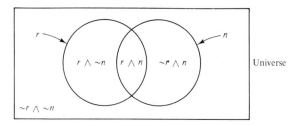

Figure 3.16   The three possible situations consistent with the imply statement: If r, then n.

The relationship between r and n in the imply statement above is one in which r is a subset of n. In the Venn diagram of Figure 3.16 the region $r \wedge \sim n$ disappears and we obtain the diagram of Figure 3.17, in which r is totally contained in n, so that r can never be true without n true at the same time. As we indicated earlier, the statement *If r, then n* can be written more compactly as *r implies n,* or $r \rightarrow n$.

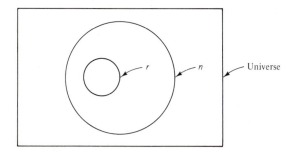

Figure 3.17   Alternative way of showing the three possible regions for the statement: If r, then n.

Let us consider now Joe's second premise, namely,

$$\underbrace{\text{If the phone rings,}}_{p} \quad \text{then} \quad \underbrace{\text{I shower}}_{r}$$

or

$$p \to r$$

This statement is true if it is never violated; that is, we cannot have a situation where p is true and at the same time r is false. Other than that, $p \to r$ permits at least one of $\sim p$ or r to be true, and therefore $p \to r$ is equivalent to $\sim p \vee r$ (in which $\vee$ designates "or"). In other words, Joe could tell us:

If the phone rings, I shower.

or what is equivalent:

I can find myself in the following situations:

$p \wedge r$, the phone rings and I shower.

$\sim p \wedge r$, the phone does not ring and I shower.

$\sim p \wedge \sim r$, the phone does not ring and I do not shower.

But I *never* find myself in this situation:

$p \wedge \sim r$, the phone rings and I do not shower.

A Venn diagram would show the region for p included inside the region for r.

To check the validity of an imply statement, we reason as follows. In the statement $p \to r$, p and r can each take on one of two truth values, T or F, and there are four combinations of these values, as shown in the following four rows below $p \to r$:

	$p \longrightarrow r$	
Row 1	T	T
Row 2	T	F
Row 3	F	T
Row 4	F	F

Of these four rows only the second, encircled row must not be possible if $p \to r$ is true. This leads to the following conclusions. Suppose that we begin with r on the right-hand side of the imply statement, assume that r is true, and inspect the corresponding truth values of p. Since p can be either T (row 1) or F (row 3) for $r = T$, there is no point in checking out these possibilities. On the other hand, if we begin by setting the conclusion r to F and consistent with this, at the same time, we succeed in showing that p can be T; then the statement $p \to r$ is false. But if r set to F can be matched only with p set to F, the imply statement is valid.

One of the prime functions of logic is to check the validity of arguments, namely, to check the claim that a conclusion follows from premises. An argument is valid if and only if the simultaneous truth of all the premises [also known as the conjunction ($\wedge$) of the premises] implies the conclusion, or if all premises are true, then the conclusion is true.

$$\underset{\text{T}}{\text{(premise 1)}} \wedge \underset{\text{T}}{\text{(premise 2)}} \wedge \cdots \wedge \underset{\text{T}}{\text{(premise } n)} \rightarrow \underset{\text{T}}{\text{conclusion}}$$

When we check the validity of an argument we do not question the credibility of the premises. We accept them to be true and check the validity of the conclusion on the basis of the accepted premises. The premises may be factual pieces of information that we have yet to obtain, such as "there are more than 400 students waiting to get into Engineering 11." If we accept this and other similar premises on a tentative basis and check the validity of our conclusion, then if the argument is invalid, it may not be necessary to establish the credibility of the premises and we can save time and effort.

There are situations in which a premise can be interpreted in one of two different mutually exclusive ways, and it will require great effort to establish which of the two was intended. Under such circumstances we can check the validity of the argument using first one interpretation of the premise, then the other, and if the argument is valid (or invalid) under both conditions, there is no need to worry about what the premise actually represented for the purpose of establishing whether the conclusion follows the premises. However, when one interpretation leads to a valid argument and the other to an invalid one, the search for the correct interpretation of the premise may be justified.

Returning now to the imply statement, we can write it in the following general form:

$$\underbrace{\text{(premise 1)} \wedge \text{(premise 2)} \wedge \cdots \wedge \text{(premise } n)}_{P} \rightarrow \text{conclusion}$$

We can represent this in a Venn diagram as shown in Figure 3.18. We aggregate

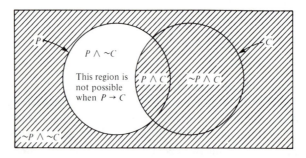

Figure 3.18 $P \rightarrow C$.

Tools for Representation   Chap. 3

all the premises on the left of the arrow in the imply statement as one region P representing all premises being true, and region C represents the conclusion being true. The region outside P that can be represented by $\sim P$ signifies one or more of the premises false. The region outside of C, $\sim C$, represents the conclusion false.

To show that an argument is not valid, we should try to show that when C is false, P can be true at the same time. But if our efforts fail, namely when C is false P is false, with at least one of the premises false, the argument is valid and all of P is included inside C, as shown in Figure 3.19, with only the three possible regions shaded in Figure 3.18.

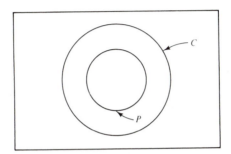

Figure 3.19 $P \rightarrow C$.

To identify premises and conclusions in general conversation or in written material, look for the following key words. Usually, sentences that follow "since," "for," "because," "whenever" are premises, while sentences that follow "therefore," "thus," "hence," "a result," and "consequently" are conclusions. For example, in "Tom cannot vote because he is not registered," the premise follows "because" and the conclusion precedes it.

Example 1

Consider the following argument: If this is a good course, then it is worth taking. Either the course is easy or it is not worth taking. The course is not easy; therefore, this is a good course.

Let us use the following notations:

g = this is a good course

ω = the course is worth taking

e = the course is easy

The three premises and the conclusion take the following form:

$$(g \rightarrow \omega) \wedge (e \vee \sim\omega) \wedge (\sim e) \rightarrow g$$

premise 1   premise 2   premise 3   conclusion

To test the validity of the argument above, we assign g a value F (false) and consistent with this, namely assign g the value F in all premises in which it appears, we try to force all premises to assume a truth value T. If we succeed, the argument is invalid; otherwise, it is valid. We illustrate the procedure in the following table of rows and columns below the statement.

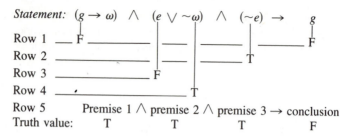

Statement: $(g \rightarrow \omega) \;\wedge\; (e \vee \sim\omega) \;\wedge\; (\sim e) \;\rightarrow\; g$

Row 1 __ F _____ |____ |_____ |____ F

Row 2 _____ |____ |____ T

Row 3 _____ F

Row 4 _____ T

Row 5   Premise 1 $\wedge$ premise 2 $\wedge$ premise 3 $\rightarrow$ conclusion

Truth value: T   T   T   F

We begin by assigning F to g on the right of the arrow and in premise 1 (row 1). Now to force premise 1 to be true (T) with $g = F$ (the equal sign stands for "assigned"), ω in premise 1 can be either T or F. So we have premise 1 = T. Now let us assign T to premise 3 (row 2), then consistent with this we must set $e = F$ (row 3) in premise 2. For premise 2 to be true (what we are trying to achieve), $\sim\omega$ must be T, because in an "or" statement, $\vee$, at least one of the statements on either side of $\vee$, must be true for the "or" condition to be true. So in row 4 we set $\sim\omega = T$. This means that we must assign F to ω in premise 1. However, premise 1 is true regardless of what truth value we assign to ω because g is false. In row 5 we note that we succeeded in proving the argument invalid because the premises can all be true when the conclusion is false.

The Venn diagram of Figure 3.20 shows the region where premise 1 is true by horizontal lines, the region where premise 2 is true by vertical lines, and the region where premise 3 is true by inclined lines. The intersection of all these lines is the region where all premises are true. When the argument is valid, this region must be totally included in the region where the conclusion is true (i.e., g). This is not the case in Figure 3.20; therefore, the argument is invalid. Note, however, that the region where all three lines intersect is totally included in the region $\sim g$. Therefore, conclusion $\sim g$ is consistent with the premises and the following argument is valid:

$$(g \rightarrow \omega) \wedge (e \vee \sim\omega) \wedge (\sim e) \rightarrow \sim g$$

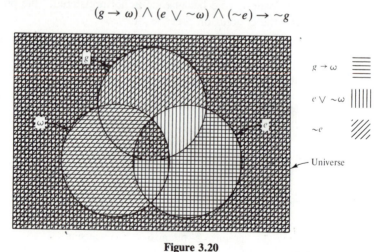

Figure 3.20

Example 2

If prices are high (p), then wages are high (ω). But either prices are not high or there are price controls (c); and if there are price controls, there is no inflation ($\sim f$). However, there is inflation. Therefore, wages are high (ω).

In the following $\underline{\vee}$ represents an *exclusive or*. In general, $A \underline{\vee} B$ is true when only one of A or B is true; otherwise, it is false; namely, when both A and B are true or both are false, $A \lor B$ is false. Beginning with the symbolic representation of the foregoing four premises and conclusion ω, we first assign F to ω in the conclusion in row 1, then look for premises where ω appears and assign it F as in premise 1. Now we continue to force the premises to a truth value T as shown below in rows 1 to 7.

$$(p \to \omega) \land (\sim p \lor c) \land (c \to \sim f) \land f \to \omega$$

	$(p \to \omega)$	$(\sim p \lor c)$	$(c \to \sim f)$	f	ω
Row 1	F				F
Row 2	F				
Row 3		T			
Row 4				T	
Row 5			F		
Row 6		F			
Row 7			F		
Row 8	Premise 1 $\land$ premise 2 $\land$ premise 3 $\land$ premise 4 $\to$ conclusion				
Truth value:	T T T T			$\to$	F

The argument is invalid because all premises are true and the conclusion is false.

An alternative way of recording information in testing the validity of arguments is shown in the following for our present example. The premises are written one below the other with the conclusion at the bottom. The truth value of each symbol (or its negation) is written above it and to the right, as the test proceeds, instead of writing it in a row as was done earlier to keep track of the sequence of steps.

Truth Value of Premise for Conclusion = F

	F F	
Premise 1	$p \to \omega$	T
	T F	
Premise 2	$\sim p \lor c$	T
	F F	
Premise 3	$c \to \sim f$	T
	T	
Premise 4	f	T
Conclusion	ω	F Argument is invalid

Example 3

If the market is free (f), company A cannot affect prices $(\sim P)$. If company A cannot affect prices, there are many companies. There are many companies (m). Therefore, the market is not free.

Truth Value of Premises for Conclusion = F

	T T	
Premise 1	$f \to \sim P$	T
	T T	
Premise 2	$\sim P \to m$	T
	T	
Premise 3	m	T
Conclusion	$\sim f$	F Argument is invalid

3.14 Communication: Novel Application of Venn Diagrams and Tables

The world can now be viewed as a single community in terms of our ability to transmit and receive information. Early in our civilization human beings communicated over distance by shouting. They could communicate at the rate of about one word per second over a distance of less than 1 mile. Then came coded smoke and fire signals, later, flag signals from ships (first used in the seventeenth century), and next, mechanical apparatus consisting of arms on towers for signaling (semaphores) about the eighteenth century. Tzar Nicholas I in Russia (nineteenth century) had a network of semaphores linking Moscow, Warsaw, and St. Petersburg. Telegraph came in the middle of the nineteenth century, then radio, TV, microwave towers, satellites, and lasers. Now we can communicate information at the rate of 10,000 words per second over distances that link us with outer space. Thus we can send or receive a signal from the moon in about 1 second.

The main elements of a communication system are shown in Figure 3.21. In oral communication the *information source* is the brain, the *encoder* is the speaker, and the voice mechanism is the *transmitter*. The sound produced by the speaker is the *signal sent* and the air is the *communication channel*. *Noise* refers to distortions of sound in transmission. The *signal received* by the listener is a combination of the signal sent and noise. The listener, *receiver, decodes* the received signal by translating it to an experience on the basis of knowledge of the language and the world. This experience becomes the delivered *message* which registers in the *destination* (i.e., the brain of the receiver).

For telephone communication, the selected message is changed by the telephone *transmitter* from sound pressure of voice to varying electrical current. The *channel* is a wire or microwave, and the signal is the varying electrical current. The decoding is done at the other end.

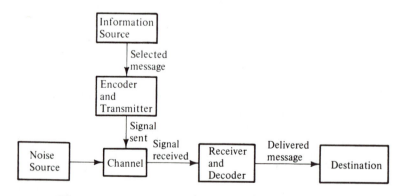

Figure 3.21   Schematic diagram of a communication system.

Transmitted messages can be coded in various ways, provided that receiver and transmitter have agreed on the encoding rules. Thus we can use a binary code to transmit decimal numbers or English words if we wish. The amount of information we transmit depends on the amount of distortion, that is, noise that corrupts the intended message as it makes its way from transmitter to receiver. Fortunately, redundancy exists in natural language. Our written language is based on complex figures that were abstracted to the form of letters of the alphabet. A letter can be recognized even when it is only partially seen, because the essential figure that it is intended to convey is not abstracted to the point where no redundancy is left.

There is also redundancy in written words: Mst ppl cn rd ths sttmnt wth lttl dffclty. Redundancy also appears in sentences; words can be omitted without loss of meaning. The same holds for paragraphs and so on.

USE OF REDUNDANCY IN COMMUNICATION

When we transmit a message by a binary code, there is also a possibility of corruption because of noise. For example, suppose that we wish to transmit information in the form of message units that consist of four binary digits (bits). Consider a pulse train as shown in Figure 3.22 as a signal sent to represent 1011.

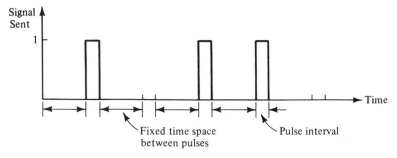

Figure 3.22 Signal sent: 1011.

A clock controls the fixed time spacing between bits. During the pulse interval, a pulse is generated when a bit 1 is sent, and no pulse is generated when a bit 0 is sent. Noise in the transmission process may cause the sent signal of Figure 3.22 to be transformed into a received signal of the form shown in Figure 3.23. The second bit in the received signal is about midway between 0 and 1. Which is it? There are clever ways to code the information by using redundancy so that errors due to noise can be detected and corrected.

In the following discussion we develop the Hamming code [29], which is a communication code that will detect and correct a *single* error in one bit out of a pulse train of seven bits in which four constitute the desired message and three are extra digits for redundancy. The development will demonstrate a novel application of Venn diagrams.

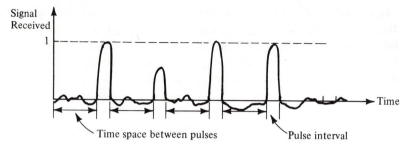

Figure 3.23   Signal received: 1011 or 1111?

HAMMING CODE

Consider a string of seven bits designated by letters a_i in which the subscript indicates the position of the bit:

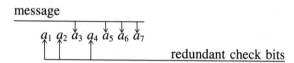

Each letter a_i can assume the value 0 or 1. The string $a_3a_5a_6a_7$ constitutes the message, and the bits $a_1a_2a_4$ are the redundant check bits added to the message to detect and correct a single error in the transmitted string of seven bits. The three redundant check bits are a function of the four bits in the message, as will be shown. Let us observe the transmitter and the receiver at work while communicating with this code.

Transmitter.   Suppose that the transmitter wishes to send the message 1011; that is, $a_3a_5a_6a_7 = 1011$. Before sending the message, she extends it by adding check bits $a_1a_2a_4$ whose values are selected using the Venn diagram of Figure 3.24. Each of the seven regions in the area bounded by the circles I, II, and III is identified by a letter a_i. The transmitter inserts the values for $a_3a_5a_6a_7$,

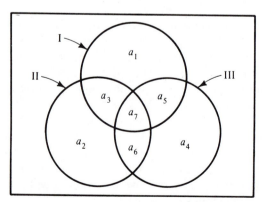

Figure 3.24   Venn diagram for Hamming code.

1, 0, 1, 1 in our case, and then she selects 0 or 1 for each check bit $a_1 a_2 a_4$ so that the sum of the bits in the four regions of each circle adds up to an even number. This is called a *parity check*. In the present case, $a_1 a_2 a_4$ are, respectively, 0, 1, 0, as shown in Figure 3.25. The transmitter sends the signal of seven bits 0110011.

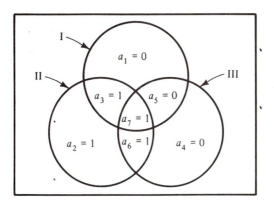

Figure 3.25 Hamming code for message 1011.

Receiver. Let us suppose that noise causes the transmitted bits 0110011 to be received as 0100011. The receiver enters each bit in the appropriate region in the Venn diagram of Figure 3.24, as shown in Figure 3.26. He now adds the bits in each circle and records 0 for a sum that is an even number, and 1 for an odd number. The resulting three bits are listed in the order III, II, I, corresponding to the results obtained with each circle. In the present case, the receiver obtains 011. This is the binary equivalent of the decimal number 3. Hence there is an error in position three; namely, $a_3 = 0$ in the received signal should be changed to 1. Now, after the correction, the parity check will yield 000, which signifies that there is no error.

The Hamming code not only detects the error, but tells you where it occurred. The parity check yields three binary digits which can stand for the

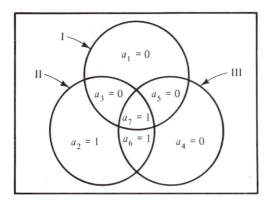

Figure 3.26

numbers 0 to 7 and represents no errors (000) or the position where a single error occurred by identifying a_1 (001) to a_7 (111).

3.15 How Does the Hamming Code Work?

Let us consider messages of four bits with the stipulation that an error can occur in only one bit. To identify which of the four bits in the message is wrong, we require a *check code* of three bits for the numbers zero to four.* But error may occur also in a check bit. Restricting ourselves to only one error, we can still use the three check bits to identify seven positions, (001, 010, 011, . . . , 111), four for the message and three for the check bits, as well as the number zero (000) to signify "no error." To make the Hamming code work as described above, we arrange the string of seven bits a_1 to a_7, as shown in the Venn diagram of Figure 3.24 with the message identified by $a_3 a_5 a_6 a_7$ and the check bits $a_1 a_2 a_4$. Each check bit is placed so that it is contained in one circle only. This way, each check bit can be entered independently for any selected message because, first, the message bits are recorded in the appropriate regions, and then the check bits are added to yield an even sum of bits in each circle separately. To check for a single error in the transmission, we add the bits in the regions of each circle. Suppose that an odd number of bits is obtained in each circle. We then write III II I = 111, which is the number seven. Hence a_7 is wrong. Note that a_7 is at the intersection of all three circles and, therefore, the error affects all of them. That is why a_7 was recorded there in the first place. Similarly, an error in position one (a_1) is identified as III II I = 001 and, therefore, only circle I is affected; that is why a_1 is in the region that is contained in circle I only. An error in a_5 is identified by III II I = 101; therefore, a_5 is at the intersection of circles III and I and outside II. You can now justify on the same basis the assignments of all a_i in Figure 3.24.

Since this is not simple and may require rereading and independent reflection, let us repeat the above by starting with the check bits. If we have three check bits, we can identify eight distinct numbers or regions: 000 will signify no error; 001, 010, and 100 will signify the three possible errors in the check bits a_1, a_2, and a_4, respectively. We have four numbers left out of the total of eight, and therefore, the message can consist of no more than four bits if we insist on identifying an error in the message. These four identification numbers are

$$011, 101, 110, 111$$

These are, respectively, the decimal numbers 3, 5, 6, and 7. Note also that the sequences of the three bits III II I in the parity check identify the eight regions of Figure 3.24; a 1 indicates that the region is in the corresponding circle, a 0 indicates the region is outside the corresponding circle. For example, 000 identifies the region outside all circles, and 111 identifies the intersection of the three circles.

*The number zero (000) in the check code signifies "no error."

You may now wish to satisfy yourself by reasoning why four check bits can be used in a Hamming code for a message of 11 bits, five check bits for a message of 26 bits, six for 57, and in general n check bits for a message of $[2^n - (n + 1)]$ bits.

USING TABLES FOR HAMMING CODE

The positions of the check bits and message bits can be identified from the following table in place of a Venn diagram for messages of four bits:

Circle or Row	Column Number						
	1	2	3	4	5	6	7
I:	0	1	0	1	0	1	0	1
II:	0	0	1	1	0	0	1	1
III:	0	0	0	0	1	1	1	1

$$a_1 \quad a_2 \quad a_3 \quad a_4 \quad a_5 \quad a_6 \quad a_7$$

check bits

To check for an error in a received message, we proceed as follows: For any $a_i = 1$, enter its identification from the table in column i; for example, for $a_7 = 1$, place three 1's in column 7 (the binary equivalent of 7). If $a_7 = 0$, place three 0's in column 7. If $a_3 = 1$, write in column 3 the binary number for 3 using the sequence III II I, which yields 011. If $a_3 = 0$, place all 0's in column 3. After entering all a_i of the message this way, add the bits in each row. Record a 1 for an odd sum and a 0 for an even sum. The sequence of bits III, II, I in the three rows identifies where a single error occurred. When transmitting a message, we record the a_i of the message and assign check bit a_1 a value of 0 or 1 as required to make the sum of bits in row I even. Similarly we assign a_2 and a_4 to make the sums of bits in rows II and III even.

For example, suppose that we receive the sequence 0100011. Then we construct this table:

I:	0	0	0	0	0	0	1
II:	0	0	1	0	0	0	1	1
III:	0	0	0	0	0	0	1	1

$$a_1 \quad a_2 \quad a_3 \quad a_4 \quad a_5 \quad a_6 \quad a_7$$

Row I: odd sum, I = 1; row II: odd sum, II = 1; row III: even sum, III = 0. Thus III II I = 011 and there is an error in a_3; namely, it should be 1 instead of 0 and the correct sequence is 0110011.

To transmit the message 1001, for example, we construct the following table ($a_1 = 0$, $a_2 = 0$, $a_4 = 1$ for this message):

I:	0	0	0	1	0	0	0	1
II:	0	0	0	1	0	0	0	1
III:	0	0	0	0	1	0	0	1

$$a_1 \quad a_2 \quad a_3 \quad a_4 \quad a_5 \quad a_6 \quad a_7$$

For a message of 11 bits with four check bits, the table takes the following form with the location of error identified by the four-bit sequence IV, III, II, I:

Row															
I:	0	1	0	1	0	1	0	1	0	1	0	1	0	1	0	1
II:	0	0	1	1	0	0	1	1	0	0	1	1	0	0	1	1
III:	0	0	0	0	1	1	1	1	0	0	0	0	1	1	1	1
IV:	0	0	0	0	0	0	0	0	1	1	1	1	1	1	1	1

$$a_1 \ a_2 \ a_3 \ a_4 \ a_5 \ a_6 \ a_7 \ a_8 \ a_9 \ a_{10} \ a_{11} \ a_{12} \ a_{13} \ a_{14} \ a_{15}$$

check bits

3.16 Hamming Distance and Hamming Code: A Generalization of Concepts

We shall now employ the concept of Hamming distance as a representation to generalize the concept of a Hamming code that can detect and correct errors in communication using sequences of binary digits.

Consider the three codes a, b, and c of Table 3.1. These codes are, respectively, for universes of eight, four, and two events. We define the *Hamming distance* between two binary sequences of the same length as the number of places in which the two sequences differ. For example, the sequences

$$101111$$

$$111100$$

Table 3.1

	Code a	Code b	Code c
	000	000	000
	001	011	111
	010	101	
	011	110	
	100		
	101		
	110		
	111		
Number of events	8	4	2

have a Hamming distance of 3. The *minimum Hamming distance* between code words is closely related to error detection and correction. The minimum Hamming distance for codes *a, b,* and *c* of Table 3.1 are, respectively, 1, 2, and 3.

To detect a single error in a code, the minimum distance between code words must be 2. For example, for a code of the two code words 00, 11, a single error can be detected in the two possible erroneous code words 01 or 10. But there is ambiguity in how to correct for the error, since each erroneous code word is one Hamming distance unit from each of the code words that could be the intended message.

For single error detection and correction (or double error detection) the minimum distance must be 3. For example, for two messages 000 and 111, all six erroneous messages with a single error can be detected and corrected using the following table:

Erroneous Code Word	Corrected Code Word
001	000
010	000
011	111
100	000
101	111
110	111

For single error correction plus double error detection (or triple error detection, in which case it could be either one or three errors and correction is not possible) the minimum distance between code words must be 4, such as, for example, the distance between 0000 and 1111. For double error detection and correction the minimum distance must be 5.

Suppose that we have a sequence of n bits for code words; therefore, 2^n unique code words can be written. Such a code will have a minimum Hamming distance of 1. Suppose that $n = 7$; then we have 2^7 code words. To detect and correct one error, we must have a minimum distance of 3. Thus from the total of 2^7 code words a smaller number must be selected to represent events, such that the minimum distance between these selected code words is 3. A single error in an intended code word will therefore be a code sequence one unit distance from the intended word, but at least a two-unit distance from any other code word. Thus we can both detect and correct the error. Conceptually, this is shown in Figure 3.27. A single code word $\alpha = 1110000$ of length 7 is surrounded by a conceptual sphere of seven code words each a unit of Hamming distance away from it representing an error in one bit only. Any other code word, β, is a minimum distance of 3 away from α (i.e., differs in at least three bits from α, say $\beta = 0000000$). β is also surrounded by a sphere of seven code words each with a single error. Since the spheres do not overlap, we can detect and correct a single error. However, if two errors are introduced in α, they can be detected

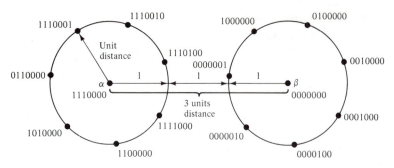

Figure 3.27

but erroneously interpreted as being a single error in code word β, when α and β are three Hamming distance units apart. For example, an erroneous code 1000000 could be α with two errors, or β with one error. Therefore, only single errors can be corrected for a minimum distance of 3.

Thus for single-error detection and correction, the total of $2^7 = 128$ code words possible with seven bits are divided into groups of eight, consisting of a code word that will be used in the language we will devise and seven code words that differ from it by one bit only and represent the results of a single error. For code words with n bits, the size of each group is $(1 + n)$ in general. Thus for $n = 7$ we can have 128/8 groups or 16 code words of events, or four bit sequences for coding events $(2^4 = 16)$. The general relation for sequences of length n bits with k bits for the message (i.e., events) and $(n - k)$ check bits for correcting a single error is

$$\frac{2^n}{n + 1} \geq 2^k$$

For $k = 4$, $n = 7$, $n - k = 3$, we have

$$\frac{2^7}{8} = 16$$

$$2^4 = 16$$

Thus the Hamming code for a message of four bits, 16 messages, has a sequence of seven bits, four consisting of the message and three check bits to indicate no error 000, or a single error in any of the seven bits.

For double-error detection and correction a minimum Hamming distance between code words must be 5, and each group for one correct code word of length n, must include all n erroneous code words with a single error (i.e., distance of one from the correct word) and all $n(n - 1)/2$ words with two errors (i.e., words with a distance of 2 from the correct one). Thus for double-error detection and correction, each group includes one code word of the language and $n + n(n - 1)/2$ neighbors representing one and two errors. This is shown conceptually in Figure 3.28 for code words α and β that are a minimum distance of 5. The general relationship for sequences of n bits of which k bits are for the message (i.e., events) and $(n - k)$ are check bits to detect and correct two errors is given by the following relation:

Tools for Representation   Chap. 3

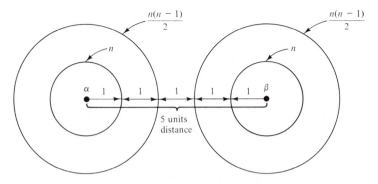

Figure 3.28

$$\frac{2^n}{1 + n + \dfrac{n(n-1)}{2}} \geq 2^k$$

In the preceding section we showed how to devise a Hamming code for detecting and correcting one error in sequences of seven bits. Four of the seven bits represent 16 messages and three of the seven bits are check bits to provide eight indicators, one for no errors and seven for a single error in any position of the seven-bit sequence. The 16 messages and corresponding check bits are given in Table 3.2. The minimum Hamming distance for these code words of length seven is 3. Table 3.2 identifies the 16 sequences that are error free out of $2^7 = 128$ sequences possible with seven binary digits. The remaining 112 $(128 - 16)$ sequences account for seven sequences with a single error in each of the 16 error-free sequences.

Table 3.2   Sixteen code sequences of a Hamming code
for messages of four bits

check bits							
1	2	3	4	5	6	7	bit position message bits
0	0	0	0	0	0	0	
1	1	0	1	0	0	1	
0	1	0	1	0	1	0	
1	0	0	0	0	1	1	
1	0	0	1	1	0	0	
0	1	0	0	1	0	1	
1	1	0	0	1	1	0	
0	0	0	1	1	1	1	
1	1	1	0	0	0	0	
0	0	1	1	0	0	1	
1	0	1	1	0	1	0	
0	1	1	0	0	1	1	
0	1	1	1	1	0	0	
1	0	1	0	1	0	1	
0	0	1	0	1	1	0	
1	1	1	1	1	1	1	

3.17 A Note on ISBN

Most textbooks carry an International Standard Book Number (ISBN) of a 10-digit code assigned by the publisher. The book *Patterns of Problem Solving* [2] has the following 10-digit ISBN:

$$\text{ISBN } 0\text{-}13\text{-}654251\text{-}4$$

The hyphens have no significance. The first digit represents some English-speaking nation, with 0 being the United States. The next two digits identify the publisher; 13 is for Prentice-Hall. The next six digits, 654251, are the book number assigned by the publisher. The last digit, 4 in our example, is a check digit derived from a weighted sum of digits modulo 11 that is generated as follows. List the first nine digits of ISBN in order in a column. Next calculate the running sums of these digits going down the column by adding each successive element to the sum obtained in the preceding step:

0	0
1	$+0 = 1$
3	$+1 = 4$
6	$+4 = 10$
5	$+10 = 15$
4	$+15 = 19$
2	$+19 = 21$
5	$+21 = 26$
1	$+26 = 27$
t	$+27 = 27 + t$

List the results in a second column to the right of the ISBN digits. Now generate the running sums of the second column and record the results in a third column as shown below. On the basis of this procedure, if the tenth digit of the ISBN is t, the entry to its right would be $27 + t$ and the entry to the right of $27 + t$ would be $123 + 27 + t = 150 + t$. As a check, t is assigned a value to make $150 + t$ divisible by 11. To make $150 + t$ divisible by 11 in our example, t is assigned the value of 4.

ISBN	first progressive sums (running sums)	second progressive sums (running sums)
0		
1	1	1
3	4	5
6	10	15
5	15	30
4	19	49
2	21	70
5	26	96
1	27	123
t	$27 + t$	$123 + 27 + t$

The tenth digit is assigned so as to make the weighted sum of all 10 digits modulo 11. When t is equal to 10, X is recorded as the last digit of ISBN. Thus the last digit of ISBN is a check digit of the code word representing the country, the publisher, and the publisher's book number.

The check sum we generated is a weighted sum of the original digits of the ISBN code. It includes 10 times the first digit of ISBN, plus 9 times the second digit, plus 8 times the third, and so on, plus finally, 1 time of the tenth digit, 4 in our case. Namely,

```
              ISBN code digits
                   ↓
        10    (0) =    0  .
         9    (1) =    9
         8    (3) =   24
         7    (6) =   42
         6    (5) =   30
         5    (4) =   20
         4    (2) =    8
         3    (5) =   15
         2    (1) =    2
         1    (4) =    4
                     154  ← weighted sum
```

3.18 Summary

Tables, matrices, Venn diagrams, tree diagrams, equations, and Karnaugh maps can be used as tools for representation. Each tool has its power and limitation in application.

Tree diagrams can be employed to structure a problem so that we can scan the field of possibilities before we embark on a course of action. Examples are given of how tree diagrams can be used in identifying a potential pool of customers for a product, how to allocate resources in a political campaign, how to classify management styles, and how to classify workers in industry or students in a school.

Venn diagrams can be used to visualize in concrete terms the distinction between conditions that are necessary and conditions that are sufficient. They are also useful in testing the validity of arguments.

It is shown how tables and Venn diagrams can be used in a novel way in a communication system in which errors can be detected and corrected. The Hamming code is developed as an example of such an application.

Venn diagrams can be used to identify logical combinations of attributes from two sets (Fig. 3.7), three sets (Fig. 3.8), and four sets (Fig. 3.9). Beyond four sets, tree diagrams or tables or algebraic statements must be employed.

Early in civilization human beings communicated at a rate of one word per second over a distance of less than a mile. At present, using modern communication systems, the rate is 10,000 words per second over distances that link the earth with outer space.

A modern communication system consists of these elements: information source, encoder and transmitter, communication channel, receiver and decoder, and destination for message from information source. These elements can be identified in oral communications. The speaker acts as information source (the person's brain), as encoder of experience into language, and as transmitter. The air is the communications channel.

Noise is a form of unwanted distortions that enter the message as it makes its way from source to destination. Redundancy can help overcome distortion introduced by noise. Redundancy exists in written natural language and can also be introduced in binary codes of modern communication alphabets. The Hamming code is an example of redundancy at work to detect and correct errors in a message. Redundancy reduces the rate of message transmission. The more errors we wish to detect and correct, the lower the rate of message transmission. The logic behind the procedure employed in detecting and correcting errors is explained in terms of the required Hamming distance between message sequences.

The International Standard Book Number (ISBN) is a 10-digit number assigned to each book by the publisher. The meaning of this code of numbers and the procedure for generating the redundant check bit in the last position of the sequence are discussed.

PROBLEMS

Test the validity of the arguments in Problems 3.1 to 3.7.

3.1. If this is a good book, it is worth buying. Either the book is on the best-seller list or it is not worth buying. But the book is not on the best-seller list; therefore, it is not worth buying.

3.2. If people did not violate the law, punishment would not be necessary. But punishment is used; hence people violate the law.

3.3. If we build the house near the river, it will be damp inside. So we will not build the house near the river; and therefore it will not be damp inside.

3.4. Next week I can either write a computer program for my job or take a vacation. If I write the program, I will meet the job deadline, but if I vacation, I will not meet the deadline. I will write the program if and only if my best friend will not join me on the vacation. My friend cannot join me on the vacation. Therefore, I will meet the deadline.

3.5. I will take the position if and only if it is in a field that is right for me. If I have time, I can choose a field that is right for me. Either I have time or I do not choose the right field. Therefore, if I take the position, I will have time.

3.6. If he is Joe's friend, he must be a "character." He is not a friend of both Joe and Jim. He is a friend of Jim. Therefore, he is a "character."

3.7. *Mystery story.* The facts: The secretary said that she saw the investigator in the front office. The front office was adjacent to the boardroom. The shot was fired in the boardroom and could be heard in all adjacent rooms. The investigator, whose hearing is good, said that he did not hear the shot.

Conclusion: If the secretary told the truth, the investigator lied.

$p =$ secretary told the truth
$q =$ investigator was in the front office
$r =$ investigator was in a room adjacent to the boardroom
$s =$ investigator heard the shot
$u =$ investigator told the truth

3.8. Is the following argument valid: If $P \rightarrow C$ is invalid, $P \rightarrow \sim C$ is valid. Use a Venn diagram to support your argument.

3.9. Suppose that $P \rightarrow C$ is invalid. Under what conditions will $P \rightarrow \sim C$ be valid or invalid? Use a Venn diagram to support your explanation.

3.10. In Section 3.13, Example 3, change the conclusion from $\sim f$ to f and test the validity of the argument. Draw a Venn diagram to explain the results shown in the example and the result you obtain in this problem.

3.11. Generate a Venn diagram for a Hamming code for a 15-bit sequence of which 11 are message bits and 4 are check bits. Identify each region a_i $(i = 0, 1, 2, \ldots, 15)$ in which $a_1 a_2 a_4 a_8$ are the regions for check bits. Why are these four the check bits?

3.12. Generate a table for a Hamming code for 26 message bits plus five check bits for single-error detection and correction. Explain how the table can be used by coding a message of your choice, then introducing a single error in an arbitrary position, reconstructing the table as a receiver to detect and correct the error. Why is a table more appropriate than a Venn diagram in this case?

3.13. Check the following ISBN codes:

$$0\text{-}470\text{-}26918\text{-}9$$

$$0\text{-}1321\text{-}2571\text{-}4$$

3.14. Generate the last digit for the following incomplete ISBN codes:

$$0\text{-}1315\text{-}2447\text{-}$$

$$0\text{-}1316\text{-}5332\text{-}$$

$$0\text{-}1391\text{-}4101\text{-}$$

3.15. How could you use a tree diagram in a way similar to the examples of Section 3.11 to allocate resources for marketing a new product?

3.16. Detect and correct a single error (if any) in the following binary sequences:

$$0011101$$

$$1110001$$

$$0000100$$

$$1010101$$

$$1001100$$

3.17. Suppose that you must transmit 100 numbers arranged in 10 rows and 10 columns. How can you introduce 21 additional "check numbers" to permit detection and correction of a single error in any of the 121 numbers you will transmit?

3.18. Discuss the powers and limitations of Venn diagrams and tree diagrams as tools for representation.

3.19. How many messages can be transmitted using sequences of seven bits if we must detect and correct as many as three errors in transmitted bits?

3.20. What are the shapes of the message sequences in Problem 3.19, and what is the minimum Hamming distance between the sequences?

3.21. What is the maximum number of messages that can be transmitted using sequences of seven bits if we must detect and correct one and two errors in transmitted bits?

3.22. How many message sequences can you actually identify in Problem 3.21? What are their shapes?

3.23. A drugstore received 10 bottles with 1000 pills in each bottle. Some of the bottles were filled by mistake with the wrong pills. Each of the wrong pills weighs 11 grams, while each of the intended correct pills weighs 10 grams. How can you identify the bottles with the wrong pills in a single weighing on a scale? (*Hint:* Every subset of the sequence 2^0, 2^1, 2^n has a unique sum.)

3.24. Explain why the final check sum in the ISBN code includes the first digit 10 times, the second digit 9 times, the third 8 times, and so on, to the check digit (the tenth), which is included once.

3.25. Show how four attributes can be represented by a Karnaugh map. Label all 16 regions in the diagram.

3.26. Which representations are limited by the number of attributes that can be treated, and which are not?

3.27. Use a tree diagram to represent three levels of motivation, high, medium, low, combined with two levels of effort, strong and weak.

3.28. When can equations be more useful than tree diagrams?

3.29. In what ways is the ISBN code similar and different from the Hamming code?

3.30. Use your own words to explain the meanings of "necessary conditions" and "sufficient conditions."

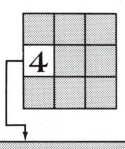

4

More Tools for Representation and Their Application: Digraphs and Matrices

4.1 Digraph-Directed Graph

There are situations when a problem is presented in a form that makes it difficult to see the relationships among elements. We demonstrated this earlier when we discussed five towns *A, B, C, D,* and *E* that were directly connected by links of equal length of travel time as follows. You can go from town *A* to town *B*, from *A* to *D*, from *B* to *C*, from *B* to *E*, from *C* to *D*, from *C* to *E*, from *D* to *A*, from *D* to *E*, and from *E* to *D*.

When we asked for a path of shortest time from town *A* to town *E* going through towns *B* to *C*, it became evident that a change of representation from English to a *digraph* (directed graph) with nodes representing towns, and edges with arrows showing direct connections between towns, gave a much better way to "see" the given information. This was shown in Figure 2.9, repeated here as Figure 4.1 for ease of reference.

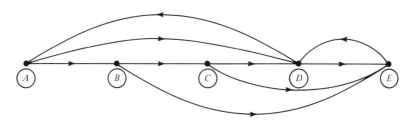

Figure 4.1 Digraph of direct connections between five towns.

An alternative representation of the direct connections between the towns is a matrix, known as an *adjacency matrix*. Towns *A, B, C, D*, and *E* of Figure 4.1 are represented by rows and columns of the matrix in Figure 4.2. The digit 1 in any position, such as row *C*, column *D*, indicates a direct connection from town *C* to town *D*. A 0 signifies no adjacency or direct connection.

$$
\begin{array}{c}
\text{To Town}\\
\begin{array}{c c c c c}
A & B & C & D & E
\end{array}
\end{array}
$$

$$
\begin{array}{c}
\text{From}\\
\text{Town}
\end{array}
\begin{array}{c}
A\\B\\C\\D\\E
\end{array}
\begin{bmatrix}
0 & 1 & 0 & 1 & 0\\
0 & 0 & 1 & 0 & 1\\
0 & 0 & 0 & 1 & 1\\
1 & 0 & 0 & 0 & 1\\
0 & 0 & 0 & 1 & 0
\end{bmatrix}
$$

Figure 4.2 Adjacency matrix for digraph of Figure 4.1.

THE SEVEN FARMS [64]

As a second example, let us consider the digraph of seven farms in Australia that is shown in Figure 2.10 and repeated here as Figure 4.3 for ease of reference. The digraph shows that farm 1 can call (directly) farm 2 and farm 4; farm 2 can call farm 3 and 5; farm 3 can call 1; farm 4 can call 5 and 7; farm 5 can call 4 and 7; farm 6 can call 2, 3, and 5; farm 7 cannot initiate any calls. The digraph provides an efficient visual representation to answer such questions as:

How can farm 3 contact farm 6? or farm 5?

How can farm 7 contact farm 3? or farm 6? or farm 2?

The direct communication ties of Figure 4.3 can be represented by the adjacency matrix of Figure 4.4. The matrix is a most efficient representation for computer manipulation of basic data given.

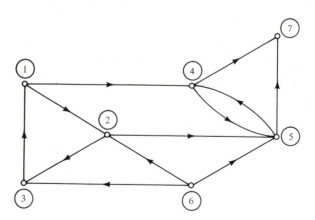

Figure 4.3 Digraph of direct communication ties between seven farms.

$$\begin{array}{c} \text{To Farm} \\ \begin{array}{ccccccc} 1 & 2 & 3 & 4 & 5 & 6 & 7 \end{array} \end{array}$$

	1	2	3	4	5	6	7
1	0	1	0	1	0	0	0
2	0	0	1	0	1	0	0
From 3	1	0	0	0	0	0	0
Farm 4	0	0	0	0	1	0	1
5	0	0	0	1	0	0	1
6	0	1	1	0	1	0	0
7	0	0	0	0	0	0	0

Figure 4.4 Adjacency matrix for digraph of Figure 4.3.

REACHABILITY MATRIX

The digraphs of Figures 4.1 and 4.3 can be transformed to *reachability matrices* by indicating whether or not a node can be reached from another node regardless of the number of intermediate nodes that must be visited in the process. For example, in Figure 4.1 we can reach town E from town A by going through B, or D, or B and C, or B and C and D. Similarly, in Figure 4.3, farm 3 can contact farm 7 by going through 1 and 4, or 1 and 4 and 5, or 1 and 2 and 5, and so on. The *reachability matrices* for Figures 4.1 and 4.3 are shown in Figures 4.5 and 4.6, respectively. A 1 in any row designated as i and any column designated as j indicates that j is reachable from i; a 0 in row i, column j indicates that j is not reachable from i. By definition each node is reachable from itself. Therefore, the elements in the matrix on the principal diagonal from the upper left corner to the lower right corner are all set to 1.

To Town

	A	B	C	D	E
A	1	1	1	1	1
B	1	1	1	1	1
From C	1	1	1	1	1
Town D	1	1	1	1	1
E	1	1	1	1	1

Figure 4.5 Reachability matrix for Figure 4.1.

To Farm

	1	2	3	4	5	6	7
1	1	1	1	1	1	0	1
2	1	1	1	1	1	0	1
From 3	1	1	1	1	1	0	1
Farm 4	0	0	0	1	1	0	1
5	0	0	0	1	1	0	1
6	1	1	1	1	1	1	1
7	0	0	0	0	0	0	1

Figure 4.6 Reachability matrix for Figure 4.3.

4.2 Weighted Digraphs

The digraphs of Figures 4.1 and 4.3 can be extended to include numbers on each arc representing a weight. Such digraphs are called *weighted digraphs*. For example, the digraph of Figure 4.7 is a weighted digraph used to study energy demand. The numbers on the directed arcs in the digraph represent the influence of a unit change in value at one node, representing a variable, on the values at the nodes adjacent to it. For example, in the weighted digraph of Figure 4.7, the weight of 2.6 on the arc between node 1 and node 3 signifies an increase in 2.6 units of number of users for each unit increase in available energy. The availability of energy can be specified in appropriate units of energy, such as

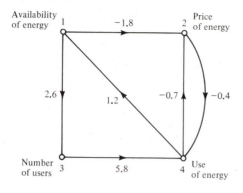

Availability
of energy 1

Price
of energy 2

−1.8

2.6

1.2

−0.7

−0.4

Number
of users 3

5.8

Use
of energy 4

Figure 4.7 Weighted digraph for energy demand.

1000 kilowatts. The number of users may be given in units of 100, 1000 people, or for a strictly industrial region it may be given in terms of number of industries or factories. The weight of −1.8 on the arc from node 1 to node 2 signifies a decrease of 1.8 units in the price of energy for each unit increase in available energy.

Of course, other nodes can be added to study the influence of energy use on environmental quality, on population size, housing, available jobs, taxes, and so on. For our purpose here to introduce concepts related to weighted digraphs, the simplified model of Figure 4.7 will suffice.

ADJACENCY MATRIX OF WEIGHTED DIGRAPH

The weight assigned to the arcs in Figure 4.7 can be represented by a matrix. Let us do this in three steps. First, let us ignore the weights assigned to the arcs and write the *adjacency matrix* for the *underlying digraph* that remains by recording 1 in row i, column j when there is an arc directed from node i to node j, and recording 0 otherwise. For Figure 4.7 we obtain the matrix of Figure 4.8. Now let us replace 1 by −1 in the matrix wherever an arc from a node i to a node j has a negative weight. The resulting digraph is known as a *signed digraph* and the corresponding matrix is the *adjacency matrix of the signed digraph*. For Figure 4.7 we obtain the matrix of Figure 4.9. If now we record the actual signed weights between adjacent vertices, the *adjacency matrix of the weighted digraph* in Figure 4.7 becomes the matrix of Figure 4.10.

1 signified a
directed arc from vertex
4 to vertex 2

$$
\begin{array}{c c}
 & \begin{array}{cccc} 1 & 2 & 3 & 4 \end{array} \\
\begin{array}{c} 1 \\ 2 \\ 3 \\ 4 \end{array} &
\begin{bmatrix}
0 & 1 & 1 & 0 \\
0 & 0 & 0 & 1 \\
0 & 0 & 0 & 1 \\
1 & 1 & 0 & 0
\end{bmatrix}
\end{array}
$$

Figure 4.8 Adjacency matrix for the underlying digraph of the weighted digraph in Figure 4.7.

$$
\begin{array}{c c}
 & \begin{array}{cccc} 1 & 2 & 3 & 4 \end{array} \\
\begin{array}{c} 1 \\ 2 \\ 3 \\ 4 \end{array} &
\begin{bmatrix}
0 & -1 & 1 & 0 \\
0 & 0 & 0 & -1 \\
0 & 0 & 0 & 1 \\
1 & -1 & 0 & 0
\end{bmatrix}
\end{array}
$$

Figure 4.9 Adjacency matrix for the signed digraph in Figure 4.7.

$$\begin{array}{cc} & \begin{array}{cccc} 1 & 2 & 3 & 4 \end{array} \\ \begin{array}{c} 1 \\ 2 \\ 3 \\ 4 \end{array} & \left[\begin{array}{cccc} 0 & -1.8 & 2.6 & 0 \\ 0 & 0 & 0 & -0.4 \\ 0 & 0 & 0 & 5.8 \\ 1.2 & -0.7 & 0 & 0 \end{array}\right] \end{array}$$

Figure 4.10 Adjacency matrix of weighted digraph in Figure 4.7.

A DIGRAPH FOR FOOD–ENERGY SYSTEM STUDY

As a second example, consider Figure 4.11. This digraph was constructed by Roberts to study food–energy systems [31]. The adjacency matrices of the underlying digraph, the signed digraph, and the weighted digraph of Figure 4.11 are shown in Figures 4.12, 4.13, and 4.14, respectively. Using the model of Figure 4.11, we can attempt to identify relationships between increased use of energy in food production and food yield. The model was generated in the context of the observation that between the years 1945 and 1970, yield of a field such as corn increased by a factor of 2.5, while the energy that was required to achieve this increase in yield has increased by a larger factor of about 3.

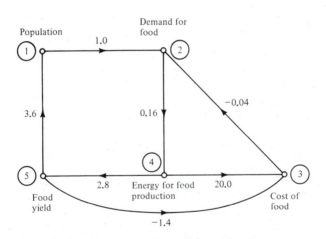

Figure 4.11 Weighted digraph for food–energy system study.

$$\begin{array}{cc} & \begin{array}{ccccc} 1 & 2 & 3 & 4 & 5 \end{array} \\ \begin{array}{c} 1 \\ 2 \\ 3 \\ 4 \\ 5 \end{array} & \left[\begin{array}{ccccc} 0 & 1 & 0 & 0 & 0 \\ 0 & 0 & 0 & 1 & 0 \\ 0 & 1 & 0 & 0 & 0 \\ 0 & 0 & 1 & 0 & 1 \\ 1 & 0 & 1 & 0 & 0 \end{array}\right] \end{array}$$

Figure 4.12 Adjacency matrix of underlying digraph in Figure 4.11.

$$\begin{array}{cc} & \begin{array}{ccccc} 1 & 2 & 3 & 4 & 5 \end{array} \\ \begin{array}{c} 1 \\ 2 \\ 3 \\ 4 \\ 5 \end{array} & \left[\begin{array}{ccccc} 0 & 1 & 0 & 0 & 0 \\ 0 & 0 & 0 & 1 & 0 \\ 0 & -1 & 0 & 0 & 0 \\ 0 & 0 & 1 & 0 & 1 \\ 1 & 0 & -1 & 0 & 0 \end{array}\right] \end{array}$$

Figure 4.13 Adjacency matrix of signed digraph in Figure 4.11.

$$\begin{array}{cc} & \begin{array}{ccccc} 1 & 2 & 3 & 4 & 5 \end{array} \\ \begin{array}{c} 1 \\ 2 \\ 3 \\ 4 \\ 5 \end{array} & \left[\begin{array}{ccccc} 0 & 1.0 & 0 & 0 & 0 \\ 0 & 0 & 0 & 0.16 & 0 \\ 0 & -0.04 & 0 & 0 & 0 \\ 0 & 0 & 20.0 & 0 & 2.8 \\ 3.6 & 0 & -1.4 & 0 & 0 \end{array}\right] \end{array}$$

Figure 4.14 Adjacency matrix of weighted digraph in Figure 4.11.

To study the systems Figures 4.7 and 4.11, we begin with the underlying signed digraph and study the bounds on the values of the variables, represented by the nodes, for which the assumed signs on the arcs between adjacent nodes will be appropriate. It is possible that a sign may be reversed as a function of the level of a particular variable. For example, in Figure 4.7 the use of energy above a particular level may cause the price of energy to go up. Similarly, when we reach the limit of available energy, the continued use of energy will reduce its availability.

Next, we can study the weighted digraph to develop confidence in the validity of the linear relationships. Since the weights remain constant and are independent of the time or the values of the variables that they link by the linear relationship, we must be careful to establish bounds on the domain within which the linearity assumption constitutes an adequate representation of the problem.

To perform a *sensitivity analysis* on system behavior, we introduce a change of a unit value at one node and observe the influence on other nodes. Using tools of mathematics, we can investigate the behavior of the system, its stability, and its response to various inputs by studying the properties of the adjacency matrix of the weighted digraph. The knowledge gained may point out errors of omission and commission, namely, variables excluded or included erroneously. Some influences that were thought to be direct may be identified as indirect influences, and vice versa. Namely, some direct arcs between nodes may be eliminated and new arcs introduced. The digraph representation provides an aid to the thinking process even without extensive calculation, in particular, in the early stages of a study.

4.3 Digraphs, Matrices, and Probabilities

There is a class of probabilistic models also called *stochastic models* that can be described by weighted digraphs. The properties of these models can be investigated by studying the weighted digraph or its adjacency matrix.

Let us begin with an example. The weighted digraph of Figure 4.15 shows five towns represented by the five vertices. The weight P_{ij} on an arc directed from town i to town j is the probability that a resident of town i will move to town j in any given year. This probability P_{ij} can also be viewed as the fraction of residents that will move from town i to town j in any given year. For any town the changes of state of residency in any given year add up to unity, because either people move to another town or they stay in the same town, in which case they "return" to the previous state of occupancy. Thus for any town i, the sum of weights from i to adjacent towns j (i can be adjacent to itself when vertex i has a loop) is unity, or

$$\sum_j P_{ij} = 1$$

For example, for town 1,

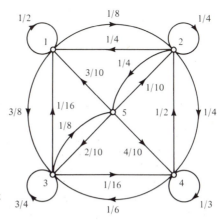

Figure 4.15 Flow of people in and out of five towns.

$$\sum_j P_{1j} = P_{11} + P_{12} + P_{13} = \frac{1}{2} + \frac{1}{8} + \frac{3}{8} = 1$$

For town 5,

$$\sum_j P_{5j} = P_{51} + P_{52} + P_{53} + P_{54} = \frac{3}{10} + \frac{1}{10} + \frac{2}{10} + \frac{4}{10} = 1$$

In town 1, on the average, $1/2$ or 50% of the residents remain in town each year, and 50% leave town for adjacent towns. In town 5, on the average, $3/10$ or 30% of the residents go to town 1, 10% go to town 2, 20% go to town 3, and 40% of the residents go to town 4. Thus, on the average, all the residents (100%) of town 5 leave town. In terms of the digraph, we can say that the sum of weights on the *outgoing arcs* at each node must add up to unity. On the other hand, the sum of weights of *ingoing arcs* at each node *does not* necessarily have to add up to unity. In town 5, on the average, all residents arrive from towns 2 and 3; $1/4$ or 25% of the residents of town 2 and $1/8$ or 12.5% of the residents of town 3 move to town 5.

TRANSITION PROBABILITIES

The weighted digraph of Figure 4.15 can be represented by an adjacency matrix called a *transition matrix* **P**. Each element P_{ij} of **P** is called a *transition probability*. A transition probability depends *only on the immediately preceding state of occupancy*. This is shown in the tree of Figure 4.16 for a transition process beginning at town 5. Regardless of how you get to town 5, once there you will be in the next step (year in our case) in towns 1, 2, 3, or 4 with probabilities $3/10$, $1/10$, $2/10$, and $4/10$, respectively. From town 2 you can go to town 1 or 4, or remain in town 2, or return to town 5 with probabilities $1/4$ each.

The probabilities P_{ij} can be considered as conditional probabilities of the following form. If we label each node (or town in our case) as a *state of occupancy*, then

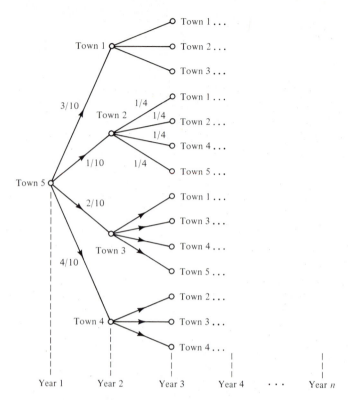

Figure 4.16 Tree of transition probabilities beginning at town 5.

$$P_{ij} = P(j \mid i)$$

in which $P(j \mid i)$ stands for the probability of a transition in one step (one arc, one year, in our case) to state j given that you start in state i.

MARKOV PROCESS OR MARKOV CHAIN

A stochastic process with transition probabilities that depend only on the immediately preceding state, namely a process in which the memory span is only one step, is a chain of steps and corresponding states of occupancy known as a *Markov process* or a *Markov chain*. For a Markov chain with n states the matrix **P** of transition probabilities P_{ij} is a stochastic matrix with the property that the sum of all elements of each row is equal to 1. Each row of matrix **P** is called a *probability* vector because of this property. Matrix **P** has n rows and n columns corresponding to the n states as shown in Figure 4.17. Matrix **P** with all its rows as probability vectors is called a *stochastic matrix,* and it is the adjacency matrix of the corresponding digraph. For Figure 4.15 we have the adjacency matrix of the weighted digraph shown in Figure 4.18.

By studying the weighted digraph of Figure 4.15 or its adjacency matrix, we can calculate future states of occupancy. For example, suppose that 1,000,000 people live in the five towns of Figure 4.15 and that the initial

$$P = \begin{array}{c} \\ \text{State 1} \\ 2 \\ \\ \\ \\ n \end{array} \begin{array}{c} \begin{array}{cccc} 1 & 2 & & n \end{array} \\ \left[\begin{array}{cccc} P_{11} & P_{12} & \cdots & P_{1n} \\ P_{21} & P_{22} & \cdots & P_{2n} \\ \cdot & \cdot & & \cdot \\ \cdot & \cdot & & \cdot \\ \cdot & \cdot & & \cdot \\ P_{n1} & P_{n2} & \cdots & P_{nn} \end{array} \right] \end{array} \qquad \sum_{j=1}^{n} P_{ij} = 1 \quad \text{for all } i = 1, 2, \ldots, n$$

Figure 4.17 Stochastic matrix **P**.

$$P = \begin{array}{c} \\ 1 \\ 2 \\ 3 \\ 4 \\ 5 \end{array} \begin{array}{c} \begin{array}{ccccc} 1 & 2 & 3 & 4 & 5 \end{array} \\ \left[\begin{array}{ccccc} 1/2 & 1/8 & 3/8 & 0 & 0 \\ 1/4 & 1/4 & 0 & 1/4 & 1/4 \\ 1/16 & 0 & 3/4 & 1/16 & 1/8 \\ 0 & 1/2 & 1/6 & 1/3 & 0 \\ 3/10 & 1/10 & 2/10 & 4/10 & 0 \end{array} \right] \end{array} \begin{array}{c} \sum_{j=1}^{5} P_{ij} \\ \hline 1 \\ 1 \\ 1 \\ 1 \\ 1 \end{array}$$

Figure 4.18 Stochastic matrix for digraph of Figure 4.15.

distribution of the population is given by the probability vector

$$\left\{ \begin{array}{c} 1/8 \\ 1/8 \\ 1/8 \\ 1/8 \\ 1/2 \end{array} \right\}$$

The distribution of the population on the average, after one year, two years, and so on, can be calculated.

We can also deal with other questions related to this model. For example, consider the nine towns of Figure 4.19. Here, all residents move each year. The

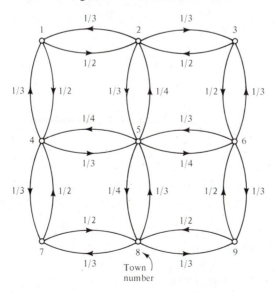

Figure 4.19 Nine towns and associated transition probabilities P_{ij} each year.

probability P_{ij} that a resident will move from town i to town j in any given year is indicated on the directed arc from node i to node j. Suppose that 24 million people live in the nine towns. Here are some possible questions of interest that can be answered by studying Figure 4.19 and its associated stochastic or transition matrix.

1. What should be the initial population distribution in order for this distribution to remain the same, on the average, in the future?

2. Suppose that we begin with some specific population distribution; what will be the expected distribution in 2 years, 6 years, and 30 years or in general in the near-, intermediate-, and long-term future?

3. What population distribution will cause an oscillation between two states of occupancy from year to year, with one state of occupancy for odd-numbered years and an alternate state of occupancy for even-numbered years?

4.4 The Fibonacci Sequence: A Pattern of Numbers as a Representation of Diverse Phenomena [32]

Unusual sequences of numbers, special equations, and patterns in general can capture the imagination of people and lead to investigations involving extensive efforts over long periods of time. One such sequence of numbers is the Fibonacci sequence. In 1963, more than 700 years after the discovery of this sequence, a group known as the Fibonacci Association was formed and began publishing a quarterly journal devoted to research on Fibonacci numbers. Hundreds of articles have been published on the subject, and the *1977 Yearbook of Science and the Future* of the Encyclopaedia Britannica featured an article on the Fibonacci sequence by Verner E. Hoggatt, Jr., editor of the *Fibonacci Quarterly* [33].

It all started in 1202, when a distinguished Italian mathematician, Leonardo of Pisa, also known as Fibonacci, published the following puzzle in a book on mathematics.

Assume that every month a pair of rabbits produces another pair, and all new pairs begin to bear young ones two months after their own birth. If you start with one pair of one month old rabbits, how many pairs of rabbits will be born in one year?

The solution to this puzzle is 377, and it is generated as shown in the tree of Figure 4.20, with P designating a pair of parents and B designating a pair of newborns.

The two basic building blocks of the tree in Figure 4.20 are the following: a single-link building block from a node B to a node P, namely, a pair of babies just born are relabeled potential parents, P, after one month; and a two-link building block from a node of parents P to two nodes: a node P and a node

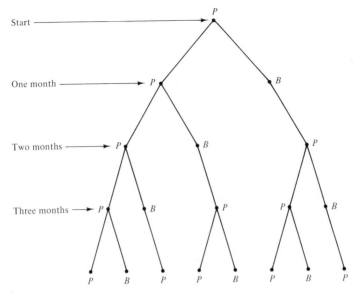

Figure 4.20 Leonardo of Pisa rabbit puzzle.

B. Namely, after one month potential parents remain parents P and give birth to pair B.

Using the tree of Figure 4.20, we have 2 pairs after one month; 3 after two months; 5 after three months; 8 after four months; and finally, 377 after 12 months. This is shown in Figure 4.21. The sequence of integers marked by the arrows in Figure 4.21 has the following form: 1, 1, 2, 3, 5, 8, 13, 21, . . . , 144, 233, 377. This sequence became known as the *Fibonacci sequence*. It has the following property. Begin the sequence with 1, and then generate each term as the sum of the preceding two terms. Thus the second term is 1 and the third term is $1 + 1 = 2$, and the three-term sequence is

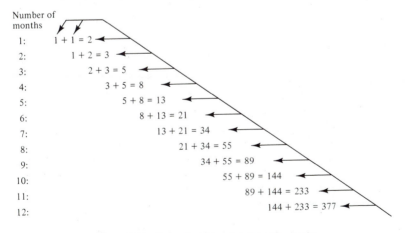

Figure 4.21 Pair of rabbits after 1 to 12 months.

$$1, 1, 2$$

The fourth term is $1 + 2 = 3$, and the four-term sequence is

$$1, 1, 2, 3$$

The fifth term is $2 + 3 = 5$, and the sequence is

$$1, 1, 2, 3, 5$$

Continuing this way by adding the last two elements to generate the following new element in the sequence, we obtain

$$1, 1, 2, 3, 5, 8, 13, 21, 34, 55, \ldots, 233, 377, 610, \ldots$$

In general the terms F_i of the Fibonacci sequence are generated from the following expressions:

$$F_1 = 1$$

$$F_2 = 1$$

$$F_i = F_{i-1} + F_{i-2} \qquad i = 3, 4, 5, \ldots, n$$

THE PASCAL TRIANGLE AND THE FIBONACCI SEQUENCE

There is an unexpected connection between the Pascal triangle and the Fibonacci numbers. Figure 4.22 shows the Pascal triangle. The diagonal lines in the figure are called *rising diagonals* of the triangle. The sum of the numbers on the rising diagonals form a Fibonacci sequence. This relation between the Pascal triangle and the Fibonacci sequence was discovered by Edouard Lucas in 1876.

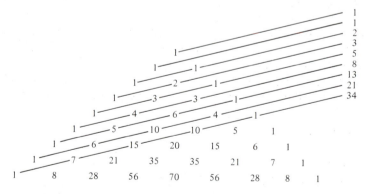

Figure 4.22 The Pascal triangle and the Fibonacci sequence.

THE FIBONACCI SEQUENCE AS REPRESENTATION OF FAMOUS PROPORTIONS AND PATTERNS

A number of geometric structures can be derived from a Fibonacci sequence: if we start with two 1×1 squares as shown in Figure 4.23, add a 2×2

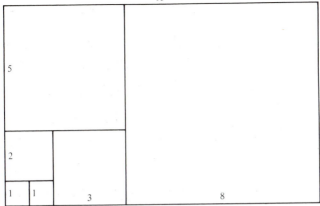

Figure 4.23 Fibonacci sequence and rectangular forms.

square, then a 3 × 3 square, then a 5 × 5 square, and finally an 8 × 8 square. The proportions generated by consecutive Fibonacci terms have been found to have aesthetic appeal. Psychologists have shown that these proportions are aesthetically pleasing to the human eye. This has been exploited commercially in label and package designs, hence the 5 × 8 card. It also found use in the design of such rectangular objects as greeting cards, pictures, mirrors, and display advertising in general.

In Figure 4.24 the involuted curve approximating a logarithmic spiral is generated. This curve appears in nature as snail shells and animal horns. It is generated by a succession of diminishing rectangles based on the Fibonacci numbers with circular arcs drawn through each square using the sides of the squares as radii.

The structure of sunflower heads, pinecones, pineapples, and the genealogy of male bees can all be described by Fibonacci sequences. And there are many more situations where the sequence surfaces as a pattern.

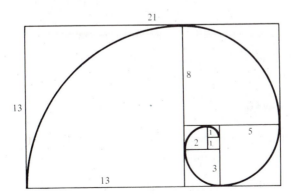

Figure 4.24 Spiral curve derived from diminishing Fibonacci sequence rectangles.

THE GOLDEN SECTION

The famous golden section is related to the Fibonacci sequence. In a golden section a line is divided into two unequal segments so that the ratio of the original length to the longer segment is the same as the ratio of the long segment to the short segment. Namely, for a line of length l, the long segment x, the short segment $l - x$, and l have the following relationship:

$$\frac{l}{x} = \frac{x}{l - x}$$

For $l = 1$, we have

$$\frac{1}{x} = \frac{x}{1 - x}$$

leading to the equation

$$x^2 + x - 1 = 0$$

with the solution

$$x = \frac{-1 \pm \sqrt{5}}{2}$$

For positive x,

$$x = \frac{-1 + \sqrt{5}}{2}$$

$$\frac{1}{x} = \frac{2}{-1 + \sqrt{5}}$$

$$\frac{1}{x} = \frac{1 + \sqrt{5}}{2} = 1.618 \ldots$$

Such a division was called by the ancients the *golden section*. $1/x$ in the golden section is the limit of the sequence

$$\frac{1}{1}, \frac{2}{1}, \frac{3}{2}, \frac{5}{3}, \frac{8}{5}, \frac{13}{8}, \frac{21}{13}, \frac{34}{21}, \frac{55}{34}, \cdots$$

Do you recognize the Fibonacci sequence in numerators and denominators? The sixth term of the sequence, $13/8$, differs from $1/x$ by 0.0070.

OTHER OBSERVATIONS

In the rectangles of Figure 4.23 we have

$$1^2 + 1^2 + 2^2 + 3^2 + 5^2 + 8^2 = 8 \times 13$$

and in general for the Fibonacci sequence,

$$F_1^2 + F_2^2 + F_3^2 + \cdots + F_n^2 = F_n \times F_{n+1}$$

Try it.

The pentagram of Figure 4.25 has properties of the golden section:

$$\frac{AB}{AD} = \frac{AD}{DB}$$

The golden rectangle, based on the golden section proportions, namely, the long-to-short side ratio equal to golden section ratio of 1.618 . . . , had influenced design throughout classical Greek culture in art and architecture. The Parthenon in Athens, the Great Pyramid in Giza, Egypt (ratios of height, slope, and base), and many structures of antiquity may have been based on golden section proportions.

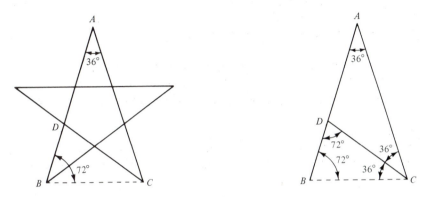

Figure 4.25   Pentagram displays the golden section property.

4.5 Statistical Representations: Tools for Thought, Not Substitutes for Thought

We employ statistical representations to study populations of similar things. A *population* is defined as a set of all possible observations of a particular attribute. The attribute may be a single measurement or observation, or a group of measurements or observations. We can speak of the population of heights of people in a certain age group in the United States, the population of all possible measurements of length of a pencil, population outcomes from the flip of six coins, and so on. A *sample* is a subset of a population.

Statistics begins with a set of measurements of the elements in the population, and one of the first activities is to order these measurements. For example, in a community with a population of 1000 families, annual incomes were recorded with a precision of the nearest $1000 and grouped as shown in Table 4.1.

Table 4.1 Annual income distribution
in a community of 1000 families

Income (dollars)	Number of Families with Income on Left
10,000	40
20,000	110
30,000	300
40,000	50
50,000	100
90,000	100
100,000	200
120,000	100

HISTOGRAM

The table gives the grouping of families that have the same income. Figure 4.26 is a *histogram* that shows a graphic representation of the data in Table 4.1. We can now aggregate the data of the population so that a single measurement becomes representative of the entire population. Let us consider three statistical measurements.

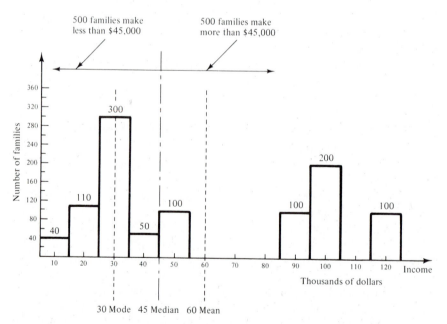

Figure 4.26 Histogram showing annual income distribution in a community of 1000 families.

MEAN

If we add the incomes of all 1000 families in the community and divide by 1000, the result is the *mean* annual income per family in the community. The mean is $59,600, or $60,000 when rounded to the nearest $1000. Note that this number is only a representation, or a model of the entire population, not necessarily an attribute possessed by any particular family within the population considered. In fact, from Table 4.1 or Figure 4.26 we observe that no single family has an annual income of $60,000.

MEDIAN

A measurement with a magnitude such that half the population has measurements of larger magnitudes and half has smaller ones is called the *median* of the population. In our example the median is $45,000.

MODE

The measurement that has the largest group in the population possessing its magnitude is called the *mode*. The mode is the measurement with the highest frequency of occurrence in the population. In our example the mode is $30,000.

When we are given a single measurement as representative of a population, we must be careful to identify how it was generated. The *mode, median,* and *mean* may create three different impressions regarding the wealth of the community. Each tells a different "story," $30,000 or $45,000 or $60,000, as representative of the population. Of course, having access to the complete data can provide the missing pieces. However, in complex problems with a lot of data, it may not be possible to have access to all the detail that makes up the population. In such cases we may study a sample of the population or resort to additional aggregated measurements such as the *range* of values for the individual measurements (i.e., the difference between the largest and smallest measurement) or the *variance* as an index of scatter or spread in the measurements of the population.

THE INCH, FOOT, AND YARD AS MEAN VALUES

It may be of interest to learn that some of the best known measurements in use are aggregate measurements representative of populations, namely, *mean* values. For example, an inch is the mean thickness of a human thumb. Some may say that it is the thickness of the average thumb, as Kenneth Boulding states in a 1979 article on the metric system [34]. But there may be no such thing as "the average thumb." The inch is an abstract representation of the thickness of all human thumbs. Similarly, the measurement of length "foot" is related to the mean length of the human foot. The yard is presumably the mean distance between the mouth and the stretched-out arm used to measure cloth.

Let us return to Figure 4.26. Suppose that we wish to calculate the probability that a family selected randomly from the population of 1000 families has an annual income of $20,000, namely, an income between $15,000 and $25,000. Since there are 110 families with this attribute out of 1000 families, the probability is 110/1000 or 0.11. Now suppose that we are given the following information: On a given holiday all the families with an annual income above $80,000 left town. If we select one of these families at random, what is the probability that it will be a family with an annual income of $120,000 (i.e., an income between $115,000 and $125,000)? We have 100 such families. But now there are 100 families out of 400 families only because the information we have caused the population or universe to be reduced to 400. The answer is 100 out of 400, or 1/4.

THE FRAME OF REFERENCE OR POPULATION IN STATISTICAL REPRESENTATION

I once met a 70-year-old man who was in a state of grave depression. He kept saying that he might as well be considered dead because the mean life span is less than 70 years. I drew for him Figure 4.27, representing approximately the life expectancy in a population. The mean life expectancy may indeed be, say, 65 years, but this is a *mean* value and is a mere representation of the entire population, not representative of a person who is 70 years old. I proceeded to convince the man that he is not the average or mean; after all, how could he be dead at 65 when he is alive at 70? The entire population of Figure 4.27 applies as a *frame of reference* to a child at birth. For a child at birth we have the probability of being alive past the age of 90 as the ratio between the area under the curve of Figure 4.27 to the right of 90 years divided by the total area under the curve. For a man who is 70 years old, the probability that he will live to be 90 or more is based on a different frame of reference or population than that for a child at birth. The man who is 70 belongs to a subset of the population that survived past 70. This is the area under the curve to the right of 70. The probability that a 70-year-old man will live to be 90 or more is the area under the curve to the right of 90 divided by the area under the curve to the right of 70. In both calculations, for a child at birth and for a 70-year-old man, the

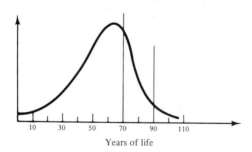

Years of life

Figure 4.27 Life expectancy.

numerator is the same. The denominator is much smaller in the calculations for the 70-year-old, say approximately four times smaller. Therefore, the probability of the 70-year-old man living to the age of 90 or more is four times larger than that for a child at birth, and larger than the probability for anyone under 70 living past the age of 90.

MEAN VALUES AND DISTORTION OF IMAGES

Suppose that you buy a new car and after four years you decide to leave it with an acquaintance while you take a two-year trip around the world. When you return your acquaintance proudly presents you with the car, telling you that it is almost in as good shape as he received it. You have a different impression. You believe the car sustained considerable abuse in two years. Who is right? The two beliefs are based on two different mean or average images. Both have the same final state images but the image of the past is different. You remember the car from the day you bought it to the day you left on your trip; therefore, the average image is not quite as perfect as the brand-new car but not quite as scratched as the day you left: namely, *an image better than the way you left it;* therefore, you believe more damage has been done to the car since you left than actually was the case. Your acquaintance has a past image of the car that is a mean between its appearance the day he received it and the present; thus *it is an image worse than the state of the car when he received it.* Therefore, he believes less damage has been done to it than actually was the case. You and your acquaintance operate from two different frames of reference.

LEVEL OF STATISTICAL SIGNIFICANCE

Suppose that a new model of a pen is introduced in the market and that 20 people who for years have used the old model of the pen are selected and asked to participate in an experiment. Ten people of the 20 are randomly selected and given the new model pen, and 10 are given the old-model pen. The old and new pens used in the experiment cannot be distinguished from each other by the 20 people, but the experimenter knows what kind of pen each person received. Let us suppose that the purpose of the experiment is to test the hypothesis that the new pen is no better than the old one. Now suppose that the 10 people who received the new pen claimed it was better than the old one; can we conclude that the new pen is indeed better than the old one? The answer is a "yes" that must be qualified. Each of the 10 people has some average image of quality of the old pen because in the past they had various qualities of this pen. Thus we could assume that if we select an old pen at random and ask a user to judge it on the average, he would claim half the time that it was better than average, and half the time that it was worse. The probability that 10 people would claim that it was better is $(1/2)^{10}$, or 1 in 1024. The number $1/1024$ represents the probability that the superiority of the new model would be observed in all 10 cases if the hypothesis of indifference between new and old model pens were true. This probability is the statistical *significance level* of the test.

CORRELATION

There are situations in which we are concerned with finding out how closely two different sets of measurements or observations are correlated, or connected with each other. In Figure 4.28 we show a straight line that represents the aggregation of data on fire damage in dollars and number of fire trucks at the site of the fire. The damage tends to increase as the number of fire trucks increases, and the two measurements are correlated. What is important to stress is not what correlation means but rather what it does not mean. Correlation does not mean cause–effect relationship between two attributes, although it may mean that sometimes. Correlation is not sufficient evidence for such a conclusion. The two correlated measurements may be caused by something else, while no causal relationship exists between them. For example, the damage at a fire is not caused by the fire trucks, but by the size of the fire. The size of the fire is also what determines the number of fire trucks dispatched to the site of the fire. Causal relationship must be based on *understanding* the connection between the variables and not based merely on a statistically generated correlation between the variables.

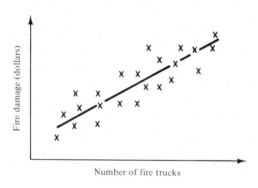

Figure 4.28 Correlation between fire damage and number of fire trucks.

4.6 Dynamic System Models and Cybernetics

SYSTEMS

A *system* is a collection of elements aggregated by virtue of the links of form, process, or function that tie them together and cause them to interact. All that is excluded from the system constitutes the *environment*. The criterion for the choice of system size in terms of what elements to include or exclude is based on the same considerations as those which guide the modeling process in general. A system model is constructed to help *understand* relationships between elements, forms, processes, and functions, and to enhance our ability to *predict* system response to inputs from the environment. This understanding may enable us to *control* system behavior by adjusting inputs to achieve a desired output whenever such control is possible.

System models have been constructed for the world population; for the economy of a country; for the learning process; for a corporation; for an airplane, an automobile, or transportation in general; for the heart; for the brain—and the list may be extended to great length. A system can be characterized in terms of an input–output model and idealized so that its *state* can be described at any time by a finite number of quantities. These quantities are called the *state variables* of the system. The temperature of an oven may represent a state variable of the oven as a system with a single state variable. The position and velocity of a moving body may represent the state variables of a vibrating mass suspended from a spring. In a model of a population plagued by an epidemic, the system state variables may be the number of people susceptible, the number infected, and the number immune.

A *dynamic system* is defined as a system whose state changes with time. The change in state is represented by the change in the state variables. The *state variables* are, therefore, in the nature of levels, such as the level of water in a container, which result from the accumulation of change as a function of time: for example, changes in the amounts of water poured in, and taken out, of a container.

A *static system,* in contrast to a dynamic system, is one whose state or level is constant and is unaffected by the passage of time. In reality it is difficult to conceive of a static system. However, we often model a dynamic system which changes very slowly with time as a static system over a limited time interval.

Dynamic systems characterize much of the natural and the human-made world. The ubiquity of dynamic systems is manifested in the human body (in which body temperature, blood pressure, and other indicators are state variables of importance) and in human patterns of behavior. The activity of problem solving is a dynamic system process in which we endeavor to go from an initial state to a desired goal state. The state, whether initial, intermediate, or final, is described by state variables that change as we progress to a solution.

FLOW OF ENERGY AND INFORMATION IN A DYNAMIC SYSTEM

A dynamic system in a most general form transforms an *input* or a *cause,* to an *output* or a *consequence.* For example, let us consider a toaster in which a dial indicator can be set at 11 different levels of toast darkness, from light to dark in varying degrees. Suppose that we set the dial at level six, which should result in medium-dark toast. If the toast is too dark, we set the dial lower the next time until we develop, with experience, a relationship between the dial setting (input) and the darkness of the toast (output). The input causes *energy* to flow in the form of heat from the electric wiring in the toaster to the bread. The observation of the consequence, namely, when we note the darkness of the toast, constitutes *information* that we use to change the input in the next step. So while *energy* flows from input to output, *information* flows from output to input. The input triggers a flow of energy *causing* an output, and the output triggers a flow

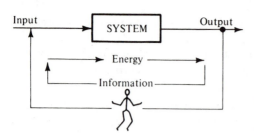

Figure 4.29 Flow of energy and information between systems input and output.

of information causing a new input. Schematically, these flows are shown in Figure 4.29. Thus, when we have a desired goal in a dynamic system, an understanding of the input–output relationship will enable us to select an input most compatible with the desired output.

CONTROL

There are two fundamentally different ways of controlling a system to achieve a desired goal output:

Case 1: Select an input and wait for an output with no interference during the waiting period.

Case 2: Select an input, observe the trend or direction of the output, and modify the input accordingly to get as close as possible to the desired goal output.

For example, when a helmsman steers a boat head-on in the direction of a lighthouse, he may proceed in one of two ways according to the foregoing schemes:

Case 1: Set the boat on the desired course and retire to his cabin.

Case 2: Set the boat on the desired course, observe the actual direction taken by the boat, and adjust the direction accordingly.

In both cases the steersman exercises control over the direction of the boat. However, in case 1 the input triggers a flow of energy causing an output, but there is no flow of information from output to a new input to close the "loop." Hence such control of consequences or output from a system is called an *open-loop control*. Case 2 is a *closed-loop control* also known as *feedback control,* because the output provides information that is fed back to the input.

For the toaster example considered earlier, we may say that each time we set the dial and wait for toast without further interference, we have open-loop control. However, considering repeated use of the toaster, trying to get a desired level of darkness by adjusting the dial on the basis of the results from each open-loop operation, we have feedback and hence closed-loop control for the total operation. Closed-loop control is exercised, however, only at discrete time intervals.

Feedback control is a key to survival; it endowed all living organisms with the system characteristics most productive for survival. The main feature in control with feedback is the flexibility that can be exercised by the controller to vary the input leading to a change in output. The species with a high degree of specialization were less likely to adapt to disturbances from the environment and therefore less likely to survive.

Control can be exercised at various levels. Human beings, for example, with the supreme goal of survival, choose lower-level goals which may enhance survival. In making such choices we exercise control over our destiny. The lower-level goals are achieved by lower-level feedback control systems. Thus control can be amplified in stages. Control can be voluntary, such as the control of temperature or blood pressure in the human body.*

The emergence of an era of automation was marked in essence by the ability to monitor a process continuously by feedback control without resorting to a human operator. Automation made great progress with the advent of the digital computer, which can process information so accurately and rapidly that the output has little time to deviate from a desired value before the information channel in the feedback loop affects a corrective change to cancel or diminish the deviation.

The feedback control mechanism is evident in government. For instance, a government may introduce economic policy regulations (control) to achieve desired levels of output such as employment, inflation, gross national product, and so on. When the actual output differs from that desired, policies and regulations are changed. The ecological system is balanced by feedback, anywhere from the balance of the number of rabbits and predators, to germs and population susceptible to them in an epidemic.

Dynamic systems with feedback in the natural and human-made world seem to be striving to achieve goals which in turn serve as inputs for the purpose of achieving higher goals yet. This hierarchy of goals and controls to achieve them can be extended to progressively higher levels until we reach a level where science, philosophy, and theology converge and meet at a junction to pose the most profound questions: To what extent are we masters of our destiny? Is there a *grand steersman* who exercises continuous closed-loop control by making observations and changing the input to achieve a *grand goal?* Or is the control open-loop, in which case a flow of energy was started at genesis to achieve a grand goal and no interference followed? Is there a supreme goal? And if so, was it fixed at genesis, or is it subject to change? And if it is subject to change, what frame of reference guides such a change?

The Bible offers models of the grand steersman, but we must stop at this point and permit each person to reflect on his or her view of the *grand model.* Such reflection can be most exciting and can help us put in perspective our

---

*There are claims that through biofeedback human beings can voluntarily control temperature, blood pressure, rate of heartbeat, and other body functions within certain bounds.

day-to-day activities. It can help us assign the proper weight to problems of deviations from lower-level goals which are subordinate to survival and to the grand goal.

CYBERNETICS

Norbert Wiener (1894–1964), one of the great mathematicians of the twentieth century, recognized the ubiquity of control and its dependence on the controlling "helmsman" and made outstanding contributions to the development of a theory of control. He named this field of study *cybernetics*, which comes from the Greek word for helmsman, *kybernet*. His book on the subject of cybernetics, published in 1948, is still a classic [35]. In view of the discussion above, it is not surprising that Wiener also published a book entitled *God & Golem, Inc.* [36], in which Golem refers to a legendary creation of a robot by Rabbi Judah Low of Prague in the sixteenth century. The legend claims that the rabbi blew the breath of life into a clay structure and made it the instrument for achieving desired goals, such as *protecting the lives of the persecuted* Jewish people in Prague. The Golem had to be destroyed when its control appeared to be getting out of hand.

GENERAL BLOCK DIAGRAM FOR DYNAMIC SYSTEM WITH FEEDBACK

Figure 4.30 is a general block diagram model of a dynamic system with feedback. This model applies to many situations in the natural and human-made world and is not limited to physical systems. Wherever a cause-and-effect relationship can be identified, conceptually, at least, a dynamic system model can be generated. For example, Figure 4.31 is a block diagram for a person's dynamic system model to achieve a desired goal. Suppose that the *goal* is to get the grade A in a course. The *plan* calls for certain levels of grades in quizzes, homework, the midterm, and the final; it may include meeting the instructor periodically and impressing her, class participation, and so on. The *decision* will select the best strategy from the available actions, and the *resource allocation* of time and effort will be made accordingly. The *achievements* are monitored (sensed) by the student and compared (comparator) with the desired goal, which may be translated to an effective overall score of 90 or better to secure an A. The *plan, decisions,* and *resource allocations* are adjusted to reduce the error e

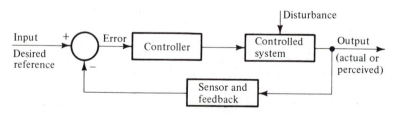

Figure 4.30 General block diagram for a dynamic system with feedback.

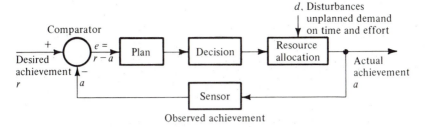

Figure 4.31 Dynamic system with feedback to achieve a goal.

between the desired achievement (reference goal) and the actual record of achievements.

ADAPTIVE CONTROL

Dynamic systems can deteriorate with time, causing change in the basic input–output characteristics. Systems are also subject to random disturbances from the environment. Since both the changes in the dynamic system and the disturbances cannot be completely predicted, it is not conceivable that a controller with fixed characteristics optimum for one set of conditions, say controlled system S and disturbance D, will also be optimal for an entire spectrum of S and D values as the systems change and disturbance D varies. Therefore, a second feedback loop, called an *adaptive controller,* can be introduced to adjust the parameters of the controller on the basis of changes in the controlled system S and the detected disturbances D so that it adapts to the new conditions. Adaptive control is being used to devise learning machines in which a punishment and reward scheme is employed. A reward is given in the form of a positive contribution to an index of performance whenever the performance is the desired performance (say, the correct weather prediction), and punishment in the form of a negative addition to the index of performance is used when the performance differs from that desired. The objective of the adaptive learning system is to establish a properly balanced scheme of reinforcement so that the performance will be statistically better than a comparable machine with no adaptive learning built in. Adaptive learning has been applied to weather prediction, to playing chess, and to a machine designed to balance an inherently unstable rod upright on a moving cart, to name some. The extension of adaptive learning to model the human learning process may prove the most novel and revolutionary advance in history. The capacity of the human nervous system is far from having been exhausted; some researchers doubt that we use as much as 10% of it. Thus we are far from having reached the constraining boundaries that may eventually limit our capacity for learning. Progress in the understanding of the human learning process could usher an era in which human beings, using the untapped capacity of their brains, will contrive novel ways to model themselves, society, the environment, and the human-made world in a form that will make decisions based on *what ought to be* our values easier to generate, and will make *what is* more compatible with the image of *what it was perceived to be.*

Adaptive control and feedback control in general can be applied at various levels. For example, the student who sets a reference goal of scoring the grade A may change his plans as he adapts to disturbances from random demands on his time and effort and to changes in his learning system such as new difficulties to concentrate, emotional stress, and other factors. However, at some point his ability to adjust his plans and decisions (i.e., changes in the controller) may prove unproductive, and goals of a higher level, of which survival is the supreme goal, will dictate a need to change the reference goal: namely, try for a B or a C. The change of the desired reference input which prescribes a desired goal is an important form of adaption which is a key to survival. What the goals ought to be in human affairs and how they ought to change depend dynamically on human values.

4.7 Summary

A graph is a collection of nodes and edges. A digraph is a directed graph consisting of a collection of nodes and edges with arrows. When a digraph represents routes between towns, the nodes represent the towns, and the edges (or arcs) represent the routes between adjacent towns. When a digraph represents a communication network, the edges represent the flow of communication between adjacent nodes. A digraph can be used as a tool of representation for the study of system behavior in many areas.

The nodes and arcs of a digraph can be replaced by an adjacency matrix.

A digraph can be transformed to a reachability matrix that indicates whether or not a node can be reached from another node regardless of the number of edges that must be used in the process.

A weighted digraph has a weight in the form of a number on each edge. The weight may represent the level of influence exerted by one node on an adjacent one.

Weighted digraphs can be used to perform sensitivity analysis and investigate the stability and response characteristics of a system.

A weighted digraph with weights that represent the probabilities of a transition from one state, represented by one node, to another state, represented by an adjacent node is known as a Markov process. The adjacency matrix of such a weighted digraph is called a stochastic matrix or transition matrix.

The Fibonacci sequence is introduced to demonstrate how the same pattern of numbers is a representation that unifies diverse phenomena from how rabbits multiply to aesthetic proportions.

Statistical measurements of mode, median, mean, and range are introduced as different aggregate representations of the same population. The frame of reference in statistical representation is discussed in relation to life expectancy.

It is shown that human beings are prone to distortion of images in aggregating impressions in a single measurement.

The meaning of statistical significance and the concept of correlation are described in qualitative terms.

A system is a collection of elements aggregated by virtue of the links of form, process, or function which tie them together and cause them to interact. A system model is constructed to help understand, predict, and control its behavior. A system is described by state variables or levels. In a dynamic system, the state variables depend on the input history.

There are two configurations of control: open and closed loop. In open-loop control, the controller selects an input, but there is no flow of information from output to new input. In closed-loop or feedback control, information flows from output, affecting the new input into the system.

Control can be exercised at various levels, and it can be voluntary or involuntary. The ubiquity of control in the natural and human-made world is manifested in its presence in the human body, in human problem-solving activities, in government, in automation, in the ecological system, and so on.

Cybernetics is the name for the field of control theory. It is derived from the Greek word for helmsman, *kybernet.*

Block diagrams describe dynamic systems by prescribing the functional relationship between input and output. A comparator can be used to measure the difference between a desired and actual output.

A general block diagram for a dynamic system with feedback is shown in Figure 4.30.

Adaptive control is a second feedback loop nested in the first one to introduce changes in the controller so that it can adapt to changes in the controlled system and to disturbances from the environment. Adaptive control is finding many areas of applications in pattern recognition, artificial intelligence, weather prediction, and learning machines in general.

An important form of adaptation is a change in the reference goal as the need arises. This is a higher level of adaptive control than changing the controller to achieve a prescribed goal.

PROBLEMS

4.1. What principal changes will take place in the model of Figure 4.7 if there is a limited amount of available energy?

4.2. Discuss the main difference in price between a resource that is viewed as infinite in abundance and one that is strictly limited in quantity.

4.3. Until recent years a customer could receive energy at a reduced unit price when the quantity used was increased. Now the unit price goes up for a quantity used above a predetermined level. How can you explain this change as a change in perception by the energy suppliers?

4.4. Create a model for a problem of your choice similar to the one shown in Figure 4.11.

4.5. Why do the entries in each row of a stochastic matrix add up to unity? Should the column entries also add up to unity? Explain.

4.6. In Figure 4.16, what is the probability of a person arriving at town 2 in the fourth year, having started at town 5?

4.7. In Problem 4.6, what is the probability of arriving in town 2 in the fourth year having started at town 5, given that the person was once in town 3 in one of the intervening years (between years 1 and 4)?

4.8. In Figure 4.19, what should the initial population be in each town for this population to remain constant, on the average, in the future? Use heuristic guides to generate a solution.

4.9. Suppose that we begin with 24,000 people in each town of Figure 4.19. What will the expected population in each town be after two years? After three years? After four years?

4.10. What population distribution in the towns will cause an oscillation between two states of occupancy from year to year? One state of occupancy will prevail in odd-numbered years and the other state in even-numbered years.

4.11. Identify two applications for Pascal's triangle of Figure 4.22.

4.12. What would motivate a person to join the Fibonacci Association?

4.13. What is the relationship between the Fibonacci sequence and the golden section?

4.14. In trying to form a group consensus, what is likely to be more acceptable as a group measurement: the mode, the mean, or the median? Discuss.

4.15. How does the relevant population change as a frame of reference in Figure 4.27? Explain.

4.16. Give an example on how you formed a distorted image in the process of averaging or aggregating impressions.

4.17. State in your own words the meaning of level of statistical significance. Give an example.

4.18. How does correlation differ from cause–effect relationship? How can correlation be misinterpreted?

4.19. Show how a toaster can be described as a dynamic system.

4.20. Identify the elements of a dynamic system for a person who is trying to control her weight.

4.21. Describe the activity of driving an automobile as a dynamic system.

4.22. Give one example each of open-loop and closed-loop control systems.

4.23. Describe a situation that you have experienced which can be modeled by Figure 4.31. Identify each element of the figure in terms of your experience.

4.24. Give an example in which adaptive control is used.

4.25. Describe the relationship between quality and price of a product as an application of feedback in a dynamic pricing model in terms of supply and demand.

4.26. Describe a control system in a living organism, such as blood pressure control, temperature control, or any other system of your choice.

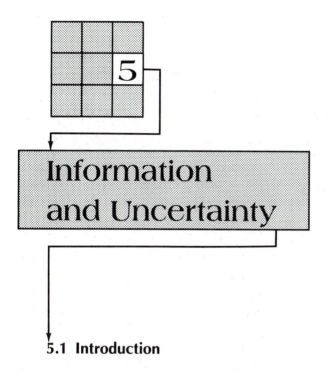

5.1 Introduction

In a world characterized by dynamic change it is productive to develop an attitude of sensitivity to new information. This attitude can provide the flexibility that will permit us to change our ideas in the face of new evidence. How much evidence is required in order for us to accept or reject an idea is a subjective matter. There is always some uncertainty left no matter how much information is available. I use the word *idea* here in the sense of an untested hypothesis. For example, the idea that a person on trial is innocent may be an untested hypothesis. As information unfolds in the court proceedings, the confidence in the idea may be enhanced, or sufficient doubt may set in to cause you to reject the idea. The idea is tested in the light of the information that is presented.

The information presented must be relevant to the case. In the court it is the judge who decides whether information is relevant. The jury decides on the credibility of the information. In fact, a member of a jury may judge the credibility of an expert witness testimony on the basis of the credibility of the expert as manifested by general appearance and style. This is particularly true when the defense and prosecution each have an expert witness providing conflicting evidence.

I mention the situation in a court because the jury is instructed to arrive at a decision "beyond reasonable doubt." This suggests that even in matters of life and death we admit that the best we can do is choose a verdict with some doubt or uncertainty.

If we are to be decision makers, we must accept the fact that we cannot wait for *all* uncertainty to be dispelled before we make decisions and take actions. In fact, if we insisted on dispelling all doubt before we decide or act, we would become paralyzed with indecision and inaction. All vitality would be driven out of our being.

To take account of information means not only to use it when it reduces uncertainty, but also when it does the reverse, namely, increases our uncertainty. Information is relevant whenever it makes a difference in our assessment of uncertainty, whether it increases or decreases it. In the discussion that follows we will develop a number of concepts that relate to information, such as how it can be measured in certain situations and how we can judge its relevance and level of credibility. In subsequent developments that deal with decision making we shall extend the concepts to include procedures for how we assess value of information. The discussion will provide a foundation for developing qualitative and quantitative concepts as tools for thought in dealing with uncertainty and information.

5.2 Universe

Let us develop some ground rules. Whenever a situation will be presented we will place it within the boundaries of what we shall call *universe*. The universe will include all events that can take place in the context of the situation that we present. For example, suppose that I lost a very valuable ancient Roman coin inside a warehouse. The warehouse is vacant and has a floor space 200 feet long and 100 feet wide, as shown in Figure 5.1. Let us suppose that the floor is constructed of square tiles each 1 foot by 1 foot in size. There are 20,000 such tiles on the entire floor. I am going to look for the coin. I choose to define as an *elementary event* in this situation the act of "finding the coin on a particular tile." The universe of this situation is therefore confined to finding the coin on any of the tiles on the floor of the warehouse. For ease of reference let us label

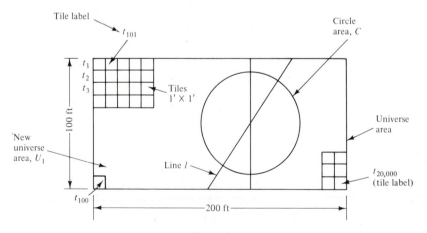

Figure 5.1

each tile by a symbol t_i, $i = 1, 2, 3, \ldots , 20{,}000$. If each tile is equally likely to have the coin and we have 20,000 such tiles, we say that the probability is 1 in 20,000 for the event of "finding the coin on a particular tile t_i ($i = 1, 2, \ldots , 20{,}000$)." Let us designate this event by the letter t_i and write

$$P(t_i \mid U) = \frac{\text{area of tile } t_i \text{ inside universe } U}{\text{area of universe } U} = \frac{1}{20{,}000} \qquad (5.1)$$

The symbols $P(t_i \mid U)$ should read as follows: "the probability of event t_i given the universe of events U." The vertical line in $P(t_i \mid U)$ separates the event of interest t_i identified on the left of the line from the universe of all possible events U identified by the symbol on the right of the line.

Suppose that we are interested in the probability of finding the coin inside the circle marked on the floor of the warehouse. The area of the circle is C. If C has an area of 8000 square tiles, we write

$$P(C \mid U) = \frac{\text{area } C}{\text{area } U} = \frac{8000}{20{,}000} = 0.4 \qquad (5.2)$$

C is a *compound event* that includes 8000 elementary events equivalent to the 8000 tiles it contains.

Now we introduce new information. I am informed that when I visited the warehouse while the coin was still in my possession, I was restricted to the area to the left of line l. If I conclude that the coin could be found only to the left of line l, I have to change the universe U to a new universe with an area U_1 equal to 14,000 square tiles. Now we have

$$P(t_i \mid U_1) = \frac{\text{area of } t_i \text{ inside } U_1}{\text{area of } U_1} = \frac{1}{14{,}000} \qquad (5.3)$$

Here t_i can have a value of 1 only for each of the 14,000 tiles in the new universe. Similarly, the probability that the coin will be found in circle C given the coin was lost in universe U_1 is given by equation (5.4).

$$P(C \mid U_1) = \frac{\text{area of } C \text{ inside new universe } U_1}{\text{area of new universe } U_1} \qquad (5.4)$$

PROBABILITY

In general, we can say the following: A probability is a ratio of two numbers. The denominator represents the universe of all possible events. The numerator represents those events in the universe on which we focus our interest. The numerator is a subset of the denominator. In the symbols $P(A \mid B)$, B is the universe and A is the subset of the universe B, B is the denominator and A is the numerator, so that

$$P(A \mid B) = \frac{\text{area of } A \text{ inside } B}{\text{area of } B} \qquad (5.5)$$

Since A in $P(A|B)$ is a subset of B, A is equivalent to A and B or AB,

$$P(A|B) = \frac{AB}{B} \qquad (5.6)$$

5.3 Probability and the Universe

From the preceding discussion we see that a probability is a positive number between 0 and 1. Since the numerator is a subset of the denominator, the smallest number we can place in the numerator is 0 and the largest is the entire denominator. Therefore, we can write for any event A,

$$0 \le P(A) \le 1 \qquad (5.7)$$

$P(A)$ should be written as $P(A|U)$ in equation (5.7). However, when a situation is first stated it is customary not to identify the universe when writing the probability of an event and write $P(A)$ instead of $P(A|U)$. The notation $P(A|B)$ is used when the universe of interest changes from U to a new universe B that is different from U.

SAMPLE SPACE AND EVENTS

The concept of universe is also known as *sample space,* and an elementary event is also known as a *simple event.* A *compound event* is a collection of simple events. In Figure 5.1, finding the coin on a tile t_i is a simple event and finding the coin in area C is a compound event.

MUTUALLY EXCLUSIVE EVENTS

Events that cannot occur at the same time are mutually exclusive. For example, if we drop a coin in the sample space (or universe) of Figure 5.2, the events A and B of the coin falling in area A and area B, respectively, are mutually exclusive. When the two areas A and B overlap as shown in Figure 5.3, A and B are not mutually exclusive.

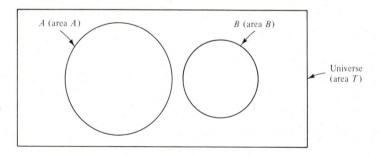

Figure 5.2   Events A and B mutually exclusive.

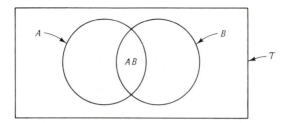

Figure 5.3 *A* and *B* not mutually exclusive.

When two events *A* and *B* are independent,

$$P(A|B) = P(A) \tag{5.8}$$

In words, this equation states that when *A* and *B* are independent, the probability of event *A*, $P(A)$, does not change when we are given the information *B*, namely that the universe has changed from *T* to *B* in Figure 5.3. This will happen in the special case when the following ratios of areas in Figure 5.3 are identical:

$$\frac{AB}{B} = \frac{AT}{T} \tag{5.9}$$

Namely, the area of *A* inside of *B* relative to *B* is the same as the area of *A* inside of *T* relative to *T*. When

$$P(A|B) \neq P(A) \tag{5.10}$$

A and *B* are dependent because knowledge of *B* changes our assessment of the probability for *A*.

5.4 Bayes' Equation and Relevance of Information

In Figure 5.3 we can write for the probability of *AB* in *T*

$$P(AB|T) = \frac{AB}{T} \tag{5.11}$$

If we multiply and divide the right-hand side of equation (5.11) by *B*, we have

$$P(AB|T) = \frac{AB}{B} \times \frac{B}{T}$$

Using our definition of probability as a ratio with the universe in the denominator and its subset in the numerator, we have (we drop here the designation of the original universe *T*, as is the custom)

$$P(AB) = P(A|B)P(B) \tag{5.12}$$

Similarly, multiplying and dividing the right-hand side of equation (5.11) by A, we obtain

$$P(AB) = P(B|A)P(A) \qquad (5.13)$$

From equations (5.12) and (5.13) we have

$$P(A|B)P(B) = P(B|A)P(A)$$

or

$$P(A|B) = P(A)\frac{P(B|A)}{P(B)} \qquad (5.14)$$

Equation (5.14) is known as *Bayes' equation* or *Bayes' theorem*. In this equation $P(A)$ is called the *a priori probability*, namely the probability before our knowledge of B, and $P(A|B)$ is the *a posteriori probability* or the probability of A after we learn that B happened. The ratio $P(B|A)/P(B)$ in equation (5.14) is a measure of *relevance* of B to A. When this ratio is equal to 1,

$$P(A|B) = P(A)$$

and the information B is not relevant to A because A and B are then independent.

5.5 Probability and Credibility

Bayes' theorem can be viewed as a rational procedure to establish whether information B relevant to A enhances or reduces the credibility of a statement or an event A. When $P(A|B) > P(A)$, the credibility of the statement "A is true" is enhanced. When $P(A|B) < P(A)$, the credibility of the statement "$\overline{A}$ is true" (or A is false) is enhanced.

DEMONSTRATIVE AND PLAUSIBLE REASONING REVISITED

Consider two statements, A and B, with B the consequence of A or $A \rightarrow B$ (A implies B). In the language of probability, $A \rightarrow B$ is equivalent to

$$P(B|A) = 1$$

because given A, B is a certainty when A implies B. Or since the area of A is completely inside area B, we are in B whenever we are in A.

In situations where the "imply" statement holds true, we distinguish two forms of reasoning: demonstrative and plausible.

Demonstrative Reasoning. Consider the following syllogism (two premises and a conclusion):

Premise 1: $A \rightarrow B$
Premise 2: $\underline{B \text{ is false}}$
Conclusion: $A \text{ is false}$

This conclusion follows directly from Bayes' theorem. For $A \rightarrow B$:

$$P(B|A) = 1$$

$$P(\overline{B}|A) = 0$$

The conclusion regarding the truth of A, given $\overline{B}$ (B false), can be written as

$$P(A|\overline{B}) = P(A) \frac{P(\overline{B}|A)}{P(\overline{B})} = 0$$

The conclusion is therefore definitive if we accept the two premises $A \rightarrow B$ and $\overline{B}$ as being true. This form of reasoning is objective, impersonal, and holds true in all fields of knowledge. It is deductive in that the conclusion is inescapable; that is, it leads from knowledge about set B (B false) to an inescapable conclusion about subset A which is contained in B, as shown in Figure 5.4.

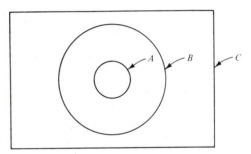

Figure 5.4 Schematic diagram illustrating $A \rightarrow B$, $B \rightarrow C$, $(A \cup B) \rightarrow C$.

Demonstrative reasoning enhances the credibility of $\overline{A}$ from $P(\overline{A}) < 1$ to a certainty $P(\overline{A}|\overline{B}) = 1$, when $A \rightarrow B$ and B is false. That is, when consequence B of cause A is false, the cause is false.

Plausible Reasoning. Consider now the following two premises and resulting conclusion:

Premise 1: $A \rightarrow B$
Premise 2: B is true
Conclusion: A is more credible

Here the conclusion is plausible; it is not inescapable, it indicates only direction. Credibility of A is enhanced, but it is a personal and subjective matter to establish how large $P(A|B)$ must be before we are willing to accept A as true.

Using Bayes' theorem, we can establish a numerical value for $P(A|B)$:

$$P(A|B) = P(A) \frac{P(B|A)}{P(B)}$$

Since $A \rightarrow B$, then $P(B|A) = 1$ (see Figure 5.4), and the last equation becomes

$$P(A|B) = P(A) \frac{1}{P(B)}$$

Considering $P(A) = 0$ to signify that A is false, and $P(A) = 1$ to signify that A is true, the last equation confirms our conclusion that when B is true the credibility of A is enhanced, because $P(A) \leq P(B) \leq 1$ (see Figure 5.4), and therefore $P(A|B) \geq P(A)$.

The smaller the probability $P(B)$ is, the more the information "B is true" enhances the credibility of A. In other words, the more unexpected B is, the more information it carries in our encoding the state of knowledge regarding A. B carries maximum information regarding A when it takes on its smallest possible value, $P(B) = P(A)$, because then A becomes a certainty when B is true. Regions A and B coincide in Figure 5.4 when $P(A) = P(B)$. B carries no information when its probability is 1, because then $P(A|B) = P(A)$. Thus, as $P(B)$ decreases from 1 to $P(A)$, $P(A|B)$ increases from $P(A)$ to 1. Stated in words: The increased confidence in the credibility of A due to the verification of B, when B is a consequence of A, varies inversely as $P(B)$. $P(B)$ is the probability of B prior to its verification (i.e., prior probability of B).

Example 1: Evidence in Court

Imagine that you are a member of a jury. The person on trial is accused of murder. The evidence, E, introduced by the prosecution is a piece of pink fabric that was found clenched in a hand of the victim. The entire court proceedings seem to hinge on whether the evidence was left by the accused. The tacit premise is that $G \rightarrow E$, namely that if someone is guilty of the crime (G), that person left the evidence (E).

From Bayes' theorem we have

$$P(G|E) = P(G)\frac{P(E|G)}{P(E)}$$

and since $G \rightarrow E$ means that

$$P(E|G) = 1$$

we obtain

$$P(G|E) = P(G)\frac{1}{P(E)}$$

Using a Venn diagram, the situation can be described as shown in Figure 5.5. In this figure each unit of area represents one person. T represents the universe in our situation. Suppose that the murder occurred in a remote isolated community. There were 10,000 people in town the night of the murder, including the residents and visitors. This total

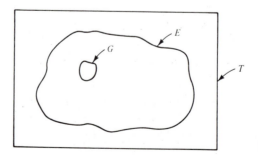

Figure 5.5 $G \rightarrow E$.

number is represented by the area T. Some members of the community were "little people," children, who were still in cribs; others were old and feeble and could not leave their homes; others were confined to hospitals. All these people are represented by the area of T outside E. They could not have left the evidence E. The murder occurred on a main street of the town. Area E represents all other people who could have left the evidence.

To prove its case, the prosecution attempts to show that the area E is the size of G, namely, that only the accused could have left the evidence, and therefore $P(G) = P(E)$ and $P(G|E) = 1$.

On the other hand, the defense wishes to show area E as large as possible under the circumstances, to suggest that the accused is as guilty as any other person who could have left the evidence, so that $P(G|E)$ is equal to 1 out of the total number of people in the community who could have been at the scene of the crime.

Let us invent two different stories, one for the prosecution and one for the defense, and observe how evidence E can be used in the court.

Story 1: The prosecution has strong evidence that the accused is the only person in town who has a pink jacket. He never parts from it and has never been seen without it. The piece of jacket in the hand of the victim matches the piece missing from the jacket of the accused. Here we have strong reason to reduce the size of E, driving

$$P(G|E) = P(G) \frac{1}{P(E)}$$

close to 1.

Story 2: The defense discovers that many people have pink jackets. In the week prior to the murder, hundreds were sold. The jackets are inexpensive and the fabric is of very low quality. Pieces of the fabric are strewn on the sidewalks and there is hardly a jacket owner who does not have a piece missing from it. Here the evidence E does not enhance the credibility of the accusation.

Example 2: Influence of New Evidence on Credibility of a Theory or a Model

As an example of how new evidence E with a small prior probability of occurrence $P(E)$ can enhance the credibility of a theory, or a postulated model, M, that is, $P(M|E) > P(M)$, let us relate the story of the discovery of Neptune that was mentioned earlier in the book, and show how it enhanced the credibility of Newton's model.

Kepler knew of six planets revolving around the sun. In 1781, about 150 years after Kepler's death, the astronomer Herschel observed a seventh planet, Uranus, revolving beyond Saturn. The observed orbit of Uranus did not agree with the predictions of Newton's model. Astronomers hypothesized that the deviations of Uranus from the orbit predicted by the model must be attributed to attraction from a planet beyond Uranus. Leverrier, a French astronomer, investigated this hypothesis and predicted the existence of an ultra-Uranian planet. He mapped the orbit of this planet on the basis of the orbit of Uranus, using Newton's model, and assigned its position in the skies. He wrote about his findings to a colleague at a well-equipped observatory and asked that the planet be observed on the night of September 23, 1846. The letter arrived on that day, and the same evening the new planet was found within 1 degree of the location predicted by Leverrier. The mass and orbit were later determined to agree also with Leverrier's prediction.

Let us use the following notations to study the enhancement of credibility for Newton's model as a result of this new evidence:

$P(M)$ = credibility of Newton's model before the evidence
$P(E)$ = probability of the evidence occurring
$P(M|E)$ = credibility of Newton's model given the evidence
$P(E|M)$ = probability of the evidence given Newton's model to be true

From Bayes' theorem we have

$$P(M|E) = P(M)\frac{P(E|M)}{P(E)}$$

If the truth of the model M implies the evidence, then $M \rightarrow E$ and $P(E|M) = 1$, and Bayes' theorem becomes

$$P(M|E) = P(M)\frac{1}{P(E)}$$

The enhancement in credibility of the model M is inversely related to $P(E)$. This probability can be considered equivalent to the probability of a random meteor appearing in a spherical cap of 2 degrees (1 degree all around the center) on the shell of a hollow sphere. Considering all 2-degree spherical caps on the shell as being equally likely to be the location for the meteor, the probability is computed as the ratio of the area of the 2-degree cap to the area of the entire shell surface. This yields 0.00007615. The credibility is enhanced more than 10,000-fold. That is to say, even a great skeptic who would assign $P(M) = 0.00007$ would become almost a "fanatic" believer in the model.

The ultra-Uranian planet predicted by Leverrier is the planet Neptune. It is interesting to note that after the discovery of Neptune, irregularities were observed in its orbit. These were also explained by Newton's model and were attributed to the existence of a small planet beyond Neptune. This small planet is Pluto, which was discovered in 1930.

What happens when the prediction does not materialize? Leverrier also observed that the planet Mercury, which is closest to the sun, displayed irregularities in its orbit. Specifically, the perihelion, which is the point of its orbit closest to the sun, was precessing around the sun describing a rosette path. Astronomers were overwhelmed by the mounting evidence that was continually enhancing the credibility of Newton's model. The model already explained the irregularities in the orbit of Uranus by predicting the existence of Neptune. Then it explained the irregularities in the orbit of Neptune (after its discovery) by predicting the existence of Pluto. It is not surprising, therefore, to learn that astronomers predicted the existence of another planet in the vicinity of Mercury to explain the irregularities observed in its orbit. So strong was their conviction that they even named this planet Vulcanus. To the present day no trace of Vulcanus has been found.

This was one of a number of observations that started casting some doubt on the domain of validity of Newton's model. It took the general theory of relativity to explain the irregularities in the orbit of Mercury. These irregularities were attributed to the curvature of space-time in the neighborhood of a large mass, such as the mass of the sun. The planet Mars also exhibits a precession of its perihelion, but this precession is smaller than that exhibited by the planet Mercury. The model of general relativity took over at the point where Newton's model reached the limit in its ability to explain and predict natural phenomena. Newton's model became, then, a subset of the more general and more powerful model of relativity.

5.6 Use of Matrices and Tree Diagrams to Assess Probabilities

Consider a rare disease D with the following statistical information compiled for 1000 people who were afflicted with it. Of these 1000 people, only 200 had survived. Of the 200 that had survived, 120 had been operated upon and 80 had survived with no operation. This information is shown in the matrix of Figure 5.6.

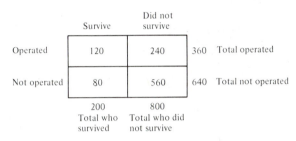

Figure 5.6

Suppose that you take a test to detect the disease D and you are told that you have it. The information of Figure 5.6 can be used as follows to help you assess your situation.

The probability of survival given that an operation takes place is 120 out of 360. This can be written in more compact form as follows, in which P represents probability and the line between Survived and Operated represents the word "given":

$$P(\text{Survived} \mid \text{Operated}) = \frac{120}{360}$$

Similarly,

$$P(\text{Did Not Survive} \mid \text{Operated}) = \frac{240}{360}$$

With no operation:

$$P(\text{Survived} \mid \text{Not Operated}) = \frac{80}{640}$$

$$P(\text{Did Not Survive} \mid \text{Not Operated}) = \frac{560}{640}$$

In each case the probability is a ratio of two numbers. The number in the denominator represents the number of people in the condition or universe that we are stipulating. For example, if we focus on the people who were operated upon, the denominator is 360, and for those who were not operated upon the number is 640. The numerator represents the number of people with a particular attribute among the total number within the condition. For example, within the condition of "operated," one attribute may be "survived"—represented by the number 120 in the matrix of Figure 5.6, and the other attribute may be "did not survive"—represented by the number 240.

Using the numbers in the matrix we can write the following probability statements in which S stands for *Survived* and $\bar{S}$ for *Did Not Survive*; OP stands for *Operated* and $\overline{OP}$ for *Not Operated*.

Given that a patient was operated upon (*first row*), the total in the given condition or universe is 360:

$$P(S|OP) = \frac{120}{360}, \text{ or 1 out of 3, 1/3}$$

$$P(\bar{S}|OP) = \frac{240}{360}, \text{ or 2 out of 3, 2/3}$$

Given that a patient was not operated upon (*second row*), the total in the given condition or universe is 640:

$$P(S|\overline{OP}) = \frac{80}{640}, \text{ or 1 out of 8, 1/8}$$

$$P(\bar{S}|\overline{OP}) = \frac{560}{640}, \text{ or 7 out of 8, 7/8}$$

Given that a patient survived (*first column*), the total in the given condition or universe is 200:

$$P(OP|S) = \frac{120}{200}, \text{ or 6 out of 10, 6/10}$$

$$P(\overline{OP}|S) = \frac{80}{200}, \text{ or 4 out of 10, 4/10}$$

Given that a patient did not survive (*second column*), the total in the given condition or universe is 800:

$$P(OP|\bar{S}) = \frac{240}{800}, \text{ or 3 out of 10, 3/10}$$

$$P(\overline{OP}|\bar{S}) = \frac{560}{800}, \text{ or 7 out of 10, 7/10}$$

The classification of each number in the matrix is obtained by reading the row label of the matrix, *Operated* or *Not Operated,* and the column label of the matrix, *Survived* or *Did Not Survive*. This can be summarized by using labels as shown in Figure 5.7. The numbers indicate the number of people in each category and the symbol ∩ for *and* stands for the intersection of the labels on each side of the symbol.

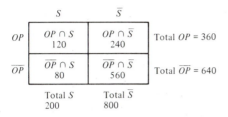

Figure 5.7

TREE DIAGRAM REPRESENTATION

The classification of the matrix in Figure 5.7 and the associated probability statements can be shown using a tree diagram as shown in Figure 5.8. Beginning with columns S and $\bar{S}$ of the matrix in Figure 5.7, we record the total numbers S and $\bar{S}$, that is, the 200 people who survived out of 1000 given, and the 800 who did not survive out of 1000 given. Going down the left branch S, we take 120 out of 200 (or 120/200) for $OP|S$, so that 120 people have the classification $S \cap P$. 80/200 are $\overline{OP}|S$, yielding 80 with classification $S \cap \overline{OP}$. The classification labels and numbers at the ends of the remaining two branches from $\bar{S}$ are generated in similar fashion as shown in Figure 5.8.

Beginning the branches of the tree with the row classifications OP and $\overline{OP}$ and then continuing with the column classification, we can obtain the tree of Figure 5.9.

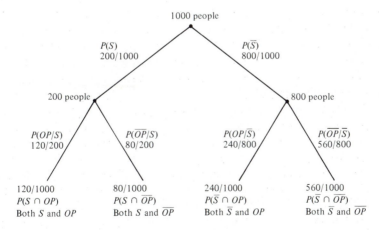

Figure 5.8

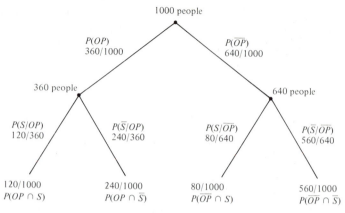

1000 people

P(OP)
360/1000

P($\overline{OP}$)
640/1000

360 people

640 people

P(S/OP)
120/360

P($\overline{S}$/OP)
240/360

P(S/$\overline{OP}$)
80/640

P($\overline{S}$/$\overline{OP}$)
560/640

120/1000
P(OP ∩ S)

240/1000
P(OP ∩ $\overline{S}$)

80/1000
P($\overline{OP}$ ∩ S)

560/1000
P($\overline{OP}$ ∩ $\overline{S}$)

Figure 5.9

INCORPORATING INFORMATION ABOUT THE ACCURACY OF A TEST

There are only four basic numbers given in the original matrix of Figure 5.6, yet there are so many different ways of looking at them. The basic question remains the following. If you take the test for disease D and are told that you are afflicted with it, *what are you to do*? If we accept the data of the past as a reasonable guide to predict the future, what is better, to operate or not to operate? Two hundred out of the total of 1000 survived (i.e., 1 out of 5). But of the 360 who were operated upon 120, or 1 out of 3, survived and of the 640 who were not operated upon 80, or 1 out of 8, survived. The odds are better for an operation.

It is important to have tools to structure the problem so that we can represent the uncertainties involved in the different courses of action (OP, $\overline{OP}$) and associated states (S, $\overline{S}$). But before we proceed with more detailed examination of these uncertainties, let us step back and view the entire situation from a higher level. What about the basic premise that you have the disease D? After all, the diagnosis of the disease was based on a test, and there are uncertainties associated with test results. Suppose you discover a study that was conducted to verify the accuracy of the test for this rare disease D. One thousand people volunteered to participate in the study. Four hundred were given a mild form of disease D, and then all 1000 were subjected to a test that was supposed to detect the presence or absence of the disease.

The test indicated either a positive result P, signaling presence of the disease, or a negative result $\overline{P}$, signaling absence of the disease. The results of the study are as shown in Figure 5.10. D stands for people who had the disease and $\overline{D}$ for those who did not.

If the test were perfect, the study would have resulted in no errors in classification, with each of the 400 people who were given a mild form of D responding positively (P) to the test, and the remaining 600 responding negatively ($\overline{P}$), as shown in Figure 5.11.

Information and Uncertainty   Chap. 5

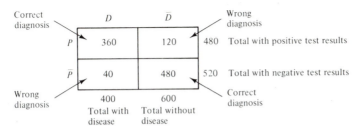

Figure 5.10 Accuracy of test for disease D.

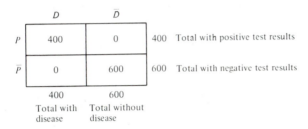

Figure 5.11 Results of a perfect test for disease D.

But the actual results of the study in Figure 5.10 show that the test was sometimes wrong. Forty cases of people with the disease got negative test results, and 120 cases of people without the disease got positive test results. If you use the numbers of Figure 5.10, then the fact that you have a positive test result P places you in the universe of the 480 people out of 1000 who had a positive test result. Of these, only 360 actually had the disease, while 120 did not. There is, therefore, a probability of 120 in 480, or 1 out of 4, that you do not have the disease D.

Now you have a new problem. We are not certain that you have the disease in the first place. How can we dispel more of the uncertainty? The key is redundancy. Take another test. Hopefully, the second test will be independent of the results of the first.

If the test presented in Figure 5.10 is to be administered again to the same 1000 people, the results would be as shown in the tree diagram of Figure 5.12. P_1 and P_2 indicate positive test results in the first and second examination, respectively, and the symbol for *and* was left out, so that $P(DP_1P_2)$, for example, stands for the probability of a person having disease D and getting positive results in two tests P_1 and P_2.

We assume that the second test will have the same record of accuracy for detection of the disease as that of the first test shown in Figure 5.10. That is, if a person has the disease (the four left branches of the tree in Figure 5.12), then in 360 out of 400 or 9/10 of the cases, the test will be positive, and in 40 out of 400 or 1/10 of the cases the test will be negative. Similarly, if a person does not have the disease (the four right branches of the tree in Figure 5.12), then in 120 out of 600 or 1/5 of the cases, the test will be negative.

In Figure 5.12 the eight labels at the end branches include two branches,

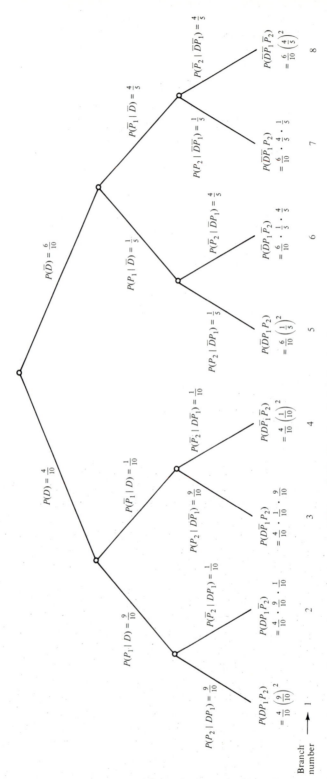

Figure 5.12 Results of administering the test twice.

160

1 and 5, in which both test results are positive; DP_1P_2 and $\overline{D}P_1P_2$. Therefore, if you have positive results in the two tests, the universe becomes $P(DP_1P_2)$ + $P(\overline{D}P_1P_2)$ and the probability that you have the disease is the share of $P(DP_1P_2)$ in this new universe, or

$$P(D|P_1P_2) = \frac{P(DP_1P_2)}{P(DP_1P_2) + P(\overline{D}P_1P_2)} = \frac{4/10(9/10)^2}{4/10(9/10)^2 + 6/10(1/5)^2}$$

$$= \frac{324/1000}{324/1000 + 6/250} = \frac{324/1000}{324/1000 + 24/1000} = \frac{324}{348}$$

Thus instead of a probability of 360/480 or 75 out of 100 after only the first positive test, we now have 324/348 or about 93 out of 100 that you have the disease after two positive test results.

Repeating the test still a third time for people with two positive results at branches 1 and 5, we obtain the probabilities of three consecutive positive test results for people who have the disease (D) at branch 1, and for people with no disease ($\overline{D}$) at branch 5. The probabilities are:

$$P(DP_1P_2P_3) = 4/10(9/10)^3 = 2916/10,000$$

$$P(\overline{D}P_1P_2P_3) = 6/10(1/5)^3 = 6/1250$$

The sum of these probabilities is the new universe of people with three consecutive positive test results. After a third positive test the probability that you have disease D would be:

$$P(D|P_1P_2P_3) = \frac{P(DP_1P_2P_3)}{P(DP_1P_2P_3) + P(\overline{D}P_1P_2P_3)} = \frac{2916/10,000}{2916/10,000 + 6/1250}$$

$$= \frac{2916/10,000}{2916/10,000 + 48/10,000} = \frac{2916}{2964}$$

This is approximately 98 out of 100. A fourth positive test would make the probability that you have the disease:

$$P(D|P_1P_2P_3P_4) = \frac{P(DP_1P_2P_3P_4)}{P(DP_1P_2P_3P_4) + P(\overline{D}P_1P_2P_3P_4)}$$

$$= \frac{26,244/100,000}{26,244/100,000 + 6/6250}$$

$$= \frac{26,244/100,000}{26,244/100,000 + 96/100,000} = \frac{26,244}{26,340} = 0.996$$

or a probability larger than 99 out of 100.

ANOTHER EXAMPLE

Suppose that people are classified in one of three categories: healthy $\equiv H$, diseased $\equiv D$, and sick (but not with disease D) $\equiv S$. Let the population, our universe, consist of 95% type H, 1.2% type D, and 3.8% type S. A test for

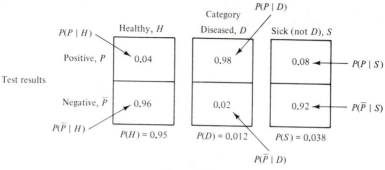

Figure 5.13

detecting disease D has the record shown in Figure 5.13. For the universe of healthy people the test is negative (correct diagnosis) 96% of the time. For the universe of diseased people the test is positive (correct) 98% of the time, and for the universe of the sick but without D the test for D is negative (correct) 92% of the time. Let us calculate the following probabilities that a randomly selected person in the population has the disease D:

$P(D)$	probability before a test
$P(D\|P_1)$	probability after one positive test result
$P(D\|P_1P_2)$	probability after two consecutive positive test results
$P(D\|P_1P_2P_3)$	probability after three consecutive positive test results
$\vdots$	$\vdots$
$P(D\|P_1P_2P_3 \ldots P_n)$	probability after n consecutive positive test results

Figures 5.14 and 5.15 show the tree diagrams for one and two test results.

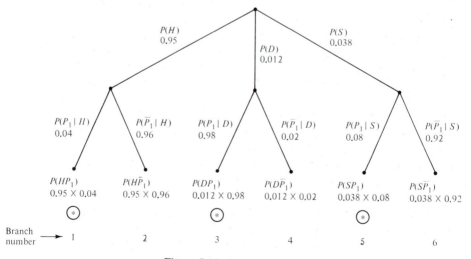

Figure 5.14 Results after one test.

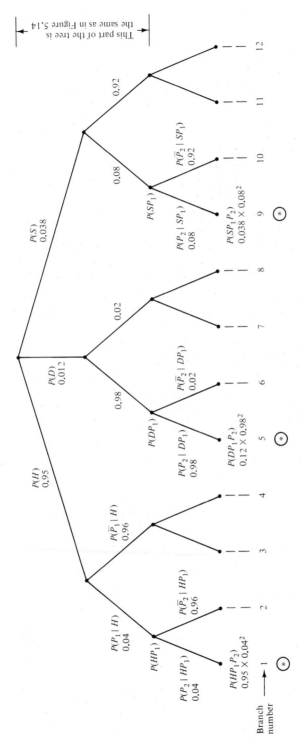

Figure 5.15 Results after two tests.

With no tests the universe, the top level of Figure 5.14, consists of

$$P(H) + P(D) + P(S)$$

Of this universe $P(D)$ has the attribute D. Therefore,

$$P(D) = \frac{P(D)}{P(H) + P(D) + P(S)} = \frac{0.012}{0.95 + 0.012 + 0.038} = 0.012$$

After one test with a positive result the universe is the sum of the probabilities at branches 1, 3, and 5, marked by asterisks in Figure 5.14.

$$P(HP_1) + P(DP_1) + P(SP_1)$$

Only $P(DP_1)$ has the attribute D. Thus

$$P(D|P_1) = \frac{P(DP_1)}{P(HP_1) + P(DP_1) + P(SP_1)}$$

$$= \frac{0.012 \times 0.98}{0.95 \times 0.04 + 0.012 \times 0.98 + 0.038 \times 0.08} = 0.2227$$

After two consecutive positive test results the universe is the sum of the probabilities at branches 1, 5, and 9 in Figure 5.15 (marked by asterisks).

$$P(HP_1P_2) + P(DP_1P_2) + P(SP_1P_2)$$

Only $P(DP_1P_2)$ has the attribute D. Thus

$$P(D|P_1P_2) = \frac{P(DP_1P_2)}{P(HP_1P_2) + P(DP_1P_2) + P(SP_1P_2)}$$

$$= \frac{0.012 \times 0.98^2}{0.95 \times 0.04^2 + 0.012 \times 0.98^2 + 0.038 \times 0.08^2}$$

$$= 0.8673$$

Extending the tree diagram of Figure 5.15 to three tests, the universe of three consecutive positive test results will be found on the expanded left legs of branches 1, 5, and 9 of Figure 5.15, to yield

$$P(HP_1P_2P_3) + P(DP_1P_2P_3) + P(SP_1P_2P_3)$$

$$= 0.95 \times 0.04^3 + 0.012 \times 0.98^3 + 0.038 \times 0.08^3$$

For n consecutive positive test results the universe becomes

$$P(HP_1P_2 \cdots P_n) + P(DP_1P_2 \cdots P_n) + P(SP_1P_2 \cdots P_n)$$

$$= 0.95 \times 0.04^n + 0.012 \times 0.98^n + 0.038 \times 0.08^n$$

The probability of the disease after n consecutive positive test results is then calculated from

$$P(D|P_1P_2 \cdots P_n)$$

$$= \frac{P(DP_1P_2 \cdots P_n)}{P(HP_1P_2 \cdots P_n) + P(DP_1P_2 \cdots P_n) + P(SP_1P_2 \cdots P_n)}$$

In summary,

$$P(D) = \frac{0.012}{0.95 + 0.012 + 0.038} = 0.012$$

$$P(D|P_1) = \frac{0.01176}{0.038 + 0.01176 + 0.00304} = \frac{0.01176}{0.0528}$$

$$= 0.2227272727$$

$$P(D|P_1P_2) = \frac{0.0115248}{0.00152 + 0.0115248 + 0.0002432} = \frac{0.0115248}{0.013288}$$

$$= 0.8673088501$$

$$P(D|P_1P_2P_3) = \frac{0.011294304}{0.0000608 + 0.011294304 + 0.000019456}$$

$$= \frac{0.011294304}{0.011605056} = 0.973$$

$$\cdot$$
$$\cdot$$
$$\cdot$$

$$P(D|P_1P_2 \cdots P_6) = \frac{0.0106301086}{4 \times 10^{-9} + 0.0106301086 + 10^{-8}} = 0.999998683$$

$$P(D|P_1P_2 \cdots P_7) = \frac{0.0104175064}{2 \times 10^{-10} + 0.0104175064 + 8 \times 10^{-10}}$$

$$= 0.999999904$$

Note that as n becomes large $P(D|P_1P_2 \cdots P_n)$ approaches unity because $P(HP_1P_2 \cdots P_n)$ and $P(SP_1P_2 \cdots P_n)$ in the denominator (universe) become vanishingly small compared to $P(DP_1P_2 \cdots P_n)$:

$$P(D|P_1P_2 \cdots P_n) = \frac{0.012 \times 0.98^n}{0.95 \times 0.04^n + 0.012 \times 0.98^n + 0.038 \times 0.08^n}$$

$$P(D|P_1P_2 \cdots P_n) \to 1 \qquad \text{as } n \to \infty$$

5.7 Use of Tree Diagrams to Assess Credibility

We shall now show an example of how to use a tree diagram to assess credibility on the basis of acquired information.

Example: Does Mr. Shackleton Have ESP?

Early studies in extrasensory perception consisted of card-guessing experiments. Special cards, called zener cards, were used. The cards were of five different types, each distinguished by one of the following markings: circle, square, cross, star, or waves.

Two subjects, a "transmitter" and a "receiver," participated in experiments that could last between one and two hours. The transmitter turned up one card at a time from a deck of zener cards that were arranged in random order. The receiver tried to guess which of the five zener cards the transmitter was observing at each turn. The two subjects in the experiment were screened from each other.

Since there were five different cards, a receiver could guess correctly one out of five cards on the average, on the basis of chance alone. But experiments performed in the early 1930s at Duke University by J. B. Rhine and his wife, Louisa Rhine, identified a number of people who consistently guessed correctly more than one in five cards. The odds against chance in these experiments were in the order of 1 million to 1 and higher [37].

Dr. Soal, a lecturer in mathematics at University College in London, learned about the experiments at Duke University and tried to repeat them. Between 1934 and 1939 he conducted experiments with 160 subjects involving 123,350 guesses using zener cards. To his disappointment he found no subjects whose performance deviated significantly from results expected on the basis of chance. He was about to give up his studies and conclude that either the results of the U.S. experiments were not credible or the English have no gift of ESP, when a coworker, Whately Carington, suggested that the data they had collected be reexamined in a revised manner. In experiments that he had conducted, Carington had noticed that some subjects are tuned to events displaced in time, namely future events about to happen rather than those taking place at present.

Carington suggested that the guesses by subjects in identifying the zener cards turned up by the "transmitter" be checked against the next card turned up or even the following one. He suggested comparing the first guess with the second card turned up, the second guess with the third card turned up, and so on, with a displacement of one future event; or checking the first guess against the third card turned up, the second guess against the fourth card turned up, and so on, a displacement of two future events in each case.

They undertook the task of reanalysis of the carefully recorded data, and to their great amazement found that one subject, Basil Shackleton, was tuned to the card that was to be turned up next by the transmitter. He guessed the card displaced by one future event of turning a card up with such remarkable consistency that the odds against chance were calculated to be 1 billion to 1.

What was even more remarkable was the fact that Shackleton was tuned to events displaced by a certain amount of time. His performance was most outstanding when cards were turned every 2.6 seconds. When the rate was increased to an average 1.4 seconds between guesses, Shackleton guessed with the same consistency the cards displaced by two events (i.e., the card turned up about 2.6 seconds later). The transmitter and receiver were in two separate rooms and the experiment was designed so that the transmitter had no way of knowing himself what card would turn up next. Cards were arranged in the deck by using a table of random numbers. So Basil Shackleton was tuned to events about 2.5 seconds in the future and his precognition communicated with the event, not the transmitter. He could not "read" the transmitter's mind because there was no way the information could be in the transmitter's mind unless he, too, had the identical precognition that characterized Shackleton's performance, a rather unlikely possibility.

How does such unusual performance render credibility to the hypothesis that some people have extrasensory perception (ESP)? Let us be skeptical and believe that the probability, $P(S)$, that a subject has ESP is a very small number ϵ, say, for example, $\epsilon = 0.00001$. Thus

$$P(S) = \epsilon$$

or the probability, $P(\bar{S})$, that a subject does not have ESP is

$$P(\bar{S}) = 1 - \epsilon$$

Suppose that we conduct an experiment with zener cards and a subject guesses correctly three cards in three experiments. The tree diagram is shown in Figure 5.16, in which we use the following symbols:

$S \equiv$ subject has ESP
$\bar{S} \equiv$ subject does not have ESP
$C_i \equiv$ correct guess in ith experiment
$\bar{C}_i \equiv$ incorrect guess in ith experiment
$mC \equiv$ m correct guesses
$p \equiv$ probability of correct guess by chance, $p = 1/5$ for zener cards
$P(mC \mid n) \equiv$ probability of m correct guesses given n experiments
$P(mC \mid n) \equiv \binom{n}{m} p^m (1 - p)^{n-m}$

$$= \frac{n!}{m!\,(n-m)!} p^m (1 - p)^{n-m}$$

The probability that the subject has ESP (S) given that he guesses correctly three cards in three experiments is given by the ratio of the probability $P(S3C)$ that the subject has ESP and guesses correctly all three cards (leftmost branch of tree) divided by the sum of the probabilities that satisfy the condition of three correct guesses, namely, the sum of the probabilities at the leftmost branch and the branch next to it (representing the chance that a subject with no ESP can guess all three cards correctly). In equation form, this becomes

$$P(S \mid 3C) = \frac{P(S3C)}{P(S3C) + P(\bar{S}3C)}$$

$$= \frac{\epsilon}{\epsilon + (1 - \epsilon)p^3}$$

As n approaches a very large number of experiments, $(1 - \epsilon)p^n$ becomes very, very small compared to ϵ, and $P(S \mid nC)$ approaches the value of 1. Namely, as $n \to \infty$,

$$(1 - \epsilon)p^n \to 0$$

and

$$P(S \mid nC) \to 1$$

The results above can be obtained directly from Bayes' equation or Bayes' theorem:

$$P(S \mid nC) = P(S)\,\frac{P(nC \mid S)}{P(nC)}$$

in which

$$P(nC) = P(nC \mid S)P(S) + P(nC \mid \bar{S})P(\bar{S})$$

Therefore,

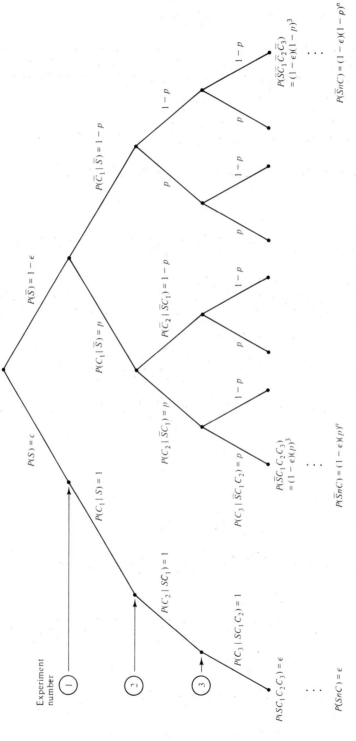

Figure 5.16 Tree diagram for three experiments with zener cards.

$$P(S \mid nC) = \epsilon \frac{1}{1 \cdot \epsilon + (1 - \epsilon)p^n}$$

As n becomes large, even the skeptic who initially assigns a very small value to ϵ, indicating little belief in the ESP gift of a subject, will become converted and assign a probability close to 1 to $P(S \mid nC)$.

5.8 How to Divide Uncertainty

HOW MANY WEIGHINGS?

Consider the following problem. There are 27 coins identical in shape and appearance. One coin is heavier than the remaining 26 that have identical weights. Given a balance, how can you identify the odd coin in only three weighings?

To solve this problem, we divide the coins into three groups of nine coins each. We weigh two groups against each other on the balance scales. If they are equal, the heavy coin is with the remaining group. If the balance tips to one side, that side has the group with the odd coin. A single weighing will identify one group of the three as the one containing the odd coin. Now we take this group of nine coins and divide it into three groups of three coins each. By the reasoning we have just used, we can identify in one weighing the group that contains the odd coin. We now separate the three coins of this group and using one more weighing, we identify the odd coin as follows. If the balance is even, the odd coin is not on the balance. If the balance tips, the side that tips down has the odd coin.

The general message in the procedure we used with the 27 coins is that problem solving can sometimes be approached by a search that involves selective rejection. The more coins we reject as not being the odd one in our problem, the closer we get to the solution. In general, in complex problems when we are in no position to know for sure that we have the best solution, we may have a number of alternatives to consider as potential solutions to a problem, and the more of them we reject on the basis of reasonable criteria, the more confidence we have in the solution we finally adopt. In such situations, even when a solution occurs to us in the first try, we should compare it with alternative solutions. The more alternative solutions we reject, the more confidence we have in our original solution.

This is similar to testing a hypothesis in the scientific method. We gain confidence in a hypothesis by rejecting efforts to prove it wrong. The more we reject, the more confident we are.

HOW MANY QUESTIONS? THE METHOD OF HALVING

As another example of selective rejection in problem solving, consider a person arriving at the intersections shown in Figure 5.17. Only one of the routes leads to a desired destination, but she does not know which. A genie stationed

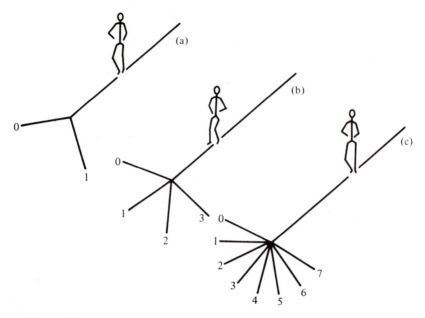

Figure 5.17 Routes at intersection: (a) two routes: 0, 1; (b) four routes; (c) eight routes: 0, 1, 2, . . . , 7.

at each intersection will respond with "yes" or "no" to any question. The answer is always credible, but there is a fixed fee per question. How many questions should the person ask at each intersection? One question, "Is it road 0?" will do for the routes in Figure 5.17a; two questions for Figure 5.17b; and three for Figure 5.17c. In general, for 2^n routes, n questions will lead to the correct route. The first question reduces the region of search by a factor of 2; that is, we reject half of the routes. This is achieved by dividing our uncertainty into two equal parts in the sense that they have equal probabilities of including the solution. For example, for eight routes, each equally likely to contain the solution (i.e., each has a probability of 1 out of 8, 1/8), our first question will be: "Is the answer in one of the first four routes?" Similarly, each successive question reduces the remaining search region by a factor of 2, each time dividing the remaining routes into two groups with equal probability of containing the solution. The selective rejection through questions continues to reduce our uncertainty as fewer and fewer routes remain as possible candidates for the solution.

An alternative way to go about the process of rejection would be to take one route at a time and ask whether it is the correct one. Suppose that there are four different routes and we are trying to find the one correct route. We could simply start with the first route and ask whether it is the correct one, and may get the answer in only one question. We would never be able to do this by dividing the routes in two and asking if the correct one is contained in one-half of them. It will always take you two questions to get the answer. By this alternative approach, we would occasionally be able to find the correct route in only one question. But sometimes it would take us three questions to get the correct answer. The preceding method guarantees that we find the correct route in only two questions. In fact, we can show that the expected value for the number of questions that we would have to ask with the alternative method is greater than 2. From Figure 5.18, we can see that after the first question of whether the correct route is the first one, there are two possibilities: a "yes" or a "no." Since there are four routes and only one of them is correct, the probability of getting a yes is 1/4 and the probability of a no is 3/4. A "yes" yields the answer in only one question. But if the answer to the first question is "no," we must ask if the correct route is the second one. Since there are three routes left, the probability of a "yes" is 1/3 (namely, we get the correct answer in only two questions) and 2/3 that we must go on to ask still another question. If we get a "no" for the second question, we must then ask if the correct route is the third one. The probability of getting a "yes" is now 1/2, since there are only two routes left. If the answer is "yes," we know that the correct route is the third one and we have gotten the correct answer in three questions. Even if the answer is "no," also with a probability of 1/2, we have still gotten the answer in three questions because the correct route must now be the fourth route. We can now calculate the expected value for the number of questions as follows.

There can be either one question, two questions, or three questions. The probability of getting the correct answer in one question is 1/4. To get the probability of finding the correct route in two questions, we must multiply down the tree diagram, considering the probability of not finding the correct route on the first question and finding it on the second. This yields 3/4 times 1/3. To get the probability of finding the correct route in three questions, we multiply down the tree again. To get a "no" in both the first and second questions, we

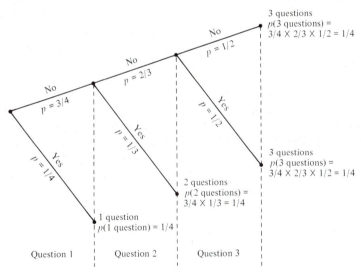

Figure 5.18 Expected number of questions for four routes by picking one route at a time.

multiply 3/4 times 2/3. Now to also get a "yes" on the third question, we multiply by 1/2; which yields 3/4 times 2/3 times 1/2 as the probability of one way of getting the correct answer in three questions. We can also find the correct route if the answer to the third question is no. That also has a probability of 3/4 times 2/3 times 1/2. The expected number of questions is, therefore,

$$\frac{1}{4}(1) + \frac{3}{4} \times \frac{1}{3}(2) + \frac{3}{4} \times \frac{2}{3} \times \frac{1}{2}(3) + \frac{3}{4} \times \frac{2}{3} \times \frac{1}{2}(3) = 2\frac{1}{4}$$

This expected value means that on the average $2\frac{1}{4}$ questions are required. The expected value of 2.25 indicates that more often three questions rather than one question will be required to find the correct route. On the other hand, the method of halving discussed earlier guarantees that the correct route can be found in only two questions. On the average, the method of halving is quicker. By halving the uncertainty with each question, we get the correct answer by the fastest method on the average. The answer to each question represents the same amount of information, because in each case, the domain of search is reduced by a factor of 2. In each case, we get a response of "yes" or "no." On the basis of this common unit of measurement, we conclude that n units of information are required to find the one correct route out of 2^n routes.

INFORMATION AND PROBABILITY

The measurement of information is related to probability as follows. If we consider the two routes of Figure 5.17a, with no knowledge as to which is more likely to be correct, we assign each a probability of $1/2$ of being the one we seek. This reflects our state of maximum doubt or uncertainty. For four routes, we assign each an equal probability of $1/4$, and for 2^n routes $1/2^n$ each. The larger the number of routes, the smaller is the probability of each route being the correct one, and the greater our uncertainty. The amount of information required to dispel uncertainty increases as uncertainty increases.

In the routes problem, each question enables us to reject one-half of the routes. In the case of the 27 coins, we divide the field of search, or our uncertainty on where the odd coin is, into three parts with equal probabilities of $1/3$ each of containing the odd coin. Because of the special nature of a balance scale, we can reject two out of three parts following each weighing, which corresponds to one question in the route problem.

5.9 Probabilities and the Morse Code

Suppose that we have eight marbles of different colors in a coffee cup. If one marble is drawn, we need three yes–no questions (binary questions) to establish the color of the drawn marble.

But now let us put in the coffee cup four red marbles, two blue, one green, and one white. Now how many binary questions do we need to establish the color of one marble selected randomly?

First we divide the uncertainty into two groups, so that one question will reject one group. The groups will be the four red marbles and the other four. Each group has a probability $1/2$ of including the marble selected randomly. So the first question will be: "Is it red?" If the response is "yes," we get the answer in one question. If the response is "no," we divide the remaining four marbles into two groups each with equal probability of containing the random one. Now we can reject one of these groups by a single question. So the second question will be: "Is it blue?" If "yes," we have the answer in two questions. If "no," one more question will do it. So we may need as many as three questions. The three questions represent a *maximum number* or an upper bound. It will not happen every time we play this guessing game.

We can treat the number of questions as some sort of "payment" and calculate the expected value of the number of questions. The probability that we will get away with one question is equal to the probability that red (R) will happen, $4/8 = 1/2$. Using a tree, we represent the results and associated probabilities for one question, two questions, and the maximum of three questions, and calculate the expected value of the number of questions. From Figure 5.19 we calculate the following expected number of questions:

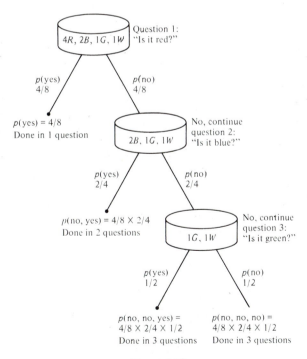

Figure 5.19

$$\frac{4}{8}(1) + \frac{4}{8} \times \frac{2}{4}(2) + \frac{4}{8} \times \frac{2}{4} \times \frac{1}{2}(3) + \frac{4}{8} \times \frac{2}{4} \times \frac{1}{2}(3)$$

$$= \frac{1}{2}(1) + \frac{1}{4}(2) + \frac{1}{8}(3) + \frac{1}{8}(3)$$

$$= 1\frac{3}{4} \text{ questions}$$

On the average, we will ask $1\frac{3}{4}$ questions to establish the color of the marble. For each real situation we will ask either one, two, or three questions as the tree shows. But if we proceeded with the sequence of questions, say in 100 situations in which we draw a marble, on the average 175 questions will be asked.

If we have two marbles of each color R, B, G, and W, the probabilities are 1/4 for each color. We need two questions, or 200 questions in 100 situations. In each situation the first question would eliminate two colors, for example, by asking "is it R or B?" The second question would identify the correct color of the remaining two colors. This is more than the number of questions we need, on the average, when the four colors have unequal probabilities of 1/2, 1/4, 1/8, and 1/8.

So we are most uncertain in the case of equal probabilities for the events of interest, and we need more questions to dispel more doubt.

In the three questions of Figure 5.19, R was identified in one question, B in 2, G and W in 3. The larger the probability of the event, the smaller the number of questions.

THE MORSE CODE

In 1938, Samuel F. B. Morse (1791–1872) devised his celebrated code using this idea. To keep the expected number of code symbols that must be transmitted small, he gave short codes to letters of high frequency of occurrence, and longer ones to the less frequent letters. He estimated the various frequencies of the letters by counting the number of type letters in the bins of a printing shop. Thus "e," the most frequent letter in English, has the shortest code, a dot.

5.10 Concepts from Information Theory [38]

HUFFMAN TREE CONSTRUCTION PROCEDURE

The Huffman tree construction procedure is an effective way to generate efficient codes and labels for events and for searching information. The information may be in the form of data stored in a computer, a book in a library, or the location of a leak in a long pipe.

BINARY CODES

Consider a universe of four events E_1, E_2, E_3, and E_4 that have the following probabilities of occurrence:

$$p(E_1) = \frac{1}{2}$$

$$p(E_2) = \frac{1}{4}$$

$$p(E_3) = \frac{1}{8}$$

$$p(E_4) = \frac{1}{8}$$

Each day one, and only one, of the four events occurs in our universe, and we inform an agent in a foreign country which event occurred. To make our model more explicit, let us assume that an omnipotent genie selects each day one marble from a container of 1000 marbles and decides on the event that will occur on that day on the basis of the label on the drawn marble. Of the 1000 marbles, 500 have the label E_1, 250 have the label E_2, 125 have the label E_3, and 125 have the label E_4. We are present at the drawing of a marble each morning and inform our foreign agent of the event.

Recently, a communication system became available. We can transmit a message on the system using a sequence of bits 0 and 1 (i.e., binary digits). The cost of transmission is linearly related to the number of bits in the message. Our objective is to devise a code for our four events $E_i (i = 1, 2, 3, 4)$ so that the cost of transmission will be as low as possible on the average.

The initial thinking might be that we should give each event as short a code name as possible, and since we have a limited number of short codes, such as two of one-bit length (0 or 1), four of two-bit length (00, 01, 10, 11), eight of three-bit length (000, 001, . . . , 110, 111), we could use the shortest codes for the most frequently occurring events. On that basis we could select the following codes:

$$0 \quad \text{for} \quad E_1$$
$$1 \quad \text{for} \quad E_2$$
$$00 \quad \text{for} \quad E_3$$
$$11 \quad \text{for} \quad E_4$$

INSTANTANEOUS CODES

The code above has a feature that we may wish to eliminate. The code cannot be interpreted instantaneously. What this means is as follows. Suppose that our agent sees the code 0. At that instance he cannot tell whether E_1 or E_3 occurred because the digit 0 could be the beginning of the code word 00 for E_3. In addition, if you receive a number of messages at the end of a number of days to inform you what transpired in those days, the message may look like this:

$$0011$$

Now you have no way of knowing which of the following events is represented by the sequence:

Four days with a sequence of events

$$E_1, E_1, E_2, E_2$$

or three days with sequence

$$E_1, E_1, E_4 \quad \text{or} \quad E_3, E_2, E_2$$

or two days with a sequence

$$E_3, E_4$$

To remove the ambiguity in the decoding, we can introduce a space between codes in the transmission, but this may add to the cost of transmission and introduces a delay in the decoding activity. Another way to overcome this difficulty is to require an *instantaneous code,* namely, a code of the events such that as soon as a complete code for any event arrives, it can be decoded uniquely as representing that event, and not possibly be the beginning of a code for a different event. This is tantamount to saying that an instantaneous code can have no single complete code of an event as a prefix of another code for a different event. *Instantaneous codes* are therefore also known as *prefix codes.*

TREE CONSTRUCTION OF CODES

A tree structure can be used to generate an instantaneous code as shown in Figure 5.20. The codes for the events are the sequences of digits along the branches of the tree. Two links emanate from each node with labels 0 and 1. Since each code word representing an event appears at the end of a complete branch, no code word is a prefix of another. This was not the case in the code words 0, 1, 00, and 11 that we devised earlier for our four events, as shown in Figure 5.21. In Figure 5.21 code words 0 and 1 appear on the first portions of branches that have code words at their ends, 00 and 11, respectively. The tree

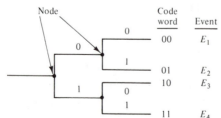

Figure 5.20 Instantaneous code.

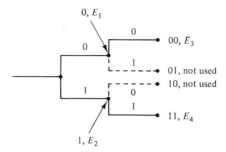

Figure 5.21 Example of code that is not instantaneous.

need not have equal length branches (i.e., equal number of links) to yield an instantaneous code as shown in Figure 5.22. The length of code word, namely, the number of bits, is equal to the number of links in the branch of the code word. Thus we can have instantaneous codes with variable-length code words, as shown in Figure 5.22.

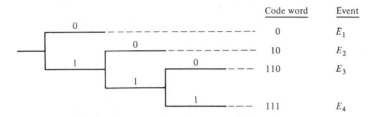

	Code word	Event
	0	E_1
	10	E_2
	110	E_3
	111	E_4

Figure 5.22 Instantaneous code with variable length words.

ENTROPY OF A SOURCE

We now return to our original problem to devise an instantaneous code for our four events E_i ($i = 1, 2, 3, 4$), so that on the average the number of bits transmitted (and hence the cost of transmission) will be a minimum. A theoretical lower bound on the average number of bits that must be transmitted, or what amounts to the same thing, the minimum *average length of code word,* is given by the *entropy, H, of the source,* namely, the entropy of our universe of four events E_i ($i = 1, 2, 3, 4$). Consider four code words for our four events with associated probabilities $p(E_i)$. Define the length l_i of each code word as the number of bits in the word; then the average length $\bar{l}$ of the four code words, or the entropy of our source, is the expected length calculated by adding the products of each length l_i by its corresponding probability of occurrence $p(E_i)$.

$$H = \bar{l} = \sum_{i=1}^{4} l_i p(E_i) \tag{5.15}$$

For n events and n corresponding code words, we have

$$H = \bar{l} = \sum_{i=1}^{n} l_i p(E_i) \tag{5.16}$$

For given probabilities $p(E_i)$, equation (5.16) can be solved for l_i values that will make the average length $\bar{l}$ minimum. The solution yields

$$l_i = \log_s \frac{1}{p(E_i)} \qquad (5.17)$$

in which s is the number of different symbols in the code: $s = 2$ for a binary code. Thus for our example,

$$H = \bar{l} = \sum_{i=1}^{4} p(E_i) \log_2 \frac{1}{p(E_i)}$$

$$= \frac{1}{2} \log_2 2 + \frac{1}{4} \log_2 4 + \frac{1}{8} \log_2 8 + \frac{1}{8} \log_2 8$$

$$= 1\frac{3}{4} \text{ bits}$$

Now the question is: How do we devise a code that will approach or achieve this limiting theoretical value? This is where the Huffman tree construction algorithm comes in.

THE HUFFMAN TREE CONSTRUCTION ALGORITHM

The Huffman algorithm for finding binary instantaneous codes of variable length that approach the minimum average length of code words follows the following steps:

1. List the probabilities of events E_i in a column in decreasing order. In our example:

$$\frac{1}{2}$$

$$\frac{1}{4}$$

$$\frac{1}{8}$$

$$\frac{1}{8}$$

2. Combine the smallest two values (circled) by using two links emanating to the right of each of these values to form a single link as shown below. Record the sum of these two smallest probabilities on the single link.

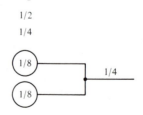

Information and Uncertainty   Chap. 5

3. Repeat step 2 with the remaining uncircled probabilities including the 1/4 that is the sum of the circled numbers and represents them. The two smallest probabilities are now 1/4 and 1/4, so we have a link emanating from each and combined in one link with a value equal to the sum of these probabilities. We circle the probabilities that were combined.

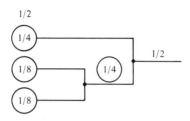

Next, combine the remaining two uncircled probabilities 1/2 and 1/2, yielding 1.0.

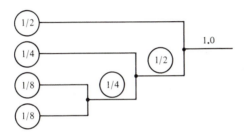

4. Stop the tree construction when the probability of the newly generated link has the value 1.0.

5. Starting from the root of the tree on the right, label the links emanating from each node to the left with 0 and 1. The code word for each event E_i with probability $p(E_i)$ is the sequence of bits on the links along the branch from the root of the tree on the right, to the end of the branch on the left. For our example, we have the following code words for the four events:

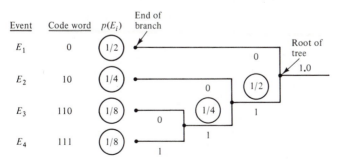

Thus 1/2 the time one bit will be transmitted, 1/4 the time two bits, and 1/4 the time three bits (1/8 the sequence 110 and 1/8 the sequence 111). Therefore, the average length of code word in our case will be

$$\frac{1}{2}(1) + \frac{1}{4}(2) + \frac{1}{4}(3) = 1\frac{3}{4} \text{ bits}$$

This is identical with the theoretical value. Hence our foreign agent will receive one, two, or three bits on any given day, with an average of $1\frac{3}{4}$ bits per day.

IS A HUFFMAN CODE UNIQUE?

Figure 5.23 shows the Huffman tree structure for six events with the associated probabilities of occurrence indicated in the figure. Notice in the figure that when the first two smallest probabilities 0.06 and 0.04 are combined, we have three values 0.1, and any two of these can be combined next. Figure 5.24 shows a code generated by combining the probabilities of E_3 and E_4 after E_5 and E_6 are combined.

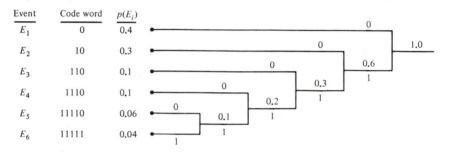

Figure 5.23 Huffman tree structure for code of six events.

The average length of code words in Figures 5.23 and 5.24 is the same. Thus although the Huffman tree construction process may not lead to a unique code, the efficiency is the same for both codes. This is shown by the following calculations. For Figure 5.23,

$$\bar{l} = 0.4(1) + 0.3(2) + 0.1(3) + 0.1(4) + 0.1(5) = 2.2 \text{ bits per event}$$

For Figure 5.24,

$$\bar{l} = 0.4(1) + 0.3(2) + 0.3(4) = 2.2 \text{ bits per event}$$

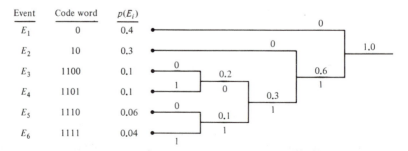

Figure 5.24 Alternative code for the events of Figure 5.23.

The theoretical lower bound on $\bar{l}$, called the *entropy* of the source, is only slightly smaller than the value we have obtained:

$$H = \bar{l} = \sum_{i=1}^{6} P(E_i) \log_2 \frac{1}{p(E_i)} = 2.14352 \text{ bits per event}$$

AGGREGATING EVENTS, CODE EXTENSION

Consider two events E_1 and E_2 with probabilities $p(E_1) = 0.8$ and $p(E_2) = 0.2$. The shortest instantaneous code we can devise is one bit per event:

Event	Code Word	$p(E_i)$
E_1	0	0.8
E_2	1	0.2

and the average length of code word is 1:

$$0.8(1) + 0.2(1) = 1$$

So if one event occurs each day, we transmit one bit per day to our foreign agent. But if we calculate the entropy, or theoretical minimum average length of code word, we obtain

$$0.8 \log_2 \frac{1}{0.8} + 0.2 \log_2 \frac{1}{0.2} = 0.7219 \text{ bits per event}$$

We can approach this value if we are willing to pay a price of time delay. Suppose that the information can be transmitted once every two days, telling our agent what happened in a sequence of two days. The messages now consist of four possible sequences as shown in Figure 5.25. The Huffman code for these

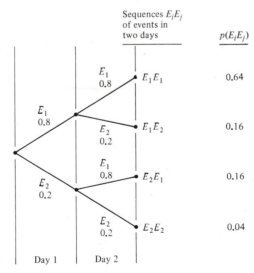

Figure 5.25

aggregated two-day events is shown in Figure 5.26, and the average length of code word for a string of two days of events is (events in consecutive days are considered independent in our calculations)

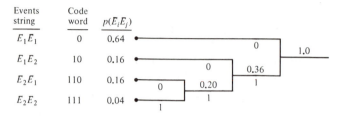

Events string	Code word	$p(E_iE_j)$
E_1E_1	0	0.64
E_1E_2	10	0.16
E_2E_1	110	0.16
E_2E_2	111	0.04

Figure 5.26 Huffman code for extended string of two events.

$$0.64(1) + 0.16(2) + 0.16(3) + 0.04(3) = 1.56 \text{ bits per string}$$

or

$$\frac{1.56}{2} = 0.78 \text{ bits per original one-day event}$$

The value of 0.78 is a little larger than the 0.7219 theoretical minimum. Extending the string to three days, namely, transmitting information at three-day intervals, we can reduce the 0.78 value further to 0.728 bits per original one-day event. The code words for the three-day extension are generated in the Huffman tree structure of Figure 5.27. In general, the closer we wish to approach the minimum average number of bits per original event, or the entropy of the source, the larger the time delay or the extension that must be coded.

Events string	Code word	$p(E_iE_jE_k)$
$E_1E_1E_1$	0	0.512
$E_1E_1E_2$	100	0.128
$E_1E_2E_1$	101	0.128
$E_2E_1E_1$	110	0.128
$E_1E_2E_2$	11100	0.032
$E_2E_1E_2$	11101	0.032
$E_2E_2E_1$	11110	0.032
$E_2E_2E_2$	11111	0.008

Average length = 0.512(1) + · · · + 0.008(5) = 2.184 bits per string
or 2.184/3 = 0.728 bit per original one-day event

Figure 5.27 Huffman code for extended string of three events.

The Huffman tree construction for compact and efficient codes has many applications. The construction process can be used in optimal merging of lists, construction of search trees, generating of high-quality computer codes (in minimizing round-off error, parallel execution time, or usage of space), compressing of data, and even checking for leaks in a pipeline.

Consider, for example, the pipeline of Figure 5.28 with a probability $P(S_i)$ for a leak in each section S_i shown in the figure. The probabilities were arbitrarily selected so that they are identical with those of Figure 5.23. Thus the Huffman structure for an event E_i signifying a leak in section S_i is identical to Figure 5.23. The search for the leak begins at the root of the tree. First check for a leak in S_1, then S_2, then S_3, and so on. If the tree structure of Figure 5.24 is used, the check sequence begins at S_1, then S_2, then the combined section of S_3 and S_4. If a leak is found there, in S_3 and S_4 combined, then check S_3; if no leak is found in S_3 and S_4 combined, then check section of S_5. This process will minimize the number of checks on the average.

Figure 5.28 Pipeline sections with probabilities for a leak.

5.11 Reliability

INTRODUCTION

The *reliability* of a system is defined as the probability that it will operate successfully. For example, the reliability of the system in Figure 5.29 depends on reliability of switches 1 and 2; that is, if a message is sent from A to B, the probability that a message transmitted from A will be received at B is dependent on both the switches operating successfully. Similarly, if the switches were arranged in parallel, as in Figure 5.30, the probability that a message transmitted from A will be received at B depends on the probability of either switch 1 or 2 operating successfully. Let us suppose that the two switches in Figures 5.29 and 5.30 are not perfect. The probabilities of successful operation are 0.9 and 0.8 for switches 1 and 2, respectively. We can now find the reliability R of each

Figure 5.29

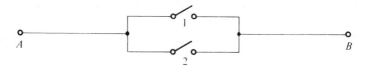

Figure 5.30

system represented by Figures 5.29 and 5.30; namely, we can calculate the probability that a message transmitted from A will be received at B. For Figure 5.29,

$$R = 0.9 \times 0.8 = 0.72$$

For Figure 5.30,

$$R = 1 - (1 - 0.9)(1 - 0.8) = 0.98$$

In Figure 5.29 the system *works* only when switches 1 and 2 both work. In Figure 5.30 the system *does not work* only when both switches fail, and this happens with probability $(1 - 0.9)(1 - 0.8)$. When at least one switch works in Figure 5.30, the system works. Therefore, subtracting the probability of failure $(1 - 0.9)(1 - 0.8)$ from the universe of 1 of all possibilities, we obtain the reliability R.

Let us generalize the concepts of reliability for systems with elements connected in series and parallel.

SERIES AND PARALLEL CONNECTION OF ELEMENTS

Let the reliability of a single element be p; then the reliability R of a system of m parallel paths of n elements each as shown in Figure 5.31 is given by

$$R = 1 - (1 - p^n)^m \tag{5.18}$$

p^n is the probability of a path surviving, and $(1 - p^n)$ is the probability of a path failing. $(1 - p^n)^m$ is the probability of all m paths failing. $1 - (1 - p^n)^m$ is the probability of at least one parallel path surviving, and this is the system reliability.

The reliability of a system of subsystems connected in series and each consisting of m parallel elements as shown in Figure 5.32 is given by

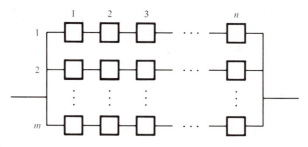

Figure 5.31 m parallel paths with n elements in series in each path (parallel–series system).

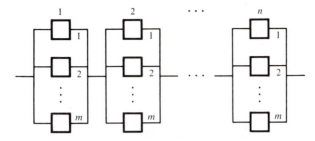

Figure 5.32 Series connection of n subsystems each consisting of m parallel elements.

$$R = [1 - (1 - p)^m]^n \qquad (5.19)$$

$1 - p$ is the probability of failure for an element, $(1 - p)^m$ is the probability of a subsystem failing, and $1 - (1 - p)^m$ is the probability of a subsystem surviving. The survival of all n subsystems in series is $[1 - (1 - p)^m]^n$, and this is the system reliability.

The reliability expressions for the systems of Figure 5.33 are shown next to each system. Each element in the systems has the same reliability p. For $p = 1/2$ the reliabilities of the four systems in Figure 5.33 become

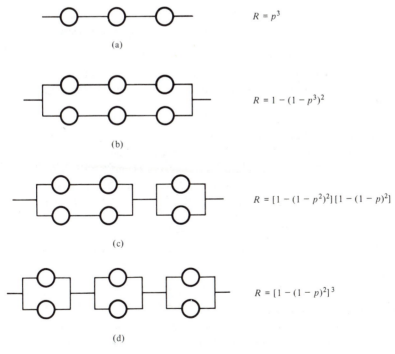

$R = p^3$

(a)

$R = 1 - (1 - p^3)^2$

(b)

$R = [1 - (1 - p^2)^2][1 - (1 - p)^2]$

(c)

$R = [1 - (1 - p)^2]^3$

(d)

Figure 5.33

(a) $R = 1/8$
(b) $R = 15/64$
(c) $R = 21/64$
(d) $R = 27/64$

5.12 Heuristic Guides to Assessing Reliability of Complex Systems [39]

Consider the five-element system of Figure 5.34. Suppose that the reliability of each element is p; namely, the element will survive the period of service required with probability p. To calculate the reliability of the system that requires that at least one path will survive between points 1 and 2, we can proceed as follows.

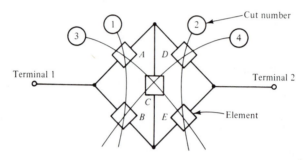

Figure 5.34 Five-element system for signal to travel between terminals 1 and 2.

The system fails if four or more elements fail. With three elements failing, there are only two possible paths for system survival, with elements A and D or B and E. The probability of system survival with three elements failing is

$$2p^2(1 - p)^3$$

With two elements failing, there are eight paths for system survival because of all 10 possible combinations, $5!/2!3! = 10$, of two elements failing and three surviving out of the five, the failures of A and B or D and E will cause the system to fail. Hence only eight paths out of the 10 are available for system survival, with two elements failing, yielding a probability of system survival of

$$8p^3(1 - p)^2$$

With one element failing there are five different ways that the system can survive:

$$5p^4(1 - p)$$

With no element failing, we have p^5.

The system reliability R is the sum of the probabilities of system survival with two elements, three elements, four elements, five elements:

$$R = \underbrace{2p^2(1-p)^3}_{\substack{\text{paths of} \\ \text{2 elements}}} + \underbrace{8p^3(1-p)^2}_{\substack{\text{paths of} \\ \text{3 elements}}} + \underbrace{5p^4(1-p)}_{\substack{\text{paths of} \\ \text{4 elements}}} + \underbrace{p^5}_{\substack{\text{paths of} \\ \text{5 elements}}} \qquad (5.20)$$

LOWER-BOUND APPROXIMATION TO SYSTEM RELIABILITY

The reliability of a system can be approximated by a technique known as the *minimal cut procedure*. This reduces the computation effort for complex systems and provides a lower bound on the reliability.

A *cut* is defined as a group of elements such that if they all fail, the system fails, independent of the state of the remaining elements of the system. A system may have many cuts, and elements may be part of more than a single cut.

A cut is also defined as a set of elements such that when they are removed from the system, the system is divided into two parts, each containing one terminal point, and there is no path from one terminal to the other. For example, in Figure 5.34 cuts disrupt paths between terminals 1 and 2.

A *minimal cut* is a cut with the following special property. No proper subset* of elements of a minimal cut can cause the failure of the system by the failure of its elements only. For example, in Figure 5.34 minimal cuts are

Elements A and B: cut ①
Elements D and E: cut ②
Elements A, C, and E: cut ③
Elements B, C, and D: cut ④

A cut consisting of elements A, C, and B is not minimal because the proper subset of elements A and B can cause system failure.

The lower bound of system reliability R_{MC} is the probability that all minimal cuts of the system survive; that is, there is failure in none of the system minimal cuts, assuming that the failures in the minimal cuts occur independently.

Let the reliability of element i contained in minimal cut ⓙ be designated as $p_i^{ⓙ}$; then the probability of failure $Q^{ⓙ}$ of cut ⓙ is the probability of simultaneous failure of all elements in the cut, that is,

$$Q^{ⓙ} = (1 - p_1^{ⓙ})(1 - p_2^{ⓙ}) \cdots (1 - p_n^{ⓙ}) = \prod_{i=1}^{n} (1 - p_i^{ⓙ}) \qquad (5.21)$$

in which i ranges over all n elements in the cut ⓙ. The probability of survival $R^{ⓙ}$ of cut ⓙ is

$$R^{ⓙ} = 1 - \prod_{i} (1 - p_i^{ⓙ}) \qquad (5.22)$$

*A proper subset has at least one less element than the set that contains the proper subset.

The simultaneous survival of all minimal cuts, or the reliability of the system, R_{MC}, in terms of the minimal cut heuristic is the probability

$$R_{MC} = \prod_j R^{\textcircled{j}} = \prod_j \left[1 - \prod_i (1 - p_i^{\textcircled{j}}) \right] \qquad (5.23)$$

in which j ranges over all minimal cuts of the system.

For example, in Figure 5.34 we have

$$R^{\textcircled{1}} = 1 - \prod_{i=1}^{2} (1 - p_i^{\textcircled{1}}) = 1 - (1 - p_A)(1 - p_B)$$

$$R^{\textcircled{2}} = 1 - \prod_{i=1}^{2} (1 - p_i^{\textcircled{2}})$$

$$R^{\textcircled{3}} = 1 - \prod_{i=1}^{3} (1 - p_i^{\textcircled{3}})$$

$$R^{\textcircled{4}} = 1 - \prod_{i=1}^{3} (1 - p_i^{\textcircled{4}})$$

$$R_{MC} = \prod_{j=1}^{4} R^{\textcircled{j}}$$

If we assume the same reliability p for each of the five elements in Figure 5.34, we have

$$R_{MC} = [1 - (1 - p)^2] [1 - (1 - p)^2] [1 - (1 - p)^3] [1 - (1 - p)^3]$$
$$= [1 - (1 - p)^2]^2 [1 - (1 - p)^3]^2$$

With $q = 1 - p$ we can write

$$R_{MC} = (1 - q^2)^2 (1 - q^3)^2$$

LOWER BOUND

The probability R_{MC} of equation (5.23) is lower than the actual reliability of the system because of the independence assumption. If no failure occurs in a minimal cut k and an element in cut k also appears in minimal cut l, the probability of survival of cut l given that cut k survived is larger than* $R^{\textcircled{l}}$, as it would appear in equation (5.22). Therefore, the actual reliability of the system is equal to or larger than that calculated from equation (5.23) using the minimal cut heuristic.

Example

For the system of Figure 5.34 we obtain the following results for reliability using the exact expression of equation (5.20) and the minimal cut calculations of equation (5.23). We assume all elements to have the same reliability p.

*It is equal to 1 because a cut fails only when all its elements fail [see equation (5.21)].

Element Reliability	Exact [Eq. (5.20)]	Minimal Cut [Eq. (5.23)]
0.99	0.9998	0.9998
0.95	0.9948	0.9948
0.90	0.9785	0.9781
0.75	$882/2^{10}$	$872/2^{10}$
0.50	$512/2^{10}$	$441/2^{10}$

5.13 Summary

Realistic decision makers know that they must often act before all uncertainty is dispelled. Relevant information may increase or decrease the perceived level of uncertainty. The tools of probability deal with uncertainty and the concept of information. To develop the foundation for these tools, the following concepts are discussed.

The universe in a situation under consideration includes all the events that can take place in the situation. A universe defines the boundaries of a problem. A compound event is a combination of elementary events.

A probability of an event is a ratio of two numbers defined in terms of a universe of events. The denominator represents the count of all possible events, and the numerator is a subset of the universe whose probability of occurrence we wish to assess.

A probability has a numerical value between 0 and 1. The universe in probability problems is known as a sample space, and an elementary event in the sample space is called a simple event.

Events are mutually exclusive when they cannot occur at the same time. Two events are independent when the probability of one event does not change when we learn that the second event had occurred.

Bayes' equation can be used to assess the relevance of information and to update the probability of an event on the basis of relevant information.

Demonstrative reasoning leads to one correct objective conclusion and is impersonal. Plausible reasoning leads to plausible conclusions that are personal and subjective in nature. The connection between plausible reasoning and credibility is discussed. Examples illustrate the nature of plausible reasoning in reaching decisions in court and in judging the credibility of a scientific theory.

Probabilities can be assessed by representing information in a matrix form or in a tree diagram. The two representations are shown side by side by an illustrative example. The tree diagram is a more powerful and useful form of representation.

A tree diagram is used to assess credibility in the study of Mr. Shackleton's ESP powers.

The concept of information is shown to be related to the concept of probability. The measurement of amount of information acquired in a situation where events are uncertain is defined as the minimum average number of binary questions required to dispel the uncertainty about the events in the situation.

The procedure employed to approach the minimum average number of questions to dispel uncertainty is known as the method of halving. Namely, the questions are posed in a way that attempts to come as close as possible to reducing the uncertainty by one-half following each binary question at each stage in the questioning process.

A number of examples are given to show how selective rejection of portions of the universe of possibilities leads us to dispel uncertainty in a most efficient way.

It is shown that the length of a binary code word that is assigned to an event is related to the probability of its occurrence. The more probable events are assigned short code names, and since we cannot assign short code words to all events, the longer codes are assigned to the less probable events.

This procedure keeps the average number of code symbols small. Morse used this procedure to create the famous Morse code. He assigned the dot, the shortest code, to the most frequent letter in the English language, the "e."

The Huffman tree is a systematic procedure for assigning binary code names to a universe of events with known probabilities of occurrence. The procedure leads to an assignment of code names that approaches the minimum average length of code name for the universe of events. This minimum average length of code name (or code word) is known as the entropy of the universe of events. The entropy, H, for n events E_i ($i = 1, 2, 3, \ldots, n$) and associated probabilities $P(E_i)$ is calculated from the equation

$$H = \sum_{i=1}^{n} p(E_i) \log_2 \frac{1}{p(E_i)}$$

The entropy H provides a lower bound on the average length of a binary code for the universe of n events E_i considered.

The Huffman tree provides the sequence for asking binary questions to dispel uncertainty in a most efficient way.

Aggregation of events E_i in strings can improve the efficiency of coding. The average length of code word can be made to approach more closely the theoretical lower bound established by the entropy H of the source by using long strings of events. However, the longer the string, the longer the time delay required before a string can be transmitted.

Reliability of a system is defined as the probability that it will operate successfully. System reliability is affected by the manner in which the system elements are connected. Elements can be connected in series and in parallel. The study of reliability of complex systems may require extensive computations. A heuristic is introduced to provide a lower bound on the reliability of a complex system using a reduced computational effort.

PROBLEMS

5.1. If two events are mutually exclusive, are they dependent or independent events? Explain.

5.2. Can two events be independent and mutually exclusive?

5.3. If two events are not mutually exclusive, are they dependent or independent events? Explain your answer using a Venn diagram.

5.4. Consider an event A in a universe T as shown in Figure 5.2. Show how the universe T can be reduced in size without a change in the probability of event A.

5.5. What are the upper and lower bounds on $p(A)$ and $p(B)$ when $B \rightarrow A$?

5.6. Consider the decision model of Figure 1.3. Let us suppose that each state of nature has the same probability of occurrence $1/3$. What actions would you take if you wish to maximize the probability of making no less than a total of $100,000 in the next two years?

5.7. Discuss the assumptions in the model of Figure 5.5 and the potential for errors. In particular, what are the implications of the premise $G \rightarrow E$?

5.8. Show how Examples 1 and 2 in Section 5.5 are related.

5.9. Calculate the probability of disease D in Figure 5.12 given that five tests were given with the first three positive and the last two negative.

5.10. How could you make more certain that medical tests are independent?

5.11. In Figure 5.12 we claim that we do not have a perfect test to detect disease D. How can we justify identifying 40% of the population as having the disease? Discuss.

5.12. What basic assumptions are made in the tree diagram of Figure 5.16?

5.13. Suppose that a box contains 20 bottles; eight are Coke, five Pepsi, four Seven-Up, two Dr. Pepper, and one Tab. Your friend takes out one of the bottles and asks you to figure out what he has. How many binary questions will you ask on the average? The first question could be: "Is it Coke or Dr. Pepper?" This leads to half the uncertainty being rejected in the first question. Or the first question could be: "Is it Coke?" This divides the uncertainty into $8/20$ and $12/20$. Which of these questions will lead to a more even division of the uncertainty for the complete sequence of questions as shown in Figure P5.13.?

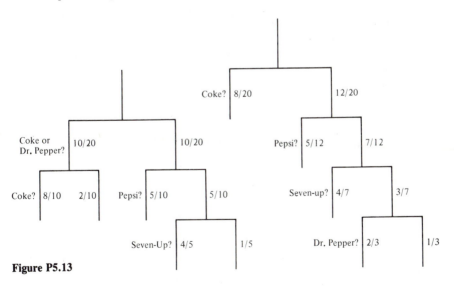

Figure P5.13

5.14. Describe the relationship between information and probability.

5.15. How does the concept of independence in probability differ from the daily use of the term "independence"? Give examples.

5.16. What is the key concept in information theory that makes it possible to identify the odd coin in three weighings in Problem 13 of Section 2.20?

5.17. Show that using 19 questions, you will identify a word selected randomly by a friend in a book that has 512 pages or less, 64 lines per page or less, and 16 words per line or less.

Find the Huffman codes for events with the following probabilities, and calculate the resulting average length of code words:

5.18. 4/9, 2/9, 2/9, 1/9

5.19. 1/2, 1/3, 1/6

5.20. 0.4, 0.2, 0.2, 0.1, 0.1

5.21. 1/3, 1/4, 1/5, 1/6, 1/20

5.22. 27/40, 9/40, 3/40, 1/40

5.23. 0.5, 0.25, 0.125, 0.100, 0.025

5.24. Generate the Huffman code for the second and third extensions of events E_1 and E_2 with probabilities 2/3 and 1/3, respectively.

5.25. We can build highly reliable systems out of less reliable elements by using redundancy of components in the system. Justify this statement and give examples to support it.

5.26. Verify the reliability expressions in Figure 5.33.

5.27. Use equations (5.20) and (5.23) to calculate the reliability of the system in Figure 5.34 for $p = 0.40$ and $p = 0.20$. Discuss the two answers.

5.28. How could you use the Huffman tree to search for an item that you have misplaced at home, in the car, or in your office? You are not sure where you last had it in your hands.

5.29. Discuss the costs and benefits of aggregating events in the code extension process. What is the relationship between benefit and time delay in Figures 5.25 and 5.26? Generate the fourth extension for the two events E_1 and E_2 with probabilities 0.8 and 0.2, respectively. How much improved efficiency in average code word length is obtained in going from a three-day to a four-day extension?

5.30. Is the Morse code an instantaneous code? Discuss.

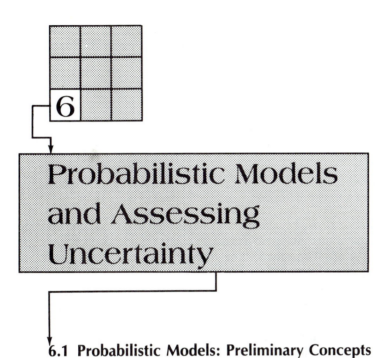

Probabilistic Models and Assessing Uncertainty

6.1 Probabilistic Models: Preliminary Concepts

LOAD-CARRYING CAPACITY OF REPRESENTATIVE NECKLACE

Let us suppose that we are producing necklaces. The necklaces have objects of varying weights suspended from them. We wish to establish a quantitative measure for the weight- or load-carrying capacity of a typical representative necklace. Each necklace is constructed from the same material and has the same dimensions. However, imperfections in the production and assembly process cause the capacity C in pounds to vary. To establish a measure of C, we design an experiment in which each necklace in a sample of necklaces is subjected to a progressively increasing load until it breaks. The breaking load is designated as C. C may, of course, vary from necklace to necklace. We can plot the results of our experiment as shown in Figure 6.1. Each time a necklace fails at loads between the limits $[C + (1/2)\,\Delta C]$ and $[C - (1/2)\,\Delta C]$, we draw one square above C. In Figure 6.1 we have such a plot for a sample of 50 necklaces, with $\Delta C = 2$ pounds. The total number of necklaces that failed for loads smaller than 41 pounds, for example, is given by the number of squares to the left of $C = 41$ pounds (i.e., 30). We can use this number to predict the probability that a necklace will fail (break) under a load smaller than 41 pounds by taking the ratio of the total number of necklaces that failed below 41 pounds divided by the total number of necklaces in the sample tested [i.e., 30/50, or, using compact notation, $P(C < 41) = 30/50 = 0.6$]. If, instead of the *number* of squares in Figure 6.1, we consider the *area* represented by the squares, the same result will

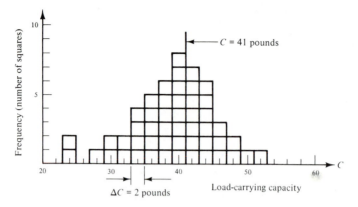

Figure 6.1 Plot of frequency versus load capacity for 50 necklaces.

be obtained for $P(C < 41)$ by taking the area to the left of $C = 41$ and dividing it by the total area of the squares. We can also adjust the area of each square so that the total area of all squares will be unity. In this case, $P(C < 41)$ will simply be equal to the area to the left of $C = 41$.

Extending the experiment to a large number N of necklaces and taking ΔC vanishing small, the plot of Figure 6.1 will approach the continuous curve of Figure 6.2 as $N \rightarrow \infty$ and $\Delta C \rightarrow 0$. Again, we can make the total area under the curve in Figure 6.2 equal to unity so that $P(C < C_1)$ will be equal to the area under the curve $p(C)$ to the left of C_1.

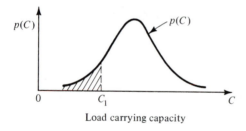

Load carrying capacity

Figure 6.2 Probability of load-carrying capacity C for necklaces.

PROBABILITY DISTRIBUTION

The function $p(C)$ of Figure 6.2 is called a *probability density function* or *distribution function* of random variable C, where in the present example C represents the load-carrying capacity of a necklace. To evaluate the area under the curve of Figure 6.2, the shape of the curve $p(C)$ must be established. This is not a simple task in most cases. For the purpose of this presentation we will assume that $p(C)$ is the *normal distribution function*, which is given by

$$p(C) = \frac{1}{\sigma_c \sqrt{2\pi}} e^{-(1/2)[(C-\mu_c)/\sigma_c]^2} \tag{6.1}$$

in which μ_c and σ_c^2 are, respectively, called the *mean* and *variance* of C. The mean μ_c is a measure of the location of the distribution (analogous to center of gravity of an area). The variance σ_c^2 is a measure of the dispersion (spread) of the distribution $p(C)$ (analogous to the moment of inertia of an area with respect to a vertical line through its center of gravity). The larger the variance, the more spread is the area under $p(C)$ about the mean. The normal distribution is completely characterized by the two parameters μ_c and σ_c^2, as seen from the equation.

The normal distribution is very important and has great utility. This is due to one of the most important theorems in mathematics, called the *central limit theorem*. To point out the significance of this theorem in terms of our present example, let us consider Figure 6.2. Suppose that in this figure each value of C represents the average load-carrying capacity of n necklaces; then, invoking the central limit theorem, it can be shown that as n gets large the distribution $p(C)$ of these average capacities C will approach the normal distribution (also referred to as the *Gaussian distribution*) irrespective of what shape the distribution $p(C)$ has when $n = 1$. The normal distribution and its use is discussed in more detail in Section 6.4 following the development of some preliminary general concepts in probabilistic models.

6.2 Population and Samples

POPULATION

A population is defined as a set which contains all the possible observations (real and hypothetical) of a particular attribute (phenomenon or measurement). For example, we may speak of the population of heights of U.S. citizens, the population of yearly incomes of U.S. citizens, the population of all possible measurements of length of a pencil, the population of outcomes resulting from the flip of a coin n times, and so on. A population can be finite or infinite in terms of the number of observations it contains. The concept of a population is similar to the concept of the universe or *universal set*. The universal set is the original complete set which contains *all the elements* in the subject of discourse. In a similar way, *population* refers to the total of all measurements or observations of interest or concern.

SAMPLE

A sample is a subset of a population. For example, we may speak of a sample of five measurements of height of five different U.S. citizens. Similarly, we may obtain a sample of yearly incomes, a sample of measurements of length of a pencil, and a sample of outcomes in the flip of a coin. Schematically, the relationship between a population and a sample from the population is shown in Figure 6.3. In the language of sets we have then the *sample as a subset of the population* (i.e., the sample is contained in the population). The population is the *sample space*.

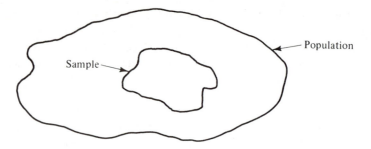

Figure 6.3 Relationship between population and sample (the population is the sample space).

AGGREGATION OF MEASUREMENTS

Let us suppose that the President of the United States desires to determine the economic well-being of the country. To do so, he requests that the income of each family in the country in the last year be presented to him. The President soon discovers that the "seven plus or minus two" limit in human information processing [2] is presenting him with a real constraint, and the only way he can get the total picture is to give up detail and aggregate the millions of numbers, or income figures, which represent the elements of the population.

Suppose that we have N families and m different incomes x_i ($i = 1, 2, \ldots, m$). $m \leq N$ because some families may have the same income, so that x_i is the income of each of n_i families and x_j the income of each of n_j families; $\sum_{i=1}^{m} n_i = N$. The President aggregates the measurements x_i into parameters to describe the population. One parameter is a measure of *central location* or the *mean* of the x_i, also referred to as *expected value* μ of x_i:

$$\mu = \frac{1}{N} \sum_{i=1}^{m} n_i x_i = \sum_{i=1}^{m} f_i x_i \tag{6.2}$$

in which

$$f_i = \frac{n_i}{N} \qquad \sum_i f_i = 1$$

f_i represents a measure of "density" (i.e., the fraction of families that have yearly income x_i). The mean μ gives an idea of income per "average family." However, it is quite possible that very few families have an income close to the mean, while many have a smaller income, and very few have a much larger income. Yet it is also possible that most families have, indeed, an income close to μ. To get a better idea as to which of those situations is more representative of reality, we aggregate the data in the form of a *parameter of dispersion* called the *population variance* σ^2, which is computed as follows:

$$\sigma^2 = \sum_i f_i (x_i - \mu)^2 \tag{6.3}$$

σ^2 is the sum of the squares of the deviations of individual family incomes x_i from the mean income μ. The smaller σ^2, the more representative μ is as a model of *family income* in the country. For the extreme case of $\sigma^2 = 0$, μ is the income of each family. The larger σ^2, the larger the dispersion in incomes and the less representative μ is as a model of family income.

POPULATION PARAMETERS AND SAMPLE STATISTICS

μ and σ^2 are population parameters descriptive of location and dispersion. In many cases these quantities are not known, cannot be computed, or require too much computational effort. In such cases, *estimates* for the population parameters μ and σ^2 are computed from a sample of the population.* Such estimates are called *statistics*. Consider a sample of size n with measurements $x_i, \ldots, x_n$. The estimate $\hat{\mu}$ for μ is the *sample mean $\bar{x}$*:

$$\hat{\mu} = \bar{x} = \frac{1}{n} \sum_i x_i \tag{6.4}$$

and the estimate $\hat{\sigma}_2$ for σ^2 is the *sample variance s^2*:

$$\hat{\sigma}^2 = s^2 = \frac{1}{n-1} \sum_i (x_i - \bar{x})^2 \tag{6.5}$$

For large sample sizes (i.e., n large), $n - 1$ can be replaced by n with little influence on the results.

DEDUCTIVE AND INDUCTIVE INFERENCE REVISITED

When a population is known, we can deduce certain conclusions regarding the attributes of a sample from the population. This is a process of deductive inference in which we go from the general to the limited, that is, from the universal set to a subset or from the population to a sample. The reverse process takes place in inductive inference, when we use the measurements from a sample (i.e., the sample statistics) to infer the population parameters. Here we attempt to go from the limited to the general, from a subset to the universal set. Inductive inference involves states of partial knowledge and therefore requires that the degree of uncertainty in the inferences be assessed.

Deductive inference can be likened to a process in which conclusions are derived from a population with no new knowledge generated. Inductive inference is a process of generalization in which new knowledge may be generated.

---

*μ and σ^2 are not the only parameters, although very commonly used. Additional parameters, such as measures of symmetry and other measures, can be generated for a more complete description of the population.

6.3 Probability Distribution Models

Consider the function $p(x)$ shown in Figure 6.4. x is the random variable and may refer to the strength of a necklace discussed in Section 6.1. Suppose that function $p(x)$ has the following properties:

1. $p(x)$ is equal to or larger than zero.
2. The area under the curve for $p(x)$ is one unit.
3. The probability $F(b)$ that a randomly selected necklace will have a strength in pounds smaller than $x = b$ is given by the area under $p(x)$ to the left of $x = b$.
4. The probability that a randomly selected necklace will have a strength x in pounds larger than a and smaller than b is given by the area under $p(x)$ between the values of $x = a$ and $x = b$.
5. The probability that a necklace will have a strength larger than $x = a$ is $1 - F(a)$.

A function $p(x)$ with the above properties is called a *probability density function** or *frequency function* of random variable x. The variable x is random when, for all we know, all extraneous influences that may affect outcomes have been removed from the model.

The *cumulative distribution function* $F(x)$ is a monotonically increasing function derived from $p(x)$ (Figure 6.4b). For example, $F(a)$ is the probability of a necklace having a strength less than a pounds, and $F(b) - F(a)$ is the probability of a necklace having a strength smaller than b pounds but larger than a pounds.

In Figure 6.4b, the ordinate $F(a)$ for $x = a$ has a numerical value equal to the area under $p(x)$ in Figure 6.4a to the left of $x = a$. Similarly, $F(b)$ has a numerical value equal to the area under $p(x)$ to the left of $x = b$. $F(b) - F(a)$ is then equal to the area under $p(x)$ between $x = a$ and $x = b$.

*The probability density function is also sometimes referred to as a distribution function.

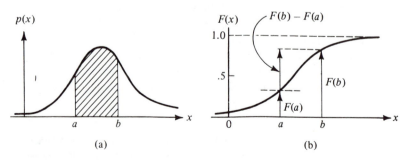

(a)   (b)

Figure 6.4 (a) Probability density function or frequency function; (b) cumulative distribution function.

There are a number of well-known distribution functions which can be characterized by a small number of parameters and can serve as models to represent various phenomena of interest. Probability density functions fall into two main classes: discrete and continuous. In a *discrete function,* the random variable takes on discrete values, such as the number of heads in the toss of 50 coins. In a *continuous function,* the variable is continuous, such as the length of pencils in a pencil factory. In Section 6.4 we discuss the most important of the continuous distribution models, the normal distribution.

6.4 The Normal Distribution Model

One of the most important and useful continuous distributions is the bell-shaped function of Figure 6.5, called the *normal distribution.* It is completely described by specifying two parameters, the mean μ and the variance σ^2 in the following equation for a random variable x:

$$p(x) = \frac{1}{\sigma\sqrt{2\pi}} e^{-(1/2)[(x-\mu)/\sigma]^2} \tag{6.6}$$

The cumulative normal distribution function $F(x)$ is equal to the area under $p(x)$ to the left of x. As seen in Figure 6.6, the larger σ^2, the more spread is the distribution. To use an analog from mechanics, the location μ can be viewed as the center of gravity of the area under the probability density function along the x axis, and σ^2 is the moment of inertia of the area with respect to a vertical axis going through μ. Namely, each strip $p(x)\,dx$ is multiplied by the square of its distance from μ, $(x - \mu)^2$; the products are added for all strips and in the limit, as $dx \to 0$, the sum becomes equal to the variance σ^2.

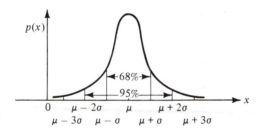

Figure 6.5

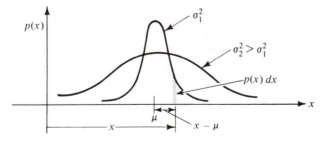

Figure 6.6

The square root of the variance is called the *standard deviation* σ. The standard deviation provides some standard measures regarding the normal distribution as follows. The probability of obtaining an observation x between the values of $\mu - \sigma$ and $\mu + \sigma$ is 0.68. Namely, the probability that x will not differ from the mean μ by more than one standard deviation or σ units is 0.68 (see Figure 6.5). Similarly, the probabilities are 0.95 and 0.998 that x will not differ from μ by more than 2σ and 3σ, respectively. For example, consider the scores in an examination to be represented by a model of the normal distribution function with mean $\mu = 65$ points and variance $\sigma^2 = 49$ (i.e., $\sigma = 7$ points). On the basis of this model we can make the following probabilistic predictions. The probabilities are 0.68 that a student will score between $65 - 7$ and $65 + 7$ points, 0.95 for a score in the range 51 to 79, and 0.998 for a score in the range 44 to 86. Since the distribution is symmetrical with respect to the mean μ with one-half the area to the right and one-half to the left, we can also answer the following questions. What is the probability of a student scoring above $\mu + \sigma$, or above $\mu + 2\sigma$, or $\mu + 3\sigma$? The probabilities are 0.16, 0.025, and 0.001, respectively, and are generated as follows. The probability of $\mu - \sigma < x < \mu + \sigma$ is 0.68. Therefore, the probability of x outside this range is $1 - 0.68 = 0.32$; but since we are only interested in the high range $(x > \mu + \sigma)$, the answer is $0.32/2 = 0.16$ because of symmetry of the normal distribution. Similar arguments lead to the values of 0.025 and 0.001. Thus the probability of a student scoring more than $\mu + 2\sigma = 65 + 14 = 79$ is 0.025, and 0.001 for more than 86.

We can easily commit to memory the numbers 0.68, 0.95, and 0.998. However, suppose that a student wishes to calculate the probability of a grade B or better in the examination, when the teacher announces that a grade of B or better requires a score above 75. This score is $\mu + (10/7)\sigma$. We know that the desired probability is smaller than 0.16, which is the probability for $x > \mu + \sigma = 72$, but larger than 0.025, which is the probability for $x > \mu + 2\sigma = 79$. To get the answer, we will need to compute the area $F(x)$ under the normal distribution curve for $\mu = 65$ and $\sigma = 7$ to the right of $x = 75$. We could calculate such areas and record the values of the cumulative distribution for values of x spaced at very close intervals such as 0.1 apart. However, for a different problem in which the normal distribution model is used, μ and σ^2 may be different and the table of $F(x)$ values for $\mu = 65$ and $\sigma = 7$ will require modification. It is, therefore, customary to resort to a standard normal distribution table, which can be used regardless of what the value of μ and σ^2 are in the model considered, as long as the variable is considered to be normally distributed.

6.5 Standard Normal Distribution and Its Use

The *standard normal distribution* is characterized as distinct from all other normal distributions by the fact that it has a mean $\mu = 0$ and variance $\sigma^2 = 1$

and hence standard deviation $\sigma = 1$. Table 6.1 gives the value of the cumulative distribution function $F(z)$ for various values of the standard normal variable, which is designated by the letter z. In general, it is customary to denote the fact that variable x is normally distributed with mean μ_x and variance σ_x^2 (the subscript x identifies the variable of the distribution) in the form $N(\mu_x, \sigma_x^2)$. Using this notation, variable z has a distribution $N(0, 1)$, that is, a normal distribution with mean $\mu_z = 0$ and variance $\sigma_z^2 = 1$. Equation (6.6) then becomes

$$P(z) = \frac{1}{\sqrt{2\pi}} e(-1/2)z^2 \tag{6.7}$$

Values of $p(z)$ for values of z from 0 to 3.0 are given in Table 6.2.

Using Table 6.1, we can find, for example, $P(z < 1.66)$, designated $F(1.66)$, by going to the value recorded in the row to the right of $z = 1.6$ under the column for 0.06, that is, $P(z < 1.66) = 0.9515$. Using this result, $P(z > 1.66) = 1 - 0.9515 = 0.0485$. The values $F(z)$ for negative values of z are obtained from the symmetry of the distribution, $F(-z) = 1 - F(z)$. For example, $F(-0.82) = 1 - 0.7939 = 0.2061$. As another example,

$$P(-0.44 < z < 1.53) = F(1.53) - F(-0.44)$$

$$= F(1.53) - [1 - F(0.44)]$$

$$= 0.9370 - (1 - 0.6700)$$

$$= 0.6070$$

USE OF STANDARD NORMAL DISTRIBUTION

Table 6.1 can be used as a model for any normal distribution $N(\mu_x, \sigma_x^2)$. This is achieved by transforming distribution $N(\mu_x, \sigma_x^2)$ of random variable x to a standard normal distribution $N(0, 1)$ of random variable z. Figure 6.7 shows on the same abscissa (horizontal coordinate) a normal distribution $N(19, 9)$ of variable x, that is, $\mu_x = 19$, $\sigma_x^2 = 9$, and the standard normal distribution $N(0, 1)$ of variable z. If we now subtract μ_x from variable x, the distribution $p(x)$ of x will be shifted to the left, as shown by the dashed-line curve $p(x - \mu_x)$ in Figure 6.7. The mean of the shifted distribution is zero; namely, it was transformed from $N(\mu_x, \sigma_x^2)$ to $N(0, \sigma_x^2)$. Next, we squeeze in the distribution symmetrically toward the mean and pull it up at the same time, so that the area under the curve remains 1, until the dashed curve $p(x - \mu_x)$ becomes identical to $p(z)$ in Figure 6.7. The squeezing reduces the horizontal scale of $p(x - \mu_x)$ by a factor of $1/\sigma_x$ and increases the vertical scale by a factor of σ_x.

Figure 6.7 shows 11 numbered rectangles, one standard deviation from the mean for $p(x)$ and $p(z)$. The sums of areas of the rectangles are identical for both distributions as is the area one standard deviation σ to the right of the mean in any normal distribution, that is, 0.34 or 34% of the total area. The squeezing operation is merely a change in the dimensions of the rectangles in $p(x)$ to those in $p(z)$ without change in area. The two-step operation described is a transformation of variable x to variable z from this formula:

Table 6.1 Values of cumulative distribution $F(z)$ for the standard normal distribution $N(0, 1)$

$F(z)$ for negative z are obtained from symmetry
$F(-z) = 1 - F(z)$. $F(1.27) = 0.8980$; $F(-0.82) = 1 - 0.7939 = 0.2061$

z	0.00	0.01	0.02	0.03	0.04	0.05	0.06	0.07	0.08	0.09
0.0	0.5000	0.5040	0.5080	0.5120	0.5160	0.5199	0.5239	0.5279	0.5319	0.5359
0.1	0.5398	0.5438	0.5478	0.5517	0.5557	0.5596	0.5636	0.5675	0.5714	0.5753
0.2	0.5793	0.5832	0.5871	0.5910	0.5948	0.5987	0.6026	0.6064	0.6103	0.6141
0.3	0.6179	0.6217	0.6255	0.6293	0.6331	0.6368	0.6406	0.6443	0.6480	0.6517
0.4	0.6554	0.6591	0.6628	0.6664	0.6700	0.6736	0.6772	0.6808	0.6844	0.6879
0.5	0.6915	0.6950	0.6985	0.7019	0.7054	0.7088	0.7123	0.7157	0.7190	0.7224
0.6	0.7257	0.7291	0.7324	0.7357	0.7389	0.7422	0.7454	0.7486	0.7517	0.7549
0.7	0.7580	0.7611	0.7642	0.7673	0.7704	0.7734	0.7764	0.7794	0.7823	0.7852
0.8	0.7881	0.7910	0.7939	0.7967	0.7995	0.8023	0.8051	0.8078	0.8106	0.8133
0.9	0.8159	0.8186	0.8212	0.8238	0.8264	0.8289	0.8315	0.8340	0.8365	0.8389
1.0	0.8413	0.8438	0.8461	0.8485	0.8508	0.8531	0.8554	0.8577	0.8599	0.8621
1.1	0.8643	0.8665	0.8686	0.8708	0.8729	0.8749	0.8770	0.8790	0.8810	0.8830
1.2	0.8849	0.8869	0.8888	0.8907	0.8925	0.8944	0.8962	0.8980	0.8997	0.9015
1.3	0.9032	0.9049	0.9066	0.9082	0.9099	0.9115	0.9131	0.9147	0.9162	0.9177
1.4	0.9192	0.9207	0.9222	0.9236	0.9251	0.9265	0.9279	0.9292	0.9306	0.9319
1.5	0.9332	0.9345	0.9357	0.9370	0.9382	0.9394	0.9406	0.9418	0.9429	0.9441
1.6	0.9452	0.9463	0.9474	0.9484	0.9495	0.9505	0.9515	0.9525	0.9535	0.9545
1.7	0.9554	0.9564	0.9573	0.9582	0.9591	0.9599	0.9608	0.9616	0.9625	0.9633
1.8	0.9641	0.9649	0.9656	0.9664	0.9671	0.9678	0.9686	0.9693	0.9699	0.9706
1.9	0.9713	0.9719	0.9726	0.9732	0.9738	0.9744	0.9750	0.9756	0.9761	0.9767
2.0	0.9772	0.9778	0.9783	0.9788	0.9793	0.9798	0.9803	0.9808	0.9812	0.9817
2.1	0.9821	0.9826	0.9830	0.9834	0.9838	0.9842	0.9846	0.9850	0.9854	0.9857
2.2	0.9861	0.9864	0.9868	0.9871	0.9875	0.9878	0.9881	0.9884	0.9887	0.9890
2.3	0.9893	0.9896	0.9898	0.9901	0.9904	0.9906	0.9909	0.9911	0.9913	0.9916
2.4	0.9918	0.9920	0.9922	0.9925	0.9927	0.9929	0.9931	0.9932	0.9934	0.9936

z	0.00	0.01	0.02	0.03	0.04	0.05	0.06	0.07	0.08	0.09
2.5	0.9938	0.9940	0.9941	0.9943	0.9945	0.9946	0.9948	0.9949	0.9951	0.9952
2.6	0.9953	0.9955	0.9956	0.9957	0.9959	0.9960	0.9961	0.9962	0.9963	0.9964
2.7	0.9965	0.9966	0.9967	0.9968	0.9969	0.9970	0.9971	0.9972	0.9973	0.9974
2.8	0.9974	0.9975	0.9976	0.9977	0.9977	0.9978	0.9979	0.9979	0.9980	0.9981
2.9	0.9981	0.9982	0.9982	0.9983	0.9984	0.9984	0.9985	0.9985	0.9986	0.9986
3.0	0.9987	0.9987	0.9987	0.9988	0.9988	0.9989	0.9989	0.9989	0.9990	0.9990

Source: *Statistical Tables and Formulas*, A. Hald, John Wiley & Sons, Inc., New York, © 1952. Reprinted by permission of John Wiley & Sons, Inc.

Table 6.2 Ordinates of the standard normal density function $N(0, 1)$

$$p(z) = \frac{1}{\sqrt{2x}} e^{-z^2/2}$$

z	0.00	0.01	0.02	0.03	0.04	0.05	0.06	0.07	0.08	0.09
0.0	0.3989	0.3989	0.3989	0.3988	0.3986	0.3984	0.3982	0.3980	0.3977	0.3973
0.1	0.3970	0.3965	0.3961	0.3956	0.3951	0.3945	0.3939	0.3932	0.3925	0.3918
0.2	0.3910	0.3902	0.3894	0.3885	0.3876	0.3867	0.3857	0.3847	0.3836	0.3825
0.3	0.3814	0.3802	0.3790	0.3778	0.3765	0.3752	0.3739	0.3725	0.3712	0.3697
0.4	0.3683	0.3668	0.3653	0.3637	0.3621	0.3605	0.3589	0.3572	0.3555	0.3538
0.5	0.3521	0.3503	0.3485	0.3467	0.3448	0.3429	0.3410	0.3391	0.3372	0.3352
0.6	0.3332	0.3312	0.3292	0.3271	0.3251	0.3230	0.3209	0.3187	0.3166	0.3144
0.7	0.3123	0.3101	0.3079	0.3056	0.3034	0.3011	0.2989	0.2966	0.2943	0.2920
0.8	0.2897	0.2874	0.2850	0.2827	0.2803	0.2780	0.2756	0.2732	0.2709	0.2685
0.9	0.2661	0.2637	0.2613	0.2589	0.2565	0.2541	0.2516	0.2492	0.2468	0.2444
1.0	0.2420	0.2396	0.2371	0.2347	0.2323	0.2299	0.2275	0.2251	0.2227	0.2203
1.1	0.2179	0.2155	0.2131	0.2107	0.2083	0.2059	0.2036	0.2012	0.1989	0.1965
1.2	0.1942	0.1919	0.1895	0.1872	0.1849	0.1826	0.1804	0.1781	0.1758	0.1736
1.3	0.1714	0.1691	0.1669	0.1647	0.1626	0.1604	0.1582	0.1561	0.1539	0.1518
1.4	0.1497	0.1476	0.1456	0.1435	0.1415	0.1394	0.1374	0.1354	0.1334	0.1315

Table 6.2 Ordinates of the standard normal density function $N(0, 1)$ (*cont.*)

$$p(z) = \frac{1}{\sqrt{2x}} e^{-z^2/2}$$

z	0.00	0.01	0.02	0.03	0.04	0.05	0.06	0.07	0.08	0.09
1.5	0.1295	0.1276	0.1257	0.1238	0.1219	0.1200	0.1182	0.1163	0.1145	0.1127
1.6	0.1109	0.1092	0.1074	0.1057	0.1040	0.1023	0.1006	0.0989	0.0973	0.0957
1.7	0.0940	0.0925	0.0909	0.0893	0.0878	0.0863	0.0848	0.0833	0.0818	0.0804
1.8	0.0790	0.0775	0.0761	0.0748	0.0734	0.0721	0.0707	0.0694	0.0681	0.0669
1.9	0.0656	0.0644	0.0632	0.0620	0.0608	0.0596	0.0584	0.0573	0.0562	0.0551
2.0	0.0540	0.0529	0.0519	0.0508	0.0498	0.0488	0.0478	0.0468	0.0459	0.0449
2.1	0.0440	0.0431	0.0422	0.0413	0.0404	0.0396	0.0387	0.0379	0.0371	0.0363
2.2	0.0355	0.0347	0.0339	0.0332	0.0325	0.0317	0.0310	0.0303	0.0297	0.0290
2.3	0.0283	0.0277	0.0270	0.0264	0.0258	0.0252	0.0246	0.0241	0.0235	0.0229
2.4	0.0224	0.0219	0.0213	0.0208	0.0203	0.0198	0.0194	0.0189	0.0184	0.0180
2.5	0.0175	0.0171	0.0167	0.0163	0.0158	0.0154	0.0151	0.0147	0.0143	0.0139
2.6	0.0136	0.0132	0.0129	0.0126	0.0122	0.0119	0.0116	0.0113	0.0110	0.0107
2.7	0.0104	0.0101	0.0099	0.0096	0.0093	0.0091	0.0088	0.0086	0.0084	0.0081
2.8	0.0079	0.0077	0.0075	0.0073	0.0071	0.0069	0.0067	0.0065	0.0063	0.0061
2.9	0.0060	0.0058	0.0056	0.0055	0.0053	0.0051	0.0050	0.0048	0.0047	0.0046
3.0	0.0044	0.0043	0.0042	0.0040	0.0039	0.0038	0.0037	0.0036	0.0035	0.0034

Source: Statistical Tables and Formulas, A. Hald, John Wiley & Sons, Inc., New York, © 1952. Reprinted by permission of John Wiley & Sons, Inc.

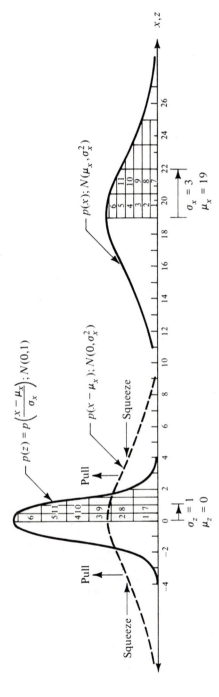

Figure 6.7 Standard normal distribution $N(0, 1)$. Distribution $N(\mu_x, \sigma_x^2)$ and transformation of $N(\mu_x, \sigma_x^2)$ to $N(0, 1)$.

205

$$z = \frac{x - \mu_x}{\sigma_x} \qquad (6.8)$$

$x - \mu_x$ is the shifting of the distribution to make the mean zero, and factor $1/\sigma_x$ is the squeezing,* or change in scale, to make the variance 1.

The transformation above reduces $N(\mu_x, \sigma_x^2)$ to $N(0, 1)$ and now Table 6.1 for standard normal variable z with $N(0, 1)$ can be used to make predictions regarding x in $N(\mu_x, \sigma_x^2)$.

For any value of x and corresponding z, from equation (6.8), we have

$$F(x) = F(z)$$

and in general,

$$P(x_1 < x < x_2) = P(z_1 < z < z_2)$$

in which

$$z_1 = \frac{x_1 - \mu_x}{\sigma_x}$$

and

$$z_2 = \frac{x_2 - \mu_x}{\sigma_x}$$

Example 1

Suppose that we wish to compute $P(x < \mu_x + \sigma_x)$ in Figure 6.7. This is equivalent to the area to the left of $x = 22$ under $p(x)$, but this area is also the same as the area to the left of $z = 1$ under $p(z)$, so we can read this value from Table 6.1 (i.e., 0.8413). In this example, $x = 22$ is transformed to $z = 1$. This transformation is obtained from

$$z = \frac{22 - 9}{3} = 1$$

Thus $P(x < 22) = P(z < 1) = 0.8413$.

Example 2

Consider a random variable x with distribution $N(65, 144)$. What is the probability of x larger than 80 [i.e., $P(x > x_1)$, $x_1 = 80$]?

$$P(x > x_1) = P(z > z_1)$$

$$z_1 = \frac{x_1 - \mu_x}{\sigma_x} = \frac{80 - 65}{12} = 1.25$$

$$P(z > 1.25) = 0.1056$$

Thus $P(x > 80) = 0.1056$.

---

*When $\sigma_x < 1$, the squeezing becomes a stretching away from the mean accompanied by a downward push of $p(x)$ to keep the area the same.

Example 3

What is the value x_1 of x in Example 2, for which the probability is 0.1788, that a random observation of x will be smaller than x_1? Namely, $P(x < x_1) = 0.1788$, $x_1 = ?$
$P(x < x_1) = P(z < z_1) = 0.1788$ from Table 6.1; z_1 must be negative because $P(z < 0) = 0.5$. It is equal to -0.92. Since

$$z_1 = \frac{x_1 - \mu_x}{\sigma_x}$$

then

$$-0.92 = \frac{x_1 - 65}{12}$$

and solving for x_1, we obtain

$$x_1 = 65 - 12 \times 0.92 = 53.96 \approx 54$$

Example 4

What is the variance σ_x^2 of a distribution $N(\mu_x, \sigma_x^2)$ if $\mu_x = 70$ and $P(x > 80) = 0.0062$?

$$P(x > x_1) = P(z > z_1) = 0.0062$$

Using Table 6.1,

$$z_1 = 2.50$$

Using the transformation of equation (6.8) yields

$$z_1 = \frac{x_1 - \mu_x}{\sigma_x}$$

with

$$z_1 = 2.50, \quad x_1 = 80, \quad \mu_x = 70$$

Then

$$2.50 = \frac{80 - 70}{\sigma_x}$$

and

$$\sigma_x = \frac{10}{2.5} = 4$$

$$\sigma_x^2 = 16$$

Example 5

Find the mean μ_x of $N(\mu_x, 36)$, given that $P(x < 75) = 0.8315$.

$$P(x < x_1) = P(z < z_1) = 0.8315$$

Thus $z_1 = 0.96$:

$$z_1 = \frac{x_1 - \mu_x}{\sigma_x}$$

with

$$z_1 = 0.96, \; x_1 = 75, \; \sigma_x = 6$$

Then

$$0.96 = \frac{75 - \mu_x}{6}$$

and

$$\mu_x = 75 - 5.76 = 69.24$$

6.6 Testing Hypotheses: Assessing Errors of Omission and Commission

In testing the validity of a hypothesis, we continue to subscribe to it as long as we do not have sufficient evidence to reject it. We do not prove it to be right or wrong in an absolute sense. Proving it right implies exhausting all possibilities of proving it wrong. This can never be accomplished since there are always the attempts of the future. Proving it wrong on the basis of an experiment implies absolute faith in the results of the experiment, but the future may show the experiment to be inaccurate or irrelevant, or the credibility of the results may be questioned. For example, the premise that the speed of light is constant may be accepted as true because no evidence exists to the contrary. However, the future may lead to new evidence. But then the evidence may be questioned at some point in time.

This indicates that our faith in a hypothesis is maintained on a tentative basis until "sufficient evidence" can be introduced as cause for rejecting it. The hypothesis may be our subscription to a particular population as a model for a problem of interest. In this section we attempt to qualify the significance of sufficient evidence through the use of information extracted from a statistical sample from which we can make an inference regarding the population that is stipulated (hypothesized) as our model. Such a sample contains incomplete information, and therefore we may commit one of two errors in our decision regarding the hypothesis. We may reject it when it is true, or continue to subscribe to it when it is false. These two types of errors are the errors of omission and commission in the modeling process in general.

Example 1

A young physician is stationed on a remote island when she discovers that an epidemic is spreading among the inhabitants. In her office she finds a large supply of little white pills which, for a moment, she thinks are the kind prescribed for this epidemic. However, on reflection she recalls that a pill very similar in appearance, taste, and size is used for a different purpose and is detrimental if taken for the present epidemic. There are no facilities for testing the composition, and the doctor is not certain about it in the first place. All the doctor can find is a statement to the effect that the pills which would help stop the epidemic have a mean diameter of 10.00 millimeters (mm) and a standard deviation of 0.60 mm. The pills detrimental to the epidemic have a mean diameter of 10.50 mm and the same standard deviation of 0.60 mm. Our doctor is inclined by her original thought to make the claim or state the hypothesis referred to as the *null hypothesis* and designated as H_0: The pills come from the population with $\mu_0 = 10.00$ mm, or $H_0: \mu_0 = 10.00$ mm. However, there is the *alternative hypothesis* H_1 which is possible: The pills come from the population with $\mu_1 = 10.50$ mm, or $H_1: \mu_1 = 10.50$ mm. The doctor takes a sample of the pills, measures the sample diameter $\bar{x}$, and now must make a decision. There are two possibilities here: accept H_0 or reject H_0 (accept H_1). The truth may be H_0 or H_1. Before proceeding with the guides to a decision rule, let us study the consequences of our decisions, something we must always do in problem solving. Table 6.3 is a model of the possible consequences.

There are two situations of correct decisions and two errors from wrong decisions. *Type I error* is rejecting H_0 when true, namely, the doctor will not use the pill when she should. *Type II error* is accepting H_0 when false (i.e., H_1 is true), namely, the doctor will use the pills when she should not. As we shall discover, for a given sample size, we can make the probability of one of the errors smaller, but at the same time increase the other. The decision rule will therefore depend on which error is more costly or more damaging. In the language of utility theory, we may wish to make the expected utility a maximum. The utility of an outcome, u(outcome), is a quantitative measure, on a scale from 0 to 1, of benefit associated with each of the four outcomes in Table 6.3. Thus, say, for example, u(error II) $= 0$, u(error I) $= 0.3$, u(correct decision) $= 1$. Thus, if the utility of the type I error, u(error I), is larger than the utility of the type II error, because it is better not to give the correct medicine than to give the wrong one, and if we designate by α and β the probabilities of type I and type II errors, respectively, we write the following equations for the expected utility $E(u)$ associated with each decision (see Table 6.4):

Decision to accept H_0:

$$E(u) = (1 - \alpha)u(\text{correct decision}) + \beta u(\text{error II})$$

Decision to reject H_0:

$$E(u) = \alpha u(\text{error I}) + (1 - \beta)u(\text{correct decision})$$

In the present example we may wish to make β smaller than α, as seen from Table 6.4. Error I will cause a larger spread of the epidemic that may lead to some deaths and a prolonged suffering on the part of the infected people who will survive. Error II can be detrimental to survival by leading to complications in both the infected and uninfected people.

Table 6.3

	H_0 True	H_1 True
Accept H_0	Correct	Type II error
Reject H_0 (Accept H_1)	Type I error	Correct

Table 6.4

	Pills Are Good	Pills Not Good
Give Pills	Correct $P(\text{correct}) = 1 - \alpha$	$P(\text{error II}) = \beta$ (can be detrimental to survival)
Do Not Give Pills	$P(\text{error I}) = \alpha$ (more people infected, suffering of infected pro- longed)	Correct $P(\text{correct}) = 1 - \beta$

Decision Rule. Let us suppose that the physician in Example 1 takes a sample of $n = 25$ pills and computes $\bar{x}$ to be 10.15 mm. Using the central limit theorem, we can assume that $\bar{x}$ is approximately normally distributed. The two distributions for H_0 and H_1 are shown in Figure 6.8.

It is plausible to decide qualitatively that for values of $\bar{x}$ close to 10.00 mm we will be inclined to consider H_0 to be true, and for values closer to 10.50 mm we will be more inclined to consider H_1 to be true. Let us suppose that we wish to be more explicit and select a value $\bar{x}$ (decision) such that, if $\bar{x} < \bar{x}$ (decision) we accept H_0, and if $\bar{x} > \bar{x}$ (decision), we accept H_1.

Figure 6.8 shows the probability α for error type I [hatched area under H_0 to the right of $\bar{x}$ (decision)], that is, accepting H_1 when the sample comes from H_0; and the probability β of type II error [dark area under H_1 to the left of $\bar{x}$(decision)], that is, accepting H_0 when the sample comes from H_1. As we move the decision value $\bar{x}$(decision) to the right, β gets larger and α smaller. The reverse is true when $\bar{x}$(decision) is moved to the left. We can make both α and β smaller for a given $\bar{x}$(decision) by increasing the sample size n, because then the variance gets smaller and each distribution is more concentrated near its mean. However, for a fixed sample size n, our choice of $\bar{x}$(decision) will depend on our choice of α or β. If we elect to choose β, α is established by this choice; conversely, if we elect to choose α, β is established.

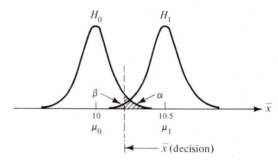

Figure 6.8 Distribution of $\bar{x}$ for H_0: $\mu_0 = 10.00$ mm and H_1: $\mu_1 = 10.50$ mm.

Probabilistic Models and Assessing Uncertainty   Chap. 6

In Example 1 it is possible that we may wish to delay a decision on whether to accept the hypothesis H_0 or reject it and decide to get more information. Instead of responding to the question "Should we accept H_0 with a 'yes' or a 'no'?", we shall admit a third response, "I do not know." This could be achieved by dividing the scale of measurement $\bar{x}$ in Figure 6.8 into three zones as shown in Figure 6.9. For $\bar{x} < \bar{x}$(lower bound) we accept H_0, for $\bar{x} > \bar{x}$(upper bound) we reject H_0, and for $\bar{x}$(lower bound) $< \bar{x} < \bar{x}$(upper bound), we state "I do not know," and we seek more information before we decide between accepting or rejecting H_0. The errors α and β are much smaller in Figure 6.9 than they are in Example 1, but the key question is: What is the cost of deciding to wait for more information, and what is the cost of obtaining the information?

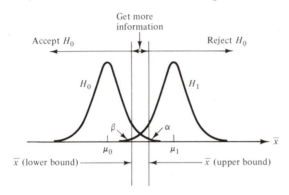

Figure 6.9   Three zones for decisions: accept H_0; reject H_0; get more information.

Example 2

You are a member of a petit jury. The hour of decision has arrived and you must cast your vote of guilty (G) or innocent (I) for the person on trial. These are the two strategies open to you. There are two corresponding states of nature (or true states of the world): innocent or guilty. The four entries in Table 6.5 designate the four possible outcomes. The first letter indicates what you say and the second what the true state is. As a rational person you study the consequence of your decisions before acting. Thus the outcome IG in which you claim the accused is innocent when in reality he is guilty may result in freedom for a guilty person. On the other hand, the outcome GI may result in punishment for an innocent person. II results in an innocent person freed, and GG results in the punishment of a guilty person. How do you assign a utility to represent your satisfaction with each of the four outcomes? We suppose that you might find it easier to rank the four

Table 6.5

		True State	
		Innocent I	Guilty G
You Claim	Innocent I	II	IG
	Guilty G	GI	GG

outcomes. For example, you might be most satisfied with II and least with GI. But how would you proceed to assess by numbers the strength of your feelings of satisfaction associated with each outcome? Your answer will depend on your values.

Consider a case in which you assign a prior probability $P(I) = 0.99$ to the probability that the person is innocent. After relevant evidence E is admitted, your state of knowledge may change. The relevance of the information submitted is decided by the judge; the judge also decides when to stop admitting evidence, and in so doing he participates in the modeling process by simplifying the case. You must now make a decision on how small $P(I|E)$ must be before you will claim, beyond a reasonable doubt (and yet some doubt, however small), that the person is guilty.

Let evidence E be the event that a piece of red fabric was found at the site of a crime where a struggle took place, and that the accused has a red jacket of the same fabric with a piece of the same size torn from it. Now we write

$$P(I|E) = P(I)\frac{P(E|I)}{P(E)}$$

in which

$$P(E) = P(E|I)P(I) + P(E|G)P(G)$$

Suppose that we have a reasonable way of calculating the relevance ratio $P(E|I)/P(E)$. How small must $P(I|E)$ be before you cast a vote for guilty?

This is a very subjective and individual matter. What is your attitude? How strong are your feelings of dissatisfaction when you are partner to the punishment of an innocent person? How strong are your feelings when a guilty person, who may endanger others, is freed? Which error should we strive to make smaller? Which error is smaller in our Western society? Is the attitude of our culture shared by other cultures? Can you describe situations in which our attitude toward the balance between type I and type II errors will change?

Using the terminology of Example 1, we can designate the null hypothesis H_0 as: The person is innocent, I, and the alternative hypothesis H_1: guilty G. Table 6.6 describes the consequences of the possible decisions.

Conceptually, the model of Table 6.6 is similar to that of Table 6.4. What is the difference with regard to information that will help to establish a decision rule? This example is to serve as food for thought and discussion regarding inference in general, which by definition is based on limited information and incomplete knowledge, and can be attended by *errors of omission* (send the guilty free) or *commission* (commit the innocent to prison).

Table 6.6

	Innocent, H_0 True	Guilty, H_1 True
Claim Innocent, H_0	Correct $P(\text{correct}) = 1 - \alpha$	$P(\text{error II}) = \beta$ (accused may hurt someone)
Claim Guilty, H_1	$P(\text{error I}) = \alpha$ (punish innocent person)	Correct $P(\text{correct}) = 1 - \beta$

Example 3

In automatic pattern recognition, a straightness ratio x is used as a parameter to distinguish the letter B from the digit 8. The value of x is established by dividing the height h of the symbol by the arc length a of the left portion between the high and low points of the symbol, as in Figure 6.10.

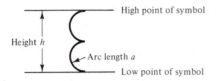

High point of symbol

Height h

Arc length a

Low point of symbol

Figure 6.10

The straightness ratio is closer to 1 for the symbol B, $x = h/a \leq 1$. Experiments with various shapes of B and 8 symbols yield the conditional probability density functions for $p(x \mid B)$ and $p(x \mid 8)$, as shown in Figure 6.11. Suppose that we use the following decision rule:

It is B for $x > 0.90$.
It is 8 otherwise.

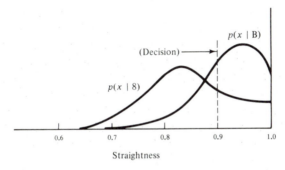

Figure 6.11 Probability distributions for straightness ratios of symbols 8 and B.

Suggested Problem 1. Identify the type I and II errors in Figure 6.11 and evaluate the corresponding probabilities of their occurrence by approximating the appropriate areas under the curves.

Consider a special case in which symbols 8 and B only are transmitted and must be identified, and suppose experience indicates that these symbols occur with probabilities $P(8) = 0.15$ and $P(B) = 0.85$, respectively. What is the probability that a symbol is B, given that the straightness ratio x is larger than $0.9 (x > 0.9)$? Using the tree diagram of Figure 6.12, we have

$$P(B \mid x > 0.9) = P(B) \frac{P(x > 0.9 \mid B)}{P(x > 0.9)}$$

Similarly,

$$P(8 \mid x > 0.9) = P(8) \frac{P(x > 0.9 \mid 8)}{P(x > 0.9)}$$

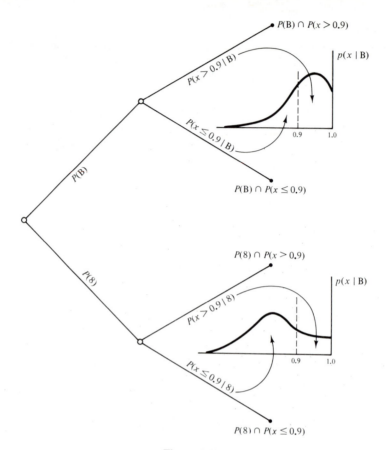

Figure 6.12

in which

$$P(x > 0.9) = P(x > 0.9 \,|\, B)P(B) + P(x > 0.9 \,|\, 8)P(8)$$

Suggested Problem 2. (a) Identify α and $(1 - \beta)$ in the equations above. (b) What is the expected number of wrong identifications in processing 1000 symbols (8 and B) if the decision rule remains: B for $x > 0.9$ and 8 otherwise? Give approximate answers working with the appropriate areas in Figure 6.11.

The choice of x (decision), such as 0.90 above, depends on the cost of errors. Let C_{8B} be the cost of claiming a symbol is 8 when it is B, and let C_{B8} be the cost of claiming a symbol is B when it is 8. Then the expected cost, $E(C)$, of errors is [x_D designates x(decision)]

$$E(C) = C_{8B}P(\text{claim } 8 \cap B \text{ true}) + C_{B8}P(\text{claim } B \cap 8 \text{ true})$$

$$= C_{8B}P(x \le x_D \,|\, B \text{ true})P(B \text{ true}) + C_{B8}P(x > x_D \,|\, 8 \text{ true})P(8 \text{ true})$$

$$= C_{8B}\beta P(B) + C_{B8}\alpha P(8)$$

The expressions for the probabilities can be identified from Figure 6.12. α and β are the probabilities of type I and type II errors, respectively. x_D can be adjusted, changing α and β to make $E(C)$ minimum.

Suggested Problem 3. Suppose that the straightness ratios of B and 8 are distributed as shown in Figure 6.13. An automatic system sorts the symbols. How could the errors α and β be reduced by introducing the option of waiting for more information? What could be the additional information?

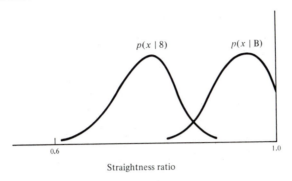

Figure 6.13

6.7 Assessing Uncertainty

One of the most important elements of a decision situation is the attitude we have to uncertainty. We can easily fall trap to biases in our assessment of levels of uncertainty and make decisions on the basis of faulty information. In the following discussion we develop an operational definition of degree of belief, or an encoding of our state of knowledge.

When we are faced with situations involving uncertainty regarding an event E, or a state of affairs, we resort to verbal expressions that represent a range of probabilities $P(E)$ for the event. Five such expressions and their approximate associated ranges of probabilities are given below:

E is almost certain to happen	$0.80 < P(E) < 0.99$
E has a very good chance	$0.65 < P(E) < 0.85$
We believe that E will happen	$0.65 < P(E) < 0.85$
E is likely	$0.50 < P(E) < 0.70$
E is probable	$0.45 < P(E) < 0.65$

The expressions are listed with an approximate range of probabilities of occurrence that the speaker may consider consistent with each statement. The following five statements are analogous to the five above and make reference to equivalent degrees of confidence or uncertainty about the nonoccurrence of an event:

E is almost certain not to happen

E has a very poor chance

We doubt that *E* will happen

E is unlikely

E is improbable

You may assign an equivalent range of probabilities to these statements, but there is no guarantee that your assignment will be acceptable to other people.

SUBJECTIVE OR PERSONAL PROBABILITY

The kind of probability we discuss here is not the "long-range relative frequency" type that is operational, in terms of frequency, namely, one for which an approximate numerical value can be obtained by observing the frequency of occurrence of an event: for example, flipping a coin and observing the number of heads. The probability considered here is not operational in this sense of frequency but can be evaluated by a person in an effort to assess the degree of confidence in the truth of a prediction. This is a *subjective* or *personal probability*. James Bernoulli presented this concept in 1713 as an alternative to the operational definition of probability viewed as a physical concept and capable of being measured from frequency of occurrence in a way similar to the measurement of other physical magnitudes such as mass, electric charge, velocity, distance, vibration, and frequency, all of which have specific operations that can be employed to find their magnitude. Bernoulli suggested that the *personal probability* or the *degree of confidence* depends on the knowledge of the person regarding the uncertain event. This was equivalent to defining a probability as a measure of state of knowledge. This definition can be equally applicable to unique as well as repetitive events. Similar definitions of probability were suggested by Laplace and by De Morgan in his *Formal Logic* (1847).

By introducing the concept of a reference gamble it is possible to employ an operational procedure to assess personal probability as shown in the following discussion.

OPERATIONAL DEFINITION OF PERSONAL PROBABILITY

Savage introduced the idea of a *reference gamble* to provide an operational definition of personal probabilities as shown by the following example.

Suppose you state that "Mr. X has a very good chance of being elected president of the United States." To assess your confidence or the state of knowledge you have in the prediction about Mr. X, we employ a reference gamble in the form of an urn with 100 marbles, 50 red and 50 white. You can win $1000 for a correct prediction of one of two events:

Event 1: The fate of Mr. X in the elections

Event 2: The color of a marble drawn at random from an urn with 100 marbles

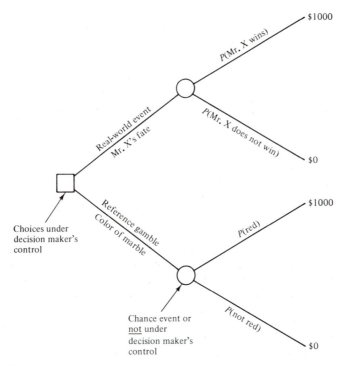

$1000

P(Mr. X wins)

Real-world event
Mr. X's fate

P(Mr. X does not win)

$0

Choices under
decision maker's
control

Reference gamble
Color of marble

$1000

P(red)

Chance event or
not under
decision maker's
control

P(not red)

$0

Figure 6.14 Choice between predicting real-world event or reference gamble event. The box indicates choices that the decision maker controls. The circles indicate chance events that the decision maker does not control.

The choice you have and the possible outcomes are shown in Figure 6.14. If you really believe that Mr. X has a better than 50% chance of being elected, you will choose to predict event 1. If you do so, we change the mix of marbles in the urn say to 99 red and 1 white and offer you again the two events, the faith of Mr. X and the new reference lottery. If you now choose the reference lottery, we reduce the number of red marbles say to 90, and increase the number of white to 10. We continue until a mix of marbles is found for which you are indifferent to a choice of the event for a prediction. Namely, a reference gamble is identified with r red marbles and $100 - r$ white marbles such that for $(r + 1)$ red marbles you choose the reference gamble, and for $(r - 1)$ red marbles you choose to predict Mr. X's fate. At this point of indifference the probability of a red marble is $r/100$, and this is the value assigned to your degree of confidence in the occurrence of the event of interest in the real world (i.e., Mr. X's election to the presidency).

Suppose that you consider a reference gamble with 70 red marbles and 30 white marbles as the mix for which you are indifferent between a prediction of the real-world event or this reference gamble shown in Figure 6.14. This encodes the level of confidence you have in the statement about Mr. X's election to the presidency.

When people assign personal probabilities, via reference gambles or directly, they normally have a tendency to overestimate their confidence. Namely, when they want an event to happen and it truly has a better than 50% chance of happening, they will assign it a higher confidence or personal probability than is justified on the basis of the available evidence. Similarly, when they wish an event not to happen and it truly has less than a 50% chance of happening, they assign a smaller probability than justified by the available evidence. Since a 0.5 probability represents a state of highest entropy or largest uncertainty, the biases above represent an overestimation of degree of confidence both for events with higher and lower than 50% chance of occurrence. This is shown in Figure 6.15, where the personal probabilities are further away from 0.5 than the probability of the actual event both above and below the 0.5 value. A perfect match between the true and personal probabilities is represented by the 45° line in Figure 6.15. Experiments that were conducted to generate Figure 6.15 included sequences of statements that had to be assessed as true or false. The actual relative frequency of true was then plotted against the estimated personal probability of true.

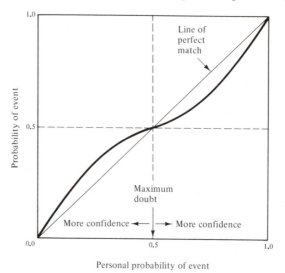

Figure 6.15 Relationship between true and personal probabilities.

OTHER BIASES IN DEGREES OF CONFIDENCE

Although Figure 6.15 indicates a tendency to overestimate degree of confidence in most cases, there are instances where the reverse is true. Consider, for example, the following situations.

Situation 1. There are 40 people in a group. What is your degree of confidence that there are two or more people in the group with the same birthday (month and day of the month only)?

Situation 2. Two urns, urn R with 70 red and 30 white marbles and urn W with 30 red and 70 white marbles, have the same outward appearance. Suppose that you take a sample from one of the urns and try to predict its content. All sampling is done with replacement. For each sample, independently assign the probability that it came from urn R.

Sample 1:   2 red and 1 white
Sample 2:   8 red and 4 white
Sample 3:   1 red
Sample 4:   2 red
Sample 5:   3 red
Sample 6:   4 red

The calculated probabilities are 0.7, 0.845, 0.927, and 0.967 (not given in the order of the sample number. We leave it as an exercise for you to match the probabilities with samples). The probability for one or more coincidence in birthday for 40 people is 0.89.

Situation 3. Suppose that we have five urns of type R and 15 urns of type W. Is a sample of eight red and four white marbles more likely to have come from an urn type R or urn type W?

The biases introduced in the level of confidence in responding to situations 1 and 2 are related to no appreciation for sample size influence on confidence. For example, did you consider the sample of two red and one white as convincing as the sample eight red and four white in situation 2 because the ratio of red to white marbles is the same in both samples? In situation 3 there is a tendency to compare the likelihoods of a sample from each class or type of urn (urn R and urn W) and ignore how representative each type is of the total universe considered. See references 40 to 42 for more discussions of biases in human information processing and their implications.

ASSESSMENT OF A PERSONAL PROBABILITY DISTRIBUTION

Suppose that you wish to guess my weight. You could establish upper and lower bounds by looking at me and concluding safely by taking a wide range that it is not less than 100 pounds and not more than 200 pounds. Now we follow a sequence of judgments that will provide more precision in the assessment. First, identify a weight W_1 such that it will divide the range between 100 and 200 pounds into two equally likely zones.

What we mean by this is the following. Suppose that you choose $W_1 = 160$ pounds. In this case we mean that if you are offered \$1000 for a correct prediction of my weight, you would be indifferent to whether you predict it to be above or below 160 pounds. Or stated another way: To win \$1000 for a correct prediction you would prefer to predict the outcome of any reference lottery in which two events have unequal probability of occurrence to predicting whether my weight is above or below W_1. Next, suppose that I step on a scale and tell you that my weight is above 160 pounds, and ask you to find a value W_2 that will divide the range 160 to 200 pounds into two equally probable zones. Say that you choose $W_2 = 170$ (if you are more certain about my weight being closer to 160 pounds, you could choose $W_2 = 165$, 163, etc.). Suppose that when I step on the scale I tell you that my weight is less than 160 pounds and now ask you to find a weight W_3 that divides the range 100 to 160 pounds into two equally probable zones. Say that you choose $W_3 = 155$ pounds. This process of dividing regions into two equally probable zones can continue to any level of precision in terms of weight. Figure 6.16 shows the values W_1, W_2, and W_3. The weights W_3, W_1, and W_2 are, respectively, the 0.25, 0.50, and 0.75 fractiles or the quartiles of the distribution. These fractiles are designated as $P_{0.25}$, $P_{0.50}$, and $P_{0.75}$, as follows:

$$P_{0.25} = P(W \leq W_3 = 155 \text{ pounds}) = 0.25$$

$$P_{0.50} = P(W \leq W_1 = 160 \text{ pounds}) = 0.50$$

$$P_{0.75} = P(W \leq W_2 = 170 \text{ pounds}) = 0.75$$

Figure 6.17 shows the cumulative personal probability distribution of my weight as judged by you.

Using Figure 6.17, we can generate the corresponding personal probability density as a histogram using the discrete values generated in Figure 6.17. If we desire, the process of dividing ranges into two equally probable zones can be

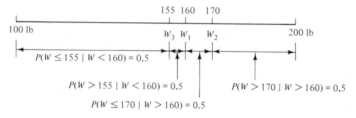

Figure 6.16 Dividing weights into zones of equal probability.

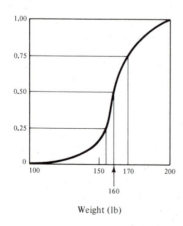

Figure 6.17 Cumulative personal probability distribution of my weight as judged by you.

Probabilistic Models and Assessing Uncertainty   Chap. 6

continued to any level of precision so that an approximate continuous distribution function can be produced.

DIGRESSION ON PRECISION AND ACCURACY

One of the words used above was precision. Since we are concerned with uncertainty and degrees of confidence, let us discuss briefly the concepts associated with the words accuracy, precision, and error. *Accuracy* refers to correctness or truth of a specification, while *precision* refers to how narrow the range of specification is. An *error* is the difference between the value considered to be true and the actual true value. For example, in considering the value of π we can write

(a) $\pi = 3.1415927$

(b) $\pi = 2.984327654$

(c) $\pi = 3$

(a) is accurate in all eight digits; (b) is most precise and least accurate because every digit is wrong; (c) is not very precise but accurate.

As another example, consider the specification for the location of a book in one of two similar buildings known as building 1 and building 2. "The book is in building 1, 7th floor, room 7549, bookcase on south wall, top shelf, second book from the right." The statement "the book is in building 1" is accurate but not very precise. Adding "7th floor" adds precision to the statement of location, and so does each additional element in the specification above. Now suppose that the book is in the location specified above but I state: "The book is in building 2, 7th floor, room 7549, bookcase on south wall, top shelf, second book from the right." This statement is as precise as the first statement, but it is not accurate since we specified the wrong building.

6.8 Summary

Probability density functions, also known as distribution functions, are used to represent relative frequency or probability of occurrence of events of interest in a universe of events.

The normal distribution function is the most important and useful of all probability distributions. This is due primarily to the central limit theorem, which states that the distributions of aggregates of measurements in the form of sums or averages of samples approach the normal distribution function as the sample size increases regardless of what distribution characterizes the individual measurements.

A population is a set that contains all possible observations of a particular attribute. A population is similar to a universal set. A sample is a subset of a population.

Population measurements can be aggregated in the form of a mean and a variance of a population. The mean is a measure of central location of the measurements. The variance is a measure of dispersion. The mean and variance are population parameters defined by equations (6.2) and (6.3), respectively.

For population size N with m different values $x_i (i = 1, \ldots, m)$ of random variable x, the mean μ is given by

$$\mu = \frac{1}{N} \sum_{i=1}^{m} n_i x_i = \sum_{i=1}^{m} f_i x_i \qquad (6.2)$$

in which $f_i = n_i | N$ and n_i is the number of elements in the population with attribute x_i.

The variance, σ^2, of the population is given by

$$\sigma^2 = \sum_i f_i (x_i - \mu)^2 \qquad (6.3)$$

The square root of the variance is called the standard deviation, σ.

A sample of a population can be used to generate estimates of population parameters μ and σ^2. Such estimates are called sample statistics.

The estimate $\hat{\mu}$ for μ is given by the sample mean, $\bar{x}$ (n is the sample size):

$$\hat{\mu} = \bar{x} = \frac{1}{n} \sum_i x_i \qquad (6.4)$$

The estimate $\hat{\sigma}^2$ for σ^2 is given by the sample variance s^2:

$$\hat{\sigma}^2 = s^2 = \frac{1}{n-1} \sum_i (x_i - \bar{x})^2 \qquad (6.5)$$

Probability density function $p(x)$ can be discrete or continuous.

Full knowledge of the parameters of a population can lead to deductive inferences about potential samples from the population. On the other hand, when only estimates of population parameters are known from a sample of the population, inductive inference is used to assess the population parameters.

The normal distribution function has the form

$$p(x) = \frac{1}{\sigma_x \sqrt{2\pi}} e^{-(1/2)[(x - \mu_x)/\sigma_x]^2} \qquad (6.6)$$

The normal distribution for random variable x with mean μ_x and variance σ_x^2 is designated by $N(\mu_x, \sigma_x^2)$. Variable x can be transformed to a standard normal variable, z, with $N(0, 1)$ by using the transformation

$$z = \frac{x - \mu_x}{\sigma_x}$$

The standard normal distribution is shown to be useful as a representation for any normal distribution. The standard normal distribution has a mean of 0 and variance of 1. In any normal distribution 68% of the population is to be found within one standard deviation of the mean; 95%, within two standard deviations; and 99% within three standard deviations.

Probabilistic Models and Assessing Uncertainty   Chap. 6

Testing hypotheses involves two errors, type I error and type II error. Type I error occurs when we wrongly reject a hypothesis. Type II error occurs when we wrongly accept a hypothesis. Examples of hypothesis testing are given in medicine, law, and pattern recognition. It is shown that the decision can be structured as two zones that may be labeled "accept" and "reject." It is also possible to create three zones, labeled "accept," "reject," and "get more information."

Considering an initial hypothesis known as the null hypothesis H_0, error type I is rejecting the null hypothesis H_0 when it is true. Error type II is accepting H_0 when it is false. The probabilities of type I and type II errors are designated by α and β, respectively.

The test of hypotheses consists of these steps:

A. Procedure based on choice of α:
1. State $H_0 : \mu = \mu_0$.
2. State alternative hypothesis, say, $H_1 : \mu = \mu_1 > \mu_0$.
3. Select α.
4. Get z_0 corresponding to α from $N(0, 1)$.
5. Compute $\bar{x}(\text{decision})$ from

$$z_0 = \frac{\bar{x}(\text{decision}) - \mu_0}{\sigma_{\bar{x}}}$$

$$\bar{x}(\text{decision}) = \mu_0 + z_0\,\sigma_{\bar{x}} \qquad \sigma_{\bar{x}} = \frac{\sigma_x}{\sqrt{n}}$$

6. Take a sample of size n and compute $\bar{x}$:

$$\bar{x} = \frac{1}{n}\sum_i x_i$$

7. Make a decision.

$$\bar{x} < \bar{x}(\text{decision}), \text{ accept } H_0$$
$$\bar{x} > \bar{x}(\text{decision}), \text{ reject } H_0$$

B. Procedure based on choice of β:
1. State $H_0 : \mu = \mu_0$.
2. State alternative hypothesis, say, $H_1 : \mu = \mu_1 > \mu_0$.
3. Select β.
4. Get z_1 corresponding to β from $N(0, 1)$.
5. Compute $\bar{x}(\text{decision})$ from

$$z_1 = \frac{\bar{x}(\text{decision}) - \mu_1}{\sigma_{\bar{x}}}$$

$$\bar{x}(\text{decision}) = \mu_1 + z_1\sigma_{\bar{x}} \qquad \sigma_{\bar{x}} = \frac{\sigma_x}{\sqrt{n}}$$

6. Take a sample of size n and compute $\bar{x}$

$$\bar{x} = \frac{1}{n} \sum_i x_i$$

7. Make a decision.

$$\bar{x} < \bar{x}(\text{decision}), \text{ accept } H_0$$
$$\bar{x} > \bar{x}(\text{decision}), \text{ reject } H_0$$

Qualitative statements of uncertainty can be assigned a reasonable range of quantitative values of probabilities. Subjective or personal states of knowledge can be assessed and assigned quantitative values by the use of a reference gamble which is compared to the uncertainty associated with the events of interest.

People are known to introduce biases in their encoding of states of knowledge. In dealing with uncertainty people tend to be overconfident when they make a choice. People are not sufficiently sensitive to sample size in making inferences from a sample.

We can use the concept of the reference gamble to generate a subjective probability distribution for the uncertainty we have regarding an event of interest.

Accuracy is shown to refer to correctness or truth, while precision refers to the level of detail in a statement, a measurement, or a specification.

PROBLEMS

6.1. Given a normal distribution with mean 150 and standard deviation 10 (i.e., $\mu = 150$ and $\sigma = 10$), find:
(a) $P(x < 130)$
(b) $P(x < 90)$
(c) $P(x > 130)$
(d) $P(130 < x < 190)$

6.2. Suppose you are given that a normal random variable x has a mean $\mu = 10$ and variance $\sigma^2 = 2.5$.
(a) How many standard deviations away from the mean is the point $x = 20$? $x = 0$?
(b) What is the probability that x lies between 0 and 20?
(c) If you were asked to find the probability that x will not differ from the mean by more than one standard deviation, then:
(i) What would this probability be?
(ii) Between what two numbers would x lie with this probability?

6.3. (a) If x is a standard normal random variable, find:
(i) $P(x > 0.3)$
(ii) $P(-1 < x < 2)$
(b) If y is a normal random variable with $\mu = 8$, $\sigma = 2$, find:
(i) $P(y > 8.6)$
(ii) $P(6 < y < 12)$
(c) Compare your answers to (a) and (b) and explain.

6.4. What is the probability that a standard normal random variable takes on a value between -3 and $+3$? Between -2 and $+2$? Between -1 and $+1$?

6.5. Mr. Commuter has a statistician friend who believes that Mr. Commuter's time of arrival, measured in minutes after 8:55, is approximately a normal random variable T, with mean 0 and standard deviation 2.5. If this approximation is valid, what is the probability that Mr. Commuter will arrive between 8:50 and 9:00?

6.6. The College Entrance Examination Board test scores are scaled to approximate a normal distribution with mean $\mu = 500$ and standard deviation $\sigma = 100$.
   (a) What is the probability that a randomly selected student will score
      (i) 700 or more?
      (ii) 580 or less?
   (b) What is the probability that three randomly selected students will score 700 or more?
   (c) What is the probability that at least two of three randomly selected students will score less than 700?

6.7. The Highway Patrol radar checks show that the average speed on the San Diego Freeway between Wilshire Boulevard and Jefferson Boulevard is 58.3 miles per hour. The standard deviation is 5.2 mph. What is the percentage of cars exceeding 65 mph if the speeds of the cars obey a normal distribution?

6.8. Results from a survey follow a normal distribution with a mean $\mu = 100$ and standard deviation $\sigma = 10$. However, the researcher considers only the middle 95% of the values to be relevant. Between which numbers should values of the results be included in the survey?

6.9. For a given population, the distribution of IQs is found to be normal with mean of 120 and a standard deviation of 15.
   (a) Draw the curves of such a distribution.
   (b) What is the probability that when five people are selected at random, two of them will each have an IQ over 140?

6.10. An archaeologist on a dig in the Middle East discovered several clay figurines near a dry river bed. He saw that the figurines were similar to those produced by inhabitants of two ancient cities, Aleph and Beth, and hypothesized that flood waters had carried the figurines to the river bed. He knows that the figurines from Aleph and Beth are indistinguishable except for weight. The weights of figurines Aleph and Beth have normal distributions with means of 7 ounces and 8 ounces, respectively, and an identical standard deviation of 0.4 ounces.

   Suppose one of the figurines that the archaeologist found in the river bed weighed 7.5 ounces. He would like to be sure that no more than 10% of the time will he identify a figurine as from Beth, when it really came from Aleph (i.e., $\alpha = 0.1$).
   (a) What is the weight below which he should claim identity Aleph, and above which, Beth?
   (b) From which town should he claim the 7.5 ounce figurine came?

6.11. Give two examples for measurements that can be represented by figures similar to Figures 6.1 and 6.2.

6.12. What do people mean by identifying a family as a typical family in terms of annual income?

6.13. Why is it possible for two populations to have the same mean but different variances?

6.14. Is it possible for two populations to have the same variance but different means? Explain.

6.15. Suppose that there are two manufacturers of light bulbs. One is known to produce bulbs with a mean life of 1000 hours and standard deviation of 10 hours. The second manufacturer produces bulbs with a mean life of 1200 hours and a standard deviation of 100 hours. Describe situations in which you may prefer one or the other of the bulbs. Explain the reason for your choice in each case.

6.16. Is it possible that a situation may arise in which you would consider the two light bulbs of problem 6.15 equally acceptable, that is, you would be indifferent to a choice between the two? Explain your answer and illustrate by a sketch where appropriate.

6.17. Consider two populations of light bulbs. Population 1 has a normal distribution for the life of bulbs with mean $\mu_1 = 1100$ hours of life and variance $\sigma_1^2 = 2500$ hours^2, namely, $N(1100$ hours, 2500 hours$^2)$. Population 2 has a normal distribution for the life of bulbs with mean $\mu_2 = 1200$ hours and variance $\sigma_2^2 = 10,000$ hours^2. Suppose that the cost of a light bulb from either population is the same. Which population would you choose if you wish to maximize the probability for a light bulb lasting:

(a) At least 950 hours   (b) At least 1000 hours   (c) At least 1100 hours

6.18. In Problem 6.17 find the specific threshold value for service life in hours for the bulbs such that if the actual required threshold is lower than this specific value you would choose population 1 and if higher you would choose population 2. The cost of bulbs is assumed to be the same for the two populations. Use a sketch of the distributions of the two populations to explain your answer in qualitative terms before you calculate the specific value.

6.19. Discuss the concepts of "population" and "sample" in the context of plausible and demonstrative reasoning.

6.20. Explain how the standard normal distribution is representative of all normal distributions regardless of mean value and variance. What is standard about the standard normal distribution?

6.21. How did 68%, 95%, and 99.8% of the area in a normal distribution (discussed in Section 6.4) become standards for probability statements?

6.22. Describe two situations for which the model of Figure 6.9 is suitable.

6.23. How could the model of Figure 6.9 be used in the pattern recognition problem described in Figure 6.11?

6.24. Use a reference gamble to select a numerical value for the probability you would assign to an uncertain event such as the election of a candidate you wish to see voted into office in your state.

6.25. How can you explain the biases that people have in encoding states of knowledge?

6.26. Use the procedure described in Section 6.7 (Figures 6.16 and 6.17) to generate your personal probability distribution for the weight of a friend.

6.27. Give examples of how people misuse the concepts of precision and accuracy.

6.28. What considerations should be used to decide which type of error, type I or type II, should be made smaller? Give one example for a situation where type I error should be made smaller and one example where type II error should be made smaller.

6.29. Discuss your thoughts on the questions raised at the end of Example 2, Section 6.6.

6.30. Discuss how you might use some of the concepts of this chapter in a qualitative way to help you deal with daily problems you may encounter.

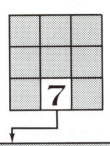

7

Tools and Concepts for Decision Making

7.1 Ubiquity of Human Decision Making

We started the book with human decision situations when we discussed the doctors' dilemma whether to treat or wait, the jury deciding on a verdict, and farmer Johnson's value driven decision to lease the land so that his daughter could go to college. Making decisions is part and parcel of everyday life. Some decisions are monumental, such as the U.S. decision to enter World War II; others are mundane, such as a decision of what to eat for dinner. All decisions require thought and the processing of information, but not to the same degree. Rational behavior would suggest that we ought to devote more time to important decisions but this is not always the case. I once read a study on committee deliberations that reported the following statistics:

Agenda Item	Approximate Cost Involved	Deliberation Time (minutes)	Resulting Disposition
Atomic reactor	$10,000,000	$2\frac{1}{2}$	Plans approved with no change
Bicycle shed	$2350	45	Plans approved with no change
Refreshments at meetings	$4.75/month	75	Decision deferred for additional information

The time taken to decide appears inversely related to the complexity of the decision. Decision making is not always a rational process. It is driven by our value system and guided by our perception of an uncertain future. Sometimes the

227

process comes to a halt when we are dominated by fear of failure and memories of postdecisional regrets. The inability to make decisions is a form of mental paralysis that drives out all vitality from the human experience of everyday life. On the other hand, making decisions and following through with steps for their implementation breeds vigor and excitement; it makes the decision maker alive. This is how the nineteenth-century Russian writer Nikolai Gogol describes his hero, Akaky Akakievich, in his famous story "The Overcoat." When poverty-stricken Akakievich realizes that his old overcoat can no longer be patched up for the coming winter, he makes a decision to buy a new one. The decision transforms indecisive Akakievich into a new man, alive, strong-willed, a man with a definite goal before him. He is now implementing a plan to cut his expenses on food, lighting, and heating oil, and put up with a little more hunger and a little less light and heat to meet his goal. Akakievich is in the cold street when he arrives at the decision and plans its implementation. The cold breeze is making its way to his body through the worn-out overcoat, but he does not feel cold. He is flushed with the excitement of the decision, he is warmed by it, he is exuberant with exhilaration. He is alive.

The psychological and mental maturity of a person is intimately connected with the ability to make reasonable decisions, to take risks, to tolerate mistakes, and to take responsibility for consequences of decisions. There is no escape from postdecisional regrets that we all have experienced at one time or another. A mature decision maker does not linger over these regrets. She learns from her mistakes. The learning does not always lead to better decisions, although it may. The learning may lead to an attitude of tolerance for uncertainty, and a better understanding of your inner environment, your values that led to your actions. I strongly believe that if we had to wait for all uncertainty to vanish before we chose to act, we would become paralyzed as decision makers and no action would take place.

Decision-making models stipulate the following elements. The *objectives* of the decision maker guided by an inner environment of a *value system*, *alternatives* identified in the outer environment, and a *criterion* for selecting an alternative following an assessment of the *uncertainties* in the potential states of the outer environment and the uncertainties in the consequences of implementing any of the alternatives. The key element is the value system, but in many situations we become aware of our *values* after we act. Thus decision making is a dynamic ongoing process. The perception of our values guides our choice of actions, and our actions give us more concrete realistic perceptions of our values; they may even cause changes in attitude. Every decision situation and the resulting experiences constitute an experiment that teaches us a little more about ourselves and the environment in which we live.

We are constantly processing information about the environment and about our reaction to it. It is productive to have a framework, a sort of structure that will help us integrate what we learn from our daily decision experiences so that we can enhance the compatibility between what we wish and what we do, and in the process develop attitudes and tools that are productive in dealing with what we can control, and learn to live with what we cannot control.

I have just returned from a meeting with the teaching staff of a course that I have created on the UCLA campus. We were trying to decide what specific content should constitute the core material for the course. I had already reviewed some potential topics and made preliminary choices of what should be included in the core. But I have a decision situation at a higher level than just content: Should I, as the originator of the course, take a position of *judge* or *leader* in establishing the content of the core? As judge I would assume a passive role. I will wait for the teaching staff to bring their alternative choices and then I shall evaluate them. Or should I take the lead by articulating the values of education, identify objectives compatible with these values, and lead the way to a successful implementation of an acceptable alternative? Namely, assume an active posture of leader.

I am more favorably disposed to assume the role of leader. But then, what about the staff? How will they perceive me in the role of leader? Will I appear too dictatorial and aggressive? Will it hinder or help the ultimate objective of the best education for the students? This is a multiattribute decision problem. How I proceed in the planning stage may have important consequences on implementation. Although the core of content must be established soon and time is important for reasons not mentioned here, I may have to slow down the process and trade off the disvalue of more time for added value in a higher level of acceptability.

Before I get carried away with the high-level decision as to whether I should assume the role of judge or leader, let me step back and ask a question that requires a decision at a higher level yet: Is a decision necessary? Actually, it is not. I could leave the task to one of the instructors and not get involved at all, not as judge nor as leader. By increasing the space of the decision situation, enlarging the context we may conclude that a decision is not necessary because we choose not to enter the more limited context.

In simpler terms, when I face the choice of leaving the house with or without an umbrella, I can decide that a choice is not necessary because I do not have to leave the house.

DECISION MODELS

Decision making requires a choice. The choice involves a process. The decision process may reflect all three modes of human consciousness: perception, emotion, and logic. How we perceive reality establishes how we see things and how we represent situations. Emotions guide our choice of values. Logic directs us to rational processes for selecting a course of action to achieve our objectives. Decision models should provide a framework for behavior which admits the contributions of all three aspects of human consciousness: perception, emotion, and logic.

Decision theory models provide productive formal structures once values, objectives, and alternative courses of action are stipulated. The information provided by studying mathematical decision models is an important input to the decision process. But in no way should the model tell us what to decide. The models of decision theory are not intended to replace sound intuitive judgment. They complement and supplement judgment but cannot replace it. Sound critical judgment is required in generating the objectives, in identifying and creating alternatives, in selecting criteria for choice, and in general in dealing with those features of a decision situation that do not lend themselves to quantitative assessment.

Choosing a career, selling or buying a house, deciding on a medical treatment, marriage and divorce, and business decisions are all complex situations. When we face such situations we can use decision theory models in some cases. But the models seldom include the entire story. There are always hidden assumptions, a larger context that could be considered; there are features that are filtered out consciously or unconsciously and elements that are a subject of more attention or focus than others. There are situations where the level of decision is not properly selected in which case a decision situation could be judged as unnecessary. The labels and description we employ in the models may "color" our thinking and force a focus on certain elements that tend to distort the total picture.

Yet despite all these difficulties the concepts and ideas underlying formal decision theory models are helpful in a most profound way. They help us perceive and think more clearly about complex problems even when the decision approach we take is more qualitative than quantitative. Decision theory provides us with perspectives, points of view, and models of thinking that are indispensable in shedding light on situations that would otherwise leave us totally in the dark. It is in this spirit that we wish to share with you, the reader, the findings of decision theory so that they can supplement, complement, and enhance your decision-making processes and potentially expedite the successful implementation of your decisions.

INFORMATION PROCESSING AND JUDGMENT

A decision maker is an information processor. The information may come from the environment, or from our internal storage in memory. We may receive information that we need and request, but we also receive information that we do not ask for explicitly.

It is perhaps reasonable to assume that we can control to some extent the information we receive from outside, but the control of the internally stored information is far more limited.

Regardless of the information source, we need to evaluate it and classify it in the context of the decision situation. We must distinguish among fact, opinion, and judgment; develop tools for assessing relevance, credibility, and value of information; and learn to correct biases that we introduce in processing information. When we drive a car or cross a street we exercise a great deal of judgment in processing information regarding speed, distance, levels of risk, and make decisions on the basis of these judgments. We can even correct for perceptual biases that make objects at a distance appear smaller, or speed to appear greater when the object is nearer. These judgments are required and are appropriate when decisions must be made rapidly, and there is no time for analytical quantitative evaluation of data and detailed information processing. The environment is dynamic and changes too quickly. The evaluation of data observed at one instant may no longer be relevant the next. That is why we drive and cross streets with our eyes open to new information, constantly. We are vigilant.

There are other situations when judgment can be enhanced by taking time to process information and presenting it in a form that contributes to better understanding of the decision situation thus leading to better-thought-out rational choices.

7.2 Representation and Decision

The models we employ may include a representation that will sort of "color" the decision situation in a way that will bias our thinking. This may be the result of the choice of words in the problem description, the arrangement of elements, timing, a form suggesting that the information was processed by the computer, approved by the boss, and so on. The representation of the decision situation coupled with the limitations of human information-processing capabilities may establish the extent that biases and distortion will enter into our decision making. Here is an example. Suppose that you are presented with the following opportunity. You will receive $1000 on the condition that you will play a game in which you can win an additional $500 or $1000, or nothing, as shown in the matrix of Figure 7.1. You must choose row A or B; a marble is taken out randomly from an urn containing 50 blue and 50 red marbles. If a blue marble is taken out, you receive 0 or $500 (in addition to the $1000 you received when you agreed to play the game in the first place) depending on whether you chose row A or row B, respectively. If a red marble is taken out, you receive $1000 or $500 (in addition to the $1000 you already have) if you chose row A or B, respectively. Which row will you choose? Think about it.

Now that you selected A or B, explain your reason for the choice. Describe circumstances that would compel you to choose A, or compel you to choose B.

Without reference to the preceding example, consider the following decision situation. You will receive $2000 on the condition that you play the game

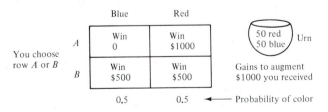

Figure 7.1

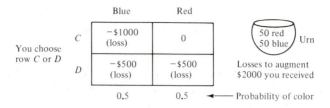

Figure 7.2

shown by the matrix of Figure 7.2. You must choose row C or D. If you choose row C, you will lose $1000 or lose nothing, depending on whether a blue or red marble is drawn from an urn of 50 blue and 50 red marbles. If you choose row D, you lose $500 regardless of what color marble is drawn from the urn. Which row will you choose, C or D? Explain the reasons for your choice. Describe circumstances that would compel you to choose C or compel you to choose D.

Now study Figures 7.1 and 7.2. They represent an identical decision situation that can lead to final total results shown in Figure 7.3. There were two different representations of the decision situation. In Figure 7.1 we started with $1000 and augmented this sum with a matrix of *gains* from 0 to $1000. In Figure 7.2 we started with $2000 and augmented this sum with a matrix of *losses* from 0 to $1000. Kahneman and Tversky (1979) presented these two decision situations to 70 people [43]. In Figure 7.1, 16% chose row A and 84% chose row B. In Figure 7.2, 69% chose C and 31% chose D. The change in representation caused a dramatic change in decision, while the actual substance of the decision situation is identical in both cases. People seemed to favor taking a risk to avoid a sure loss of $500 in row D of Figure 7.2, but favored not taking risk when there was a sure gain of $500 in row B of Figure 7.1.

The same sort of inconsistency was in evidence when Tversky and Kahneman (1981) presented the following decision situation to over 150 people [44]:

> You are given reliable and credible information that 600 people will die for sure in an epidemic if you are not going to choose one of two alternatives A or B shown in Figure 7.4. The probabilities of states 1 and 2 are $1/3$ and $2/3$, respectively. The fate of the 600 people will be as given in the matrix, showing the four possible intersections of your two alternatives and the two states.

72% of the participants in the exercise chose alternative A, 28% chose alternative B.

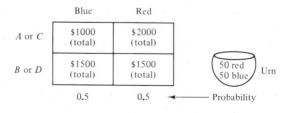

Figure 7.3

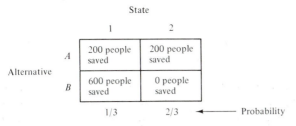

Figure 7.4

When Tversky and Kahneman presented the same decision situation to another group of over 150 people but changed the representation, the response was drastically different:

You are given reliable and credible information that 600 people will die for sure in an epidemic if you are not going to choose one of two alternatives C or D shown in Figure 7.5. The probabilities of states 1 and 2 are 1/3 and 2/3, respectively. The fate of the 600 people will be as given in the matrix, showing the four possible intersections of your two alternatives and the two states.

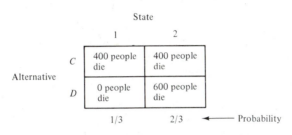

Figure 7.5

Twenty-two percent of the participants in the exercise chose alternative C, 78% chose D. The words "save" and "die" employed in the two representations play a crucial role in the choice of an alternative. Faced with a sure loss (death) in alternative C of Figure 7.5, most people favored a fighting chance to avoid a sure death of 400 people (although at a risk of death to 600) and chose D. Faced with a sure survival of 200 people in Figure 7.4, most people avoided the risk of putting this positive sure result in jeopardy and chose alternative A. Yet the decision situations in Figures 7.4 and 7.5 are identical.

DECISION MAKING AND BIASES IN ASSESSING INFORMATION

We demonstrated in the preceding discussion that representation has a profound influence on our perception of the context in which a decision situation becomes nested in our mind. We retrieve attitudes and general heuristics that guide our decision making based on the representation. To become aware of potential influence of a representation, it is productive to employ more than one representation of a decision situation whenever possible. This will enrich the spectrum of attitudes and heuristics that we will consider as guides to a decision, and thus reduce the possibility of undue influence of one representation.

In our earlier discussion of problem representation we pointed out a number of sources for biases in human assessment of information. In this section we discuss the implication of these biases in decision making. Awareness of the biases is an important first step in an attempt to correct for them. But to remove them from the decision-making process will require the aid of some mathematical tools. These tools have been well established and they deal with our concepts of information and uncertainty in a way that can help us construct conceptual models that are more true to the reality of the decision situations we face.

7.3 Labels and Decisions: The Wristwatch Story

A few years ago we were about to board a plane from Amsterdam to New York when a three-hour delay in departure was announced. What does an experienced traveler do in such a case? Of course, take advantage of the airport duty-free shop. This was precisely what we did. For many years now my wife has been insisting on a new wristwatch for me. I resisted the idea because my old simple Timex was part of me. I was used to it and it never failed me in more than 10 years. It did require winding every day and it lost about 5 minutes a week. My wife reminded me of these negative features as we passed by a large display of wristwatches in the duty-free shop of the airport. But I argued that I was not going through life in such a hurry to be concerned with a 5-minute delay on any occasion. My resistance to purchase a wristwatch was no match to the argument that we have a God-sent opportunity, because of the delay in departure, to get the wristwatch in a duty-free shop, the implication being that *duty free* connotes a bargain. After studying a number of models and consulting with the salesman, we bought a *duty-free* Constellation Automatic Omega Chronometer, a self-winding latest-model wristwatch. The duty-free price was $475.

Two weeks after we returned home I happened to be on a main street near my home when I noticed a large display of wristwatches in a store front. I passed by this store on many occasions in the past but never stopped to inspect the merchandise. This time it was different. I wanted to find out how much I *had saved* by this God-sent opportunity at the duty-free shop in Amsterdam. Indeed, I was lucky; in a large display of Omega wristwatches I spotted the very same model that I had purchased. My attention was not on the watch, but rather on the white piece of paper attached to it by a string. I could not believe my eyes! The price tag was $100 less than what I had paid. Perhaps, I thought, the number was not the price. The dollar sign was not clear on the price tag. I had to find out. I entered the store and inquired about the watch. The salesman, who was the owner of the store, as I later learned, took out the watch, showed it to me and praised its quality and precision. When I asked for the price, he quoted what I could not believe. It was $100 less than what I had paid. My face must have revealed my disbelief because as soon as I said "thank you" and turned around to leave, the salesman called after me, "Wait, if it is too much I will give you a better deal."

I have learned my lesson. The duty is free; the prices may be outrageous. One does not contradict the other. I had attributed to *duty free* much more than "free of duty," which is all it really means.

The lesson was worthwhile; I have no regrets. I wear the watch as a constant reminder of high-level presuppositions that may become the source of the biggest mistakes in decision making. I never hesitate to enter a store labeled as "expensive." I have often discovered the expensive merchandise in so-called "inexpensive" stores. The labels may even be accurate in a general sense when averaged over all the merchandise. But the average may not apply to the item I need, and often it does not. Of course, price is not the only feature that guides decision making. There is the reputation of the seller, his or her attitude to defective merchandise that a buyer may take home, and other features to be considered depending on the particular decision situation.

7.4 Main Elements of Decision Making

A decision-making model contains these five elements:

1. *Alternative actions,* which decision makers control because they can select whichever action they wish.
2. *States of nature,* which constitute the environment of the decision model. The decision maker does not control the states of nature.
3. *Outcomes,* which are the results of a combination of an action and a state of nature.
4. *Utilities,* which are measures of satisfaction or value that the decision maker associates with each outcome.
5. *An objective,* which is a statement of what the decision maker wants.

The prevailing objective in decision theory is *maximization of expected utility.* The objective constitutes the *decision rule* or *criterion* which guides decision makers in their choice of a course of action.

The elements above can be identified in the models discussed at the beginning of the book. There is one more element of the decision model which is important, and that is the assessment of the decision maker's *state of knowledge* regarding the states of nature. This can be achieved by assigning probabilities to the states of nature.

There are four basic categories of decision situations:

(a) *Decision under certainty:* Each action results in one known outcome which will occur with certainty.

(b) *Decision under risk:* Each action can result in two or more outcomes, but the states of nature have known objective probabilities.

(c) *Decision under uncertainty:* Each action can result in two or more out-comes, but the probabilities of the states of nature are unknown.

(d) *Decision under conflict:* The states of nature are replaced by courses of action open to an opponent who is trying to maximize his or her objective function. Decision making under conflict is the subject of *game theory*.

Decision under conflict is not discussed here. See references 15, 61, 62, and 63 for a treatment of this topic.

7.5 Decision Making under Certainty Using Heuristics

Decision making under certainty occurs when we know with certainty which state of nature will occur. In other words, there is a single column in the *payoff matrix* or the matrix of outcomes in the decision model. This seems a rather simple decision problem because all that is required is to select the action that leads to the maximum utility. However, there are many problems in which the number of possible courses of action open to the decision maker is so enormous that an exhaustive list of all of them is not feasible and the modeling process of reducing their number requires heuristic tools of problem solving.

For example, consider a factory with 20 different machines and 20 con-tracts for parts which these machines can produce [45]. Since the machines are different, they may require different costs for each contract. Hence, to compare costs and select the optimum assignment of contracts to machines, we should consider all possible assignments. The contracts can be assigned in $20 \times 19 \times 18 \times \cdots \times 2 \times 1$ ways, or a number which is larger than 2×10^{18}. Each of these assignments constitutes an alternative action or one row in the *payoff matrix*. Since the outcomes are assumed certain, we have a single column. To impress you with the magnitude of the task required to compute the costs for all the alternatives, let us use some calculations. Suppose that a computer can calculate the costs for each of $2,000,000 = 2 \times 10^6$ alternatives in 1 second (this is a very large number of calculations, because each alternative requires 20 multiplications and 20 additions). Since a year contains about 32×10^6 seconds (31,558,000 is closer), the computer can calculate the costs of about 64×10^{12} alternative actions in one year. To complete the calculations for all 2×10^{18} alternatives, $(200/64)10^4$ or about 30,000 years of computer time are required.

All this was merely to impress you with the fact that even decision making under certainty may become a problem that is not tractable. It also serves to illustrate that decision theory is a link in problem solving. Here the modeling aspect of problem formulation requires actions that cannot be placed on a strictly prescriptive and systematic basis; at best these actions are plausible and are guided by heuristics.

Let us suppose that you are the owner of 20 machines and you have 20 contracts for parts that the machines can produce. You wish to assign one contract to each machine to meet your commitments. The machines are different and require different costs for each contract. The costs of assigning contracts to machines are summarized in the following matrix:

$$
\begin{array}{c}
\text{Machine Number} \\
\begin{array}{cccccc}
 & 1 & 2 & 3 & 4 & \cdots & 20
\end{array} \\
\begin{array}{c}
\text{Contract}\ \ \\
\text{Number}
\end{array}
\begin{array}{c}
1 \\ 2 \\ 3 \\ 4 \\ \cdot \\ \cdot \\ \cdot
\end{array}
\left[
\begin{array}{cccccc}
15 & 66 & 19 & 12 & & \\
28 & \cdot & \cdot & 75 & & \\
17 & \cdot & \cdot & & & \\
46 & \cdot & \cdot & \cdot & & \\
 & & \text{Costs of assigning} & & \\
 & & \text{contracts to machines} & &
\end{array}
\right]
\end{array}
$$

To compare costs and select the least costly assignment of contracts to machines, you should consider all possible assignments, and this will require 30,000 years of computer time, as we calculated above.

This will not be the case if in the matrix of costs above there are 20 numbers with the following properties. Each of these 20 numbers occupies a unique row and column position and is the smallest entry of both this row and column. These numbers identify the assignments and their sum constitutes the associated minimum total cost. For example, in the following matrix for three contracts and three machines:

$$
\begin{array}{c}
\text{Machine Number} \\
\begin{array}{ccc}
1 & 2 & 3
\end{array} \\
\begin{array}{c}
\text{Contract} \\
\text{Number}
\end{array}
\begin{array}{c}
1 \\ 2 \\ 3
\end{array}
\left[
\begin{array}{ccc}
26 & \circled{15} & 16 \\
\circled{18} & 22 & 23 \\
19 & 20 & \circled{14}
\end{array}
\right]
\end{array}
$$

we have three such numbers identified by circles:

18 is the smallest entry in row 2, column 1.

15 is the smallest entry in row 1, column 2.

14 is the smallest entry in row 3, column 3.

Therefore, the minimum cost is achieved by assigning contracts 1, 2, and 3 to machines 2, 1, and 3, respectively, for a total cost of $15 + 18 + 14 = 47$.

The unique situation we are describing here does not occur very often. For example, for the following matrix of costs:

$$
\begin{array}{c}
\text{Machine Number} \\
\begin{array}{ccc}
1 & 2 & 3
\end{array} \\
\begin{array}{c}
\text{Contract} \\
\text{Number}
\end{array}
\begin{array}{c}
1 \\ 2 \\ 3
\end{array}
\left[
\begin{array}{ccc}
17 & 21 & 16 \\
20 & 22 & 18 \\
19 & 13 & 14
\end{array}
\right]
\end{array}
$$

only the entry 13 in row 3 (contract 3) and column 2 (machine 2) is the smallest entry for both row 3 and column 2. No other entry has this property and we need two more such values for the unique situation we are discussing here.

However, it will be worth exploring the possibility of such a unique set of numbers when all it takes is a few minutes even for 100 contracts and 100 machines, and it certainly beats waiting for years of calculations. But even when we fail to discover such a unique situation we can employ algorithms that can still reduce the search effort considerably. Let us present two such algorithms and show how their power can be enhanced by employing heuristics to guide the search for solutions.

BREADTH-FIRST AND DEPTH-FIRST SEARCH ALGORITHMS

Consider the tree of Figure 7.6 as a collection of routes from a starting point at node a to a terminal node such as j, n, o, q, r, u, v, x, z, or the unlabeled node below node y. The objective is to find the route of shortest distance from node a to some terminal node.

There are systematic procedures such as breadth-first or depth-first search algorithms to achieve our objective. These are, in a sense, blind or unguided search procedures, because the order of the search follows a fixed and exhaustive sequence that is established in advance and is unaffected by the intermediate calculations, or by the location of the desired terminal goal node.

In the *breadth-first* search we progress with the calculations from higher levels to lower levels of the tree in the order in which the nodes are generated. In Figure 7.6 we begin at node a and go to b, c, d, and e and calculate the path lengths 23, 14, 1, and 3, respectively. Then we move to nodes f, g, h, i, j, k, then to the next level of nodes l to s, and so on.

In the *depth-first* search we conduct the calculations by exploring a path from the most recently visited node. If we reach a terminal node, we back up to the preceding most recent node we visited. In Figure 7.6 a depth-first search begins at node a and goes to b, f, l, t, x, recording the length of the path to each node (i.e., 23, 24, 26, 27, 28). At x we back up to t and explore the path from t to y to the unlabeled node recording lengths 38 and 39 at y and at the unlabeled node, respectively.

HEURISTIC GUIDES IN SEARCH

Instead of using the breadth-first or depth-first algorithms in an unguided search, we can employ heuristic guides of a holistic or global nature to help us identify the more promising paths to explore first. These heuristics will reduce the search effort on the average compared with blind search methods, and will permit us to use the results generated in the course of the calculations as information to guide the direction of the search.

Let us use a heuristic to guide the search for the shortest path in Figure 7.6. Starting at node a, we proceed to record the length of each path to the node at the next level (i.e., at b, c, d, and e). Of these lengths the path of length 1

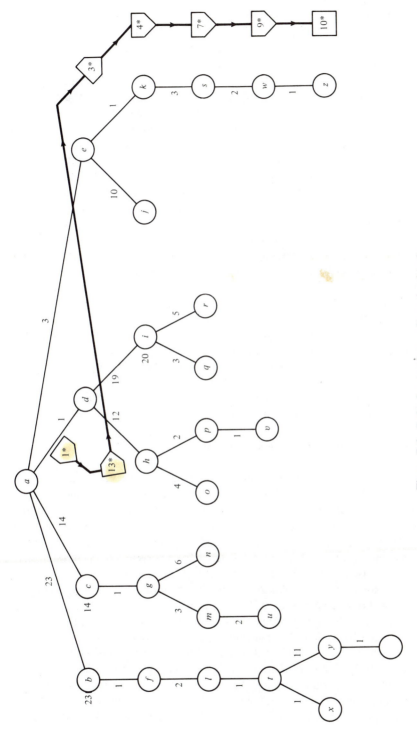

Figure 7.6 Paths from node *a* to lower-level nodes.

(marked by an asterisk) from a to d is the shortest. We continue from node d to its successor nodes h and i and record the length of the path from the starting node a to them (i.e., 13 and 20, respectively). 13 is smaller, so we mark it by an asterisk. Now compare this value of 13 with length of paths recorded at the nodes of the level above node h that were not expanded to lower levels. These are the length, 23, 14, and 3 at nodes b, c, and e, respectively. Since 3 at node e is the shortest, continue the exploration there. From e to k is shorter than to j. Total length of path to k is 4. This value of 4 is smaller than any length we explored so far, so we continue to s. Again compare the length of 7 with the values recorded earlier and continue from s if the length to it is still shorter than all paths calculated earlier. We finally reach terminal node z. Since the path from a to z of length 10 is still smaller than the paths from a to b (23), a to c (14), a to h (13), a to j (13), path a to z is of minimum length. The nodes explored in our search are d, h, e, k, s, w, and z, as shown by the boxed numbers and arrows in Figure 7.6.

Another heuristic guide for the search in Figure 7.6 could proceed as follows. Establish a lower bound on any path starting from a and going through a node at the next level, say node d. From a to d we have a length of 1, from d to its immediate successor nodes h and i 12 is the shortest distance, from h and i to their immediate successors the link of length 2 is shortest. Since some nodes at this level are terminal, let us stop and add the lengths of links we have so far, $1 + 12 + 2 = 15$. This is a lower bound on the length of path from a through d to a terminal node. No path going through d can be shorter than 15, and a path of length 15 may or may not be possible. In fact, the shortest path through d is of length 16 (a, d, h, p, v).

Now if we can find any path from a to a terminal node that is of length 15 or less, then the paths from a through d would not have to be explored further.

REFINEMENTS IN HEURISTIC SEARCH [46]

The heuristic search can be improved by adding reasonable estimates from any node to the goal node. For example, consider the road distances in miles between the European cities shown in Figure 7.7. To find the shortest path from Paris to Vienna, we can use at each intermediate city i an estimate of the air distance from that city i to Vienna and add it to the road distance from Paris to i, thus obtaining an estimate of total distance from Paris to Vienna through city i. A more realistic estimate may approximate road distance between city i and Vienna as the air distance plus 20%. This information can then be used to guide the search. For example, start at Paris. The successor nodes (cities) are Brussels and Genoa. A path through Brussels is 225 road miles plus 672 miles estimated distance from Brussels to Vienna calculated as air distance plus 20% (see Table 7.1). The total is $225 + 672 = 879$ miles. From Paris to Vienna through Genoa we have $629 + 522 = 1151$ miles, which is larger than 897 miles, so continue the exploration of routes through Brussels by going to its successor nodes of Amsterdam, Bern, Genoa, and then from Amsterdam to Hamburg and Munich.

Complete the problem of Figure 7.7 and show that only routes through

Tools and Concepts for Decision Making   Chap. 7

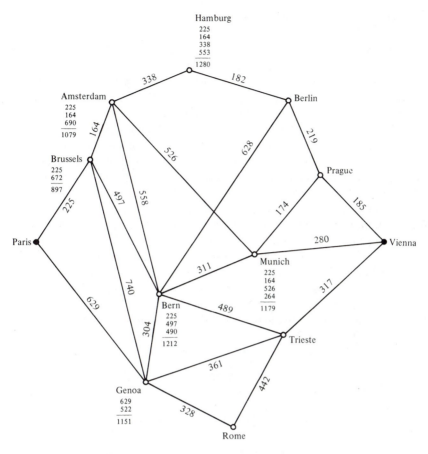

Figure 7.7 European road distances in miles.

Brussels, Genoa, Amsterdam, and Munich need to be explored and the shortest route of 1195 miles is Paris–Brussels–Amsterdam–Munich–Vienna. So the only city explored that is not on the path is Genoa.

Table 7.1 Estimates of air distances to Vienna

City	Air Distance + 20% (miles)
Paris	760
Brussels	672
Genoa	522
Amsterdam	690
Bern	490
Munich	264
Hamburg	553
Trieste	206
Rome	570
Berlin	386
Prague	186

The 3 × 3 matrix in Figure 7.8 represents the cost of assigning three different contracts to three different machines. The objective is to minimize the cost of the assignment under the constraint that each machine must be assigned exactly one contract. There are six possible assignments, as shown in Figure 7.9. Using the heuristic guides discussed in dealing with the problem of Figure 7.6, we find the solution path for minimum cost to be along nodes a, b, e, k. Namely, machine i gets contract i for $i = 1, 2, 3$. The search proceeded from node b to e, d, j, k, c, g, p. The numbers in parentheses next to these nodes identify the order of exploration. Suppose now that the numbers in the matrix of Figure 7.8 are profits instead of costs. Then our objective is to find an assignment of maximum profit with the same constraint of exactly one contract per machine. We can employ our procedure for finding the shortest path in a tree by converting the maximization to a minimization problem. We do this as follows: Find the largest entry in Figure 7.8, which is 7 in our case, and subtract each entry from this largest entry. The resulting matrix is shown in Figure 7.10. The assignment of lowest total value in Figure 7.10 is identical to the assignment of largest profit in Figure 7.8. The tree diagram for the values in Figure 7.10 is shown in Figure 7.11. The solution is along the path of nodes a, c, h, n. Namely, contract 1 goes to machine 2, contract 2 goes to machine 3, and contract 3 goes to machine 1, and the profit is $6 + 6 + 7 = 19$ (see Figure 7.8).

Machine Number

		1	2	3
Contract	1	2	6	4
Number	2	5	3	6
	3	7	3	4

Figure 7.8 Costs of three contracts assigned to one of three machines.

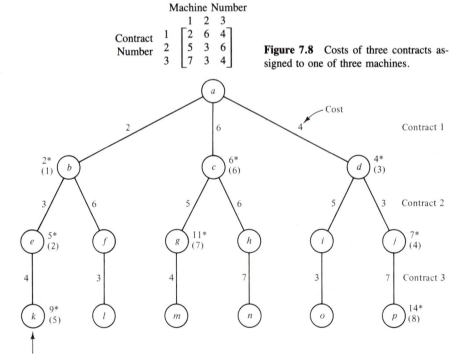

Figure 7.9 Tree diagrams for assignments of contracts to machines in Figure 7.8.

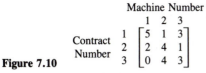

Figure 7.10

Machine Number

$$\begin{array}{c} \text{Contract} \\ \text{Number} \end{array} \begin{array}{c} 1 \\ 2 \\ 3 \end{array} \begin{array}{ccc} 1 & 2 & 3 \\ \begin{bmatrix} 5 & 1 & 3 \\ 2 & 4 & 1 \\ 0 & 4 & 3 \end{bmatrix} \end{array}$$

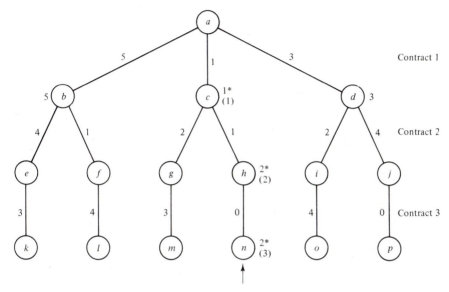

Figure 7.11

LARGER PROBLEMS AND SATISFACTORY SOLUTIONS

Consider the following problem. A factory has five machines and five different contracts for parts that can be produced by each of these machines. The costs are different for each contract, depending on the machine used to produce the parts, as shown in the following matrix of Figure 7.12:

Machine Number

		1	2	3	4	5	
	1	5	7	3	6	2	
Contract	2	6	3	5	5	5	← cost (thousands
Number	3	1	2	3	2	3	of dollars)
	4	4	6	7	5	4	
	5	3	4	3	4	4	

Figure 7.12 Cost matrix.

The contracts can be assigned to the machines in $5 \times 4 \times 3 \times 2 \times 1 = 5!$ different ways. The objective is to find the assignment of minimum cost. Although this may not seem to be a difficult task for the present problem, the amount of calculations required increases very rapidly as the number of machines and contracts increase. As shown earlier, if we have 20 contracts and 20 machines, there are 20! different possible assignments. To calculate the cost of all these assignments will require 30,000 years if a computer can compute the cost of 2,000,000 assignments each second.

Instead of attempting to find the best solution, let us focus on finding a satisfactory solution. To be more explicit regarding what we mean by "satisfactory," let us return to our 5 × 5 matrix of contracts and machines of Figure 7.12. A feasible solution is one that assigns one contract to each machine. This means that once contract i is assigned to machine j, element ij of the matrix represents the cost of this assignment, and row i and column j are deleted from the matrix. A feasible assignment will include five costs, or entries in the matrix, such that each column and each row can have only one entry included in the final assignment. All possible feasible assignments can be generated by constructing a tree such as in Figure 7.13, where we begin with the rows (i.e., the contracts). Contract 1 can be assigned to any one of the five machines, contract 2 to the remaining four available, contract 3 to the remaining three available, and so on. Figure 7.14 shows the assignment tree starting with columns (i.e., machines assigned to contracts).

If we take the smallest entry across each level of the tree in Figure 7.13, it is the same as taking the smallest value of each row in the matrix of Figure 7.12, as shown in Figure 7.15. If we add these row minima, we obtain a sum of numbers that may represent an assignment that is not feasible, as it does in our case, but certainly no feasible assignment could have a smaller total cost than this sum, which is 13 in our case. We could similarly go across the tree in Figure 7.14 selecting the smallest entries. This is equivalent to generating the column minima in Figure 7.15. The sum of these minima is 10 in our case and again represents an assignment that is not feasible, the minima of columns 1 and 2 are in the same row 3; namely, contract 3 is assigned to two machines. But again the sum 10 represents a lower bound on any actual assignment. Since 10 < 13,

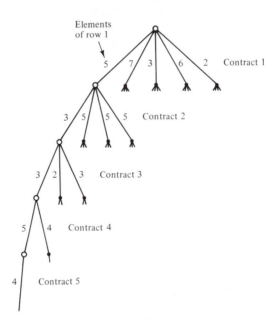

Figure 7.13

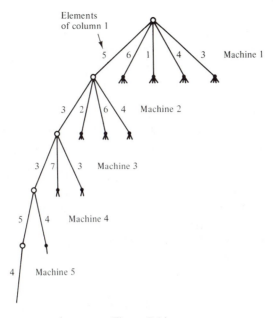

Figure 7.14

the sum of the row minima of 13 represents a more realistic bound. Since in both Figures 7.13 and 7.14 we end up with all the possible assignments, then whichever sum of minima across the levels is higher constitutes a more realistic lower bound on the solution. After all, we could say that no assignment can be smaller than 0 since all entries are positive, or smaller than $1 + 2 + 2 + 2 + 3 \, (=10)$ since these are the first five smallest numbers in the matrix; however, 13 is a better bound since it approaches the true minimum more closely. For a problem in which entries in the matrix are profits (i.e., a maximization problem), a

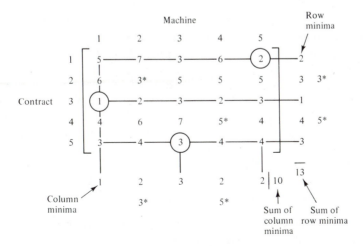

Figure 7.15

realistic upper bound would be the sum of row maxima or sum of column maxima, whichever is smaller.

A heuristic approach to get a satisfactory solution can employ the following procedure. Find a realistic bound on the solution. Try a feasible solution, say the elements on the principal diagonal of the matrix. If this assignment is close enough to the bound, you may stop. In our case the cost of this assignment, in which contract i is assigned to machine i, is $5 + 3 + 3 + 5 + 4 = 20 > 13$. This is more than 50% above our bound, so let us continue our heuristic search. In Figure 7.15 draw a horizontal line to the left of each row minimum and a vertical line above each column minimum, and identify the entries that are both their row and column minima, such as the element ① in row 3 column 1, the ② in row 1 column 5. Circle these elements in the matrix and delete the corresponding rows and columns in which they appear. Now concentrate on assigning the remaining contracts to the remaining machines. In our problem (Figure 7.15) contracts 1, 3, and 5 are assigned to machines 5, 1, and 3, respectively and at costs of 2, 1, and 3 units. The best assignment for remaining contracts 2 and 4 to machines 2 and 4 can again employ the procedure of recording row and column minima, as was done with the original matrix. These are the numbers 3 and 5 marked by asterisks. The result we obtain is 14, only 1 unit cost above the lower bound of 13 that is not feasible. This is the best assignment for this problem.

BRANCH-AND-BOUND TECHNIQUES [47]

The procedure we employed here to generate bounds on the solution to an assignment problem is the basis of the *branch-and-bound technique*. For example, in Figure 7.12 we can select one assignment that is feasible with contract 1 assigned to machine 5, 2 to 4, 3 to 2, 4 to 1, and 5 to 3 for a total cost of 16. Now we can look at contract 1 assigned to machine 2 and inspect it as follows. Cross out row 1, column 2 from the matrix of Figure 7.12 and find the row and column minima of the remaining matrix. Take the largest sum of these minima and add it to entry 1, 2, (i.e., the cost of assigning contract 1 to machine 2). If the result is larger than the cost of the feasible assignment you already have, contract 1 should not be assigned to machine 2. In Figure 7.13 there would be no point in searching the tree for a solution down from the second branch to the left. If the result is smaller than the cost 16 of the feasible assignment you already have, then try to find a feasible assignment starting with contract 1 assigned to machine 2, that is lower in cost than 16 of the first feasible solution. If such a new feasible solution is found, it becomes the new bound for the search. The search (branching) and establishing bounds to limit the search space can be continued at all levels of the assignment tree.

SEARCH METHODS IN GENERAL

Search methods are important because in many ways problem solving in general involves search activities at all stages:

First, we search for a meaningful problem. Namely, we use intelligence to find facts; then we interpret the facts to help us identify a problem area of importance.

Next, we synthesize a model for the problem by searching for relevant alternatives that are candidate solutions.

Finally, we search for the "best" or satisfactory alternative.

All three stages are important and they interact. However, the more programmable procedures are more common when we get closer to the final stage. Heuristic guides are more common when we get closer to the first stage, but they may also be present in the final stage, as we have shown here in assignment problems when the number of alternatives is too large to search by programmed methods.

7.6 Decision Making under Risk

When the states of nature can be assigned objective probabilities of occurrence on the basis of a great amount of available information, we have a situation of decision making under risk. Let us suppose that this is the situation of the farmer in the model of Figure 7.16. The numbers in the payoff matrix represent the subjective degrees of *satisfaction* or *utilities* that the farmer believes he will derive. The utility incorporates the assessment of the monetary value, the risk, as well as additional related consequences that go with a particular outcome.

If the objective is to maximize the expected value of utility, the farmer calculates the following three expected values $E(S_1)$, $E(S_2)$, and $E(S_3)$ for the three strategies S_1, S_2, and S_3:

$$E(S_1) = 0.15(10) + 0.60(1) + 0.25(-2) = 1.6$$
$$E(S_2) = 0.15(8) + 0.60(4) + 0.25(0) = 3.6$$
$$E(S_3) = 0.15(3) + 0.60(3) + 0.25(3) = 3.0$$

Since $E(S_2)$ yields the largest expected utility of 3.6, the farmer will plant crop B.

TREE REPRESENTATION OF DECISION SITUATION

The decision model of Figure 7.16 can be represented by a tree structure as shown in Figure 7.17. In this figure a box represents a decision node. The box is a state under complete control of the decision maker. In our example the

	State of nature for crops		
Strategy	Perfect	Fair	Bad
S_1: plant crop A	10	1	-2
S_2: plant crop B	8	4	0
S_3: hothouse	3	3	3
	0.15	0.60	0.25 ← Probability

Figure 7.16

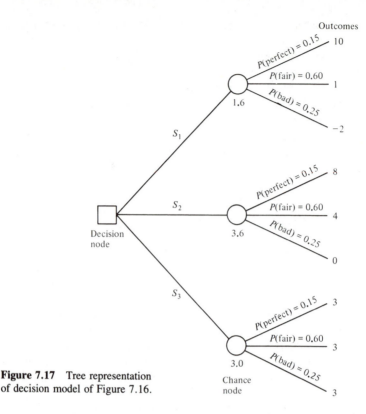

Outcomes

$P(\text{perfect}) = 0.15$ — 10

$P(\text{fair}) = 0.60$ — 1

1.6

$P(\text{bad}) = 0.25$ — −2

S_1

S_2

$P(\text{perfect}) = 0.15$ — 8

$P(\text{fair}) = 0.60$ — 4

3.6

$P(\text{bad}) = 0.25$ — 0

Decision
node

S_3

$P(\text{perfect}) = 0.15$ — 3

$P(\text{fair}) = 0.60$ — 3

3.0

$P(\text{bad}) = 0.25$ — 3

Figure 7.17 Tree representation
of decision model of Figure 7.16.

Chance
node

farmer can select one of three strategies S_1, S_2, and S_3. A circle represents chance events that the decision maker cannot control such as the states of nature in our case. The chance events are identified on the tree by the probabilities associated with their occurrence. The numbers at the end of the tree branches are the outcomes for the strategies and associated states of nature.

The tree structure proceeds from left to right according to the sequence of events. First select a strategy, then wait for a state of nature to occur, and finally obtain the resulting outcome. The calculations for the best decision are conducted by working backward. We start at the right and work our way to the left. Average out the outcomes for each chance node and record it next to the circle. Compare these values and select the largest, 3.6 in our case. The strategy that corresponds to this largest value is S_2, and this is your choice for this problem. The process we have described is known as *averaging out and folding back*. It is essentially the technique of dynamic programming discussed in more detail later.

7.7 Decision Making under Uncertainty

The most complicated case of decision making is that in which no objective probabilities are available for the occurrence of the states of nature. This could describe the situation when war and peace are the relevant states of nature, and many other examples. We can distinguish a number of different attitudes to decision making under uncertainty, as demonstrated by the following descriptions of decision makers. To make the discussion simpler to follow, let us consider the farmer's decision problem in Figure 7.16 and maintain that the region where the crops are to be planted is unknown to the farmer and that no data are available to establish objective probabilities for the states of nature.

THE SUBJECTIVIST

If the decision maker subscribes to the concept of a subjective probability as a measure of his state of knowledge, he can assign equal probabilities to all states of nature and thus indicate his highest state of ignorance or maximum entropy. He may assign unequal values when he has more knowledge. Using the criterion of maximum expected value of utility, he can then find a course of action consistent with this criterion. Thus for the subjectivist, the decision under uncertainty is reduced to one under risk.

A decision maker who does not subscribe to the concept of subjective probability can select a different rule or criterion for decision making under uncertainty, depending on his attitude as an experienced decision maker in the real world (i.e., the *pessimist,* the *optimist,* or the *regretist*).

THE PESSIMIST

The pessimist reasons that if anything can go wrong, it is sure to happen to her. She may be the person who tells you that she is out of luck. When she buys stocks, they go down in value; when she sells, they go up; when it rains, her umbrella is home; and when she has it, it does not rain. A pessimist adopts the criterion of *maximin* or the maximum of the minima. Namely, she studies the consequences of her actions by considering what is the minimum utility associated with each action, and then she selects the action that yields the maximum of these minima.

For the decision model of Figure 7.16 the pessimist proceeds with the analysis as shown in Figure 7.18. On the right-hand side of the payoff matrix the minimum of each row is recorded. These numbers represent the worst results for each course of action. Since the pessimist takes the attitude that the worst always happens to her, she selects the best of the worst results, that is, the maximum of the row minima, which is referred to as the *maximin*. This is the

	State of nature			
	Perfect	Fair	Bad	Row minima
S_1: plant crop A	10	1	−2	−2
S_2: plant crop B	8	4	0	0
S_3: hothouse	3	3	3	③ maximin

Figure 7.18 Maximin criterion.

value of 3 in our case (circled), and therefore the decision is hothouse crops. Note that the pessimist is now guaranteed 3 units of utility.

If we were to remove the last course of action from our model (because all outcomes of 3 are replaced by -5 and are therefore dominated by the other two alternatives, for instance), the pessimist would decide on crop B. In such a case she would be certain to realize no less than a zero utility. However, if nature is kind to her, she could realize as much as 8 units of utility.

The pessimist is, therefore, a risk averter. She is happy to settle for a guaranteed minimum satisfaction instead of taking a chance on realizing less, but also realizing more, than the guaranteed minimum.

THE OPTIMIST

The optimist is the risk lover. In each situation he has high hopes for the best outcome. His decision rule or criterion is to choose the best of the best. This is known as the *maximax criterion*. For each action he singles out the maximum and of all these, he selects the best (i.e., largest utility), as shown in Figure 7.19. On the right-hand column the row maxima are listed and of these, the optimist selects the highest value (i.e., the maximax). Hence he decides on strategy S_1: plant crop A.

	State of nature			
	Perfect	Fair	Bad	Row maxima
S_1: plant crop A	10	1	-2	(10) maximax
S_2: plant crop B	8	4	0	8
S_3: hothouse	3	3	3	3

Figure 7.19 Maximax criterion.

THE REGRETIST: LOSS OF OPPORTUNITY

The regretist is the person who is often heard saying: "I could kill myself for what I did. I could have done so much better had I selected a different course of action." Such a person is always full of regret for the difference between the outcome that he realizes and the maximum that he could have realized for the particular state of nature which prevails. For example, in Figure 7.18, if the state of nature turns out *Perfect* and he selects S_1, he would have no regret. However, had he selected S_2 or S_3, he would regret the *loss of opportunity* of 2 or 7 units of utility, respectively, namely, the difference between the best possible for this state of nature and the outcome which he realizes.

The regretist's objective is to make his regret as small as possible. For this purpose, the original payoff matrix is rewritten with the outcomes representing his losses due to imperfect foresight. Such a matrix is called a *regret matrix*. The regret matrix for the model of Figure 7.18 is shown in Figure 7.20.

State of nature

	Perfect	Fair	Bad	Row maxima
S_1: plant crop A	0	3	5	5
S_2: plant crop B	2	0	3	③ minimax
S_3: hothouse	7	1	0	7

Figure 7.20 Regret matrix.

To guarantee a lower bound for the maximum regret, we record the maximum regret for each row in a column on the right-hand side of the regret matrix and select the strategy corresponding to the minimum of these maxima. We have then the criterion of *minimax* regret. The outcomes in the regret matrix are also called *opportunity costs*. In situations where it is possible to obtain more information on the states of nature, the opportunity costs provide the criterion for the upper bound on the value of the information. For example, to a decision maker in Figure 7.18 who decided on S_2, information leading to certainty about the occurrence of the state *Bad* is worth no more than 3 units. This is the cost of opportunity for the outcome (S_2, Bad), as shown in Figure 7.20.

7.8 Utility Theory

The task of assigning numerical values to the possible outcomes in the decision model is within the domain of utility theory.

Famous mathematician and philosopher Daniel Bernoulli (circa 1730) suggested that utility $u(M)$ of a sum of money M could be measured by using the logarithm of M, that is, $u(M) = \log(M)$. French naturalist Buffon suggested that if you have a sum M and it is increased by m, the increase in your utility $u(M)$ should be computed from

$$u(m) = \frac{1}{M} - \frac{1}{M + m}$$

Cramer proposed a square-root function for utility.

Von Neumann and Morgenstern [48] developed an axiomatic approach to utility theory. The axiomatic approach guarantees the existence of a cardinal* utility function if the decision maker subscribes to the axioms. The von Neumann–Morgenstern utility model brings into consideration the decision maker's attitude toward risk by considering her preferences with respect to gambles that involve outcomes, in addition to her rational preferences for the outcomes. This will become clearer as we proceed to state the axioms. The subject is treated in detail in reference [49].

---

*A cardinal utility function assigns distinct numerical values to each outcome. This is distinguished from an ordinal utility which ranks only the outcomes.

Notation. Let the symbols *A, B,* and *C* represent three outcomes or prizes resulting from a decision. These could be, for instance:

A: A tuition-free college education (four years)
B: Three summer trips for archaeological diggings in Turkey, the Sinai Desert, and South America; all expenses paid
C: A cash award of $18,000

You may think, of course, of many other possible outcomes. They could all be cash awards of different sums or all noncash.

We use the symbols $>$ and $\sim$ to indicate preference and indifference, respectively. Thus $A > B$ means that the decision maker prefers *A* to *B*. $B \sim C$ means that the decision maker is indifferent between the outcomes *B* and *C*.

Axiom 1. Preferences can be stated and they are transitive; namely,

$$A > B \text{ and } B > C \text{ implies } A > C$$

and

$$A \sim B \text{ and } B \sim C \text{ implies } A \sim C$$

A rational decision maker faced with outcomes *A, B,* and *C* will be able to state his preference without violating the transitivity property.

Suppose that you cannot decide which you prefer, a blue or a red dress; then you violate the axiom because you cannot state a preference that could be one of the following:

$$\text{blue} > \text{red}$$

$$\text{red} > \text{blue}$$

$$\text{blue} \sim \text{red}$$

If your preferences among red, blue, and green dresses are

$$\text{blue} > \text{green}$$

$$\text{green} > \text{red}$$

$$\text{red} > \text{blue}$$

then you violate the transitivity property and cannot play our "game" for generating a utility for outcomes. It is only rational to insist that we know what our preferences are before we can speak of degree of satisfaction, or utility, derived from outcomes. For example, the irrationality that results from the violation of transitivity can best be illustrated by considering the second preference list of dress colors. Suppose that the store owner gives you the green dress. As you are about to leave, he calls you back and suggests that you trade the green for the blue dress by paying him $1. Since you prefer the blue dress, you pay the dollar. Now the store owner offers you to trade the blue for the red dress for $1. You agree to that, too. But then he offers to exchange the red for the green dress for $1. Since you prefer the green to the red, you accept the offer. You have paid $3 so far and you are back where you started with the green dress in your possession. The store owner can start a second cycle earning $3 and continue to take your money until, of course, you decide that something is wrong; namely, you are behaving in an irrational manner because transitivity is violated.

Note, however, that preferences in general are an individual matter. An avid archaeology student who values the experience of the particular diggings in the three summers of outcome B mentioned earlier may prefer B over A or C. A young man who does not intend to go to college, or one who is through with his college education, may prefer C. We consider A, B, and C mutually exclusive.

Preliminary Concepts and Notations Applicable to Axioms 2 and 3. Consider a game in the form of a lottery, as shown in Figure 7.21. A pointer spins in the center of a circle. When the pointer is set spinning, it is equally likely to be pointing in any direction when it comes to rest. A lottery ticket to play the game entitles you to prize A when the pointer stops in region A, and to prize B when it stops in region B. With each outcome there is an associated probability of occurrence. In Figure 7.21 the probabilities are computed from the area of each region divided by the total area.

The lotteries of Figure 7.21 are also shown by tree diagrams in Figure 7.22.

A further abstraction represents each lottery by symbols as follows:

$$L_1 = [P(A), A; P(B), B]$$

$$L_3 = [P(A), A; P(B), B; P(C), C]$$

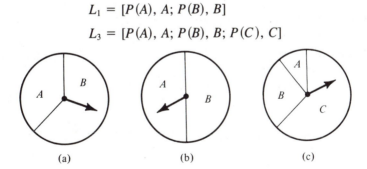

(a)　　　　　(b)　　　　　(c)

Figure 7.21 (a) Lottery L_1; (b) lottery L_2; (c) lottery L_3.

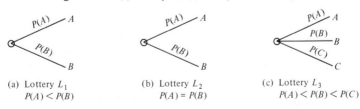

(a) Lottery L_1　　　(b) Lottery L_2　　　(c) Lottery L_3
$P(A) < P(B)$　　　$P(A) = P(B)$　　　$P(A) < P(B) < P(C)$

Figure 7.22 Tree diagram representation of lotteries.

Each outcome is separated by a comma from its probability of occurrence, and a semicolon separates the outcomes. Consider, for example, the following compound lottery. You are given a ticket to play lottery $L_1 = [P(A), A; P(L_2), L_2]$.

Here you receive a prize A with probability $P(A)$ and prize L_2 with probability $P(L_2)$. However, L_2 consists of a ticket marked L_2, which entitles you to play lottery $L_2 = [P(B), B; P(C), C]$. The complete compound lottery will finally result in one of the three prizes or outcomes A, B, and C. This can be written as

$$[P(A), A; P(L_2), [P(B|L_2), B; P(C|L_2), C]]$$

The information within the inner brackets is L_2. As can be verified from Figure 7.23, the compound lottery can also be written in this form:

$$[P(A), A; P(B|L_2)P(L_2), B; P(C|L_2)P(L_2), C]$$

This represents symbolically also a single lottery in which outcomes A, B, and C can occur with the probabilities indicated. Such a lottery $L*$ is shown in Figure 7.24.

Axiom 2. When a decision maker prefers an outcome A to an outcome B (i.e., when $A > B$), then

$$[P*(A), A; (1 - P*(A)), B] > [P(A), A; (1 - P(A)), B]$$

if, and only if, $P*(A) > P(A)$. Namely, when $A > B$, then of two lotteries involving A and B, a decision maker prefers the one in which the probability of her preferred outcome is larger.

Axiom 3. The decision maker is indifferent to the number of lotteries in a decision situation and is concerned only with the final outcomes and associated probabilities. Thus the decision maker is indifferent to the compound lottery of Figure 7.23 and the equivalent single lottery $L*$ of Figure 7.24. In Figure 7.23 a pointer may be spun twice, once in L_1 and once in L_2, and there may be fun

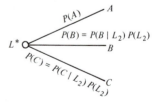

Figure 7.24 Representation of compound lottery of Figure 7.23 as a simple single lottery: $L* = [P(A), A; P(B), B; P(C), C]$.

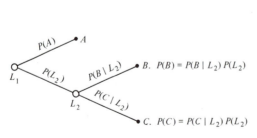

Figure 7.23 Compound lottery involving L_1 and L_2.

in the excitement of suspense,[†] but not to our "rational" decision maker, who would consider $L*$ of Figure 7.24 equivalent, although there a pointer is spun only once to yield one of three outcomes A, B, or C. In summary,

$$[P(A), A; P(L_2), L_2] \sim [P(A), A; P(B), B; P(C), C]$$

in which $L_2 = [P(B|L_2), B; P(C|L_2), C]$:

$$P(B) = P(B|L_2)P(L_2)$$

$$P(C) = P(C|L_2)P(L_2)$$

Axiom 4. If $A > B > C$, there exists a probability p for outcome A such that the decision maker is indifferent to a lottery $[p, A; (1 - p), C]$ involving her most preferred outcome A and least preferred outcome C, or receiving an intermediate outcome B with certainty. Namely,

$$B \sim [p, A; (1 - p), C]$$

As an example, consider the outcomes A, B, and C to stand for $A = \$100$ prize, $B = \$20$ prize, and $C = \$0$ prize. If the decision maker's preferences are

$$A > B > C$$

then axiom 4 requires that the decision maker be able to select a probability p such that

$$B \sim [p, A; (1 - p), C]$$

This is reasonable, as can be deduced from the following argument. If we set $p = 0$ in the lottery above, B is preferred because the lottery will yield C with certainty and $B > C$. On the other hand, for $p = 1$, the lottery is preferred because it will yield A with certainty and $A > B$. Thus

For $p = 0$: decision maker prefers B

For $p = 1$: decision maker prefers the lottery

At some point between $p = 0$ and $p = 1$, the decision maker is indifferent between the lottery and outcome B. The choice of p reflects the decision maker's attitude to risk.

UTILITY FUNCTION

Adhering to the constraints of the four axioms, it is possible to guarantee the existence of a *utility function*, which is a rule for assigning a number to each outcome or to a corresponding equivalent lottery (axiom 4). The utility function is written in the form $u(A)$, or $u(B)$, and so on, signifying the utility associated with the outcome in parentheses. The utility function has these properties:

[†]This fun can be included in the assessment of benefit (utility) associated with the outcomes.

Property 1

$$u(A) > u(B)$$

if, and only if,

$$A > B$$

$$u(A) = u(B)$$

if, and only if,

$$A \sim B$$

Property 2. The expected value of the utilities in a lottery L involving outcomes A and C is equal to the utility of the outcome B when $B \sim L$. Or, when

$$B \sim [p, A; (1 - p), C] = L$$

then

$$u(B) = \text{expected value of } u(L)$$

or

$$u(B) = pu(A) + (1 - p)u(C)$$

The utility of lottery L is the expected value of the utilities of the outcomes in the lottery.

The concept of a utility as a rational basis for comparing values or degrees of satisfaction applies to any type of outcome, as will be demonstrated by some examples.

Property 3. The choice of a reference value for the utility of the worst (or best) outcome, and the choice of a scale factor, which separates the utilities of the best and worst outcomes, are arbitrary. This is similar in concept to the reference value and scale in the measurements of temperature.

Example 1

We return to Figure 1.1 at the beginning of the book and consider the assignment of utilities to the three outcomes:

$$A = \text{cure}$$

$$B = \text{paralysis}$$

$$C = \text{death}$$

Ginsberg and Offensend [1] devised a lottery named "A Game with a Witch Doctor" in order to assign utilities to the three outcomes. The witch doctor is all-powerful. The decision-maker doctor playing the game is told that he can play only once as follows:

Make a choice between an outcome B guaranteed by the witch doctor or a lottery involving the other two outcomes. The lottery consists of an opaque bottle with a total of 100 pills. A game consists of drawing at random a pill from the bottle, with each pill being equally likely to be drawn. There are only two colors of pills, white and black. Drawing a white pill yields outcome A, and a black pill yields outcome C.

Now consider a doctor decision maker whose preferences are

$$A > B > C$$

From the properties of the utility function, we know that

$$u(A) > u(B) > u(C)$$

The question is: Where does $u(B)$ lie on the scale between $u(A)$, the best, and $u(C)$, the worst? For this purpose, $u(A)$ and $u(C)$ are assigned arbitrary values [consistent with transitivity, $u(A) > u(C)$] $u(A) = 100$ and $u(C) = 0$.

Now consider a lottery $[p, A; (1 - p), C]$ in which p is the fraction of white pills in the opaque bottle of 100 pills.

For $p = 0$: doctor prefers B because the lottery guarantees C (death) and $B > C$

For $p = 1$: doctor prefers the lottery because the lottery guarantees A (cure) and $A > B$

For what value of p is the decision maker indifferent between B and the lottery?

Ginsberg and Offensend [1] report that one doctor selected $p = 0.4$. Namely, he was indifferent between paralysis (B) and a lottery of cure (A) and death (C) when the bottle had 40 white pills (see Figure 7.25a).

$$u(B) = 0.4u(A) + (1 - 0.4)u(C) = 40$$

A second doctor arrived at $u(B) = -150$ when $u(A) = 100$ and $u(C) = 0$. Since the reference value for the utilities is arbitrary, the second doctor's utility assignment tells us that consistent with her utilities,

$$u(A) > u(C) > u(B)$$

her preferences were

$$A > C > B$$

She was indifferent to death (C) or the lottery shown in Figure 7.25b, in which the opaque bottle has 60 white and 40 black pills.* Drawing a white pill guarantees cure (A), and a black pill paralysis (B). If we assign $u(B) = 0$ and $u(A) = 100$, then

$$u(C) = 0.6u(A) + 0.4u(B)$$

$$= 60$$

*Note that the black pill now represents paralysis.

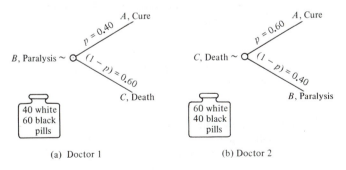

(a) Doctor 1   (b) Doctor 2

Figure 7.25

If we subtract from all utilities 60 [i.e., shift the reference basis so that $u(C) = 0$ for both doctors], then $u(A) = 40$, $u(C) = 0$, and $u(B) = -60$. To make $u(A) = 100$, we multiply the utilities by 2.5 yielding $u(B) = -150$.

In summary the utilities of doctor 2 were generated as follows (for comparison we also show the utilities of doctor 1):

	Doctor 1	Doctor 2	−60	×2.5
A. Cure	$u(A) = 100$	$u(A) = 100$	40	100
B. Paralysis	$u(B) = 40$	$u(B) = 0$	−60	−150
C. Death	$u(C) = 0$	$u(C) = 60$	0	0

Example 2

Consider the problem of self-insurance [51], in which a business manager has a shipment of goods worth $10,000. There is a probability that the shipment may be destroyed in transit. The insurance company requires a $1500 premium to insure the shipment. How small must be the probability p of safe shipment for her to buy insurance? Suppose that the total assets of the manager are $15,000. Then, if she buys insurance, she is guaranteed $15,000 - 1500 = \$13,500$. Call this B. If she does not buy insurance, she is effectively playing a lottery:

$$[p, \$15,000; (1 - p), \$5000]$$

Namely, the shipment arrives safely with probability p, and she has $A = \$15,000$; the shipment is destroyed with probability $(1 - p)$, and she has $C = \$5000$. Clearly,

$$A > B > C$$

To decide on a value for p above which she does not insure and below which she does, she equates the utility of B, $u(B)$, to the utility of the lottery:

$$u(B) = pu(A) + (1 - p)u(C)$$

Now suppose that she uses a utility function which is the logarithm to the base 10 of the total assets. Then

$$\log 13,500 = p \log 15,000 + (1 - p) \log 5000$$

$$4.13 = p(4.17) + (1 - p)(3.70)$$

$$p = \frac{0.43}{0.47}$$

$$= 0.915$$

Note: When p is known from experience, we can use the equation above to establish what value is feasible for the premium B.

Example 3

Consider a decision maker whose utility function for money from zero to $100 is curve (a) of Figure 7.26. The satisfaction associated with each additional increment say of $10 (above the first) diminishes, as is reflected from the decrease in increments of utility in the figure. For example, from $30 to $40 the utility increases by 0.1, while from $90 to

Tools and Concepts for Decision Making   Chap. 7

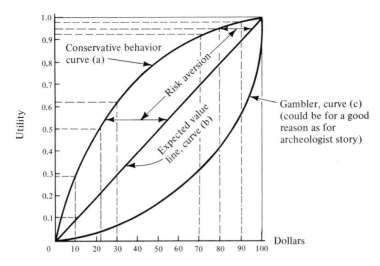

Figure 7.26 Utility function for dollars from 0 to 100: (a) conservative; (b) expected value; (c) gambler.

$100 the increase is 0.02. This is quite typical in the sense that the utility of an additional sum of money depends on how much you have.

The decision maker has $30. He is offered the chance to pay the $30 for a ticket to a lottery $L = [p, \$100; (1 - p), \$0]$. How big must p be before he decides to buy the ticket and gamble?

Let

$$A = \$100 \text{ assets for best outcome}$$

$$C = \$0 \text{ assets for worst outcome}$$

$$B = \$30 \text{ guaranteed assets}$$

$$A > B > C$$

The solution is obtained from the equation

$$u(B) = pu(A) + (1 - p)u(C)$$

From Figure 7.26, $u(100) = 1.0$, $u(0) = 0$; hence,

$$u(B) = p = 0.62$$

Note: By assigning to the best outcome A a utility of 1.0, and to the worst outcome C a utility of 0, the utility of an intermediate outcome B is equal in numerical value to the probability p when

$$B \sim [p, A; (1 - p), C]$$

Namely,

$$u(B) = pu(A) + (1 - p)u(C) = p$$

because $u(A) = 1$ and $u(C) = 0$.

Example 4

In Example 3, suppose that the lottery is $L = [1/2, \$70; 1/2, \$0]$. Would you pay \$30 to play the lottery?

Using curve (a) of Figure 7.26,

$$u(30) = 0.62$$

$$u(L) = \frac{1}{2}u(70) + \frac{1}{2}u(0)$$

$$= 0.46$$

Since $u(30) > u(L)$, you should not play the lottery.

How much should you pay to play a lottery $[1/2, \$70; 1/2, \$0]$, when you have \$30 in assets? Suppose that you should pay a sum S ($S < \$30$). Then the states of your assets are:

Best outcome: $A = (30 - S) + 70 = 100 - S$
Worst outcome: $C = (30 - S) + 0 = 30 - S$
Guaranteed state: $B = 30$

$$u(30) = \frac{1}{2}u(100 - S) + \frac{1}{2}u(30 - S)$$

or

$$1.24 = u(100 - S) + u(30 - S)$$

From curve (a) of Figure 7.26, by trial-and-error selection of values for S, we obtain $S = 20$ because

$$u(80) + u(10) = 0.95 + 0.29 = 1.24$$

or

$$u(30) = \frac{1}{2}u(80) + \frac{1}{2}u(10)$$

Example 5

Consider a young archaeologist who, in the course of her studies, discovers an ancient manuscript that describes a statue and discloses its location on a remote island. The archaeologist travels to the island to search for the statue. After a year of effort in vain, frustrated and with total assets of \$30, she decides to leave. As she is ready to depart, one of the natives approaches her with the authentic statue that she sought. When the archaeologist offers to buy the statue, the native insists on a price of \$31 for it. Our distressed archaeologist runs to the island "casino" and pays her \$30 for the only game on the island, a lottery $L = [p, \$31; (1 - p), \$0]$.

What are the best (A), worst (C), and guaranteed (B) outcomes in this case? Suppose that $p = 1/4$. Is our archaeologist rational? Does the utility curve (a) of Figure 7.26 apply in the present case? If you were the archaeologist, what utilities would you assign the three outcomes?

This example should serve to illustrate the subjective nature of utility.

The three utility curves of Figure 7.26 are distinctly different in terms of the rate of change of utility as a function of wealth (dollars):

In curve (a), the rate of increase in utility gets smaller with wealth.

In curve (b), the rate of increase in utility is constant regardless of wealth.

In curve (c), the rate of increase in utility gets larger with wealth.

Which of the three utility curves applies to our young archaeologist?

Why is it reasonable, in general, to label the curves above and below the expected value line in Figure 7.26 as *conservative behavior* and *gambler,* respectively? When is the label *gambler* not appropriate? Give examples.

7.9 Utility Assignments and the Decision Models

In a decision model involving many outcomes, the decision maker can proceed to assign utilities by first ranking the outcomes. The most preferred outcome, A, is assigned a utility $u(A) = 1.0$, and the least preferred, C, is assigned $u(C) = 0$. Any intermediate outcome B is compared to a lottery $[p, A; (1 - p), C]$. The value of p for which the decision maker is indifferent to B or the lottery is equal to the utility $u(B)$ of outcome B.

All this sounds, of course, much simpler in theory than in practice. People are not accustomed to thinking in terms of probabilities. In addition, experience of many investigations indicates that people do not behave as if their objective is to maximize the expected value of the outcomes, but rather to maximize the expected value of some function of the outcomes (i.e., a utility function). For example, when people are asked to bid on a game with a lottery [1/2, $0; 1/2, $100], the average bid is about $20 [52] and not $50 as would appear to be the case on the basis of expected value of the outcome,

$$\frac{1}{2}(0) + \frac{1}{2}(100) = 50$$

A conservative decision maker [curve (a) of Figure 7.26] with zero assets would be indifferent between a cash prize of $22, $u(22) = 0.5$, and the lottery $L = [1/2, \$0; 1/2, \$100]$, $u(L) = 0.5$.

In general, it is difficult for people to distinguish between various values of very small probabilities, such as 0.0003 or 0.00006. The same is true for values close to 1, 0.9973, 0.979, and so on. It is, therefore, simpler at times to establish utilities by fixing the probabilities in the lottery L as 1/2, because people do have a feeling for a 50-50 chance, and ask them to select a guaranteed outcome which is equivalent to the lottery. That is, find B for which $B \sim [1/2, A; 1/2, C]$ when $A > B > C$.

PRESCRIPTIVE (OR NORMATIVE) AND DESCRIPTIVE UTILITIES

Utilities can be established by selecting a mathematical function which is derived axiomatically and which tells people essentially what rule they should follow if they wish to behave in a rational, consistent manner. Such a utility is called a *normative* or a *prescriptive utility.*

The actual behavior of people in the marketplace may be quite different, however. Establishing the utilities in the marketplace as they are, and not as they ought to be, leads to a descriptive utility. However, in many instances when people become aware of their inconsistencies, they may change their utilities accordingly and thus come closer to not violating the axioms of rational behavior. The framework of decision and utility theory can uncover such inconsistencies and make decision makers aware of how they behave in the decision-making phase of problem solving. Such awareness will bring about more consistency, more rationality, and, we hope, more success in meeting objectives in a manner that is compatible with the decision maker's attitude toward risk and his value system.

Some Results of Descriptive Utilities. Swalm [53] studied utilities of money for executives. He devised hypothetical situations and asked the executives to make choices between lotteries involving risk and guaranteed outcomes. On the basis of these questions, he plotted utility functions.

For example, consider an executive who is indifferent to $B = \$1,000,000$ with certainty or a lottery $L = [1/2, \$0; 1/2, \$5 \times 10^6]$. The lottery might represent a contract in which there is a 50-50 chance of outcome 0 or $\$5 \times 10^6$. We write, then,

$$u(\$10^6) = \frac{1}{2}u(\$0) + \frac{1}{2}u(\$5 \times 10^6)$$

We now arbitrarily assign $u(\$0) = 0$ and $u(\$5 \times 10^6) = 10$ utiles (units of utility). On that basis, $u(\$10^6) = 5$ utiles. This information provides three points on the executive's utility curve for money.

Next, the executive is asked to choose between a contract with a 50-50 chance of making $\$10^6$ or nothing, or a cash prize B for selling the contract. Suppose that he is indifferent between $L = [1/2, \$0; 1/2, \$10^6]$ and $B = \$300,000$. Then

$$u(\$300,000) = \frac{1}{2}u(\$0) + \frac{1}{2}u(\$10^6)$$

$$= 0 + \left(\frac{1}{2}\right)(5)$$

$$= 2.5$$

Now, a situation is considered where a loss is involved. The executive is asked to bid on a contract. If successful, the contract will net $300,000; if unsuccessful, it will cost $200,000. Of course, he could elect not to bid (i.e., $B = 0$). For what probability p of success would he be indifferent to $L = [p, \$300,000; (1 - p), -\$200,000]$ or $B = 0$, that is,

$$u(0) = pu(300,000) + (1 - p)u(-\$200,000)?$$

Suppose that the executive is indifferent for $p = 3/4$. Then we can compute $u(-\$200,000) = -7.5$ utiles. The utility curve obtained by fitting a curve to the points we have generated so far is shown in Figure 7.27.

Some of the results reported by Swalm [53] are shown in Figure 7.28. The

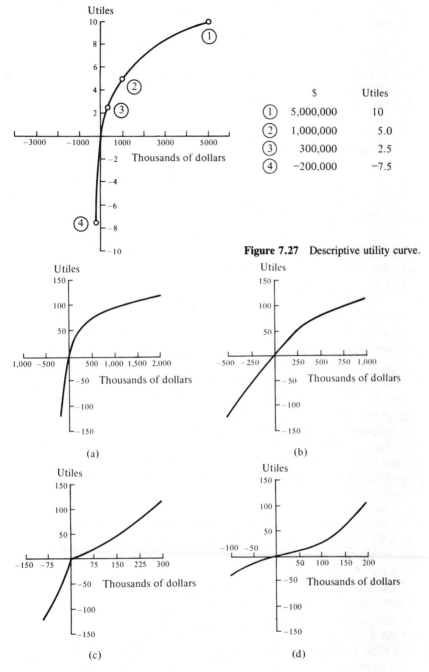

	$	Utiles
①	5,000,000	10
②	1,000,000	5.0
③	300,000	2.5
④	−200,000	−7.5

Figure 7.27 Descriptive utility curve.

(a)

(b)

(c)

(d)

Figure 7.28 Descriptive utility curves for executives: (a) extremely conservative; (b) conservative; (c) inclined toward risk; (d) gambler. Reprinted by permission of *Harvard Business Review*. An exhibit from "Utility Theory–Insights into Risk Taking" by Ralph O. Swalm (November-December 1966). Copyright © 1966 by the President and Fellows of Harvard College; all rights reserved.

executives whose utility functions are described by these curves range all the way from what appears to be an extremely cautious executive to a gambler. Swalm has found that attitudes toward risk vary widely for executives within the same company. In general, he speculates on the basis of his studies that U.S. executives in the business world are not the big risk takers they are thought to be. In many cases, they consistently avoid risks which in the long run, viewed from the overall company welfare, would be considered worth taking.

7.10 Group Decision Making

When a group involving two or more members is faced with a decision problem, we can still apply the tools that we discussed for a single decision maker, provided that they agree on:

1. The model (i.e., the alternatives that should be considered)
2. The assessment of probabilities
3. Utilities of outcomes

Seldom does a group agree on all of these items. As a basis for joint action, a majority rule could be adopted to establish group preferences. However, a simple example will illustrate that the transitivity property may be violated, leading to inconsistent results, when the majority rule is applied to three persons, P_1, P_2, and P_3, faced with the problem of choosing one of three strategies, S_1, S_2, and S_3. Suppose that the three persons rank the strategies as shown in Figure 7.29. Using a majority rule, we proceed as follows:

Decide on group preference between S_1 and S_2. Since both P_1 and P_3 prefer S_1 to S_2, the group preference is $S_1 > S_2$. Considering next S_1 and S_3, P_2 and P_3 prefer S_3 to S_1. Hence majority rule preference is $S_3 > S_1$. Then considering S_2 and S_3, we conclude that $S_2 > S_3$. This violates transitivity because

$$S_2 > S_3, \; S_3 > S_1, \text{ and } S_1 > S_2$$

The fact that transitivity is violated leads to the possible choice of any of the three strategies S_1, S_2, and S_3, depending on the order in which we make choices between pairs of strategies by the majority rule:

Beginning with S_1 and S_2, the choice is S_3.
Beginning with S_1 and S_3, the choice is S_2.
Beginning with S_2 and S_3, the choice is S_1.

	Persons		
	P_1	P_2	P_3
First choice	S_1	S_2	S_3
Second choice	S_2	S_3	S_1
Third choice	S_3	S_1	S_2

Figure 7.29

Therefore, the group choice by majority rule is arbitrary. Such a choice is irrational because it leads to an inconsistency in the decision process. The example above is known as the *Arrow paradox* [54].

The problem of establishing societal or group utilities as contrasted with individual utilities is a problem of great importance in our democratic society, which operates on majority rule. There is growing interest in this area and studies are being conducted to establish societal utilities by rational procedures. For example, the problem of an individual and societal utility function applied to welfare programs is examined in reference 55.

7.11 Summary

Decision making is ubiquitous. It is an integral part of daily life for all human beings. Decision making is not always a rational process; it can be influenced by fear of failure and postdecisional regrets. Inability to make decisions is a form of mental paralysis that can drive out all vitality from the human experience. On the other hand, setting goals, making decisions, and acting on them breeds vigor, vitality, and excitement. Psychological and mental maturity are intimately connected to the ability to make decisions and take responsibility for their consequences.

Decision-making models include a statement of objectives, a value system, alternatives, uncertainties, and a criterion for choosing an alternative. Decision making can be structured in a hierarchy of decision levels. The higher-level decisions govern those at a lower level. The decision process involves human perception, emotion, and logic. Decision theory provides a formal structure for rational choice, and it should complement, not replace, intuitive judgments. Decision models provide perspectives and can help simplify and clarify complex obscure situations.

Representation may exert a profound influence on decision making. This is illustrated by examples in which a change in one word may cause a change in choice of an alternative. The words "lose" and "die" lead to a different contextual framework for decisions than do the words "gain" and "survive" or "save." Biases in assessing information may influence decision making. Awareness of these biases is a first step in an effort to correct for them in our thinking and decision making.

There are four categories of decision situations:

Decision under certainty
Decision under risk
Decision under uncertainty
Decision under conflict

Decision under certainty may involve such a large number of alternatives that heuristics must be introduced to reduce the search for a solution to a reasonable amount of time and effort. Heuristic search methods are discussed in connection with assignment of tasks to machines. The breadth-first and depth-first search algorithms are developed and heuristics are suggested to guide and thus reduce the search effort in the algorithms. Possible refinements in the search heuristics are also introduced.

It is shown that when the search for a maximum-profit solution or minimum-cost solution is replaced by a search for a reasonable or satisfactory solution, heuristics can be employed to arrive at such a solution with a considerably reduced search effort.

The branch-and-bound technique of searching a tree for an optimum solution is discussed.

Decision making under risk is introduced in both matrix and decision tree representation. Averaging out and folding back is used to identify the alternative with the maximum expected utility of outcomes.

Decision under uncertainty is discussed in the context of four decision attitudes for potential decision makers:

    Subjectivist

    Pessimist

    Optimist

    Regretist

The regretist attitude leads to a regret matrix in which the outcomes represent opportunity costs. The regret matrix is a loss matrix (i.e., loss of opportunity).

Numerical values are assigned to outcomes in decision models using utility theory.

Utility theory guarantees that a utility function for outcomes exists if the following axioms hold true:

Axiom 1. Transitivity is not violated:

$$A > B \text{ and } B > C \text{ implies } A > C$$

$$A \sim B \text{ and } B \sim C \text{ implies } A \sim C$$

Axiom 2. When $A > B$,

$$[P^*(A), A; (1 - P^*(A)), B] > [P, (A), A; (1 - P(A)), B]$$

$$\text{if, and only if, } P^*(A) > P(A)$$

Axiom 3. The decision maker is indifferent to the number of lotteries if the final outcomes and associated probabilities are the same:

$$[P(A), A; P(L_2), L_2] \sim [P(A), A; P(B), B; P(C), C]$$

    two lotteries   one lottery

$$L_2 = [P(B|L_2), B; P(C|L_2), C]$$

$$P(B) = P(B|L_2)P(L_2)$$

$$P(C) = P(C|L_2)P(L_2)$$

Axiom 4. If $A > B > C$, there exists a lottery involving A and C with a probability p for which

$$B \sim [p, A; (1 - p), C]$$

Properties of Utility Function:

Property 1. $u(A) > u(B)$ if, and only if, $A > B$

$u(A) = u(B)$ if, any only if, $A \sim B$

Property 2. When $B \sim [p, A; (1 - p), C]$

$$u(B) = pu(A) + (1 - p)u(C)$$

Property 3. The choice of reference value and scale for units of utility is arbitrary.

Both normative (prescriptive) and descriptive utilities can be generated.

Operational definitions for utility assignments are described. Results of descriptive utility curves for executives are discussed.

Group decision making differs from individual decision making. It is shown that in a group, transitivity may be violated by the group while it is not violated by each individual in the group.

PROBLEMS

7.1. Give three examples of major decision situations and three minor decision situations. Use examples from your own experience.

7.2. Suggest a possible explanation to the times spent on the three agenda items atomic reactor, bicycle shed, and refreshments described at the beginning of Section 7.1.

7.3. Give an example of a situation where a person is paralyzed by the inability to make decisions.

7.4. Describe a situation that requires decisions at three levels or more.

7.5. What purpose do decision models serve?

7.6. What is the relationship between human information processing and judgment?

7.7. Present the models of Figures 7.1 and 7.2 to a number of your friends. Guess in advance what their choices might be. Discuss the actual choices that were made. Explain any disagreements with your predictions.

7.8. Repeat Problem 7.7 for Figures 7.4 and 7.5.

7.9. Give an example from your own experience in which a bias in assessing information had a marked influence on a decision.

7.10. What is the general lesson that can be learned from the stories in Section 7.3?

7.11. What are the main elements of a decision model? Can all the elements be evaluated objectively? Discuss.

7.12. Why do we encounter difficulties with decision making under certainty? After all, if all consequences are known for sure, why can't we make a quick decision?

7.13. Decribe a situation in which you would employ a breadth-first search for a solution.

7.14. Describe a situation in which you would employ a depth-first search for a solution.

7.15. How could heuristics guide your search in Problems 7.13 and 7.14?

7.16. Describe how a person would approach marketing a new product:
(a) When the best possible result is stipulated as an objective.
(b) When a satisfactory or a satisfying goal is stipulated.

7.17. Discuss why in real-world situations it is more pragmatic and reasonable most often to strive for satisfactory solutions rather than optimum or ideally "best" solutions.

7.18. Give an example of a qualitative use of the branch-and-bound technique.

7.19. Describe a situation for the model of Figure 7.16 that will justify the use of strategy S_3.

7.20. Describe a situation for the model of Figure 7.16 that will justify the use of strategy S_1.

7.21. Could the same person justify the use of any one of the three strategies S_1, S_2, and S_3 in Figure 7.16 depending on his or her circumstances, or does each strategy characterize one person and one personality? Discuss and give examples of circumstances that establish a context for choice of strategies, or describe personalities associated with particular strategies.

7.22. Discuss what is meant by opportunity cost. How can opportunity costs guide a business or an individual in accepting or rejecting opportunities presented to them?

7.23. Discuss how the excitement of being involved in a risky situation can be considered without violating axiom 3 of Section 7.8.

7.24. Plot your own utility function for money. Use a realistic range (for you) for monetary values from reasonable negative net worth to a substantial positive net worth. Compare your plot with that of Figure 7.27 and discuss similarity and difference. Why does Figure 7.27 show a high disutility for loss?

7.25. Discuss the role of context in the decision situation of Example 5, Section 7.8. Should the archaeologist play the game when $P = \frac{1}{2}$ in lottery L? Explain your answer.

7.26. What are the difficulties you encountered in plotting the utility curve for money in Problem 7.24? What aids can you suggest to make the task of assigning utilities more manageable?

7.27. What conclusions can be drawn from the Swalm study summarized in Figure 7.28?

7.28. Discuss what makes group decision making different from individual decision making.

7.29. Is transitivity always violated by a group? How can violation of transitivity be detected from the shape of the utility curve?

7.30. Discuss the difference between an individual and a group in the model construction phase where alternatives and states are identified and then probabilities and outcomes are assigned numerical values.

7.31. Consider two people P_1 and P_2 who agree that their problem consists of two states of nature W_1 and W_2 and two alternatives a_1 and a_2. They each assign, however, different values to the outcomes and probabilities as shown in Figure P7.31. How should P_1 and P_2 choose between a_1 and a_2 if they must act as a group on one alternative only?

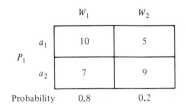

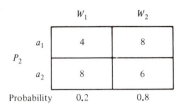

Figure P7.31

7.32. Suppose that the values assigned by the two people P_1 and P_2 in Problem 7.31 are averaged out and a composite group model results as shown in Figure P7.32. What will be the group decision? Discuss the implications of this procedure.

	W_1	W_2
a_1	7	6.5
a_2	7.5	7.5
Probability	0.5	0.5

Figure P7.32

7.33. Problems 7.31 and 7.32 bring in the issue of deciding how to decide when group decision making is involved. Suggest ways of dealing with this issue.

7.34. Legend has it that once two partners came to King Solomon and asked for advice on how to divide their property in an equitable manner because they could not agree on a process to do so and dissolve the partnership. King Solomon suggested that one of them will do the dividing and the other will have first choice, and that they should draw lots to decide who should do the dividing and who will have first choice. Give at least two examples where this or a similar procedure could be used by a group.

7.35. What kind of processes would you suggest to turn a group of people in an industrial organization into an effective team? What do you think distinguishes a group from a team? Will the best team in a sport, say basketball, be formed by taking the right number of best players from the existing teams? Discuss.

7.36. How was your decision making influenced by the study of this chapter? Give specific examples if possible.

7.37. Try to obtain the minimum-cost assignment for the following matrix.

		Machine Number			
		1	2	3	4
	1	26	15	16	20
Contract	2	30	25	26	14
Number	3	19	20	9	25
	4	20	5	20	15

7.38. Consider the entries in the matrix of Problem 7.37 to be profits. Find the assignment for maximum profit.

7.39. The matrix below represents the costs of assignments for 10 contracts and 10 machines. Find a realistic lower bound on the solution and generate a reasonable satisfactory assignment that is less than 70% above that bound, and a better one yet that is less than 50% above the bound.

		Machine Number									
		1	2	3	4	5	6	7	8	9	10
	1	64	89	55	53	97	4	22	7	53	59
	2	18	1	78	72	63	17	9	34	35	90
	3	96	87	92	61	29	87	49	71	54	58
Contract	4	8	82	69	50	59	21	82	47	89	44
Number	5	34	63	96	14	54	95	3	59	80	49
	6	35	83	43	31	34	98	97	51	36	4
	7	65	59	18	94	56	11	96	28	15	34
	8	42	81	15	96	99	60	65	87	97	88
	9	4	55	17	94	20	97	83	96	54	49
	10	11	4	20	73	26	49	47	35	12	49

7.40. Suppose that the entries in the matrix of Problem 7.39 represent profits. How would you transform the matrix so that the branch-and-bound technique could be used to find the assignment of the 10 contracts that will yield maximum profit?

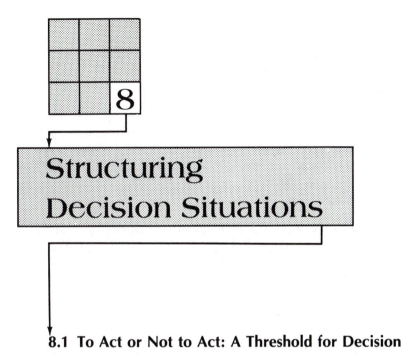

8

Structuring
Decision Situations

8.1 To Act or Not to Act: A Threshold for Decision

The dilemma of a doctor whether or not to perform an operation on a patient, the dilemma of the member of a jury whether to vote guilty or not guilty, or the predicament of the chief engineer of a nuclear power plant whether or not to shut it down are only some situations in which decisions must be made under conditions of uncertainty. In this section we develop the framework for calculating a threshold probability that will constitute a boundary between deciding to act or not to act. The implicit assumption is that we must choose only one of the two: *to act* or *not to act*. The threshold probability is associated with the probability of an undesired state. Namely, the patient has the disease (and could benefit from an operation), the person on trial is guilty of a crime (and society could benefit by a verdict of "guilty"), the nuclear power plant has a malfunction (and we could all benefit from a shutdown).

The decision model is assumed to consist of two states: the *undesirable state* (S) or its *negation* ($\bar{S}$), and two alternatives *to act* (A) or *not act* ($\bar{A}$), as shown in Figure 8.1. We consider action A desirable when S occurs and no

	Undesirable state, S	Not undesirable state, $\bar{S}$
A	U_{AS}	$U_{A\bar{S}}$
$\bar{A}$	$U_{\bar{A}S}$	$U_{\bar{A}\bar{S}}$

Figure 8.1 Decision model. $P(S) = p$ $P(\bar{S}) = 1 - p$

action $\bar{A}$ desirable when $\bar{S}$ holds true. The utilities of the outcomes, at the intersections of actions and states, are given by U_{AS}, $U_{\bar{A}S}$, $U_{A\bar{S}}$, and $U_{\bar{A}\bar{S}}$. U_{AS} and $U_{\bar{A}\bar{S}}$ represent the utilities of outcomes with no errors. $U_{\bar{A}S}$ and $U_{A\bar{S}}$ represent, respectively, the utilities of errors of omission and commission. $U_{\bar{A}S}$ is the utility of not acting when we should, and $U_{A\bar{S}}$ is the utility of acting when we should not. When the undesirable state, S, is true, the benefit B is given by the difference between U_{AS} and $U_{\bar{A}S}$:

$$B = U_{AS} - U_{\bar{A}S} \qquad (8.1)$$

namely, the difference between utilities of *acting* (doing the right thing) and *not acting* (error, not doing the right thing) when an undesirable state S can be removed by action A. When $\bar{S}$ is true, the cost C that we may incur is given by the difference between $U_{\bar{A}\bar{S}}$ and $U_{A\bar{S}}$:

$$C = U_{\bar{A}\bar{S}} - U_{A\bar{S}} \qquad (8.2)$$

namely, the difference between the utilities of *not acting* (when not acting is the right thing to do) and *acting* (the error of acting when we should not). Figure 8.2 shows the decision tree corresponding to the matrix of Figure 8.1.

The expected value of utility for each alternative is given by

$$E(A) = pU_{AS} + (1 - p)U_{A\bar{S}} \qquad (8.3)$$

$$E(\bar{A}) = pU_{\bar{A}S} + (1 - p)U_{\bar{A}\bar{S}} \qquad (8.4)$$

When probability p approaches the value of 1, S is true and action is preferred over no action, namely

$$E(A) > E(\bar{A}) \qquad (8.5)$$

because

$$U_{AS} > U_{\bar{A}S}$$

and when p approaches 0, $\bar{S}$ is true and no action is preferred over action, namely,

$$E(\bar{A}) > E(A) \qquad (8.6)$$

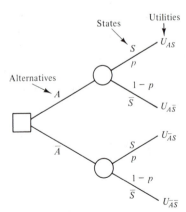

Figure 8.2 Tree diagram corresponding to matrix of Figure 8.1.

because

$$U_{\overline{A}\overline{S}} > U_{A\overline{S}}$$

We choose the alternative with the higher expected value. Since the expected value of each alternative depends on p, we can find a threshold value of p, p^*, such that for $p > p^*$, $E(A) > E(\overline{A})$ and we choose A, and for $p < p^*$, $E(\overline{A}) > E(A)$ and we choose $\overline{A}$. p^* is calculated by equating $E(A)$ and $E(\overline{A})$ of equations (8.3) and (8.4) and solving for the corresponding p^*.

$$p^*U_{AS} + (1 - p^*)U_{A\overline{S}} = p^*U_{\overline{A}S} + (1 - p^*)U_{\overline{A}\overline{S}} \qquad (8.7)$$

or

$$p^*(U_{AS} - U_{\overline{A}S}) = (1 - p^*)(U_{\overline{A}\overline{S}} - U_{A\overline{S}}) \qquad (8.8)$$

Substituting from equations (8.1) and (8.2) in equation (8.8), we obtain

$$p^*B = (1 - p^*)C \qquad (8.9)$$

$$p^*(B + C) = C$$

$$p^* = \frac{C}{B + C} \qquad (8.10)$$

$$p^* = \frac{1}{(B/C) + 1} \qquad (8.11)$$

Equation (8.11) gives a relationship between the threshold probability and the benefit-to-cost ratio B/C. A plot of equation (8.11) is shown in Figure 8.3. The region above the curve represents $p > p^*$.

Example 1: To Operate or Not to Operate [50]

A physician examines a 15-year-old boy who has pain in the right lower quadrant. On the basis of the symptoms, fever 38°C, a urinalysis, and a white-cell count, the physician assesses the probability of acute appendicitis, state S, to be 0.3, and the probability of

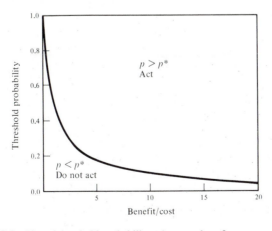

Figure 8.3 Plot of threshold probability p^* versus benefit-to-cost ratio B/C.

gastorenteritis (inflammation of the stomach and intestines), state $\bar{S}$, to be 0.7. If the state is S, immediate surgery, action A, is required. If the state is $\bar{S}$, action $\bar{A}$ is prudent (i.e., waiting for further observations).

Considering survival statistics for a group of patients with similar characteristics, the same age group, the same health status, namely, a cohort of the 15-year-old boy, the following data are available.

Survival with surgery is 99.9% for both states S and $\bar{S}$. For untreated appendicitis there is a 50% chance of perforation if surgery is delayed and a mortality rate of 2% for patients with perforation. Therefore, there is a 1% probability of mortality or 99% probability of survival without surgery when it is necessary because state S is true.

Suppose that we calculate the utilities of the outcomes as being direct measures of survival probabilities. On that basis we have the matrix of outcomes shown in Figure 8.4. The utility $U_{A\bar{S}}$ could be made smaller than that of U_{AS} because of the cost and discomfort resulting from unnecessary surgery; however, for our purposes here we decided to focus on survival as the only measure contributing to utility.

If we now calculate the threshold probability $p*$ from equation (8.11) and compare its value with $P(S) = 0.3$, our decision will be

$$\text{Operate for } P(S) > p* \quad \text{(see Figure 8.3)}$$

$$\text{Do not operate for } P(S) < p* \text{ (see Figure 8.3)}$$

$$B = U_{AS} - U_{\bar{A}S} = 0.999 - 0.990 = 0.009$$

$$C = U_{\bar{A}\bar{S}} - U_{A\bar{S}} = 1.000 - 0.999 = 0.001$$

$$p* = \frac{1}{(B/C) + 1} = \frac{1}{(0.009/0.001) + 1} = 0.1$$

Since the assessed probability of appendicitis $P(S) = 0.3$ is larger than the threshold probability $p* = 0.1$, immediate surgery is the preferred alternative.

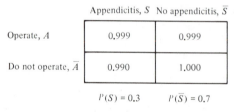

Appendicitis, S No appendicitis, $\bar{S}$

	Appendicitis, S	No appendicitis, $\bar{S}$
Operate, A	0.999	0.999
Do not operate, $\bar{A}$	0.990	1.000
	$P(S) = 0.3$	$P(\bar{S}) = 0.7$

Figure 8.4 Probabilities of survival in surgery or no surgery for appendicitis or no appendicitis.

Example 2: To Vote Guilty or Not Guilty

A person is on trial for murder and the jury must decide on a verdict. The decision model is shown in Figure 8.5, in which G stands for guilty. The benefit B in this case is represented by the difference in the utilities when the person on trial is guilty, namely, a difference between the utility of a verdict of guilty when the person is guilty U_{GG}, and the utility of a verdict of not guilty when the person is guilty $U_{\bar{G}G}$, or

$$B = U_{GG} - U_{\bar{G}G}$$

In other words, it is the difference between punishing a guilty person and acquitting a guilty person.

The cost C is the difference in utilities when the person on trial is not guilty, or

$$C = U_{\bar{G}\bar{G}} - U_{G\bar{G}}$$

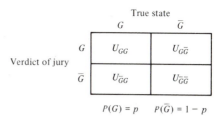

Figure 8.5 Model for jury verdict in a trial.

$$P(G) = p \qquad P(\bar{G}) = 1 - p$$

Namely, it is the difference between acquitting an innocent person and punishing an innocent person.

The threshold probability p^* can be calculated from equation (8.11) and compared with $P(G)$ once we know B and C above. But how do we measure the utilities in the matrix of Figure 8.5? And how do we assess the probability $P(G)$? There are no set answers to these questions, and it is doubtful that members of a jury could agree on values for utilities and probabilities. Yet the model we have here is useful as an aid to the thinking process and to deliberations. The final decision is based more on reasonable thinking than on precise quantification of utilities and probabilities. After the model has been used to study and justify reasons why a "guilty" verdict may be appropriate, you may still decide that it is most reasonable to vote "not guilty."

8.2 Value of Information in a Decision Situation

Consider a farmer who is studying the model of Figure 8.6 as a basis for a decision. He can plant lettuce (L) or tomatoes (T) in his fields next season, and these choices are mutually exclusive in his model. In the past 100 seasons, 60 were wet (W) and 40 were dry (D). On the basis of this information the farmer concludes that if the future will on the average be no different from the past, 60 out of 100 seasons will be wet on the average, and 40 out of the 100 will be dry. Or the probabilities of wet and dry seasons are, respectively, 0.6 and 0.4. Figure 8.6 gives the profits in thousands of dollars resulting from each alternative action coupled with a wet or dry season.

Suppose that the farmer plants lettuce L in each of 10 seasons; then on the average in six seasons, he will receive \$100,000 and in four seasons \$25,000, for a total of

$$6 \times 100{,}000 + 4 \times 25{,}000 = \$700{,}000$$

The average per season will be \$70,000, and this is the expected value, $E(L)$, per season from the choice of lettuce; that is,

$$E(L) = 0.6 \times 100{,}000 + 0.4 \times 25{,}000 = \$70{,}000 \qquad (8.12)$$

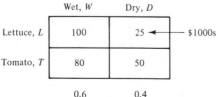

Figure 8.6

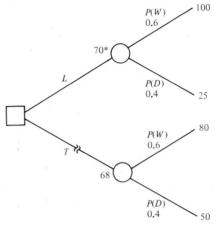

$P(W)$
0.6
100

70*

L

$P(D)$
0.4
25

$P(W)$
0.6
80

T

68

$P(D)$
0.4
50

Figure 8.7

The choice of tomatoes yields an expected value $E(T)$:

$$E(T) = 0.6 \times 80{,}000 + 0.4 \times 50{,}000 = \$68{,}000 \qquad (8.13)$$

These results are shown in Figure 8.7, and since $E(L) > E(T)$, the choice is lettuce. In Figure 8.7 a box indicates a decision junction, and a circle is a junction of chance events consistent with the symbols introduced in Section 7.6, Figure 7.17.

PERFECT INFORMATION: THE GENIE

Let us suppose that a perfect source of information in the form of a genie is available. The genie knows in advance what will happen each season. Thus, if the genie says that next season will be wet, the farmer should plant lettuce, and if he says "dry," he should plant tomatoes. On the average the genie will say "wet" and "dry" 60% and 40%, respectively, because this is how often these states occur. Therefore, with the help of a genie the farmer can expect $E(G)$:

$$E(G) = 0.6 \times 100{,}000 + 0.4 \times 50{,}000 = \$80{,}000 \qquad (8.14)$$

VALUE OF PERFECT INFORMATION

The difference between this value of $80,000 and the best the farmer can expect without the genie's help, $70,000, is the value of perfect information. In our case it is $80{,}000 - 70{,}000 = \$10{,}000$.

IMPERFECT INFORMATION: CONSULTANT

Consider now a consultant who made predictions of "wet" or "dry" for the past 100 seasons with a record given by Figure 8.8. He predicted correctly "wet," w, 42 seasons out of 60 that were wet (W). But he was wrong 18 out of 60 wet seasons. He was correct in his prediction 36 out of 40 dry seasons and wrong 4 out of 40. In Figure 8.8 the lowercase letters w and d indicate the

Structuring Decision Situations   Chap. 8

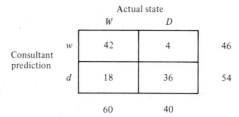

	Actual state		
	W	D	
w	42	4	46
d	18	36	54
	60	40	

Figure 8.8 Consultant record (100 seasons)

consultant predictions "wet" and "dry," respectively, and uppercase letters *W* and *D* designate true states.

Figure 8.9 shows a decision tree for the farmer when he incorporates the consultant record of Figure 8.8. First, he must decide whether to use the consultant (get information) or not. The lower branch "No Information" leads to Figure

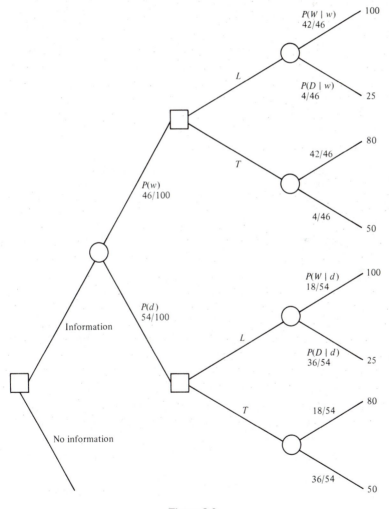

Figure 8.9

8.7 with a maximum expected value of $70,000. In the upper branch, "Information," we assume that the consultant's record in the future will be no different from his record of the past. Then 46 out of 100 seasons he will predict w and 54 out of 100 he will predict d. After the consultant makes a prediction we can choose L or T. The season may turn out either W or D.

Thus, given that the consultant predicts w, we have

$$P(W\,|\,w) = 42/46$$

$$P(D\,|\,w) = 4/46$$

The outcome from L with a wet season, W, is $100,000, and with a dry season, D, $25,000. The expected value from planting lettuce L when the consultant predicts w is

$$E(L\,|\,w) = \frac{42}{46} \times 100,000 + \frac{4}{46} \times 25,000 = \frac{1}{46} \times 4,300,000 \text{ dollars}$$

The expected value from planting tomatoes when the consultant predicts w, $E(T\,|\,w)$, is

$$E(T\,|\,w) = \frac{42}{46} \times 80,000 + \frac{4}{46} \times 50,000 = \frac{1}{46} \times 3,560,000 \text{ dollars}$$

Since

$$E(L\,|\,w) > E(T\,|\,w)$$

then if the consultant predicts w, the farmer should select L and expect $1/46 \times 4,300,000$ dollars on the average. However, he can expect this profit only as often as the consultant predicts w, and this will happen 46 out of 100 seasons.

Given that the consultant predicts d, we use similar calculations to obtain the expected values from planting lettuce L or tomatoes T,

$$E(L\,|\,d) = \frac{18}{54} \times 100,000 + \frac{36}{54} \times 25,000 = \frac{1}{54} \times 2,700,000 \text{ dollars}$$

$$E(T\,|\,d) = \frac{18}{54} \times 80,000 + \frac{36}{54} \times 50,000 = \frac{1}{54} \times 3,240,000 \text{ dollars}$$

Since

$$E(T\,|\,d) > E(L\,|\,d)$$

the farmer should plant tomatoes when the consultant predicts d and expect a profit of $1/54 \times 3,240,000$ dollars on the average. This will happen as often as the consultant will predict d, or 54 out of 100 seasons.

The total expected value $E(C)$ with the consultant information becomes

$$E(C) = \frac{46}{100} \times \frac{1}{46} \times 4,300,000 + \frac{54}{100} \times \frac{1}{54} \times 3,240,000 \qquad (8.15)$$

$$= \$75,400$$

Note that this value is larger than the $70,000 expected without any information, and less than the $80,000 expected with perfect information.

ALTERNATIVE FORM OF CONSULTANT RECORD

When the consultant record is given in terms of conditional probabilities as shown in Figure 8.10, they can be converted to joint probabilities as of Figure 8.11, and finally to conditional probabilities of Figure 8.12 that are used in the decision tree of Figure 8.9.

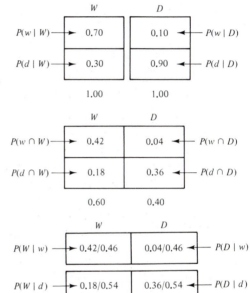

Figure 8.10 Record in form of conditional probabilities.

Figure 8.11 Converting probabilities of Figure 8.10 to joint probabilities for $p(W) = 0.60; p(D) = 0.40$.

Figure 8.12 Converting joint probabilities of Figure 8.11 to conditional probabilities of states given prediction.

8.3 Precision of Information for Decisions

PRECISION OF INFORMATION

Consider the payoff matrix of Figure 8.13. Let us suppose that we must make a choice between product d_1 and d_2 for next year. The profits from each choice depend on the state of the economy designated as Strong (S), Medium (M), or Weak (W). Four genies are available to us. Their information is accurate, but each provides information in a different form. *Genie P*, the most precise genie, tells whether the economy will be S, M, or W. The remaining three genies are less precise than genie P but accurate. The information they provide is as follows. *Genie S* only tells whether the economy will be strong (S) or not strong $(\bar{S})$. *Genie M* only tells whether the economy will be M or $\bar{M}$, and *genie W* tells whether the economy will be W or $\bar{W}$. Which of the four genies should we use with the payoff matrix of Figure 8.13?

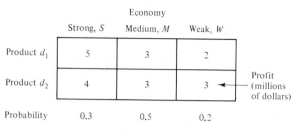

Economy

	Strong, S	Medium, M	Weak, W
Product d_1	5	3	2
Product d_2	4	3	3
Probability	0.3	0.5	0.2

Profit (millions of dollars)

Figure 8.13

If we must know the state of the economy, only genie P will always give us complete information. On the other hand, if our objective is to obtain no more information than that required to decide on a choice of product d_i for maximum profit, genie S and genie W are just as precise for us as genie P. Because if genie S says S, we choose d_1, and if he says $\bar{S}$, we choose d_2 regardless of whether M or W will happen. Similarly, when genie W says W we choose d_2, and when he says $\bar{W}$ we choose d_1. Genie M does not give us the needed information, because when he says $\bar{M}$ we must know whether S or W will happen before we make a choice of product for maximum profit. When genie M says M, we can choose either d_1 or d_2. Thus with reference to information about the states of the economy, genie P is more precise than genies S, M, or W. But with reference to a choice of action, genies S and W are as good as genie P, and genie M is inferior to the others. The level of precision of information required in a decision situation depends on the payoff matrix and often we can do just as well with partial information as with the most precise information possible in the context of the problem.

PRECISION OF PROBABILITIES OF STATES

In the absence of genies we may wish to establish the probabilities associated with each state of the economy. Let us consider two examples.

Suppose that we can choose one of two alternatives a_1 and a_2 for investment. Profit depends on whether the economy will be strong, S, or not strong, $\bar{S}$. The payoff matrix is shown in Figure 8.14. We are uncertain about what the state of the economy will be, and therefore, we are uncertain about what to choose, a_1 or a_2. Suppose that we decide to choose the alternative that yields the largest expected value. Then if p designates the probability that S will occur, that is, $P(S) = p$, $P(\bar{S}) = 1 - p$, and $E(a_1)$ and $E(a_2)$ designate the expected values from alternatives a_1 and a_2, respectively, we have

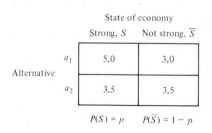

State of economy

	Strong, S	Not strong, $\bar{S}$
a_1	5.0	3.0
a_2	3.5	3.5

$P(S) = p$ $P(\bar{S}) = 1 - p$

Alternative

Figure 8.14

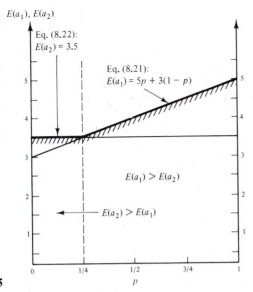

Figure 8.15

$$E(a_1) = 5p + 3(1 - p) \tag{8.16}$$

$$E(a_2) = 3.5p + 3.5(1 - p) = 3.5 \tag{8.17}$$

Equations (8.16) and (8.17) are equations of straight lines representing the expected values of the alternatives as a function of probability p. These two equations are plotted in Figure 8.15.

From this figure we can see that for $0 \leq p < 1/4$, $E(a_2) > E(a_1)$, and for $1/4 < p \leq 1$, $E(a_1) > E(a_2)$. When $p = 1/4$, $E(a_1) = E(a_2)$. Therefore, we do not need to know p with more precision than that provided by the following statement: The probability p of a strong economy is smaller than $1/4$; or the probability p of a strong economy is larger than $1/4$. Once we know the answer in terms of either statement, we know what to do.

Let us consider a second example with two states of the economy, but this time with four alternatives, as shown in Figure 8.16. Suppose again that we are uncertain about what the state of the economy will be and we wish to choose the alternative that yields the largest expected value. Then if we designate $P(S) = p$

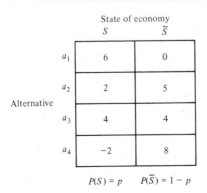

	State of economy	
	S	$\overline{S}$
a_1	6	0
a_2	2	5
a_3	4	4
a_4	-2	8

Alternative

Figure 8.16 $P(S) = p$ $P(\overline{S}) = 1 - p$

as the probability of a strong economy, the expected values from alternatives a_1, a_2, a_3, and a_4 are

$$E(a_1) = 6p \tag{8.18}$$

$$E(a_2) = 2p + 5(1 - p) \tag{8.19}$$

$$E(a_3) = 4p + 4(1 - p) = 4 \tag{8.20}$$

$$E(a_4) = -2p + 8(1 - p) \tag{8.21}$$

The four equations above are equations of straight lines representing the expected values of the alternatives as a function of probability p of a strong economy. These equations are plotted in Figure 8.17.

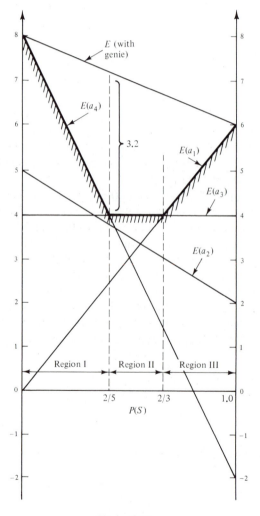

Figure 8.17

The information required for the decision is limited to establishing whether $P(S)$ is in region I, II, or III of Figure 8.17. In each region a different alternative yields the largest expected value:

In region I, where $0 \le P(S) \le 0.4$, alternative a_4 yields the largest expected value.

In region II, where $0.4 < P(S) \le 2/3$, alternative a_3 yields the largest expected value.

In region III, where $2/3 < P(S) \le 1$, alternative a_1 yields the largest expected value.

Suppose that a genie is available for the model of Figure 8.16. Then for $P(S) = p$, the expected value E(with genie) is

$$E(\text{with genie}) = p6 + (1 - p)8 \qquad (8.22)$$

Equation (8.22) is represented by the highest straight line in Figure 8.17. From Figure 8.17 we note that the largest difference between the expected value we can realize with the aid of the genie and on our own occurs when $P(S) = 2/5$. This maximum difference is 3.2, and this is the upper bound on the value of genie information.

$$E(\text{with genie}) = 0.4 \times 6 + 0.6 \times 8 = 7.2$$

$$E(\text{without genie}) = 0.4 \times 4 + 0.6 \times 4 = 4.0$$

$$E(\text{with genie}) - E(\text{without genie}) = 7.2 - 4.0 = 3.2$$

Note also in Figure 8.17 that alternative a_2 should never be used because it is dominated by at least one other alternative in each region.

8.4 Relevance Tree Representation of Multiattribute Decision Problems

CONSTRUCTING A RELEVANCE TREE

Multiattribute decision problems can often be represented by a relevance tree that provides a convenient way to establish the relative weights of importance of the attributes.

The attributes are first described in broad categories at a high level of aggregation. For example, in a problem of choosing an automobile, cost and performance are broad categories; in a problem of selecting a job, location and compensation are broad categories; in selecting a university, reputation and education opportunity are broad categories.

To construct a relevance tree, we begin with a list of the broad categories at the top of the tree. These describe the *inner environment* of the problem solver in terms of desired objectives. The objectives are those relevant to the problem at hand. Irrelevant attributes are those that make no difference in choosing between the alternatives being considered. The alternatives represent the *set of opportunities* provided by the *external environment*. For example, if location of a job makes *no difference* to you, exclude location from the relevance tree. On the other hand, if proximity to your friends is important, location should be included.

The number of categories of attributes you select should be small so that you can compare them and assess their relative importance without too much difficulty. Two or three top-level categories would be ideal.

The next step is to decompose each major category into lower-level attributes that relate to them. Again, the partitioning of each category should be into two or three elements, if possible, so that elements can be assigned relative weights of importance with ease.

Figure 8.18 shows a relevance tree for a job selection problem [56]. At each node we assign relative weights of importance to the categories on the branches that emanate from the node. The sum of the weights is 1. The relative importance of the attributes at the bottom of the tree is obtained by multiplying down the branches. For example, the rating of importance of starting salary is computed as follows (see Figure 8.18):

$$0.33 \times 0.7 \times 0.9 = 0.208$$

The decomposition should continue this way, with each node containing a relatively small number of lines until we reach a level where the labels of the attributes appear explicitly measurable either objectively or subjectively. For example, the category of cost in the purchase of an automobile becomes more explicitly measurable in terms of the subattributes of initial cost and cost of maintenance. Under maintenance, fuel economy, average monthly cost of repair, yearly cost of license, and tire replacement cost are more explicit.

The objectives and the associated lower-level attributes should include both positive and negative aspects, namely, both that which we wish to achieve and that which we wish to avoid. You may include color as an attribute in the choice of car because you love red and you are indifferent to other colors, or because you hate red and you are indifferent to other colors. Similarly, in selecting a university you may include proximity to relatives because you wish to be close to them or far from them, but in either case you care, you are not indifferent.

As an example, consider a person trying to select one of four jobs that were offered to him. These constitute his alternatives or the *opportunity set* provided by the external environment. The four jobs are described in Figure 8.19 in terms of the attributes at the bottom of the relevance tree in Figure 8.18.

Each job opportunity or alternative a_i ($i = 1, 2, 3, 4$) is studied in terms of its contributions c_{ij} to each attribute j at the lowest level of the relevance tree shown in Figure 8.18.

Studying the alternatives this way you may sharpen the calibration of your scales for assigning relative values to categories; you may identify missing attributes that make a difference in your choice. In sum, you may learn something about yourself as a problem solver.

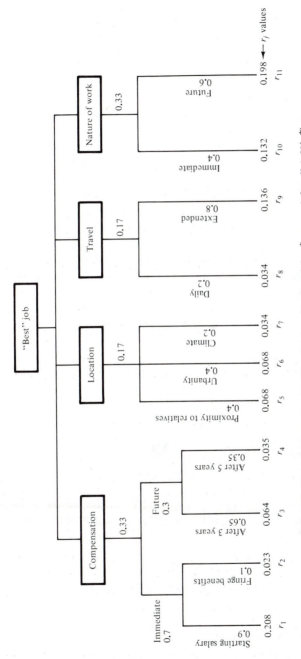

Figure 8.18 Relevance tree for job selection. For best job a_β^*, $c_{\beta j} = 1$ for all j, $V(a_\beta^*) = \sum c_{\beta j} r_j = 1$. For worst (barely acceptable) a_w^0, $c_{wj} = 0$ for all j, $V(a_w^0) = \sum c_{wj} r_j = 0$.

Attributes, j	Job Opportunities or Alternatives, a_i			
	a_1	a_2	a_3	a_4
1. Starting salary (dollars)	32,400	33,000	35,000	34,200
2. Fringe benefits (dollars)	4,900	6,200	6,300	5,100
3. Three-year salary (dollars)	45,000	38,000	42,000	42,000
4. Five-year salary (dollars)	60,000	42,000	46,000	46,000
5. Proximity to relatives (hours)	0	0	5	1
6. Urbanity	2.5	2.5	1.0	15.00
7. Climate	*	*	*	*
8. Daily travel (hours)	5	1	0.25	1.25
9. Extended travel (days)	0	10	0	35
10. Nature of immediate work	*	*	*	*
11. Nature of future work	*	*	*	*

Figure 8.19 Job alternatives $a_i (i = 1, 2, 3, 4)$ described in terms of attributes.

A weight of 0, $c_{ij} = 0$, implies the lowest level of contribution of job i to the realization of attribute j, just short of the job opportunity not being acceptable as an alternative on the grounds of failing to meet the threshold of acceptance in attribute j. $c_{ij} = 1$ signifies the largest contribution of job i to the realization of attribute j within the horizon of what appears most feasible and realizable to the problem solver.

CALCULATING THE VALUE $V(a_i)$ FOR EACH ALTERNATIVE a_i

The value $V(a_i)$ of each alternative a_i is obtained by multiplying the contributions c_{ij} for alternative a_i by the rating of importance r_j of each attribute j:

$$V(a_i) = \sum_{j=1}^{m} c_{ij}r_j \qquad i = 1, 2, \ldots, n \qquad (8.23)$$

In matrix form equation (8.23) becomes

$$\mathbf{V} = \mathbf{cr} \qquad (8.24)$$

The worst acceptable alternative, which barely satisfies the threshold for each attribute, will have $c_{ij} = 0$ for all j. The best possible alternative in terms of the horizon of feasibility will have $c_{ij} = 1$ for all j. Thus

$$V(a_{\text{worst}}) = \sum_j c_{ij}r_j = 0$$

$$V(a_{\text{best}}) = \sum_j c_{ij}r_j = \sum_j 1 \cdot r_j = 1$$

Intermediate alternatives will have values $V(a_i)$ between these limits of 0 and 1.

Figure 8.20 gives the ratings of importance, r_j, of the attributes in Figure 8.18 and the contributions c_{ij} of each job alternative to these attributes. We obtain the following results ($m = 11$ in Figure 8.18):

		Alternatives			
		a_1	a_2	a_3	a_4
Attribute Number, j	Relative Weight, r_j	c_{1j}	c_{2j}	c_{3j}	c_{4j}
1	0.228	0.68	0.7	0.75	0.73
2	0.023	0.6	0.7	0.7	0.6
3	0.064	0.75	0.6	0.7	0.7
4	0.035	0.75	0.45	0.5	0.5
5	0.068	1.0	1.0	0.7	0.5
6	0.068	1.0	1.0	0.7	0.8
7	0.034	0.7	0.7	0.9	0.6
8	0.034	0.6	0.5	0.9	0.4
9	0.136	1.0	0.7	1.0	0.4
10	0.132	0.5	0.9	0.8	0.9
11	0.198	0.5	0.75	0.75	0.85
↑	↑	↑	↑	↑	↑
j	r_j	c_{1j}	c_{2j}	c_{3j}	c_{4j}

c_{ij} contribution of alternative or opportunity i to attribute j

Value $V(a_i) = $ 0.71   0.75   0.74   0.69

$$V(a_i) = \sum_{j=1}^{m} c_{ij} r_j$$

a_i are alternatives in opportunity set, $i = 1, 2, 3, 4$ in our case

Figure 8.20

$$V(a_1) = \sum_{j=1}^{m} c_{1j} r_j = 0.71$$

$$V(a_2) = \sum_{j=1}^{m} c_{2j} r_j = 0.75$$

$$V(a_3) = \sum_{j=1}^{m} c_{3j} r_j = 0.74$$

$$V(a_4) = \sum_{j=1}^{m} c_{4j} r_j = 0.69$$

Alternative a_2 has the highest value with a_3 very close to it.

WHAT YOU CAN LEARN FROM THE MODEL

If the choice of best alternative based on the relevance tree model does not agree with your "feelings" about the choice, go back and study the model. Perhaps your ratings of importance do not represent properly your feelings. Did you leave out an important attribute? Did you overestimate the contributions of an alternative to some attributes? Did you underestimate some values? Did you get sufficient information in some areas? Did you sort out the information carefully and question its credibility?

8.5 Nine Steps to Construct Relevance Trees in Multiattribute Decision Models

We summarize now the procedure for constructing a relevance tree representation for multiattribute decision situations. We list the nine steps of the procedure using the example of Section 8.4 as a reference to provide concrete meaning to each step.

Step 1. Establish broad categories relevant to the problem. In the job selection model of Section 8.4, these are compensation, location, travel, and nature of work. Limit the number of categories to five. If you initially have more than five, group some of them together into broader categories.

Step 2. Assign numerical values between 0 and 1 to each broad category. The sum of the assigned values should equal 1. The larger the value, the greater its importance. In Figure 8.18 "compensation" and "nature of work" each constitute 1/3 of the relevant considerations. The remaining 1/3 $(1 - 1/3 - 1/3)$ is divided evenly between "location" and "travel." The value of 0.17 does not indicate whether the problem solver likes to travel or not, it simply says that travel is relevant in choosing a job.

Step 3. Subdivide the broad categories into more specific components. In Figure 8.18, "compensation" is divided into "immediate" and "future," "location" is divided into "proximity to relatives," "urbanity," "climate," and so on. Assign relative values to these components so that the sum of the divisions under each category equals 1. Thus the relative values for "immediate compensation" and "future compensation" add up to 1, and the relative values for the three aspects of location add up to 1.

Step 4. Examine the model to be sure that each category is as specific as necessary. Continue dividing the headings until you are satisfied with the degree of detail. In Figure 8.18 "immediate compensation" and "future compensation" are further broken into fractional parts.

Step 5. Multiplying down the branches of the model gives a relative value of importance for each attribute at the bottom of the tree. For example, proceeding with the first branch on the left of Figure 8.18, we have

$$0.33 \times 0.7 \times 0.9 = 0.208$$

The value of 0.208 indicates that "starting salary" has an importance rating of 20.8% in any job consideration. Similarly, "extended travel" has a rating of 0.136 or 13.6%.

Step 6. In a separate chart list the attributes that are at the bottom of the relevance tree. Next to these attributes list each of your alternatives in terms of what they offer to each attribute such as starting salary, fringe benefits, and so on, as shown in Figure 8.19. If, for any attribute, you have a threshold value, namely you will not accept an alternative that does not reach this level, do not list options that fail to achieve one or more threshold levels. For example, if a job alternative a_5 starts at $20,000 and you will *only* accept a job that pays $28,000 or more, do not list job a_5 in Figure 8.19. Temporarily leave blank spaces for those features of an alternative that depend on qualitative evaluations, such as "nature of work" or job satisfaction and "climate." These spaces are marked by asterisks in Figure 8.19.

Step 7. Establish reasonable minimum and maximum limits for each attribute. For example, for "starting salary" the limits could be $28,000 and $36,000 for minimum and maximum, respectively. Evaluate the contributions c_{ij} of each job i to each attribute j according to its position within these boundaries, and assign relative values c_{ij} between 0 and 1. Zero means the job ranks as poorly as possible with regard to that attribute, and a 1 indicates the best on your predetermined scale. For "starting salary" $28,000 will be assigned 0 and $36,000, 1. Do this for both qualitative and quantitative characteristics, namely salaries as well as nature of work and climate.

Step 8. Record in a table the contributions c_{ij} from step 7 and the ratings of importance r_j for the attributes from step 5 (the bottom of the relevance tree in Figure 8.18). Such a table is shown in Figure 8.20. Multiply the ratings of importance r_j calculated in step 5 by the contribution c_{ij} of each job obtained in step 7. Add up these products for each job to get a total value for each job. This step constitutes the application of equation (8.23).

$$V(a_i) = \sum_{j=1}^{m} c_{ij} r_j$$

Step 9. Compare the results from step 8 with your anticipated results and see what is revealed about your values and thoughts. Adjust the relative weights and values if necessary. The most important contribution of the model may be realized when you will ponder what you learned about yourself as a problem solver and decision maker.

8.6 Value Judgment and Resource Allocation: An Extension of the Relevance Tree Model

Acts of judgment are inseparable from the fundamental act of matching. The doctor matches a medicine to a disease, the judge matches a punishment to an offense, and in common speech we match words to objects, experiences, thoughts, and so on. Indeed, judgment as a matching activity is closely related to the concept of classification, because the act of judging what is like and what is unlike is at the very foundation of human thought process in classification.

Value judgment is the act of matching behavior, or a course of actions, to values. To be more specific, when we claim that activity or policy a is good for the purpose of realization of value v, we have performed an act of judgment in the sense of matching an activity or a policy to a value. It is conceivable, however, that an act may contribute to the realization of a number of values v_j $(j = 1, 2, \ldots, m)$. In that case, we must use judgment to match a number with the relative intensity of the contribution of the act to each value. We use the word "value" here in a sense that is similar to our use of the word "attribute" in Sections 8.4 and 8.5.

Since values can be viewed as means, values that contribute to the realization of an end value, we may use judgment to assign a rating r_j in the form of a number which matches the importance of the means value v_j, or how much v_j matters, to the realization of the end value, as we have done in Sections 8.4 and 8.5.

Consider, for example, the design of an urban transportation system. Suppose that the model consists of n alternatives a_i, and that the hierarchy of values consists of the end value "quality of life" and three means values v_j $(j = 1, 2, 3)$ convenience, safety, and aesthetics. We note that the list of values could be expanded and that each may be considered as an end value within a substructure of lower-level values. To assess the utility of each alternative, we write an equation similar to equation (8.23):

$$u(a_i) = \sum_{j=1}^{m} c_{ij} r_j \qquad i = 1, 2, \ldots, n \qquad (8.25)$$

in which r_j is the importance rating of value v_j and c_{ij} is the relative contribution of alternative a_i to the realization of value v_j.

In matrix form, equation (8.25) becomes

$$\mathbf{u}(a_i) = \mathbf{cr} \qquad (8.26)$$

The criterion for selecting an alternative can be max $\mathbf{u}(a_i)$, that is, the alternative which yields the maximum utility.

This model is, of course, very simple. It is not stipulated here that the linear model of equation (8.25) is the most descriptive or appropriate. In addition, the assignment of values r_j may be quite a complicated task if we consider interactions of the following nature. Consider four values v_j. It is conceivable that the assignment of a particular importance rating r_k will depend on the probabilities and extents of realization of the other three values. The number of combinations is infinite because both the probabilities and the extents of realization are on a continuous scale. In Chapter 7 we considered problems in which a utility was generated for a particular outcome B by the mechanism of a conceptual lottery. The most desired outcome A was assigned a utility of 1, the least desired outcome C was assigned a utility of 0, and the utility $u(B)$ assigned to B was the probability p in the following lottery:

$$[p, A; (1 - p), C]$$

Efforts have been made to extend this fundamental approach to situations in which multiple attributes are involved [57, 65–67].

Public and private agencies are often confronted with the problem of allocating resources to alternative programs of research and development. When values v_j can be stipulated and their importance rating r_j assessed, equation (8.25) can be used in a model of value judgment among alternative programs. Since each program may require a different level of resource allocations, a ratio of benefit, or accrued expected utility, to cost can be generated and used as an index of desirability for each program.

Cetron [58] employed such an approach in comparing the desirability of the following two research and development programs for the U.S. Navy.

Program a_1: Enhance Tensile Strength of Metals
Program a_2: Improve Metal Corrosion Resistance (in Seawater)

The programs were compared in terms of their value to the country, their cost, and their probability of success, using these steps:

1. The national values v_j or goals and their ratings r_j were established.
2. The contributions c_{ij} of programs a_1 and a_2 to the realization of values v_j were assessed.
3. A probability was assigned to the likelihood of success for each program in meeting its objective (say, a certain level of tensile strength for program a_1, and a certain level of corrosion resistance for program a_2).
4. The costs for each program were estimated at three levels of funding:
   (a) A threshold level below which the program should not be undertaken.
   (b) A maximum level which represents the amount of funding for the program under conditions of unlimited resources (i.e., the program can progress at a rapid pace to meet the stipulated objective).
   (c) An optimum level to proceed at an optimum rate which is compatible with normal but productive procedures.

Figure 8.21 lists the values,* their ratings r_j, and the contribution coefficients c_{ij} of the two programs. The ratings r_j were assigned on the basis of

$$\Sigma_j r_j = 100 \quad \text{and} \quad 0 \le r_j \le 100$$

From the information in Figure 8.21, the national utilities $u(a_1)$ of the programs were calculated by applying equation (8.25):

$$u(a_1) = \sum_{j=1}^{16} c_{1j}r_j = 0.8 \times 14 + 0.3 \times 12 + \cdots + 0.9 \times 2$$

$$= 51.5 \text{ utiles for program } a_1$$

*The values are from Lecht [59]. The ratings r_j and coefficients c_{ij} are those used by Cetron [58].

National Goals, j (values, v_j)	Ratings, r_j	Contribution c_{ij} to Realization of Goal	
		c_{1j}, Program a_1: Tensile Strength	c_{2j}, Program a_2: Corrosion Resistance
1. National defense	14	0.8	0.9
2. Social welfare	12	0.3	0.0
3. Education	8	0.1	0.0
4. Urban development	8	0.9	0.0
5. Health	7	0.1	0.0
6. Area development	7	0.7	0.1
7. Housing	6	1.0	0.3
8. Agriculture	6	0.2	0.4
9. Manpower retraining	6	0.0	0.0
10. Transportation	5	0.9	0.6
11. Consumer expenditure	5	0.2	0.0
12. Private plant and equipment	4	0.8	0.0
13. Space	4	0.6	0.1
14. Research and development	3	1.0	0.9
15. International aid	3	0.0	0.0
16. Natural resources	2	0.9	0.8

Figure 8.21 Contributions c_{ij} of two programs to the realization of national goals (values) and their ratings, r_j. From *Industrial Applications of Technological Forecasting*, by Martin J. Cetron and Christine A. Ralph. © 1971 John Wiley & Sons, Inc.

$$u(a_2) = \sum_{j=1}^{16} c_{2j} r_j$$

$$= 0.9 \times 14 + \cdots + 0.8 \times 2$$

$$= 25.2 \text{ utiles for program } a_2$$

The probabilities of success were 0.9375 and 0.75 for programs a_1 and a_2, respectively. These values were calculated on the following basis. Four independent efforts* were considered in progress in program a_1, each with probability 0.5 of success. Since the success of one effort or more is equivalent to the success of the program, $P_{\text{success}}(a_1) = 1 - P_{\text{failure}}(a_1) = 1 - (0.5)^4 = 0.9375$. Two independent efforts were considered for program a_2, each with a probability 0.5 of success; therefore, $P_{\text{success}}(a_2) = 1 - P_{\text{failure}}(a_2) = 1 - (0.5)^2 = 0.75$.

Thus the expected utilities of the programs were calculated as

$$E[u(a_1)] = P_{\text{success}}(a_1) \times u(a_1)$$

$$= 0.9375 \times 51.5$$

$$E[u(a_2)] = P_{\text{success}}(a_2) \times u(a_2)$$

$$= 0.75 \times 25.2$$

*Possibly different approaches to achieve the same objectives of the program.

The optimum fundings for the programs were \$1 billion for program a_1 and \$0.516 billion for program a_2. Therefore, the expected utility per billion dollars, or the index of desirability D_i, was calculated for each program as follows:

$$\text{Program } a_1: \quad D_1 = \frac{0.9375 \times 51.5}{1} = 48.3 \text{ utiles/billion dollars}$$

$$\text{Program } a_2: \quad D_2 = \frac{0.75 \times 25.2}{0.516} = 36.6 \text{ utiles/billion dollars}$$

8.7 Sequential Decisions

Dynamic programming is a technique for making decisions in sequence by working backward. The technique applies to both outcomes that are deterministic and random. Let us illustrate the technique by examples.

Figure 8.22 shows a network of links between nodes. The number on each link designates the cost of travel along it between the two adjacent nodes. Suppose that you wish to get from node A to node B. You are constrained to move between the nodes heading only north or east. There are $5!/2!3! = 10$ different possible routes which do not violate the constraints on the directions of travel. A possible route is one that achieves the desired goal state from an initial state, without violating the constraints, namely, without doing that which is not to be done in the problem considered. Possible solutions in this context are also referred to as feasible or acceptable solutions.

To select the optimum route in Figure 8.22, one approach is to compute the cost of each of the 10 possible routes and find the one of least cost. The optimum is marked by heavy lines in the figure and represents a cost of 17 units. In more complex problems, such an approach for finding the optimum path may not be possible with the constraints of reasonable time and effort for the search. Consider, for example, a grid of 20×20 instead of the 2×3 in Figure 8.22. In such a grid there are $40!/20!20!$ possible routes from A to B. This is a number larger than 13×10^{10}. To obtain the cost of each route will require the addition of 40 numbers (one for each of the 40 links), and a computer that can perform 2×10^6 additions per second will require about one month of continuous computations. For a grid of 100×100, the computations are not possible in a lifetime. In view of these enormous numbers of possible solutions, methods are

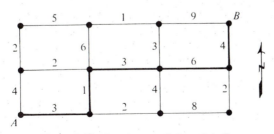

Figure 8.22 Least-cost path from A to B.

needed to reduce the extent of the search and associated computations and still identify the best of all possible solutions (i.e., the optimum) in reasonable time and effort. One such method is the method of *dynamic programming*.

The method of dynamic programming is based on the mathematical concept of recursion. It essentially converts a problem in which an optimum policy involving n components is desired to a sequential decision process of n separate stages dealt with in a recursive fashion. The method is based on Bellman's principle of optimality, which states [60]:

> An optimal policy has the property that, whatever the initial state and initial decision are, the remaining decisions must constitute an optimal policy with respect to the state resulting from the first decision.

What the principle is telling us is that if we know how to proceed with the best course of action from any intermediate state to a final desired goal state, we should follow this course of action regardless of how we get to the intermediate state from an initial state. This is illustrated conceptually in Figure 8.23. If we know the best* path, between nodes, from an intermediate state, say node i, to the desired state, node n, then regardless of how we get to node i from node 1, we should proceed along this best path from i to n, say, path $ijkln$ in the figure. The principle of optimality points out the recursive nature of the method. We can now say that if we know the best path from node 1 to node n in Figure 8.23, then, regardless of how we arrive at node 1 from earlier states preceding it, we should proceed along this best path. Each node should be viewed as a state where a decision must be made. The decision is characterized conceptually by selecting a link from the node to a neighboring adjacent node. The sequence of links between nodes (i.e., the path from the initial state to the final desired goal state) constitutes a decision policy. The object of dynamic programming is to find the optimal policy with respect to a reference criterion by using a sequential

---

*Best with respect to a reference criterion such as cost, time, distance, profit, utility, and so on. The conceptual diagram of Figure 8.23 applies to problems of travel as well as other problems as is illustrated by the examples that follow.

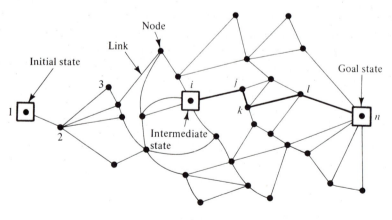

Figure 8.23

decision-making process which is computationally efficient in that it reduces greatly the search for the "best." The method can be used for problems in which the outcomes of our decisions are known with certainty as well as problems in which the outcomes are probabilistic.

Example 1: Maximum Utility

Suppose that you wish to reach node B from node A in Figure 8.24, heading only north and east, along a path of maximum utility. The utility associated with each link is marked on the links between nodes. The designation of levels along the dashed inclined lines is used to identify all the nodes at a particular stage in the decision process. At level 8, a decision leads to one of the nodes at level 7, and a decision at one of the nodes of level 7 leads to level 6, and so on, from level i to level $i - 1$, until the destination is reached at level 0. Thus eight decisions must be made between A and B. Each level number identifies the number of decisions that must still be made before the destination is reached. There are a total of $(5 + 3)!/3!5!$, or 56, different paths between A and B, each consisting of eight links. Which is the best? We can, of course, identify all paths, compute the associated utilities, and select the best. This procedure will prove rather inefficient as the number of north and east blocks increases, and will become an impossible task as the grid is of the order of, say, 100×100, as indicated earlier. Dynamic programming provides us with a method that not only makes manageable the impossible task of dealing with a large grid, but also reinforces a basic concept of problem solving: Do not always start at the beginning; sometimes starting at the end and working backward may prove productive.

Dynamic programming solution. Let us go to the end, and position ourselves at level 1, only one level away from the goal B. At node a we can travel only east to B with a utility of 9. This is indicated by the circled number at node a. The arrow on the circle indicates the direction of travel. At b we have 4 in the circle. Now we move back to level 2. At node c we can proceed only to node a with 5 units of utility; but since we have 9 units from a to B, the total from c is 14. At d we can move to a or b. But going to a yields 1 unit and from a we have 9, so the total is 10. On the other hand, going to b, the total is 11. We, therefore, select the best of the two regardless of how we get to d. The best, which is 11, is entered in the circle, and the arrow points to b. At e we have 5. Now we

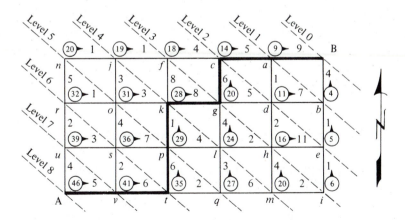

Figure 8.24

move to level 3 and proceed the same way. For example, at node g we have 6 units going to node c, but from c on we have 14, as recorded in the circle at c; the total is 20. Going to d, the total is 16; therefore, we go to c. Proceeding this way from level to level, we inspect each node and make a binary decision, namely, a choice between two options: going north or east to the next level. Each option requires adding two numbers, the utility of the link to the adjacent node and the circled number at the node ahead. To emphasize this point again, suppose that we are at level 6 node s. Going to o we have 4 units and from o, regardless of how we get there, the best path has 31 units; the total is 35. Going to p, the total is 36, so we go to p, and the best or maximum utility path from s to B is 36 units regardless of how we get to s. This best path from s follows the nodes $spkgcaB$, as indicated by the arrows on the circles at each node, starting from node s. Finally, by working backward we reach level 8, node A, and find that the optimum path from A to B yields a utility of 46 units and goes through the sequence of nodes $AvtpkgcaB$ marked by the heavy line in the figure.

Example 2: Minimum Distance

Let us suppose that the numbers on the links of Figure 8.24 represent units of distance, and we wish to minimize the distance of travel from A to B. The solution is shown in Figure 8.25, in which the circled numbers represent the shortest distances to B. The optimum path, marked by the heavy line in the figure, is $AvtqmiebB$, with a length of 27 units of distance.

Note that the shortest distance from A to B goes through v and not through u. This demonstrates that beginning the decisions at the initial state, instead of working backward, would have led to a nonoptimal path. It also demonstrates that dynamic programming leads to an optimum for the entire problem of n levels or stages from initial to goal state, and in the process local optima between intermediate stages may be sacrificed.

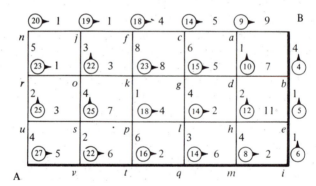

Figure 8.25

8.8 Sequential Decisions with Random Outcomes

Dynamic programming can also be applied in situations where the outcomes are not certain and have probabilities associated with their occurrence. The decision tree model of Section 8.2 had such outcomes. Indeed, the procedure for solving the decision tree problem of section 8.2 is an application of dynamic programming. In these problems we chart the courses of action at the decision junctions by going to the end of the tree, averaging out outcomes and folding back toward the root of the tree or the initial state. We average outcomes and compare the averages at each stage the same way as we compare utilities or distances in the dynamic programming examples of Section 8.7. The folding back in the decision tree is the process of working backward in which we identify the routes that should be taken from each node to the destination regardless of how we got to the node.

Let us present an example to show how we use dynamic programming for sequential decisions with random outcomes. The similarity of the procedure to the averaging out and folding back process used in Section 8.2 will become apparent.

Example

Suppose that you are presented with an opportunity to play the following game for a fee of $5. A die is tossed a maximum of six times. After each toss you must decide whether to stop the game or continue with the next toss. If you decide to stop, you receive an amount of money in dollars equal to the outcome from the toss. If you decide to continue, you receive no money and you wait for the outcome of the next toss, which may become your reward in dollars if you decide to stop then. You can receive only the amount resulting from a single toss out of six. If you decline to accept any of the outcomes of the first five tosses, and decide not to stop the game, you *must* accept the outcome of the sixth toss, which is the last possible toss of the game. Thus a game can stop after one toss or continue on to a maximum of six tosses.

If you decide to play the game, what would be your strategy? How would you chart the courses of action at all possible stages of the game?

What you must do is establish a decision rule to guide your action at each stage of the game. At each stage we must determine a value that will constitute a threshold for stopping. For example, suppose that you have just seen the result of the second toss and you must decide whether to stop or continue when there are four tosses to go. Let d_4 be an amount of money in dollars such that if the outcome x_4 from the second toss is equal to it or larger, we stop the game and take x_4; otherwise, we continue with a third toss. At any stage i of the game with i representing the number of remaining tosses, we have the following decision rule:

$$\text{For } x_i \geq d_i \quad \text{stop, accept } x_i$$
$$\text{For } x_i < d_i \quad \text{continue, wait for } x_{i-1} \qquad i = 6, 5, 3, \ldots, 1, 0$$

x_i is the result from a toss when there are i tosses to go and can take on the values from 1 to 6. Each d_i stands for the threshold value for the decision when there are i tosses to go.

Let us proceed with calculations for the threshold values d_i by working backward.

Stage 6, $i = 0$, no more tosses to go: x_0 can be 1, 2, 3, 4, 5, or 6 with a probability of 1/6 for each value. Therefore, the expected value of x_0 at stage 6 is

$$E(x_0) = \frac{1}{6}(1 + 2 + 3 + 4 + 5 + 6) = \frac{21}{6} = \$3\frac{1}{2}$$

Stage 5, $i = 1$, one more toss to go: Since in stage 6 you can expect $3\frac{1}{2}$ on the average, this value becomes the threshold d_1:

$$d_1 = \$3\frac{1}{2}.$$

If $x_1 \geq \$3\frac{1}{2}$, stop. This will happen when x_1 assumes the value 6, 5, or 4 each with a probability of 1/6.

If $x_1 < \$3\frac{1}{2}$, continue. This will happen with probability 3/6 when x_1 assumes the values 1, 2, or 3. Therefore, the expected value at stage 5 is calculated as follows. If you stop, the value can be 6, 5, or 4, each with a probability of 1/6. If you continue, you will expect $\$3\frac{1}{2}$ in the future, and this will happen with a probability of 3/6. Thus the total expected value at stage 5 is

$$6 \times \frac{1}{6} + 5 \times \frac{1}{6} + 4 \times \frac{1}{6} + \frac{21}{6} \times \frac{3}{6} = \frac{17}{4} = \$4\frac{1}{4}$$

Stage 4, i = 2, two tosses to go: Since in stage 5 you expect $\$4\frac{1}{4}$ on the average, this value becomes the threshold d_2:

$$d_2 = \$4\frac{1}{4}$$

If $x_2 \geq \$4\frac{1}{4}$, stop. If $x_2 < \$4\frac{1}{4}$, continue. You will stop for $x_2 = 6$ or 5 with probabilities 1/6 each, and will continue when $x_2 = 1, 2, 3,$ or 4 and expect $\$4\frac{1}{4}$ in the future with a probability of 4/6. The expected value at stage 4 becomes

$$6 \times \frac{1}{6} + 5 \times \frac{1}{6} + \frac{17}{4} \times \frac{4}{6} = \frac{14}{3} = \$4\frac{2}{3}$$

Stage 3, i = 3, three tosses to go: Following the procedure used in stage 4, we obtain

$$d_3 = \$4\frac{2}{3}$$

and the expected value at stage 3 becomes

$$6 \times \frac{1}{6} + 5 \times \frac{1}{6} + \frac{14}{3} \times \frac{4}{6} = \frac{89}{18} = \$4\frac{17}{18}$$

Stage 2, i = 4, four tosses to go:

$$d_4 = \$4\frac{17}{18}$$

and the expected value is

$$6 \times \frac{1}{6} + 5 \times \frac{1}{6} + \frac{89}{18} \times \frac{4}{6} = \frac{277}{54} = \$5\frac{7}{54}$$

Stage 1, i = 5, five tosses to go:

$$d_5 = \$5\frac{7}{54}$$

and the expected value is

$$6 \times \frac{1}{6} + \frac{277}{54} \times \frac{5}{6} = \$5\frac{89}{324}$$

Stage 0, i = 6, six tosses to go:

$$d_6 = \$5\frac{89}{324}$$

d_6 represents the expected value of the game before you start playing.

The calculations for the preceding stages 6 to 0 are shown in summary form in the tree structure of Figure 8.26.

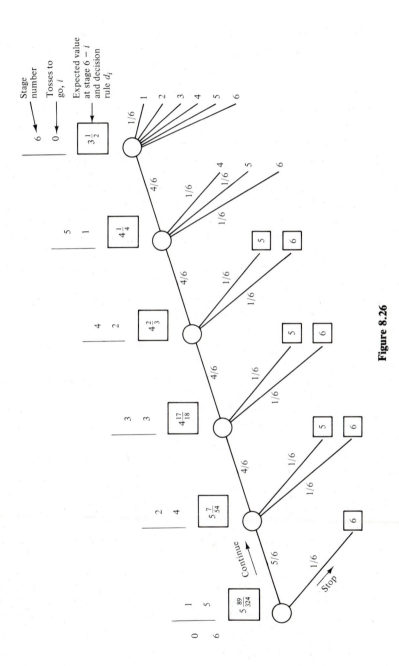

Figure 8.26

8.9 Summary

A dilemma we often face is whether or not we should act under conditions of uncertainty when we have a choice between acting, A, or not acting, $\bar{A}$. Considering two possible states of nature $\bar{S}$ desirable to us and S undesirable, we can calculate a threshold probability for the undesired state to guide our decision. The threshold probability $p*$ is a function of benefit B and cost C and is given by equation (8.11):

$$p* = \frac{1}{(B/C) + 1} \tag{8.11}$$

The benefit B is the difference between the utilities of acting and not acting when it is prudent to act:

$$B = U_{AS} - U_{\bar{A}S}$$

The cost C is the difference between the utilities of not acting and acting when it is prudent not to act:

$$C = U_{\bar{A}\bar{S}} - U_{A\bar{S}}$$

When the probability p of undesired state S is larger than the threshold probability $p*$, the utility of action is greater than that of no action. When p is smaller than $p*$, the utility of no action is greater. When $p = p*$ the utilities of action and no action are the same.

Examples are given for models dealing with decision for surgery and a jury's choice of verdict.

When decisions must be made under conditions of uncertainty, the expected utility can be increased by using relevant information. The value of the information depends on its accuracy. Information from a perfect source of information has the highest value. The value of imperfect information can be assessed by using the past records of predictions of the source. The value of perfect information constitutes an upper bound for the value of less than perfect information.

An example is given in which value of information is assessed. The assessment procedure uses conditional probabilities of the source being correct or wrong given it made a prediction for a state of nature. These conditional probabilities become entries in a decision tree in which averaging out and folding back are employed to calculate the action of maximum expected utility with the aid of the information.

Precision of information must be considered in the context of a decision model before we expend efforts to obtain the information. It is shown that the level of precision may vary depending on the actual outcomes in a decision model. It is quite possible for information to be coarse and still provide as much guidance to a choice of action as the most refined detailed information. This is illustrated by examples.

It is also shown that the probabilities for the states of nature may be specified in the form of a range of values, instead of a specific value, and provide the necessary and sufficient level of precision to guide the choice for action that maximizes expected utility.

Multiattribute decision problems can be represented by a relevance tree to establish relative weights of importance for the attributes.

The relevance tree represents the inner environment of the decision maker. The alternatives represent the set of opportunities or the outer environment. The value of each alternative is calculated in terms of its contributions to the attributes of the inner environment, and the alternative with the largest value is chosen by the decision maker.

The relevance tree model can help the decision maker calibrate the process for assigning numerical values to ratings of importance.

The following nine steps are given to construct a relevance tree for multi-attribute decisions:

1. Establish broad categories relevant to the problem.
2. Assign a weight to each broad category.
3. Subdivide the broad categories into more refined components.
4. Continue step 3 to a satisfactory level of refinement.
5. Calculate the ratings of importance r_j for the attributes.
6. Assign values to the contributions c_{ij} that each alternative a_i makes to attribute $j = 1, 2, \ldots, m$.
7. Establish reasonable upper and lower limits for each attribute.
8. Calculate the value $V(a_i)$ of each alternative a_i using equation (8.23):

$$V(a_i) = \sum_{j=1}^{m} c_{ij} r_j$$

9. Study the results of step 8 and modify your model where necessary.

The relevance tree can be extended to serve as a model for resource allocation. An example illustrates the use of such a model for the allocation of funding for research and development programs.

Dynamic programming is useful in problems of sequential decisions and is based on the principle of optimality, which states:

An optimal policy has the property that, whatever the initial state and initial decision are, the remaining decisions must constitute an optimal policy with respect to the state resulting from the first decision.

The solution procedure in dynamic programming works backward, using a recursive relationship. Dynamic programming can be applied to random outcomes. Decisions are made sequentially based on maximum expected value at each node. The entire process is based on "averaging out and folding back."

PROBLEMS

8.1. Discuss the implications of Figure 8.3.

8.2. The matrix in Figure P8.2 shows a record of a consultant who *never* predicted the state of the economy correctly. What would you do in the model of Figure 8.13 when he says *s*? You can answer this without resorting to trees or any calculations for this matter. Is the information relevant? What would you do when he says *w*? No calculations are needed here either. What would you do when he says *m*?

When state of economy was:

		Strong, S	Medium, M	Weak, W
	Strong, s	0	0.4	0.5
Consultant said:	Medium, m	0.7	0	0.5
	Weak, w	0.3	0.6	0

Figure P8.2

8.3. Consider the payoff matrix of Figure 8.13 and the consultant record of Problem 8.2. Use a decision tree similar to Figure 8.9 to establish the consultant maximum fee.

8.4. A genie will say *s* (strong), *m* (medium), *w* (weak) for the model of Figure 8.13 with the same probabilities 0.3, 0.5, and 0.2 as *S*, *M*, and *W* respectively actually occur. Suppose that a consultant will say *s*, *m*, and *w* with the same probabilities as *S*, *M*, and *W* actually occur, respectively. Is he necessarily a genie with perfect information? Is it possible for him to be wrong always even with this record? Discuss.

8.5. If you must decide what to do in Figure 8.13, d_1 or d_2, which of the four genies of Section 8.3 would you use given that their fees for a single prediction are as follows:

Genie *P*: $100,000

Genie *S*: $70,000

Genie *M*: $50,000

Genie *W*: $15,000

Discuss your answer. Recall that genie *P* gives you precise information about the state of the economy, while genie *S* tells you only whether *S* will or will not happen, genie *M*—whether *M* will or will not happen, and genie *W*—whether *W* will or will not happen.

8.6. Let us suppose that in Problem 8.5 you must know in advance precisely how much profit you will obtain next year. Which genie or genies will you employ for this purpose?

8.7. Work Problems 8.5 and 8.6 given that genie *W* raises his fee to $40,000.

8.8. Create a multiattribute model for the purchase of one of five automobiles. Use a relevance tree and generate values for the attributes you consider for the five alternatives.

8.9. What is the optimum path of maximum utility in Figure 8.24 subject to the constraint that the path must go through node *l*?

8.10. What is the optimum path of shortest distance in Figure 8.25 subject to the constraint that it must go through node *g*?

8.11. Find the path of shortest time between UCLA and Disneyland. The road map shown in Figure P8.11 gives the travel time between nodes. Travel is constrained to follow the directions of the arrows.

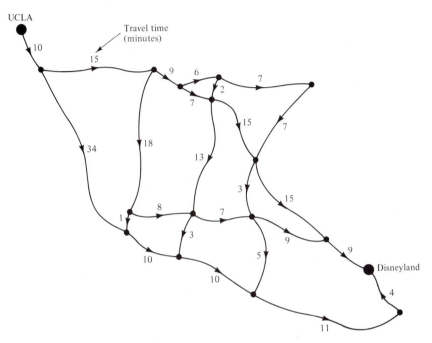

Figure P8.11   Find route of shortest time.

8.12. The numbers in the grid shown in Figure P8.12 on page 304 represent travel time between nodes. If you can move only north and east, what is the route of shortest travel time between *A* and *B*?

8.13. What is the route of least time in Problem 8.12 if the route must go through *C*?

8.14. How would you proceed to find the path of shortest time in Problem 8.12 if you could travel north, east, and south from each node?

8.15. You are an executive considering a choice between products d_1, d_2, and d_3 with probabilities of the states of the economy and outcomes as shown in Figure P8.15. There are three genies who have access to perfect information; however, each gives information regarding the states of the economy in a different form:

Genie 1: Will tell only whether the economy will be *Strong* or *not Strong*

Genie 2: Will tell only whether the economy will be *Medium* or *not Medium*

Genie 3: Will tell only whether the economy will be *Weak* or *not Weak*
     (a) Calculate the value of information for each genie.
     (b) Describe the strategies you would use with each genie.

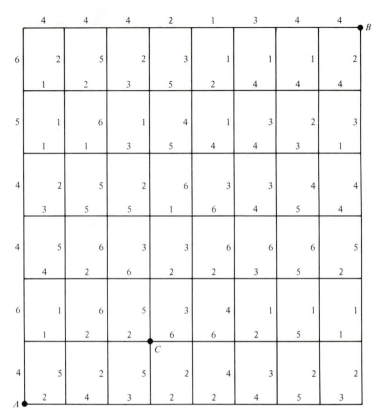

Figure P8.12

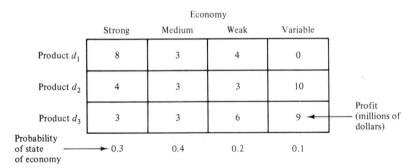

Figure P8.15

8.16. In the payoff matrix shown in Figure P8.16, the states of nature θ_1 and θ_2 occur with probabilities p and $1 - p$, respectively.
(a) Calculate the range of p values for which you will use a_1, a_2, or a_3.
(b) For what value p^* of p is the value of perfect information a maximum? What is this maximum value?
(c) For what value of p is the decision maker most uncertain as to what to do in the absence of information?

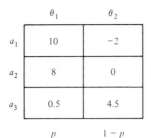

	θ_1	θ_2
a_1	10	−2
a_2	8	0
a_3	0.5	4.5
	p	$1-p$

Figure P8.16

8.17. Farmer Jones subscribes to the utility curve shown in Figure P8.17. He must decide whether to plant peas or soybeans, and the payoff matrix below summarizes the various possibilities:

	θ_1: good weather	θ_2: bad weather
S_1: plant soybeans	$5000 profit	$2000 loss
S_2: plant peas	$3000 profit	$1000 loss

From experience Jones knows that the weather is good 40% of the time. Dr. George is a world-famous meteorologist. When the weather was good, Dr. George predicted it correctly 90% of the time, and when it was bad, she predicted it correctly 80% of the time. Dr. George charges $250 for her prediction.

Farmer Jones' current assets are $5000 and the profit or loss associated with any outcome will augment these assets.

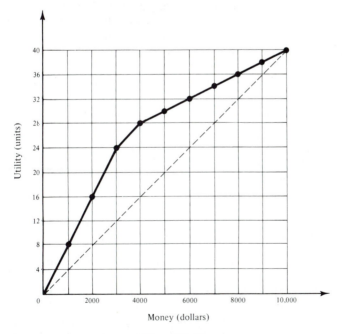

Figure P8.17

(a) Draw a decision tree to determine whether farmer Jones should buy the opinion of Dr. George. Show all calculations.

(b) Calculate the value of perfect information.

(c) Calculate the value of Dr. George's opinion.

8.18. A doctor has the task of deciding whether or not to carry out a dangerous operation on a person suspected of suffering from a disease. If he has the disease and the doctor operates, the chance of recovery is only 50%; without an operation the similar chance is only 1 in 20. On the other hand, if he does not have the disease and the operation is performed, there is 1 chance in 5 of his dying as a result of the operation, whereas there is no chance of death without the operation. Assume that there are always only two possibilities, death (D) or recovery (R). Set $u(D) = 0$ and $u(R) = 1$. For what range of probabilities p of the patient having the disease should the doctor operate (OP)?

8.19. A woman must sell her house in the next three months. The house is located away from the center of town and she expects three offers, one each month. She committed herself to accept the third offer, whatever it might be.

The house is a standard type and of 100 such houses sold recently

30 sold for $50,000

60 sold for $55,000

10 sold for $60,000

(a) What decision rule should the woman follow if she wishes to maximize the expected value of the accepted offer?

(b) What is the expected value of the accepted offer?

8.20. The owner of an original painting wishes to sell it. He expects three offers, one in each of the following three weeks. The probability distribution for offers is shown in Figure P8.20. What strategy should the owner use if he must accept the third offer? What should he accept as a lower bound for the first offer, and for the second offer? Show all calculations.

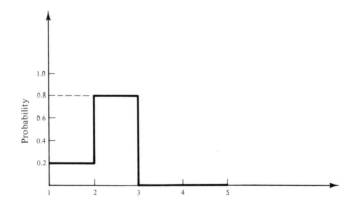

Figure P8.20 Normalized scale of offers in units of $20,000.

8.21. A part of an aircraft engine can be given a test before installation. The test has only a 75% chance of revealing a defect if it is present, and the same chance of passing a sound part. Whether or not the part has been tested, it may undergo an expensive rework operation which is certain to produce a part free from defects. If a defective part is installed in the engine, the loss is L (utiles). If the rework operation costs $L/5$ utiles and 1 in 8 of parts are initially defective, calculate how much you could pay for the test and determine all the optimum decisions.

8.22. Rework Problem 8.18, where recovery can now mean either complete recovery (R) or partial recovery (PR). If the operation is performed and recovery results, it is always complete. If the operation is not performed and recovery results, it will be partial if he has the disease, and complete otherwise. Assume that the operation cannot be performed later, if the patient lives. Set $u(PR) = \lambda$, $0 \leq \lambda \leq 1$, and $u(R) = 1$, $u(D) = 0$. For what probabilities of the patient having the disease should the doctor operate? Solve in terms of λ.

8.23. An automobile manufacturer installs catalytic converters in exhaust systems of its cars. A nondestructive leak test, T, can be conducted before installation. The test is not perfect and costs \$2. You can reseal a converter at a cost of \$10 with a guarantee that it will be sealed. A leaky converter will be detected in the final inspection and will cost \$30 to replace. Converters are 6% defective. The test T identifies correctly properly sealed converters 90% of the time and leaky converters 70% of the time.
(a) Construct a decision tree.
(b) List the strategies available.
(c) What strategy should the automobile manufacturer choose?
(d) What is the minimum expected cost per converter?
(e) How can you answer part (c) very quickly by considering only the cost of testing, the cost of replacing a leaky converter, and the percentage of defective converters.

8.24. Discuss the value of the model of Figure 8.5 as a frame of reference in deliberation by a jury.

8.25. How would you change the model of Figure 8.5 to apply to a person on trial considering a choice between pleading guilty or not guilty? What could the stakes be in this case? Discuss.

8.26. Consider a farmer with a utility for money shown in Figure P8.26a on page 308. The farmer is considering two alternative courses of action, a_1 and a_2, as shown in Figure P8.26b.
(a) Calculate the value of perfect information.
(b) Calculate the value of the consultant information for the record shown in Figure P8.26c. E_1 and E_2 are the actual states of nature; e_1 and e_2 are the consultant's predictions.

8.27. Suppose that you have applied to three graduate schools: A, B, and C. You calculate your probability of acceptance to each school at 0.5. You will be notified of the status of your application before April 1 with probability 50%, and after April 1 with probability 50%. This applies to each school. If you have been accepted to a school before April 1, you must commit yourself by April 1 or you will be considered rejected by that school. The utility associated with going to each school is $A = 4$, $B = 3$, $C = 2$. Once you accept a school you forfeit an opportunity to attend any other school.
What should you do on April 1st so that your utility is maximized?

8.28. The water master of a combination flood control/water supply reservoir must decide whether or not to open the spillway gates and lower the reservoir level in the face of a later season storm. The two states of nature are: The resulting runoff

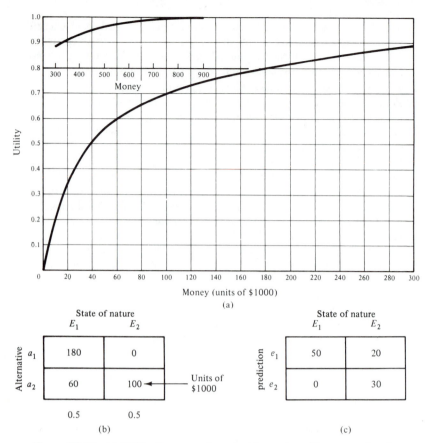

Figure P8.26 (a) Utility for money for a decision maker; (b) courses of action; (c) consultant record.

will be greater than or equal to flood stage, or less than flood stage. The utilities of the four possible outcomes are shown in the matrix in Figure P8.28a, where S = (runoff $\geq$ flood stage), $\bar{S}$ = (runoff $<$ flood stage), A = open gates, and $\bar{A}$ = don't open gates. The probability of S is 0.05.

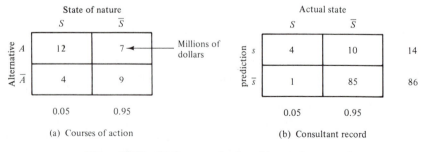

Figure P8.28 (a) Courses of action; (b) consultant record.

(a) Use a decision tree to determine the best alternative.

(b) Determine the threshold probability for action A.

(c) If information from the weather service is available with the past record of prediction accuracy shown in Figure P8.28b, what is the value of the information for the decision faced by the water master?

8.29. In Las Vegas you can bet on pro football games where the house advantage is 10%. That is, if you lose a bet, you lose $11 for every $10 you could win if you win the bet. There are 16 games played each week and a particular consultant sells his predictions on the 10 games on which he is most confident. In the past he has been accurate 60% of the time on the 10 games he predicted. If you ask him advice on a particular game without knowing that it is one of the 10 games he would normally predict, how much would his advice be worth to you? Assume that you cannot win more than $1000 per game.

8.30. Discuss the limitations of the relevance tree model for multiattribute decision making.

References

1. "An Application of Decision Theory to a Medical-Diagnosis Treatment Problem," A. S. Ginsberg and F. L. Offensend, *IEEE Transactions,* Vol. SSC-4, No. 3, September 1968, pp. 355–362.

2. *Patterns of Problem Solving,* Moshe F. Rubinstein, Prentice-Hall, Englewood Cliffs, N.J., 1975.

3. "Contributions of Harmony to Productivity," Moshe F. Rubinstein, *California Engineer,* Vol. 59, No. 3, March 1981, pp. 11–13.

4. "Hierarchies, Clans, and Theory Z: A New Perspective on Organization Development," William G. Ouchi and Raymond L. Price, *Organizational Dynamics,* Autumn 1978.

5. *The Japanese and the Jews,* Isaiah Ben-Dasan, Weatherhill, Tokyo, 1972.

6. *Motivation and Personality,* A. H. Maslow, Harper & Row, New York, 1964.

7. *The Structure of Scientific Revolution,* Thomas Kuhn, University of Chicago Press, Chicago, 2nd Edition, 1970.

8. *Perception and Change,* John Platt, University of Michigan Press, Ann Arbor, Mich., 1970.

9. *The Image,* K. E. Boulding, University of Michigan Press, Ann Arbor, Mich., 1956.

10. *Your Erroneous Zones,* Wayne W. Dyer, Funk & Wagnalls, New York, 1976.

11. *The Psychology of Science: A Reconnaissance,* Henry Regnery, Chicago, 1969.

12. *Methods of Heuristics,* Rudolph Groner, Marina Groner, and Walter F. Bischof, eds., Lawrence Erlbaum, Hillsdale, N.J., 1983.

13. "Problem Solving and Education," Herbert A. Simon, in *Problem Solving and*

Education—Issues in Teaching and Research, David Tuma and Frederick Reif, eds., Lawrence Erlbaum, Hillsdale, N.J., 1980, pp. 81–94.

14. *The Art of Clear Thinking,* R. Flesch, Collier Macmillan, West Drayton, Middlesex, England, 1962.

15. *Concepts in Problem Solving,* Moshe F. Rubinstein and Kenneth R. Pfeiffer, Prentice-Hall, Englewood Cliffs, N.J., 1980.

16. *Problem Solving and Creativity in Individuals and Groups,* N. R. F. Maier, Brooks/Cole, Monterey, Calif., 1970.

17. *Gödel, Escher, Bach: An Eternal Golden Braid,* D. Hofstadter, Jr., Vintage Books, New York, 1979.

18. *Pattern Recognition,* M. Bongard, Spartan Books, Bensalem, Pa., 1970.

19. "Problem Solving on Both Sides of the Brain," Moshe F. Rubinstein, *Chemtech,* Vol. 11, No. 11, November 1981, pp. 654–657.

20. *The Psychology of Consciousness,* Robert E. Ornstein, W. H. Freeman, San Francisco, 1972.

21. *The Active Society,* Amitai Etzioni, Macmillan, New York, 1968.

22. "Learning Strategies and Individual Competence," G. Pask and B. C. E. Scott, *International Journal of Man–Machine Studies,* Vol. 4. 1972, p. 217.

23. "CASTE: A System for Exhibiting Learning Strategies and Regulating Uncertainties," G. Pask and B. C. E. Scott, *International Journal of Man–Machine Studies,* Vol. 5, 1973, p. 17.

24. "Technology Assessment from the Stance of a Medieval Historian," Lynn White, Jr., *The American Historical Review,* Vol. 79, No. 1, February 1974.

25. *The Information Machines,* Ben H. Bagdikian, Harper & Row, New York, 1971.

26. "Problem Solving and Educational Policy," Richard M. Cyert, in *Problem Solving and Education—Issues in Teaching and Research,* David Tuma and Frederick Reif, eds., Lawrence Erlbaum, Hillsdale, N.J., 1980.

27. *How to Solve the Mismanagement Crisis,* Ichak Adizes, Dow Jones-Irwin, Homewood, Ill., 1979.

28. *Management of Organizational Behavior,* P. Hersey and K. H. Blanchard, Prentice-Hall, Englewood Cliffs, N.J., 1977.

29. "Error Detecting and Error Correcting Codes," R. W. Hamming, *Bell System Technical Journal,* Vol. 29, 1950.

30. *Coding and Information Theory,* Richard W. Hamming, Prentice-Hall, Englewood Cliffs, N.J., 1980.

31. *Graph Theory and Its Applications to Problems of Society,* F. S. Roberts, NSF-CBMS Monograph 29, SIAM Publications, Philadelphia, Pa., 1978.

32. *Excursions in Number Theory,* Stanley Ogilvy and John T. Anderson, Oxford University Press, New York, 1966.

33. "Number Theory: The Fibonacci Sequence," Verner E. Hoggatt, Jr., in *1977 Year Book of Science and the Future,* Encyclopaedia Britannica, Chicago.

34. "Numbers Count," Kenneth Boulding, *Science,* Vol. 19, No. 8, October 1979.

35. *Cybernetics,* Norbert Wiener, The MIT Press, Cambridge, Mass., 1948.

36. *God & Golum Inc.: A Comment on Certain Points Where Cybernetics Impinges on Religion,* Norbert Wiener, The MIT Press, Cambridge, Mass., 1964.

37. *The Roots of Coincidence,* Arthur Koestler, Random House, New York, 1972.

38. *Information Theory and Coding,* Norman Abramson, McGraw-Hill, New York, 1963.

39. *Introduction to Reliability in Design,* Charles O. Smith, McGraw-Hill, New York, 1976.

40. "Judgment under Uncertainty," Amos Tversky and Daniel Kahneman, *Science,* September 25, 1974, pp. 1124–31.

41. *Human Inference,* Richard Nisbett and Lee Ross, Prentice-Hall, Englewood Cliffs, N.J., 1980.

42. "Human Information Processing and Adjudication: Trial by Heuristics," Michael J. Saks and Robert F. Kidd, *Law and Society Review,* Vol. 15, No. 1, 1980–1981, pp. 123–160.

43. "Prospect Theory: An Analysis of Decision under Risk," D. Kahneman and A. Tversky, *Econometrica,* Vol. 47, 1979.

44. "The Framing of Decisions and the Psychology of Choice," A. Tversky and D. Kahneman, *Science,* Vol. 211, January 30, 1981, pp. 453–458.

45. *The Structure of Human Decisions,* David W. Miller and Martin K. Starr, Prentice-Hall, Englewood Cliffs, N.J., 1967.

46. *The Thinking Computer,* B. Raphael, W. H. Freeman, San Francisco, 1976.

47. *Introduction to Methods of Optimization,* L. Cooper and D. Steinberg, W. B. Saunders, Philadelphia, 1970.

48. *Theory of Games and Economic Behavior,* John von Neumann and Oskar Morgenstern, Princeton University Press, Princeton, N.J., 1947.

49. *Games and Decisions: Introduction and Critical Survey,* R. Duncan Luce and Howard Raiffa, Wiley, New York, 1957.

50. "Therapeutic Decision Making: A Cost–Benefit Analysis," S. G. Pauker and J. P. Kassirer, *The New England Journal of Medicine,* Vol. 293, No. 5, July 1975.

51. *Decision Analysis,* Howard Raiffa, Addison-Wesley, Reading, Mass., 1968.

52. "A Tutorial Introduction to Decision Theory," North, D. Warner, *IEEE Transactions,* System Science and Cybernetics, Vol. SSC-4, No. 3, September 1968, p. 203.

53. "Utility Theory—Insight into Risk Taking," Ralph O. Swalm, *Harvard Business Review,* December 1966.

54. *Social Choice and Individual Values,* Kenneth Arrow, Wiley, New York, 1951.

55. "Individual and Societal Utility," David S. Roberts and Richard C. Clelland, *Environmental Systems,* Vol. 1, No. 1, March 1971, pp. 19–36.

56. "A Systematic Procedure for Assessing the Worth of Complex Alternatives," J. R. Miller III, Mitre Corp., Bedford, Mass., November 1967. Prepared for EDP Equipment Office, Electronic Systems Division, U. S. Air Force.

57. "Preferences for Multi-attributed Alternatives," Howard Raiffa, Memorandum RM 5868-DOT/RC, The RAND Corporation, Santa Monica, Calif., April 1969.

58. "A Method for Integrating Goals and Technological Forecasting into Planning," Marvin J. Cetron, *Technological Forecasting,* Vol. 2, No. 1, 1970.

59. "Manpower Requirements for National Objectives in the 1970s," Leonard A. Lecht, Center for Priority Analysis, National Planning Association, 1968.

60. *Applied Dynamic Programming,* Richard Bellman and Stuart Dreyfus, Princeton University Press, Princeton, N.J., 1962.

61. *The Strategy of Conflict,* Thomas C. Schelling, Harvard University Press, Cambridge, Mass., 1960.

62. *Paradoxes of Rationality,* Howard Nigel, The MIT Press, Cambridge, Mass., 1971.

63. *Game Theory and Politics,* S. J. Brams, The Free Press, New York, 1975.

64. "Problem? What Problem?" Moshe F. Rubinstein, *Chemtech,* Vol. 14, No. 4, April 1984, pp. 204–207.

65. *Decisions with Multiple Objectives,* Ralph L. Keeney and Howard Raiffa, Wiley, New York, 1976.

66. *The Analytical Hierarchy Process,* Thomas L. Saaty, McGraw-Hill, New York, 1980.

67. *Multiobjective Decision Analysis with Engineering and Business Applications,* Ambrose Goicoechea, Don R. Hansen, and Lucien Duckstein, Wiley, New York, 1982.

Index

Error(s) (*cont.*)
  in Hamming code, 104–105
  detection, 109–111
    in Hamming code, 104–105
  in diagnosis, 158–159
  double, detection and correction,
    110–111
  in dynamic system, 140–141
  by jury, 4
  of omission, 4, 38, 208–214
  single, detection and correction, 109–110
  type I, 209
  type II, 209
  and values, 4
ESP, 165–169
Estimates, statistic, 197
Etzioni, Amitai, 56, 311
Euler diagram, 82
Europe, city distances in, 241
Events:
  aggregates of, 180–181
  compound, 147, 148
  dependent, 149
  elementary, 146
  independent, 149
  mutually exclusive, 148–149
  sample space and, 148
  simple, 148
  universe of, 146
Evidence:
  in court, 212
    defense use of, 153
    prosecution use of, 153
  credibility of, 4
  relevance of, 4
  sufficient, 208
"Exclusive or," in symbolic logic, 100
Expected value, 196
  utility function, 259
External environment, for decisions, 284

F

Facts:
  consequences of ignoring, 34
  and problem representation, 33
Farmer:
  decision model for, 275–279
  and values, 4–6
Feasible solutions, 244, 293
Feedback control, 138
Fibonacci sequence, 126
  aesthetics and, 129
  golden section and, 130

and Pascal triangle, 128
  rectangular forms and, 128–129
  spiral curve and, 129
Filtering, 43–49
Flesch, R., 311
Flexibility, and frames of reference, 24
Focusing, 43–49
Folding back, in decision tree, 297
Foot measurement, origin of, 133
Force of gravity, 54
Form:
  of model, 11, 38
  of representation, 3
Frames of reference:
  change of, 19
  and concepts, 22
  Einstein and, 22–23
  and flexibility, 24
  and learning, 22
  in life expectancy, 134
  and paradigms, 20
  and perception, 23–24
  Picasso and, 22–23
  and representation, 6
  in statistical representation, 134
Funding, levels of, 291
  maximum, 291
  optimum, 291
  threshold, 291
Fuzziness, tolerance of, 55

G

Game(s), 66–74
  star, 68
  against strong and weak players, 70
  theory, 236
  triangle, 69
Gaussian distribution, 195
Ginsberg, A. S., 256, 257, 310
Goals:
  national, 292
  of problem, 7–10
Goicoechea, Ambrose, 313
Golden section, 130
  pentagram and, 131
  structures of antiquity and, 131
Golem, 140
Graph, directed. *See* Digraph
Graphic representation, 38–40
Gravitation, model of, 54
Great Lakes, acronyms for, 31
Groner, Marina, 310
Groner, Rudolph, 310

demonstrative, 93–94, 150–151
plausible, 93–94, 150–152
Receiver:
  in communication, 102
  in Hamming code, 105
Recursion, 294
Redundancy:
  accuracy and, 159–165
  in communication, 103
  in Hamming code, 104
  language and, 103
  uncertainty and, 159
Redundant bits, 104
Reference criterion, in decision making,
  294
Reference gamble, 216–217
Reference lottery, 217
Regnery, Henry, 310
Regret:
  matrix, 250–251
  postdecisional, 228, 234–235, 265
Regretist, in decision making, 250
Reif, Frederick, 311
Relationship:
  causal, 136
  removing, 53–54
Relevance:
  Bayes' equation and, 149–150
  of evidence, 4
  independence and, 150
  information, 12–13, 145–146
Relevance tree, 283, 288–289
  alternatives, values of in, 286–287
  construction, 283–285
  for job selection, 285
  learning from, 287
  for resource allocation, 289–293
Relevant question, 2
Reliability:
  definition, 183
  heuristics to assess, 186–188
  lower-bound approximation, 187–189
  minimal cut procedure for, 187
  parallel connections, 184–185
  parallel-series connections, 184–185
  series connections, 184–185
Re-presentation, 6
Representation:
  abstract, 43
  apple grower problem, 35–36
  attributes, 78–88
    four, 86
    three, 83, 85
    two, 84
  change, 35–38

  by adding, removing, and rearranging,
    41–43
  and hangar design, 38
  and invention of canals, 38
  for knights problem, 36–37
  for number scrabble, 36
  verbal to graphic, 38–40
  choice of, 87
  communication system, 102
  compound lottery, 254
  and concepts, 22
  concrete, 42
  context and, 233
  and decision, 231–234
  digraph, 117–121
  of doctors problem, 2
  equation for, 82
  of farmer's problem, 5
  Fibonacci sequence and, 128–131
  form, 3
  and frame of reference, 6
  as framework for thought, 6
  Hamming distance, 108–111
  and heuristics, 233
  importance of, 6
  influence, in decisions, 233–234
  International Standard Book Number,
    112–113
  jury verdict, 3–4
  Karnaugh map, 82–83
  lottery, 253
    compound, 254
  matrices, 78–80, 117–121
    for probability assessment, 155–159
  of numbers:
    by Greeks, 38
    by Hebrews, 38
  and perception, 233
  of phenomena, diverse, 126–131
  pictorial, 42, 43
  relevance tree, 283–287
  removing elements from:
    by filtering, 43–49
    by focusing, 43–49
  as re-presentation, 6
  statistical, 131–136
    frame of reference in, 134
  tables, 78–80
    for Hamming code, 107–108
  and thinking, 80
  as tool for thinking, 6
  tools for, 78
  tree, 81–82
    decision, 247–248
    for probability assessment, 155–165